Routledge Revivals

Hausa Tales and Traditions

Hausa Tales and Traditions

Translated and edited by
Neil Skinner

Volume I

Routledge
Taylor & Francis Group

First published in 1969 by Africana Publishing Corporation

This edition first published in 2018 by Routledge
2 Park Square, Milton Park, Abingdon, Oxon, OX14 4RN
and by Routledge
52 Vanderbilt Avenue, New York, NY 10017, USA

Routledge is an imprint of the Taylor & Francis Group, an informa business

Publisher's Note
The publisher has gone to great lengths to ensure the quality of this reprint but points out that some imperfections in the original copies may be apparent.

Disclaimer
The publisher has made every effort to trace copyright holders and welcomes correspondence from those they have been unable to contact.
A Library of Congress record exists under ISBN:

ISBN 13: 978-0-367-13693-2 (hbk)
ISBN 13: 978-0-367-13694-9 (pbk)
ISBN 13: 978-0-429-02810-6 (ebk)

Hausa Tales and Traditions

Hausa Tales and Traditions

An English Translation

of

TATSUNIYOYI NA HAUSA

Originally compiled by Frank Edgar

Translated and edited by
NEIL SKINNER

With a foreword by M. G. SMITH

In three volumes

VOL. I

AFRICANA PUBLISHING CORPORATION · NEW YORK

First Published in 1969 by
FRANK CASS AND COMPANY LIMITED
67 Great Russell Street, London, W.C.1

Published in the United States of America in 1969
by Africana Publishing Corporation
101 Fifth Avenue
New York N.Y. 10003

SBN 8419-0021-3

Library of Congress Catalog Card No 74-89679

Printed in Great Britain

Contents

FOREWORD BY M. G. SMITH   vii

TRANSLATOR'S INTRODUCTION   xxiii

GLOSSARY   xxxi

PART I MAINLY ANIMALS   I

     1   Spider   3
     2   Hare   58
     3   Jackal   69
     4   Lion   89
     5   Cat   97
     6   Goat   100
     7   Hyena   110
     8   A Miscellany   129

PART II CARICATURES—ETHNIC
AND OTHER STEREOTYPES   155

     1   Maguje   157
     2   Fulani   176
     3   Gwari   178
     4   The Kano Man   181
     5   Sokoto Men   190
     6   Kanuri   194
     7   Tuareg and Buzu   196
     8   Nupe   203
     9   Stupid Country Folk   204
     10   The Malam   206
     11   The Barber   209
     12   All Hausas   210

PART III MORALISING   213

     1   Women   215
     2   Poverty   240

CONTENTS

3 *Gratitude and Ingratitude*   246

4 *The Will of God*   251

5 *Miscellaneous Morals*   257

PART IV MEN AND WOMEN YOUNG MEN AND MAIDENS 287

PART V DILEMMA TALES   379

PART VI CASES AT LAW   405

APPENDIX   435

Table of Cross-References to Original Edition

Foreword

Neil Skinner probably invited me to contribute this Foreword to his translation of Frank Edgar's Hausa folk stories as a gesture of friendship and because he knows my admiration for Edgar's work and for the Hausa people. In accepting, I am struck by the strange indirect association of these two men which dates in my experience beyond 1958 when Neil Skinner showed me a mass of Edgar's unpublished writings which he had purchased while on leave in Britain the year before for the Northern Region Literature Agency (NORLA) from the estate of Frank Edgar's widow. Assisted by a Hausa Arabist of the NORLA staff at Tudun Gaskiya, Zaria, I spent an exciting week with these papers; all clearly handwritten on foolscap, they filled three shelves, each five feet long. To list them I catalogued these papers by their titles, and grouped them in provisional categories by topic or region. If Edgar's published corpus is in fact the most extensive collection of African folklore yet issued by a single author, these and other works published by Edgar in his lifetime represent merely a portion of his total literary output, little of which was written in English. Surely among the many scholarly officials who have devoted their lives to the study of Northern Nigeria, Edgar can have few peers as a field collector of folklore and tradition.

In 1963 when Neil Skinner was teaching Hausa at the University of California, Los Angeles, Professor William Bascom of Berkeley asked him to translate the three volumes of *Tatsuniyoyi Na Hausa*, Edgar's major work, thereby making it available to scholars unfamiliar with Hausa. Without thought of possible publication, Neil Skinner agreed and returned to New Zealand with a photo-copy of Edgar's text, long out of print. For the next three years he worked at the translation of Volumes I and II of the *Tatsuniyoyi*, whenever he could. Only then and with some urging did he contemplate the prospect of publication. To translate a work of such heterogeneity and character is no mean feat; and to under-take this task as an end in itself without ulterior purposes illus-trates remarkable devotion; but perhaps in the wearier stretches the translator recalled the bulk of Edgar's work, unpublished and perhaps prepared without thought of publication. It is odd, the indirect association of these two men, spanning half a century, both former Administrative Officers in Northern Nigeria, both talented linguists, both steeped in the lore and language of the North, both undertaking major literary tasks for their own sake, the older man as collector, the younger as translator. It is odd too that the man who finally translated Edgar's compendium of Hausa folklore should earlier have rescued the greater part of Edgar's remarkable work from loss or destruction by purchasing it, on his own initiative, for Northern Nigeria where this treasure rightly belongs; and it is quite fitting that as the former Director of NORLA, Neil Skinner should have volunteered for this strenuous task of translation, one commensurate perhaps with Edgar's initial compilation.

Edgar's published collection of Hausa folklore was made primarily in Sokoto Province at the direction of Major John Alder Burdon, the first Resident of Sokoto, who in 1910 gave Edgar some Hausa texts written in the Ajemic script for transliteration into Roman characters as reading matter 'of real use to Hausa students,' that is, to Europeans who wished to learn Hausa. Together with some extracts from the Maliki Law book and other texts that he had collected himself, Edgar prepared the first volume of the *Tatsuniyoyi* for publication in 1911. The two later volumes contained materials he collected himself.

Burdon had two major interests in directing Edgar to prepare a collection of Hausa folk tales and texts for publication: firstly, to provide British Administrative Officers with suitable materials for Hausa language study, and secondly to increase their knowledge of Hausa society and culture by presenting these folk tales and traditions. Both interests reflect the pattern of Indirect Rule by which the British sought to administer the large Hausa–Fulani Emirates through their traditional rulers and institutions. Such administration required British officials to have a sound knowledge of the native language, history and culture. With this end in view, officials strove to collect folk tales and historical traditions, proverbs, riddles, statements of native custom and belief, and manuscripts on religious, legal and historical subjects from Hausa and Bornu. Besides Burdon and Edgar, H. R. Palmer, E. J. Arnett, A. J. N. Tremearne, R. S. Rattray, J. R. Patterson and others undertook such enquiries in Hausaland and in Bornu.

Thus it is to Lugard's system of Indirect Rule that we owe the relative abundance and high quality of the documents on the history and customs of these Central Sudanic Emirates, their languages and folklore, compiled by Administrative Officers during the first decades of this century. By comparison with other African regions of similar size, this official contribution to the study of Hausa and Kanuri culture and history in Northern Nigeria is outstanding alike in its depth, quality, variety and volume. In this stimulating milieu, Frank Edgar compiled his enormous corpus of Hausa folk literature.

By 1913 Edgar had published his *Grammar of the Gbari Language* with attached Dictionary, together with the three volumes of *Tatsuniyoyi Na Hausa*. Thereafter he published a Hausa selection from the Thousand and One Nights in Roman script. His unpublished manuscripts now at the Regional Archives in Kaduna, Northern Nigeria, reveal the range of his interests and efforts. These scripts include, besides a monumental Hausa–English Dictionary, some poems in Ajemic and Roman script, a store of proverbs, riddles and similar word-plays, numerous folk tales and historical texts on Bornu, Bauchi, Zaria, Katsina, Biu, Jukun, Potiskum, Fika, Kano, Gobir, Kebbi and Sokoto. In addition there are many old texts on legal, political, theological and historical subjects in Arabic, Hausa Ajemic and Roman Hausa versions. Apparently most of these materials were collected after the publication of the *Tatsuniyoyi*; and perhaps the greater portion consists of historical texts with varying character and range, from terse king lists of local states to extensive accounts of particular incidents and personalities. How many of these scripts were included in the *Tatsuniyoyi* I cannot say.

The Hausa whose folklore Edgar recorded so industriously are the largest ethnic group in Northern Nigeria and number many millions. Settled in the north-western quarter of that territory, for centuries Hausa have been open to influences from North Africa and from the Middle East as well as from other Central Sudanic states. For centuries also Hausa have traded eastwards to Bornu and west to Gao and the Niger Bend, north to Ghadames and Ghat, southwards to Yoruba and Nupe. Settled on the high fertile savannahs that stretch north to the sahil below the desert, Hausa were simultaneously enriched by trade and exposed to military and political domination for much of their history. Of foreign influences that bore upon them, medieval Islam was both the most complex and important. Then, after centuries of religious syncretism, the traditional Hausa chiefdoms, nominally Muslim but still attached to heathen idioms, were challenged and subdued by a movement of militant Islamic reform led by Shehu dan Fodio, a local Fulani cleric; between 1804 and 1810 the region experienced a major upheaval as the Shehu and his followers, mainly Fulani, overpowered the various Hausa states and established their theocratic regime. Since then most Hausa chiefdoms have had Fulani rulers who claim authority and descent from the Shehu's lieutenants; and despite the British occupation of 1900 to 1903 under Lugard, the Fulani have retained their dominance until and since 1960, when Hausaland passed from British rule as part of the independent Nigerian Federation.

Since at least the fifteenth century, Hausa have lived in contiguous centralised chiefdoms whose capitals were large fortified towns where the ruler's palace and the central market stood. For centuries before the Jihad of Shehu dan Fodio the Hausa people were organised in a series of overlapping social strata based on hereditary occupational classes. In each state the royal family and the official nobility had precedence, followed by the Muslim intelligentsia of native and immigrant clerics, jurists, preachers, teachers and scribes, *sherifai* descended from the Prophet and wandering holy men or marabouts. Next came the wealthier merchants engaged in local and long-distance trade (*fatauci*); then craftsmen and other traders such as the commission-agents, vendors of salt or slaves, weavers, leather workers, silversmiths, dyers, master builders and blacksmiths, few of whom in the cities probably farmed for subsistence, though their rural counterparts generally did so. Then as now, the mass of Hausa people lived in rural villages and hamlets, farming the sorghum and millet staples and the cotton they wove for cloth. Besides this free population were the slaves, some captive or purchased, others born locally to whom Hausa language and culture were native. Chiefs and a few others had eunuchs in their households, and in several states eunuchs served as senior administrators in palace and public affairs. The traditional society was further complicated by the presence of several relatively endogamous ethnic groups whose ancestors, attracted by the prosperity and prospects of these Hausa societies, had moved and settled there; such immigrants included Arab traders from Ghadames, Tuareg from Asben and Air, Berbers from Bornu, Nupe from Bida, some Yoruba from Old Oyo, settled and nomad Fulani, some Mandinka, and yet others. Thus the traditional Hausa society, before as after the Holy War of 1804–10, was a complex of overlapping strata, communities and groups differentiated by religion, language and ethnicity, by connubium, by political and legal status as Muslim or pagan, free, eunuch or slave, rulers or ruled, aristocrats by birth or nobles by office, city folk and countrymen, farmers, craftsmen, traders of various sorts, the Muslim intelligentsia (a hereditary group), the wealthy and the destitute, the old, the mature and the younger men.

Excluding Tuareg, all ethnic groups in this society stressed paternal descent in residence, inheritance and succession to office or to civic status. Compounds enclosed families linked through the agnatic kinship of their male heads; polygyny was common as well as preferred; on marriage, women moved to live in their husband's home, generally among his close kinsfolk; and first marriages were normally arranged between first cousins. However, under pressure from Islam the old pagan lineages had been transformed by proscriptions of exogamy and levirate and by differentiation of descent lines and inheritance subdivisions.

This traditional society had also official Muslim courts, Koranic schools for children and for adult scholars, elaborate military and civil organisations, youth associations, hereditary occupational groups, cults for the worship of pagan spirits by possession, institutions for long-distance trade, guilds of prostitutes under titled head women, currency, markets, a literate intelligentsia, slave estates attached to particular offices or owned by individuals, and various other social formations characteristic of a complex, prosperous society with relatively high levels of technological development and social differentiation.

In this society women, though central to the private domain of kinship and marriage, remained minors at law under the guardianship of their senior male kin who commonly acted on the advice of an elderly kinswoman. This co-ordinate situation enabled women to divorce their husbands at will with support from their kin; alternatively, spirited women, rejecting their subservient status, might leave husband and kin to join the prostitutes in another town or state.

This, briefly, was the traditional pattern of Hausa society in which the Shehu proclaimed his *jihad* and to which most of the stories and traditions recorded by Edgar relate. For its members, differences of social and ethnic status provided a broad framework in which other differences of individual situation, temperament and fortune were easily appreciated. A fine and firm web of institutional-ised relations distributed constraints and opportunities for initiative unequally among individuals of differing social categories. Relations of clientage and bond-friendship allowed men to select their patrons or peers for personal or structural considerations. To those who sought fortune (*arziki*) in commercial success, the market offered exciting opportunities; warriors and others pursu-ing political position might move from one Hausa chief to the next by changing their patrons. Devout Muslims could combine adventure and travel with the search for grace and knowledge by pilgrimage to the Holy Places of Islam; other scholars could pursue their religious and legal studies at home or on periodic journeys within the Central Sudan; slaves might seek their master's favour or even manumission; adepts of the pagan *bori* (spirit) cult, prostitutes, wastrels and immigrants were free also within Islamic limits to pursue their interests in a tolerant, eclectic milieu. Some of the following stories illustrate these qualities of the traditional society; others exhibit its less pleasant features – ethnic intolerance, chiefly high-handedness, the depressed position of women, slaves, and so on.

After the tradition of folk literature, Edgar's narratives assume the reader's familiarity with these variegated patterns of Hausa society; and, except for a few remarks on grammar and ortho-graphy, Edgar neither discusses his materials nor reports their sources nor the methods of their collection. Evidently he enjoyed his task as collector of native folklore; his activities were justified by the current demand among British officials for suitable Hausa reading materials in Roman script. Edgar accordingly converted Arabic or Ajemic texts into Roman Hausa and gave little thought to their analysis. Lacking explicit academic interests, he was con-tent merely to record and to transliterate; and on retiring to Britain Edgar seems to have ceased work on his massive collection, except perhaps for fair copying and transliteration. Nothing suggests that he seriously considered its analysis beyond the natural categories of the folk classification, in which *tatsuniyoyi* or fables were separated from other materials (*labaru* or *labarai*), most of which referred to real persons, events, customs or situations.

However, Edgar's practice sometimes invalidates this broad distinction. As fables, and thus wholly fictitious, the *tatsuniyoyi* are distinguished from old folk literature which treats situations of real life, whether in poems, proverbs, legal codes, historical scripts, descriptions of custom and ethnic types, or legends of uncertain validity. Even so, many of these *labaru* seem quite as fabulous as some *tatsuniyoyi*. Though Edgar, writing in Hausa for officials familiar with Hausa society, was unconcerned by such anomalies or by the grossness of the folk classification he employed, it is necessary in translating these materials for presentation to a wider audience to develop a more meaningful organisation. H. A. S. Johnston, another ex-official of Northern Nigeria, in his recently published *A Selection of Hausa Stories** which is based largely on Edgar's work, has organised its eighty-six items for Westerners unfamiliar with Hausa culture in six categories; and Neil Skinner in presenting the 443 fables and 240 *labaru* of Edgar's compilation, has ordered the former in fourteen classes, the latter in twelve. Clearly these two reclassifications are in part designed to facilitate the orderly presentation of these very diverse and exotic materials to Western readers, including specialists in comparative folklore. By provisionally adopting Edgar's gross distinction between fables and *labaru*, we can tentatively distinguish their contents and contexts and thus indirectly indicate some of their values for the study of Hausa ethnography and culture history.

Neil Skinner distinguishes certain folk tales which treat the marvellous, sometimes offering etiological explanations, or Just So Stories about common everyday things. Many of these tall stories deal with animal or mythical beings who inhabit a curiously Hausa world and conduct themselves after the fashion of Hausa. Since the etiological value of such tales is minimal, while they are clearly pleasurable and generally non-didactic, it seems that they are related for entertainment rather than instruction, or perhaps to

* H. A. S. Johnston, *A Selection of Hausa Stories*, Oxford, 1966.

xiii

pass the time pleasantly. Sometimes these fantasies or fables treat problem situations current in Hausa society, though in idealised forms.

Another group of tales centres on relations between the sexes, with marriage, adultery and child nurture as its major themes. These stories are often ribald, rarely sentimental and only in a gross way moral. Many present male comments on the attractions and defects of the opposite sex, but most seem morally indifferent and few are etiological in any sense. All presuppose standard Hausa patterns of relations between individuals of specified sex, age, status and kinship, so that as a group these stories of men and women provide a broad indirect account of heterosexual relations in Hausa society.

Though many stories treat Hausa Islamic beliefs, institutions and representatives, sometimes satirically, fewer present local beliefs in *dodos*, witchcraft, tree serpents, *kwari*, the impersonal supernormal power Polynesians call *mana,* or *iskoki*, the named spirits personified through possession in the bori cult. Edgar provides little information on the characters and doings of these pagan spirits by comparison with A. J. N. Tremearne.* Undoubtedly these omissions reflect Edgar's dependence on literate Hausa who belonged to the Muslim intelligentsia for much of his materials. Such men were unlikely to possess a wide knowledge of the *iskoki* cult or to admit familiarity with its lore.

To seek a single function for these folk tales, despite their differing genres, presupposes their functional uniformity. Often such questions assume mistaken equations of function and purpose. Whereas purpose involves conscious intention, function denotes the latent and unintended effects of particular modes of social action. Thus to say that, while these tales are related for their entertainment value, their primary function is broadly educational, involves no inconsistency. Hausa tale-tellers and audiences share certain institutional orientations and conceptions which are largely embedded in Hausa speech. When the narrator relating his stories seeks to dramatise events to achieve appropriate effects, these

---

* A. J. N. Tremearne, *Hausa Superstitions and Customs*, London, 1913. A new edition with an introduction by M. Hiskett is in preparation by Frank Cass, A. J. N. Tremearne, *The Ban of the Bori*, London, 1914. Reprinted Frank Cass. 1968.

histrionic efforts presuppose accepted canons of thought and conduct common to himself and his audience. Without this shared background, the dramatic gestures would often misfire, thereby destroying the tale. Because the story has its context and meaning in the common culture, the audience responds by evaluating its incidents, characters and presentation in terms familiar to them, drawn from their own social experience, thereby indirectly re-vitalising the cultural norms and social models to which they were socialised. Indeed, folk tales, even when dealing with fabulous creatures and events, serve as media for the socialisation of succes-sive generations of Hausa children who are gradually inducted from realms of cultural phantasy in which animals talk and act like Hausa adults into the lore of white (good) and black (bad) spirits, of magic and the mysterious, and so, with certain trans-formations and changing stress, into the complex workaday society where differentials of birth, status and power are often interpreted in mystical terms, as for instance when abrupt changes of fortune are explained by possession of a *dodo*. In a traditional society where schools are devoted to the study of religious texts in a foreign tongue, folk tales, proverbs, historical legends and etiological narratives that represent approved and deviant be-haviours and their consequences are, virtually for lack of com-petition, among the most influential instruments for the trans-mission and reinforcement of customary values and attitudes. Such broadly educational effects do not imply that such folklore has an educational purpose, solely or primarily; but its educational value is surely enhanced by its qualities as entertainment. More-over, in a traditional preliterate society, folk education consists mainly in the transmission and reinforcement of stereotyped folk attitudes, values and conceptions, rather than in the transfer of technical 'knowledge', data or moral maxims.

How or why these tales and other forms of folk literature took their present shape, we do not know. Clearly, while some tales were diffused among Hausa by contacts with foreign peoples, including immigrants, others were probably indigenous; tales of either sort vary in their age and purity; but whether borrowed from abroad or fashioned locally, for their preservation among the Hausa, these tales depend on their appeal and their meaningfulness for Hausa narrators and audiences. So, regardless of their differing origins, Hausa folk tales are socially selected items of local lore, reworked and simplified or amplified in the processes of transmission. Various versions of Edgar's tales, collected in the same or different Emirates, illustrate certain features of these transforming processes, including omissions or reallocations of roles, recombinations of motifs, events and the like. Clearly in such processes those items which lack immediate intelligibility or cogency are most likely to be modified or omitted, while those which have local relevance will be retained and perhaps elaborated or transferred to other narratives.

To substantiate some of the preceding remarks we may review briefly the contexts in which *tatsuniyoyi* and *labaru* of differing sorts are generally told. Some tales that deal with animals, the marvellous, and so on, are identified with old women who relate them to groups of young children in family compounds at night, often in the old dame's hut where the children will sleep. Baba of Karo, an old Hausa lady who narrated her life history, makes frequent references to these nightly tale-tellings.* Hausa describe such sessions as *hira*, a term which includes conversation or gossip. *Hira* thus has as many varieties as situations, audiences, and types of discourse. For example, the tales which are told by old dames to children differ in content from those that are appropriate for old men to tell. Old men avoid the miraculous and animal stories, preferring instead to discuss the legendary foundations of their community or chiefdom, the family genealogy and history, traditions of local saints, of marabouts, princes or warriors – that is, events or personalities believed to belong to the real world of Hausa society. In Koranic schools, at craft sessions, during Ramadan and at certain festivals, old men may tell such tales to children and adolescents. However, fathers are segregated from children and women in the daily round, and perhaps elderly men addressed their stories mainly to their last-born (*auta*), the favourite child, and to grandchildren, their joking relations.

In youth groups and as apprentices to some craft whose traditional lore summarises its distinctive ethos and relations with other segments of Hausa society, young boys take part in special social contexts, each with its appropriate lore. Perhaps among the crafts,

* Mary Smith, *Baba of Karo: A Woman of the Moslem Hausa*, pp. 52–55, 59–60, 75, 152, 177, 179, 251, London, 1954.

long-distance traders (*fatake*), butchers, blacksmiths, and praise-singers maintain the richest special traditions, if we exclude the spirit-possession cults, clerics and officialdom. Young girls have also their own lore, linked with bond-friendship, betrothal, sex, petting (*tsarance*), marriage and the magico-religious complex which includes, besides witchcraft (*maita*), magic (*boka*), medicines (*magani*), the pre-Islamic nature spirits (*iskoki, bori*), and Islamic charms (*layu*) or prayers (*addu'a*). Girls also learn a lore of marketing by peddling wares around the village and find contexts in their own youth associations for Hausa lore about relations between the sexes.

Ribald stories that treat of sexual matters are told to mixed audiences of younger adults in *hira* sessions nightly at the local brothel or at the salon of some leading prostitute (*karuwa*). Such tales may also circulate on certain festive occasions, such as marriage, among co-wives and female guests within a compound, or among men segregated by work or on journeys, idled by rain, darkness or other circumstances. The lore of *iskoki*, the old Hausa spirits, their praise-songs, genealogical and other relations, attributes, powers and needs is vested in bori cult-groups, each locally anchored in the prostitutes' guild; thus the stories and music of the spirit-possession cult are indirectly linked with lewder tales through recital by the same persons in the same milieu. More specialised information about particular spirits, their diseases, susceptibilities and powers, is available privately from bori specialists who preserve and know them. Not all of these devotees are women; nor are all female cultists prostitutes.

Yet other folklore traditions are centred in the capitals, concentrated among the elderly savants of particular wards and especially at and around the ruler's court. There we should find the major oral traditions of the chiefdom's history, often apparently bizarre and uneven. These include, besides legends of the state's foundation and origin, cryptic king-lists, some of which specify the length of each king's reign, tales of pre-Fulani rulers and their deeds, of local battles during the Shehu's *jihad*, tales of the Shehu's miraculous powers and leadership, of Fulani Emirs and their wars, their characters and difficulties, of civil commotion and strife, of the coming of the British and their early forceful years. Tales of rulers and events nearer in time can still be checked against narratives by old men who witnessed or heard directly of these events from those who witnessed them. For earlier histories we must seek either the narrator's source and authority, following the model of a Muslim *isnad*, or admit the folk element in the narrative and its interpretation equally. Such quasi-historical tales form the majority of Edgar's *labaru*. They centre about the actions of chiefs and have their most authentic sources at or near the court, especially in Edgar's case the imperial courts of the Sultan and Vizier (Waziri) of Sokoto. Some of these tales are well known to older men, even in rural areas; others that detail events more finely, may be private to official or aristocratic circles; and even these latter are often found in differing versions that express corresponding political alignments.

Yet other stories, which purists might exclude from Hausa folklore, are related by clerics, having their core in Traditions of the Prophet and his Companions, supplemented by tales of famous Sudanic figures such as Shehu dan Fodio and his brother Abdullahi, Mohammed Askia of Gao, Bawa Jan Gwarzo of Gobir or Kanta of Kebbi. This clerical tradition also includes legends that exalt the cleric's mystical powers over heathen magicians and his role in assuring the success of his clients in their search for fortune – princes for the throne, officials for office, women for children, peasants for various boons and Emirs for victory in the field.

Thus in this corpus each major body of folklore and narrative has its appropriate milieu and content, and most represent the traditions of special groups in the complex, differentiated Hausa society. The tales are thus differentially associated with differing Hausa institutions such as praise-singing and prostitution, the pagan bori cult or the Muslim intelligentsia, youth associations and the premarital petting sessions known as *tsarance*, kinship ceremonials of betrothal and marriage, childbirth and the following ablutions, bond-friendship and the routine round of compound life in city, rural town or bush hamlet, the market place, the law court, the palace, officialdom and the army, and with particular chiefdoms. There are tales also of wells, or fishermen and of hunters, of hereditary thieves and other craft specialists, tales of madness and personal misfortune and social stereotypes of various ethnic groups – Maguzawa or pagan Hausa, the Bugaje (s. Buzu) or Tuareg serfs, Fulani pastoralists and Nupe craftsmen, Gwari pagans, Arab merchants from Ghat or Ghadames, the Kanuri and the country bumpkins ill at ease in town. Beyond the lore of these specialised contexts stand the cycles of fables and wonder stories that old women relate to the young.

These folk tales accordingly offer very diverse and valuable evidence on particular institutional contexts and differentiated groups of the traditional Hausa society. They also provide many comments on the structures they describe and on the stereotyped situations and ethnic and social categories they feature. Besides such indirect information and commentary, Edgar also collected many texts which describe Hausa customs, such as marriage or inheritance directly, and others that summarise folk evaluations of ethnic and occupational groups or people of different states such as Kano or Katsina, of women, conjugal relations, relations between co-wives, siblings, commoners and chiefs or clerics and their clients. Such direct descriptions and evaluations delineate important features in the contexts of many traditional tales; they also furnish an excellent account of Hausa practice and cultural orientations at the turn of this century, before European influences had taken their present effect. Used with caution, they can thus serve to identify later changes.

Although non-narrative and explicitly descriptive, such direct statements form a natural part of Hausa folklore, since the conceptions and attitudes they express are important elements of the folk tradition. These summary descriptions always refer to concrete social situations and to local types. They are thus quite distinct from the strictly Islamic texts that declare or discuss the Law, the Faith, Prophetic Traditions or the norms of Muslim government. Such Islamic materials differ in source, character, manifest purpose and range from local lore. They express, in Hausa form, the universalistic orientations of Islam which contrast sharply with the ethnic axes of Hausa society.

Historical and quasi-historical texts, not all of which are narrative, also form an extremely valuable section of Edgar's compilation. Besides several king-lists of certain states, often given in different versions, these texts include origin legends for the Hausa states and some local communities, apocryphal tales of Kanta, Bawa and the Shehu, some stories that illustrate important features of traditional government, and others that characterise particular rulers, such as the Sultans Umaru and Abdu Danyen Kasko of Sokoto, or the Emir Abdullahi of Kano, together with a mass of illuminating incidental materials on historical events and personalities during the century of Fulani domination that followed the *jihad*. If we accept the folk interpretation of unusual events by reference to destiny (*rabo*) or magic, and the unavoidable variants of a common tale, we have no reason to doubt the intended accuracy of many of these 'historical' traditions, though naturally such intent cannot guarantee their historicity. To assess this, we should first correlate these variant versions with any others still available and identify their similar or dissimilar contents, sequences, characters and interpretations. It may then be possible to collate an abstracted probable or common sequence with other data drawn from the Emirates to which specific narratives relate, to determine the probable historical situation and sequence. Naturally such procedures presuppose adequate bodies of independently derived data for the events under study, and also substantial consistency, detail, and credibility among the various traditions. However, much historical information can still be gathered by field enquiries in Hausa emirates and checked by the study of official and other records*

Setting aside their uncertain historical values, these tales of past events show how Hausa conceive the histories of their states, the characters of their rulers, and their institutions of government and law. These traditions are thus equally important as documents of folk thought and as historical sources.

The academic values of Edgar's collection are many and various; to students of Hausa culture and history, it provides a comprehensive body of diverse materials, much of which, being explicitly fictive, is of great ethnographic significance as a projection of Hausa attitudes and practice on to other planes. Together these texts, descriptive and narrative, supply rich firsthand materials on Hausa institutions, inter-ethnic relations and social stratification, supplementing such standard sources as the Kano Chronicle and

* M. G. Smith, 'Field Histories Among the Hausa', *Journal of African History*, vol. 3, No. 1, pp. 87–101.

S. J. Hogben and A. H. M. Kirk-Greene, *The Estimates of Northern Nigeria: A. Preliminary Survey of their Historical Traditions*, London, 1966.

other Emirate histories*, and presenting, with insight and economy, the characteristic failings, virtues and orientations of Hausa differentiated by rank, sex, age and circumstance. Directly, and in narrative obliquely, the texts also present many insights into Hausa values, beliefs and social orientations. As documents that transmit the flavour of Hausa life and the background of individual experiences, they have few rivals. Within this compilation we can also distinguish various items that derive from different levels of Hausa social history, thereby indicating certain broad courses of Hausa cultural development. Many tales, for example, centre on Fulani Emirs; though they express the broadest traditions of Hausa lore, others dwell upon ancient Hausa chiefs and yet others, of uncertain age, seem rather more ancient in content and manner. Perhaps by employing our knowledge of major developments and cultural innovations in Hausa society we may provisionally identify historical periods to which such tales and traditions relate; and thus by procedures of exclusion, we may perhaps reduce part of this corpus to a reasonable chronological order. For folklorists and others not directly concerned in Hausa culture history, these abundant materials invite and permit other analyses, thematic, stylistic and distributional, independently or in comparative contexts. For those readers with a general interest in the customs and conditions of life in exotic countries at earlier periods, this remarkable collection needs no further recommendation.

* H. R. Palmer, 'The Kano Chronicle', *Journal of the Royal Anthropological Institute*, vol. 38, pp. 58–98.
S. J. Hogben and A. H. M. Kirk-Greene, 1966, *op. cit.*

M. G. SMITH
*University of California
Los Angeles*

Translator's Introduction

Litafi Na Tatsuniyoyi Na Hausa by Frank Edgar, to give it its full title – hereafter it is referred to as TATS – appears to have been published in 1911 (Volumes I and II) and 1913 (Vol. III); but the edition of the first two volumes from which this translation has been made is dated 1924 on the title page (though the Preface bears the original date of 1911). Major Edgar was one of the early British Political Officers in Northern Nigeria. Appointed in December 1905, he retired in July 1927 and died about ten years later. He and Major J. Alder Burdon, first Resident of Sokoto Province, collected large numbers of manuscripts in Hausa, written in Arabic script. He transliterated them himself into Roman script, then just starting to be used for Hausa, and published them while on leave in Britain.

The material was hardly sorted or edited, though Edgar did include short notes on the Hausa of the first volume, and are a remarkable miscellany: fables, history, quasi-history, proverbs, riddles, a few songs or poems (there is only one Hausa word for the two things), tongue-twisters, brief letters and notes (some of quite ephemeral interest), and religious and legal items. A collection of similar MSS – including some of the originals of these – obtained from Edgar's executors was handed over by the translator in 1958 to the newly-formed regional archives at Kaduna.

The three volumes have been unobtainable for some time, and until 1966 none had been translated. In this year, H. A. S. Johnston published translations of some sixty of them in *A Selection of Hausa Stories*. The versions in these volumes have been compared with his and reference is made where applicable, using the abbreviation J. References are also given, for each story, to the numbers in Edgar's original work, so that those able to consult it and wishing to compare the English and the Hausa may do so. Other references have been given to variant versions in other collections of Hausa tales. Edgar made a dichotomy in each volume between *tatsuniyoyi* and *labarai,* the former being mostly fables and tales of fancy; the latter being historical and other traditions, Muslim material and miscellanea. This dichotomy has been retained to the extent that the first two volumes of the present work contain mainly *tatsuniyoyi* and the last *labarai*. In fact though, in the Hausa, a *tatsuniya*,* which is also freely referred to as *almara*, will also very often be called *labari*.* A *labari* (history, tradition) will, on the other hand, not be called a *tatsuniya*.

Other than translation, the only major change has been in the order of the tales. They have been classified, the *tatsuniyoyi* into fourteen sections; and the *labarai* into twelve. From the nature of the former, the task has been a difficult one. So many of them have the characteristics of several categories, and whereas a Spider Tale or a Tall Story is a fairly easily distinguishable genre, some of the other categories set up are by no means so. The story titles, which were usually just a list of the main characters, have mostly been left unchanged. Where, however, the story is included in a sub-category named after a principal character, his name has been omitted from the titles of the individual stories, to avoid tedium. A small number of titles has also been changed for aesthetic reasons, for the sake of clarity, or perhaps to indicate why it was felt that the story was categorised as it was. It is noteworthy that the best criterion of the story's genre is often to be found, not in the title, which, as stated, is a mere *dramatis personae,* but in its tail. The art of the story-teller is to keep the punch-line till the end.

Few textual emendations have seemed necessary, and these have usually been noted at the foot of the page. In particular, Arabic script does not use capitals, nor does it punctuate in the same way as does Roman, and Edgar's choice in this matter has sometimes been departed from. If anything has been omitted, because it is not understood, such omission is duly noted. In this connexion, the reader of fifty-five years later may perhaps smile at Edgar's words written in 1913: 'Many of the tales, of course, cannot for obvious reasons be translated into English, but as it is important to get an insight into the minds and habits of natives, I have felt justified in including them.' What would his comment on *Fanny Hill* have been, I wonder?

In Hausa the story usually begins *ga ta ga ta nan* ('see it, see it here'), to which the audience can reply *ta je ta komo* ('let it go, let it come back'), or a *ta zo, mu ji* ('let it come, for us to hear'). So a *gatanan* is often another name for a *tatsuniya*. The traditional finish is *kungurus kan kusu* (probably 'the rat's head is off'). *Bera,* the

* Singular.

commoner word for 'rat', sometimes replaces *kusu*, and *kungurus* (an ideophone, perhaps to be rendered by 'chop-chop') has the variants *kunkurus* and *kurungus*. Other endings, less common, are 'I ate the rat, not the rat me'; 'it wasn't because of Spider that I made it up – I was making it up in any case' (Rattray, however, prefers this to be a question, 'You don't think I should have made it up if it hadn't been for Spider do you?'); and the longest one, rare in TATS, which can be read at III/17,† and is also quoted by Tremearne. In TATS – perhaps because they were given to Edgar in written form – the initial and final formulae are often omitted, or something more mundane or Muslim inserted by the scribe. So we have, for the beginning, often merely 'a tale' or 'another tale' and, for the ending, *haza wassalamu*, 'this with peace', the normal epistolary ending, or even the Arabic *tammat* (rendered 'finis').

The story tellers are the mothers and grandmothers and the motifs are, of course, well known. In 1954 the North Regional Literature Agency advertised, offering 5s. for a good story, and in the following months received several thousands, mostly sent in by schoolboys. In fact, the quantity proved embarrassing. They are now also broadcast from Kaduna.

The language of TATS, as would be expected with such a large number of pieces collected from various sources, is fairly variable. On the whole, though, it tends to exhibit characteristics of the language as spoken in Sokoto and Katsina rather than the now standard (for writing) Kano speech. This is truer of the first two volumes than of the third. The third volume also shows far fewer archaisms and anomalies than the first two. One example of this difference is in the use of the word *amma* (usually rendered 'but', but far rarer than 'but' is in English). This is an Arabic loan-word, whose meaning has undergone change since being adopted by Hausa. In the two earlier volumes, the word is not infrequently used in the Arabic way; also in a rather bewildering variety of usages, as if the scribes were experimenting with something that was not yet firmly established. In the third volume, on the other hand, the modern usage has almost completely established itself* – probably because Edgar here employed scribes from a different area, whose idiom was the modern one.

* See article on this word in *J. African Languages*, Vol. VI, Pt. 2 (1967).
† See Appendix.

There is not space in this introduction to mention more than one or two of the main characteristics of the language of TATS. Many of these are of the nature of spoken Hausa – but less so of Hausa as increasingly written in 1966, or indeed as used for speeches:

1. The style is staccato. The sentences are short. There are none of the cumbrous monstrosities of modern newspaper writing, introducing strings of subordinate clauses, due to the influence of bureaucratic English. Even the use of Hausa particles is kept to the minimum. The overwhelming preponderance among them of *sai* ('then, thereupon, etc.') taxes the ingenuity of the translator to avoid monotony. This is perhaps especially true of Volume I and, in it, of those pieces about Argungu history, presumably contributed by Argungu scribes. Nor do we get the more recent Arabic loan-words and phrases, many of which have been borrowed to meet the increasing complications of modern society. It goes without saying that English loan-words are virtually non-existent (see Glossary under 'Cowries'). On the other side of the picture – words that have since dropped out of use – there are not many of these that occur frequently in TATS. The word for 'cowries' (*kudi/kurdi*) has become the word for modern money, but other idioms used in connection with cowries are now obsolete; also a number of words and phrases used in connection with the institutions of slavery and old-style warfare (such as *goron yaki,* 'cola-nuts of war', bestowed by the chief on one determined to do or die.) Nor, other than *kudi*, do many of them seem to have survived with altered connotation. *Dakare* (infantryman) gave way for a short time to *askar* (Arabic 'soldier'), but very rapidly *soja* prevailed. The practical Hausa realised that this was a new genus, not a mere variant, for whom the same word could be extended. Perhaps this resistance of the language to change indicates that, for all its ready welcome of English and Arabic loans, the solid core of Hausa has changed little.

2. Direct speech is always preferred to indirect. In the only story where the opposite is true, I have suggested that this is occasioned by its being a translation from the Arabic. Here again the translator is taxed by the monotonous Hausa use of *ce* ('say'), where in English there would be a wide range of expressions such as 'exclaim, ask, reply, answer, suppose, say to oneself' not to

mention all the adverbial expressions, such as 'angrily, shocked, in surprise, indignantly,' etc. Hausa leaves it to the teller to express all these by his voice. The most it does by way of indication to a reader is to put an interjection at the beginning of the quoted passage, which gives some guidance as to the feelings of the speaker. Thus, for example, *Sai tace 'Wayyo!* ...' ('she said "Alas..."') will bear translating – though I have not usually done so – as 'She answered sorrowfully'.

3. TATS is unbelievably repetitive. Not only is this true of plots and motifs – understandable in folklore (for, once again, such repetition gives the teller scope to exhibit his powers of playing different roles, and the audience the opportunity of joining in, knowing well what is coming next). But it is true also of the language. A passage such as this would be impossible in English:

> 'The chief told the boy to go and fetch the girl. The boy went and fetched the girl. The boy said to the girl, "Come." The girl came.'

and yet this is of the very stuff of TATS and occurs in paragraph after paragraph. In translation, again to avoid monotony, I have used phrases like 'He did so' and 'He obeyed'; also I have made greater use of pronouns and surrogates such as 'the former', 'the latter', 'the other' and the like.

Next, a word about the translation itself. Looking back over it, I am conscious that the style has changed as the work proceeded. The latter half is far more literal than is the earlier part and, perhaps for this reason, does not read so well in English. I decided at the start to translate literally the Hausa masculine and feminine pronouns. This was perhaps a mistake, since whereas 'he' and 'she' have connotations of sex difference in English, *ya* and *ta* cannot have these in the same way in Hausa. There is no natural basis for the Hausa division into masculine and feminine of the vast majority of nouns. As a result, there are some interesting anomalies. For example, in III/66 the *shirwa* (kite-hawk) is the husband, but the word is feminine; so in the same sentence, where we are being told that the bird was the husband of Auta's sister, the pronoun switches from feminine to masculine, thus avoiding absurdity, at the expense of syntactical regularity. In contrast with this, in Mischlich,* No. 4, there is a case where the *damisa* (usually

* See p. xxx

feminine, but with this teller apprently masculine) becomes feminine when he is speaking of a leopardess.

Sarki I have rendered by either 'emir' or 'chief' but not 'king'; *Sarkin Musulmi* (the Hausa equivalent of *amīru lmu' minīn*, 'commander of the faithful') I have rendered 'Sultan' in accordance with modern usage. *Zakara* I have translated sometimes as 'cock', sometimes, in deference to American usage, as 'rooster'; *damo* is sometimes 'land-monitor', at others 'iguana', but it is the same reptile; *bera/kusu* in Hausa may be either 'rat' or 'mouse'. *Gida* has usually been 'compound', but frequently 'home'. *Cikin gida* which is the inner part of an important man's compound, or alternatively, for others, just 'inside the compound', has also varied. *Rafi* strictly means 'stream' and has usually so been translated, but the phrase *ta je rafi* means 'she went to the source of water' and will, as often as not, be a well; so, in some places where 'stream' has been used, this may very likely be inaccurate. *Bebe* is given by Bargery in his dictionary as 'deaf-mute', but, unlike Johnston, I have usually rendered it simply as 'dumb', since the inability to hear usually seemed irrelevant to the story. *Tsarance* will be found in the Glossary, but I have sometimes translated it as 'courting' or 'dating' or even 'petting'.

Which brings us to other sexual and excretory words. I have been as colourless and scientific as I could, unless I felt the Hausa was being deliberately vulgar and shocking, in which case I permitted myself an English vulgarism. This was particularly so in the matter of breaking wind, where it was referred to in a proverb; I felt here that something so folksy required 'fart'. In general, Hausa – as Greenberg noted – uses the Arabic loan-word, rather than the native one as the polite word in such instances, and it is these mostly that the scribes of TATS have given us.

Wānē, 'So-and-So' is quite often used either where the storyteller wishes to indicate that a name is used, but as most of the characters are anonymous, he is forced to use this surrogate; or because the speaker is avoiding using the name (probably because of name-avoidance customs). I have sometimes rendered this literally, but felt it very awkward in English, and more often presumed that it was the former case and turned e.g. 'he said "Hey, So-and So"' into 'he addressed him by name'. The same applies to *kazā*, 'such-and-such', used of place names.

Zane, 'cloth', usually a woman's body-cloth or wrapper, has been rendered simply as 'cloth'. On one or two occasions the phrase *ta dauki zane*, 'she took up the cloth' has been literally rendered, where it probably connotes that she actually wrapped it round herself as well. *Sallama*, 'say *sallam alaikum*' (obligatory for Muslims coming to another's presence or home) has usually been translated as 'made formal greeting' to distinguish it from the less formal greetings that follow. Difficulties with *ce*, 'say' have been mentioned above, but other ubiquitous combinations which occur have also necessitated varying renderings in the interests of readibility. Such are:

1. *ya/ta/*etc. *ce 'To'*   =   'he/she/etc. said "OK" '
2. *ana nan* at start of paragraph =   'one-being there'
3. *sun zauna* at end of story   =   'they sat'

1. which seems to give expression to the Muslim attitude of acceptance, I have varied as much as I could. There are at least two places where it follows after the speaker has been told that he or she is to die, where to render it 'She said "OK" ' in English would be, to put it mildly, frivolous. 2. is usually 'Time passed', 'Presently', 'Things continued thus for a while', 'After a while' and the like. 3. I have been unable to bring myself to translate as 'They lived happily ever after', though it takes the place of this in our own tales. The idea of happiness seems foreign to the spirit of Islam, so I have usually made it 'They settled down again' or 'Everyone relaxed again'.

Some titles are explained in the Glossary, others I have simply rendered as 'the Ubandawaki', 'the Yarima' without further explanation. 'Prince', etc., are surely inapplicable in a translation such as this.

The many biblical echoes of the translation may reflect my own basic vocabulary, but I think more probably are a result of trying to be as literal as possible, and Hausa, being a member of Greenberg's Afro-Asiatic family of languages and so related to Hebrew, seems to lend itself to the sort of English that King James's translators found appropriate to Scripture.

Lastly, acknowledgements are gratefully made to Professor Bascom, who prompted the translation; Tom Lanagan, without whose Herculean achievement of xerographing the UCLA copy of the Hausa, I should have had nothing to translate; the African Studies Center at VCLA, who provided funds for the xerographing; Mike Smith, without whose encouragement the work would never have been published; B. M. McFarlane, for information about Frank Edgar, and M. Ahmadu Ingawa, for his answers to a number of queries, where the dictionaries and my own knowledge of Hausa failed me.

NEIL SKINNER

January 1967   *University of Wisconsin*

Publications Referred To In The Text

Abbreviation

Edgar, *Tatsuniyoyi Na Hausa*, Vols. I, II and III   TATS
References are to the story or tradition by arabic or roman numeral. Thus the sixth story in Volume II is II/6; and the thirtieth tradition in Volume I is I/XXX.   See Appendix.

Abraham, R. C. *Dictionary of the Hausa Language*. London.
1962   ABR

Charlton, L. *A Hausa Reading Book*. Oxford. 1908   C

Diederichs, E. *Der Geist Des Quorra*. Jena. 1924   D

Fletcher, R. S. *Hausa Sayings & Folklore*. London. 1912   F

Johnston, H. A. S. *A Selection of Hausa Stories*. Oxford. 1966 J

Labaru Na Da da Na Yanzu.* Education Department. Nigeria.
1931 (This is the only one of these publications where the stories have not been translated either into English or into German.) Reprinted 1968. N. Nigerian Publishing Company,
Zaria   LND

Mischlich, A. *Neue Marchen Aus Afrika*. Leipzig. 1929   M

Olderogge, D. A. *Skazky Khausa*. Afrikanskiy Etnograficheskiy
Sbornik V p. 259, etc. Leningrad. 1963   O

Rattray, R. S. *Hausa Folklore*. Oxford. 1913   R

Schön, J. F. *African Proverbs, Tales and Historical Fragments*.
1886   S

Smith, Mary. *Baba of Karo*. London. 1964   BABA

Tremearne, A. J. N. *Hausa Superstitions and Customs*. London.
1913. New ed. Cass. 1968   TR

Glossary

acca (sometimes, in older style, *acha*)
Small cereal, *Digitaria exilis*; not now part of Hausa diet, but grown on the Plateau by non-Hausa tribes.

alewa (probably from Arabic *ḥ l w*)
Boiled sweet (candy), made from sugar or honey or a number of fruits and involving (as Edinburgh Rock) much pulling from a suspended hook.

aya
Tigernut, *Cyperus esculentus*.

baure
Ficus gnaphalocarpa, grown for both shade and fruit.

ɓukka
Temporary shelter, beehive in shape, made by nomad Fulani of a frame of sticks covered with leaves or grass. In the text this is sometimes translated 'booth' or 'shelter'.

cediya
Ficus Thonningii, grown for both shade and fruit.

cowrie-shells
These gave way to the British currency rapidly at the start of the century, the rate being 100 to ½d.; so rapidly in fact that there are several tales in TATS where *sule* and *kwabo* occur – the only English loan-words in the corpus, with the exception of military words in the accounts of the Satiru rising.

daddawa
Small black cakes made from the fermented seeds of the locust-bean tree and used for flavouring *miya*, q.v.

dara
The Hausa version of draughts, each player having six rows of six holes, and twelve draughtsmen, those of one player being stones, of the other, sections of cornstalk.

dinya
Vitex Cienkowskii, a tree whose plum-like fruit are used for a number of purposes.

durmi
Ficus syringifolia, grown for both shade and fruit.

fura	The usual morning meal, preferably of millet, mixed with buttermilk and 'drunk'. Its preparation involves pounding, winnowing; pounding, winnowing – five or six times; washing; back into the mortar for a last pounding; making into balls and putting into boiling water; taking out and pounding again until quite smooth; rolling in flour; putting into a calabash with buttermilk and mashing.
gawasa	Gingerbread-plum tree, *Parinarium macrophyllum*.
geza	Various species of *Combretum*.
haza wassalamu	'This with peace' – see Translator's Introduction.
imam (Hausa) (Arabic, *limam*)	The chief *malam* of the village or town, who leads the prayers at the Friday mosque.
jekadiya	Female messenger of a chief or notable (being female she has access to purdah compounds).
kalgo	*Bauhinia reticulata*, whose bark is much used for rope-making.
kanya	African ebony tree, *Diospyros mespiliformis*.
kihshi	Thin strips of meat dried in the sun, sprinkled with pounded nuts and grilled.
kirari	'Praise-songs', epithets, personal slogans or theme tunes.
kungurus kan kusu/bera	See Translator's Introduction.
kunu	A gruel, that is quick to make as a substitute for *fura* or *tuwo*, and so, not popular as a food. The grain is ground and then, apparently, only pounded once. Then a lump of dough is put in a calabash and hot water poured over it and it is stirred till viscous.
kurna	*Zizyphus Spina-Christi*.

Magajiya	Title of the chief prostitute (Hausa *karuwa* which strictly=any mature woman not married; see BABA, p. 25), having a number of other social roles in addition.
Maguje	See Introduction to Section 2.
maiwa	*Pennisetum spicatum* millet.
malam	Muslim cleric, the standard of whose scholarship varies from a nodding acquaintance with the Koran to an extensive knowledge of the Book, the Hadiths and the Maliki legal treatises. At the lower levels he is much involved in the traffic in charms (see Trimingham J. S., *Islam in West Africa*).
maroki	Praise-singer, panegyrist, 'beggar-minstrel'.
miya	Soup, or sauce, poured over *tuwo* before eating; usually *romo*, 'broth' thickened with various condiments such as *daddawa* and baobab leaves.
nakiya	Sweetmeat made of pounded guinea-corn (or other grain) mixed with honey, and peppers.
tsarance	This is defined in BABA as 'institutionalized love-making between unmarried youths and girls.' In TATS it has sometimes been left untranslated, sometimes rendered as 'dating' or 'courting'.
tuwo	The usual evening meal – the Hausa food *par excellence* – taken with *miya* and 'eaten'. Millet, guinea-corn or – less commonly – maize is used. As with *fura*, it involves five or six poundings and winnowings, and washing before proceeding to cook. The rougher flour is put into the boiling water first; later the finer flour. Various stages of simmer and cool follow, before dishing out into a wooden bowl. Then the *miya*, which has been prepared separately, is poured over; and, probably, groundnut oil, which has been heated, added on top.

waina (or *masa*)   A small fried cake made from guinea-corn, millet or rice. It does not require such intensive pounding as *fura* and *tuwo*. Then, having been mixed with water, the mixture is left overnight to get acid. Next morning it is spooned into the different compartments of the *tanda*, groundnut-oil is poured over, and it is then fried, turning over, when the one side is done. 'Remove each *waina* as it is done and sell for 1 *anini* (tenth of a penny) each' (c. 1930). One of the sources of women's income is the hawking of such, though nowadays they would sell for more like ½d. each.

wasawasa   A food made from bean-flour.

zagi   One of the retainers of a chief, whose function is to walk before him (or sometimes run) when he is riding. He carries usually, as a mark of his office, a red blanket over his shoulder. The number that a chief has varies in accordance with his status.

zana   Thick grass screen used for fencing or for roofing (between framework and outer thatch). A single *zana* might be eight feet by twelve, made of stout, feathery grass.

PART I

MAINLY ANIMALS

These are arranged under the name of the leading character of each tale. Rightly or wrongly, I have made each animal male or female according to whether the Hausa word is masculine or feminine.

SPIDER

Spider [*Gizo*] and His Wife Koƙi*

TATS does not, unlike Rattray, attempt to render the poor pronunciation of Hausa, that Gizo (as a foreigner) is supposed to have. This is not to say that the story-teller did not add it, when speaking the part. R. No. 6 gives a tale about the origin of Gizo – which is nearly the ordinary name for 'spider' in Hausa – telling how he came into existence when the lion trampled on a smith thus giving him many legs.

One of the concluding formulae, involving Gizo, which occurs several times, would appear from Rattray to be 'Do you think I would have made it up if it hadn't been for Gizo?', but the versions in TATS sometimes differ slightly from this.

The Crested Cranes and the Lion†[I/₃]

One day twelve crested cranes made a journey to eat the fruit of a *baure* tree in the middle of a river. As they were leaving they passed Spider's house. One of the figs fell into Spider's house. Said he to them 'Stop, you crested cranes.' So they stopped. Said he

---

Koƙiƙoƙi in Hausa is a kind of mantis.

† Cf. I/153; also TR. No. 36; also M. No. 35 (where the throwing of eggs into the fire is made part of a game): but the start of this tale appears as the opening of M. No. 36, a different version of the tale. Cf. also R. No. 27 (for the second half) and R. No. 28 (for the first half – a much fuller version). Also D. No. 88 (for second half) and D. No. 91 (for first half). Cf. also S. p. 92 and p. 165.

'Crested cranes, won't you take me with you to eat of the *baure*?'
Said they 'But, Spider, you have no wings!' Said he 'Pluck me
one each from yours.' And each of them plucked him a feather
from his own wing.

Then they took him along and went with him to eat of the *baure*.
But Spider prevented them from eating of it. Whereupon they, in
their turn, took back their wings and flew off, leaving him asleep on
the *baure*. After a while he woke, straightened himself to take off –
and fell into the river.

Now, in this river there was a big town. It was into this that he
fell. He greeted the townspeople 'Peace be upon you'; and they
replied 'Welcome, stranger!' Then said their chief 'Take him to the
fishes' hut.' Spider settled down. Then said he to the Chief of the
Water (head ferryman) 'Bring me the children that I may teach
them to read.' The children were collected together for him. He
kindled a fire in the school*.

Then he chanced to see ten crocodile's eggs. So he picked one
up, put it in the fire and said to the children 'If you hear a pop,
say "Stranger's fart, stranger's fart".' This he continued doing till
he had used up† the ten eggs. Then he said to them 'Tell the Chief
of the Water to have me taken home' and he was entrusted to ten
fishes to take him to the bank.

When they had brought him to the bank, he said to them 'Come
out a little way on to the land and let's play the entering-bag game.'
Out they came. Said he 'If I enter, don't strike it!' Then he got into
the bag and out again, and said to them 'Now it's your turn to
enter.' But when they were in the bag, he tied up the mouth of the
bag with them in. Then he kindled a fire and began to grill them.
As he finished grilling them up comes the lion. Says the lion 'Peace
be upon you, Spider.' Says Spider 'Welcome, Big Brother.' And
the lion says 'Give me some fish!' and he took the fish. Whereupon
Spider burst into tears. Says the lion 'Crying for the fish, Spider?'
And Spider replied 'No, it's the smoke.'

They were sitting there when a guinea-fowl got up, and Spider,
speaking of her, said 'Shameless creature, just as if it wasn't me
who gave her her markings!' Then a bush-fowl got up and Spider
said 'Look at her! I'm just preparing to give her some markings

* An open-air one, likely.
† Or, perhaps, to be taken literally – 'eaten up'.

too, when off she goes!' Says the lion 'Can you really do those markings, Spider?' and Spider replies 'Of course I can!' Then the lion says 'Do you think you could give me markings like that?' and Spider answered 'Get a rope of ox-hide.' And he brought him one.

Then Spider seized the lion and tied him to a tree-trunk; and he put an iron rolling-pin* in the fire till it was red-hot. Then pressed it against the lion's body, cauterizing him, and off he ran. Along came the termite and said to the lion 'You're tricky, ungrateful people: if one gives you day, you return night.' Says the lion 'I won't return night to you.' So she chewed through the ox-hide rope and the lion made off.

He went to look for Spider. When Spider heard that the lion was seeking him, he took the corpse of an oribi, dried up, and put it on his body. Then he met the lion, who said to him 'Oribi, have you heard news of Spider?' And the oribi answered the lion 'Run, lion, run. Don't you know, if Spider looks angry at a man, he'll fade, or die. You've been warned!' And the lion set off running.

Big Fleas and Little Fleas† [¹/₆]

Spider was sick. When he got up, he said to his wife 'I haven't any meat.' And he said, sitting at the door of his compound 'I invite all the wild beasts to help.' So she went off and told them, saying 'You are all invited, Spider summons you all to help him.'

Next morning first thing along comes the cockroach, he's the first. Says he to Spider 'Here I am, answering your call to help.' And Spider answered 'Into a hut with you before the others come!' Next up comes the cock. Says he to Spider 'Where are all the others?' and Spider said 'The cockroach is in the hut – in you go and kill

---

* For ginning cotton.

† Cf. I/5 and I/75 for the meat craving, a common motif; cf. the next tale and III/145; and for a variant of this common story M. Nos. 42 and 43; R. No. 26 (where the dung-beetle replaces Spider as the trickster); and F. p. 99.

him!' and the cock went into the hut, killed the cockroach and down he sat.

A little later up comes the cat. Says he to Spider 'Where are all the others?' and Spider answered 'There's the cock in the hut there. Go and kill him!' Into the hut went the cat and killed the cock, and there was the cock, in the hut, dead.

And there was the cat too, when up comes the dog. Says he to Spider 'Where are all the others?' and Spider answered him 'Into the hut with you! The cat's there, go and kill him.' And in he went and killed the cat.

And as he sat in the hut, up came the hyena and said to Spider 'Here I am, come to help.' And Spider said 'There's the dog in the hut. Go and kill him!' And the hyena went in and killed the dog.

And she settled in the hut. Then along came the leopard and said to Spider 'Here I am, come to help' and the Spider said to the leopard 'There's the hyena, go in and kill her!' And the leopard went in and killed the hyena. And while she was still in the hut, up came the lion. Says he to Spider 'Here I am, come to help' and Spider said to him 'There's the leopard, go and kill her!' Then the lion and the leopard both came out and joined battle. And as they fought, Spider came up and ground up a pepper fine, and, taking some, threw it in the lion's eyes. Then he took some more and threw it in the leopard's eyes. And they shut their eyes and couldn't see. Then he took a stick and started beating the lion, beating the leopard, saying

'Leave off, lion; leave off, leopard! For who may enter the fight of you great ones?' until he killed them. And he got meat enough to satisfy him. And he ate and grew fat.

A Variant* [$^I/_{94}$]

It is said that once Spider recovered from an illness and felt the desire for meat. Not finding any he summoned all the beasts of

* Cf above, I/159, III/38, III/125; also see J. p. 7 (a composite version, introducing the important motif of the spear, missing from this, rather bare one).

the bush to come to his compound and do some work for him.

When it was light, the first to arrive was the cockroach. 'Peace be upon you' said he. 'And upon you peace' said Spider. 'Haven't the others come yet?' asked the cockroach, and Spider answered ' Go into a hut and sit down, till they arrive' and the cockroach entered a hut and sat down.

After a while the rooster arrived. 'Peace be upon you' said he to Spider. 'And upon you peace' answered Spider. 'Haven't the others come?' he asked, and Spider answered 'Only the cockroach has come so far. He's there in the hut. Go on in and kill him.' So the rooster went in and killed the cockroach. Then he too sat down in the hut and waited.

After a while the cat came along. Says he to Spider 'Where are the others?' and Spider answered 'They haven't collected yet. The rooster is the first to come. He's there in the hut. When you go in, kill him!' Then the cat went into the hut, and killing the rooster, sat down and waited. And Spider just went on sitting there at the doorway of the entrance-hut.

After a while the dog came along, and asked Spider 'Haven't the others come yet?' 'Not yet' said Spider. 'Just the cat so far – he's there in the hut. When you get in, kill him!' So the dog went and killed the cat and sat down and waited in the hut.

After a while the hyena came along. 'Haven't the others come yet?' says she to Spider. 'No' says Spider. 'Just the dog so far.' 'Where's he?' says she. 'In the hut' says Spider. 'When you go there, kill him!' and in went the hyena and killed the dog, and she too sat down in the hut and waited.

After a while, along comes the leopard. 'Where are the others?' says she to Spider. 'Haven't they collected yet?' 'Not yet' says Spider. 'Except for the hyena – she's here. She's sitting in the hut there. If you go in, kill her!' So the leopard went in, killed the hyena and sat down in the hut and waited.

After a while, along came the lion. Said he to Spider 'Haven't the others collected?' 'No' said Spider. 'Not yet – except only the leopard, she's there in the hut. Go and find her, and kill her!' So the lion went on and found the leopard in the hut, and he seized the leopard, and the leopard in her turn seized him and they fought.

Now Spider had had some pepper pounded up for him and put it by. When he heard the lion and leopard fighting, he went up to them, and taking some of the pounded pepper he threw it in the lion's eyes. And taking some more, he threw it in the leopard's eyes. Then the eyes of both of them were closed and they couldn't see, and Spider, picking up a big stick, began to hit them both hard, saying as he did so 'Lion, leave off! Leopard, leave off! For who may enter the fight of you great ones?' And he went on hitting the lion and the leopard in turn until he had killed them and there they were, dead. Then he called Mrs. Spider and they gathered up the meat, and ate and ate, and had their fill of meat. *Kurungus kan kusu.*

The Malam and the Hyena*[I/7]

One day a certain malam set out on a journey. And as he rode along on his mare, up came a hyena and said to him 'Where are you going?' And he answered 'I'm going to school.' And she said 'May I come too?' and he answered 'Certainly, come along!'

As they went along, the malam's mare collapsed and could go no farther. Then said the hyena 'Malam, give me the mare to eat. Get on me and we'll get along.' And the malam said to her 'Very well, take her and eat her!' So she took her and ate her, and then ran off, leaving the malam with his saddle and bridle.

He put his saddle up on his head and set off, and as he went along he met with Spider. Says Spider 'Malam, where are you off to?' and he answered 'I came out and met a hyena as I was going. She asked me to give her my mare to eat, saying I could ride her. But when I gave the mare and she had eaten her, she ran off, and I haven't seen her since.'

Says Spider 'Where's the place she ate your mare?' and the malam answered 'Come along with me and I'll show you!' Off they went and he showed Spider where the hyena had eaten her. She had left the liver, the head and the hooves. Spider took the liver and put it in his bag. Then he said to the malam 'You stay here!' And

* Cf. R. No. 9.

the malam sat down waiting for Spider, while Spider went off to look for the hyena.

A little later he met with the hyena and said to her 'Where are you going?' and she answered 'I'm on the run. I ate a malam's mare, after telling him a lie.' Says Spider 'Come along, we'll go and I'll take you to some meat.'

As they went along Spider said to the hyena 'Today you'll eat meat till you're full.' Says the hyena 'I say, Spider, you wouldn't be after taking me to that malam would you?' and he answered 'No.'

Then Spider said to the hyena 'If we're to get along briskly, I must ride you' and the hyena answered 'O.K., hop on and let's go.' And Spider got on the hyena.

Then, as they were going along, Spider said 'Here, I'm not comfortable riding you, hyena' and she said 'Put that thing of the malam's on me, that'll be comfortable for you.' So Spider put the bridle on the hyena, and the saddle, and spurs too. And he got on her and spurred her. And the hyena said 'I say, Spider, you wouldn't be after taking me to that malam would you?' and he answered 'No. If you're doubtful, see here, here's meat. Have some! Eat!' and he took the liver in the bag and gave it her to eat. And she said 'O.K., let's go!' And Spider's sitting there on top of her.

Now, when they got near to the malam, Spider spurred the hyena and brought her to where the malam was. When they reached him, the malam said 'Thank God! For He has caught you, hyena.' Then he got on her and travelled on with her for three days. But when he had got off and was resting, the hyena again ran off, leaving the malam where he sat.

Then the hyena went off in search of Spider. She met him as he went along, and said 'Thank God – I've found you, Spider, you treacherous devil.' But Spider said to the hyena, 'Come on and I'll take you to some meat!' She answered 'No you don't, Spider–you'll take me to the malam–won't you?' And he answered 'Hyena, hyena, don't you know, the malam's gone?' And she said to him 'O.K., lets go!'

Off they went, till they came to a place where a trap had been set, with a leg of beef in it. And the people were all around it. Then Spider said to the hyena 'Hyena, here's meat, come and eat!' Up came the hyena to take the beef, but as she made to take it, the trap closed on her neck, and she said 'Spider, Spider is this what you have done to me!' But before she could say more, the people had clubbed her to death.

Then the malam said 'My thanks to you for killing for me this hyena that told me a lie.'

The Iguana (Land-Monitor) [$^I/_9$]

Spider and the iguana lived together, each with his wife. It was the time of heat just before the rains, and they set out one day to their farms to sow. But while the iguana was busy sowing guinea-corn, Spider just fried his guinea-corn and ate it, sowing nothing. Then came the time for hoeing, and they hoed. The iguana had guinea-corn to hoe, but Spider had nothing.

Then the iguana collected his guinea-corn together, and built two store-bins, one for the bundles, one for the threshed grain. But Spider got into the iguana's store-bin and stole guinea-corn from it, two baskets full. And when the iguana came and looked into the bin he saw two baskets of guinea-corn missing. And he said to himself 'No one else could have robbed me but Spider' and again 'I'll be even with Spider for what he has done to me!'

Then said the iguana to his wife 'Chop me up and put me in a pot and cook me with rice and take me to Spider!' And she chopped up the iguana and put him in a pot and cooked him with rice and took him to Spider.

And she said to Spider 'Here's meat for you – the iguana said to bring you *tuwo*.' And Spider said 'Thank God! I am grateful.'

Then Spider took the meat and ate it and finished it all up. He had started on the *tuwo*, when the iguana moved in his inside and said 'And *now*, Spider, if you don't bring out my guinea-corn, I'll pierce your stomach and come out, and you'll die.' Then said Spider to his wife 'Hi, Koki! Bring that guinea-corn, but keep a bit out!' And she brought the guinea-corn but kept a bit out. And the iguana started hitting Spider's inside again. And Spider shouted

'Oh! Oh! My God! Hey, bring him all of his guinea-corn.' And she brought all of the guinea-corn and gave it to the iguana. Then Spider went and squatted down, and the iguana came out and went off home.

Then said Spider to himself 'Now it's *my* turn to get even with the iguana for what he did to me.' And he said to his wife 'Take me and chop me up and cook me and take me to the iguana. Say to him 'Spider says "Here's some meat for you".' 'O.K.' says she and takes hold of him to chop him up. Then he hollers out 'Ow! That hurts. Just take me like this. Put me in a wooden bowl and cover me up with gravy.'

Then she picked up Spider and put him in a wooden bowl and took it to the iguana's compound. Says she to the iguana 'Here's meat for you, Spider said I was to bring it.' 'Thank God' says the iguana.

Then says the iguana to Spider's wife 'You know, we tailors always prick a thing over with a needle before we eat it.' But when Spider heard that the iguana was going to prick him as he was in the bowl, out he got and ran off. And after that he didn't again share a home with the iguana.

The Man and his Wife and the Heads* [I/22]

There was once a man who had quarrelled with his wife and he was on his way to the home of his in-laws to persuade her to come back. As he went along he came to the foot of a shea-butter tree. As he was resting there, a shea-nut fell down and he picked it up and ate it. He threw away the stone, when out popped a head. The head said to him 'Hey, you. Where are you off to?' and he answered 'I'm away to call on my in-laws.' And the head said 'I'll come with you, but you must take me up and put me in your trousers.' 'Right' says the man and taking up the head, put it in his trousers.

* Cf. D. No. 105 and C. p. 38.

So they went on till they came to the home of his in-laws. There he made formal greeting at the door and the people of the house answered. They then enquired after each other's health and the visitors were taken to where they were to sleep. And whenever food was brought them, the head would take it and eat it up. Whenever *fura* was brought, the head took it and drank it up.

Thus it was for three days. The man got very thin and came near to dying of hunger. Then said he to his in-laws 'I'm going to return home, now that I have made my call on you.' And they replied 'Very well, but take your wife with you.' And they gave him back his wife and off he went.

And as he went, he got back to the foot of the shea-butter tree where he had rested when he was on his way. Again he sat down and again he rested. When he had rested, he got up and was going off, when the head said to him 'What, man! Are you going to leave me just like this, after my coming with you to get your wife back? Now, you just divide your wife up and give me my share.' But he refused.

And while they were arguing, two more heads popped out. And they said 'Hey there, man! What are you arguing about?' And the head answered 'It's like this – I went with him to get his wife back and now he says he won't divide her up with me.' And the other heads said 'Since you went with him, by all means he should divide and share her with you – and with us too, though we didn't go!'

They were hard at it, when twenty more heads popped out and said 'Hey, what goes on here?' And the two heads said 'We went with him to get his wife back, and now he says he won't share her with us.' And they said 'Since you went with him, by all means he should divide her with you – and with us too, even though we didn't go.'

And they went on and on and the husband began to get frightened and said to himself 'What on earth can I do about these heads?'

But as he was lamenting, who should come by but Spider. He came up to the man and said to him 'Hey there, what's the matter?' And he answered Spider 'I went to get my wife back. I got here and, while I was resting, these heads said I should divide and share my wife with them.' And Spider said to him 'Leave them to me, you'll have no more trouble from them.'

Then Spider picked up a shillelagh,* aimed carefully at one head and hit it, and the head shattered. He looked at another and struck it. Whereupon all the heads scattered and left the man and his wife. Then the two of them went off home. That's all. *Kurungus kan kusu.*

The Hyena and the Goat†[$^{I}/_{31}$]

They say that once the hyena was walking in the fields near a town and came near to the house of a man who kept goats. And she saw a goat that had just produced a kid, licking her son. And she said 'My God! Some people have all the luck! (*lit.* those with possessions can feed during the day). Look at that goat licking her son!'

Well, it happened that Spider was watching her and followed her closely wherever she went, till she came to her lair. There he saw her children, and they had eaten fat meat, eaten their fill of it, and one little hyena had even taken a piece of fat and had put it on her head and was playing with it. Then said Spider 'Some people are always lucky.' (*lit.* those with possessions have possessions). Then the hyena said to him 'Hey there, Spider! What makes you say that?' and Spider answered 'When *you* saw the goat had produced a kid and was licking her son, why did *you* say "Some people have all the luck"?' The hyena replied 'Well!! Because I saw the goat licking her son, neither eating him nor leaving him alone. That's why I said "Some people have all the luck".' Spider replied 'And *I*, it's because *I* saw your children eating meat, eating their fill of it and taking the fat and putting it on their heads – it was obvious they had more than enough meat, so I said "Some people are always lucky".' The hyena answered 'Spider, you are too fond of pettifogging questions. I'll have nothing to do with you. Be off with you!'

---

* *guduma* is actually a throwing-stick, with a knob on the end.
† Cf. M. No. 37.

The Foolish Boy* [I/8₃]

There was once a foolish boy whose parents left him in charge of the home, telling him that they were going off to the farm. 'In a little while' said they, 'Cook beans† for us to eat when we get back.' 'Certainly' said he.

When they had gone, he took a single bean† and put it in a large pot. He poured in a pitcher full of water, and putting it on the fire-place, made a good fire under it, which he kept going till the evening when his parents returned from the farm. They asked him 'Where are the beans that you have cooked?' and he answered 'There it is, in the pot.' But when they looked, all they saw in the pot was the one bean, and they said to him 'Tomorrow, you must take out a lot to cook for us, do you understand?' 'Yes' said he.

And so, each day he took out a lot of beans as they had told him and cooked them for them. Now their house was much troubled by gazelles which came and did harm there. One day Spider came along and saw what was happening. Says he 'Foolish boy, do gazelles come to your home?' 'Yes' says the other, and Spider said 'Tomorrow I'll bring a trap and we'll catch them. Do you understand, foolish boy?' 'O.K.' says he.

And so Spider went off home and brought a trap. When he came back, he had with him a female donkey and a large, hide bag. When they had set the trap beneath the ground, they caught twelve gazelles. They skinned them all. By then the sun was red as it neared its setting and Spider said to the foolish boy 'See the fire over there? Go and get some.' But the foolish boy said to Spider '*You* go and get some, and by the time you get back, I'll have packed the meat into your bag.' 'O.K.' says Spider and goes off to get some firing.

Meanwhile the foolish boy took all the meat and threw it into the corn-bin, only leaving out one piece. Then he took the stomach contents and tipped them into the bag, and picking up the one piece of meat, added that on top, in the mouth of the bag, and tied it up. But Spider's donkey was watching as the foolish boy put the offal into the bag.

* Cf. TR. No. 17 and I/157.
† In Hausa the singular form of this word also serves for the plural.

Then Spider returned, saying he hadn't managed to get any fire, and the boy said 'Very well, let's lift your bag and put it on to your donkey. You must get along, it's nearly night.' 'O.K.' says Spider, and they lifted the bag on to the donkey and off went Spider, driving his donkey before him.

But as they went along, the donkey kept saying 'It's offal, it's offal that we've got.' Then Spider said to her 'Here! Stop saying "It's offal that we've got"—say "It's pieces of meat that we've got"'. At length they got home and when Spider's cat saw them, she began miaowing. Says Spider to her 'Today you'll have meat to eat, more than you can manage', and taking the piece of meat from the mouth of the bag, he threw it to her and she took it. Then said he to Mrs. Spider 'Bring a wooden bowl for us to put the meat in. She brought one and they were going to tip the meat in, when they saw that it was the contents of the beasts' stomachs. 'Well, well' says Spider. 'So that's what the foolish boy has done to me.'

Then he went back to the foolish boy's house, whom he found covered with ashes from head to foot. 'Peace be upon you' said Spider and the foolish boy answered 'And upon you peace.' 'Fancy your treating me like that, foolish boy' says he, and the foolish boy answered 'All right, all right – look, those gazelles we caught belonged to the chief, and now they've sent for my father and asked him what has become of the gazelles his son caught; they've told him to bring them back at once as they belong to the chief. I don't know what I'm going to do.' 'God make it easy for you' says Spider [and aside] 'I intended this.' That's all.

Butorami* [^{I}/144]

This is a tale of Butorami, who is a sort of huge wild beast. If he is going hunting, he makes his wife grind flour and fry large amounts of it, so that he'll have enough. Then when he gets to a river†, he pours the flour into the river and drinks up the whole river, leaving

* Cf. TR. No. 33 and I/90.
† Cf. No. I/90.

only sand, and then he goes on with his hunting. If he sees elephants in the distance, he hurls abuse at them. And when they say 'Who are you abusing?' he replies 'Your chief'. Whereupon they charge him and he shoots their leader and kills him, and taking the meat, goes off home. And that keeps him going for months.

Well, one day Spider came to the compound for some embers. He saw the meat that Butorami's wife had, and she threw him some. He took the embers, but let them go out as he was going. So he went back to her and again she threw him some meat. This happened five times!

Then one day when Spider came he asked Butorami 'Where did you get the meat?' 'In the bush' said the other. 'Please take me with you' said Spider. So they went off together and brought back more meat. But afterwards, Spider set out with Mrs. Spider on his own, and when they got there he made her go and abuse the elephants. She did as she was told and came running back to Spider. But the elephants followed her and squashed them both flat.

——————

The Hyena and The Lion* [I/153]

Here's a long tale. One day Spider and the hyena set off for a walk together. They both spotted a guinea-fowl and the hyena said 'What beautiful marking that guinea-fowl has!' 'Oh yes' said Spider. 'It was I did it for her.' 'Won't you do it for me too?' said the hyena, and Spider answered 'If I do it to the hyena, I know I'll have to do it for a hundred other people.' 'Nonsense' said the hyena 'why should doing it to me mean doing it for a hundred others?' 'Then' said Spider 'you must pay me for the work.' 'What shall I give you?' asked the hyena. Now they had previously got some meat, so Spider said to her 'You must give me your share of the meat we divided between us – then I'll do it for you.' So she gave him that, and then he said 'Do you think you can take it?' 'I can take it' she answered. 'But I'll have to tie you up first' he said. And she agreed to this.

* Cf. I/3 and R. No. 27.

So he took hold of her and tied her up, and then put a branding-iron in the fire. When it was red-hot he picked it up and applied it to her body. And when she felt the heat, she yelled loudly. Each time he applied the branding-iron to her, she howled. And he kept picking up a piece of meat, throwing it on the fire and saying 'There's one fat piece you won't eat', until he had finished up all the meat.

Then he went off leaving her there tied up. He met the lion, and the lion greeted him 'How's things?' 'Have you seen the guinea-fowl's markings?' said Spider. 'Well, it was I who did them for her.' 'I'd like you to do some for me too' said the lion. And Spider answered 'I'll do some for you, but only if you can take it.' 'Certainly I can take it' said the lion. 'Then' said Spider to the lion 'you must get hold of a seven-year-old bull and roast it, and while you're eating it, I'll put the markings on you.'

So the lion went off to where some cattle were corralled and, killing a bull, brought it along. 'Good' said Spider. 'But before I start marking you, I must tie you up.' And the lion expressed agreement.

So he took hold of the lion and tied him up. Then Spider started to eat the meat, and ate and ate, until he was full. Then he went off, leaving the lion there tied up.

So he left him and went and fetched the hyena. And the hyena came back with him and they both ate of the meat together. Then they left the lion there still tied up. So now you know how the lion fared with Spider. That's the end of that tale. If cold doesn't kill a naked man, heat won't kill a gowned one.

The Woman and Her Foolish Son* [^{I}/₁₅₇]

There was once a woman who had never borne a child, and she prayed to God 'Give me a child, even though he be a foolish one!' God heard her prayer and gave her a son, a simpleton. And he grew into a youth. One day she set out for the bush, telling him to

* Cf. I/83 and TR. No. 17.

cook beans for her. 'O.K.' said he. Then he filled a huge water storage-jar with beans and cooked them. When she got back she said 'Why ever did you cook enough beans for a large party?' 'You should have told me to cook just a few beans' said he. So she said to him 'Tomorrow just cook a few.' 'O.K.' said he, but he cooked just as many as before. This vexed his mother very much, but she said 'A man must resign himself to what God has given him.'

When Spider saw what was happening, he gathered together a large party of gazelles to come and eat up half the beans. When the foolish boy's mother returned, she asked 'Who's eaten up half the beans?' and he answered 'It was Spider. He gathered a large party of gazelles and they did.' 'Well' said she 'if they come again, you say to them "My mother says we must play the tie-up tie-up game before I give you the beans. You tie me up and I'll tie you up".' The gazelles agreed to this and so the foolish boy tied them up.

Then Spider said 'Let's have the slaughter slaughter game and the skinning skinning game!' and the gazelles agreed and lay down; and were slaughtered and skinned.

Spider divided up the meat. He separated the meat and the bones into two lots, saying 'The one with something, Squelch; the one without something, Thud.' Then, having finished dividing it up, he said 'Foolish Boy, go and drive my donkey here!'

But when he got to her, he drove her off into the bush and returned, saying to Spider 'The donkey has run off.' So up jumps Spider saying to the foolish boy and his mother 'I'll go myself and get the donkey. But, while I'm away you put the meat into the panniers. There they are, the one with something, Squelch and the one without something, Thud.'

Whereupon the two of them took the gazelles' stomachs and put them into the pannier, and pouring the stomach contents on top, they closed it up. Then they took the livers and put them in the other pannier, and poured more of the stomach contents on top before closing that one up too.

When Spider got back he asked them 'Have you put the meat in?' 'Yes.' 'Then load the panniers on to the donkey for me' and they did so.

So Spider set off driving his donkey and beating her as he went. And the donkey sang as they went 'Stomach and liver and stomach contents is what we are taking.' Then he beat her the more. But she repeated it, and he said 'You should say "Meat is what we are taking" .' But she wouldn't, and so they reached home. 'Hey, Mrs. Spider' said he. 'Come and help me unload this donkey! And bring the huge calabash that belonged to the ancestor of your mother and father!'

She brought it, and he undid the pannier. Putting his hand in, he brought out a stomach and threw it to the dog. Putting it in again, he brought out liver and threw it to the cat. Then putting it in again, he found nothing. He called the dog, but it had run off. He called the cat but it had run off too.

Turning back, he found himself in a quarrel with Mrs. Spider. 'Liar' said she. 'You've got nothing. You tell me to bring the big calabash, and all you have is stomach and liver, and you give them to the dog and the cat!' And Spider was silent. He had nothing to say.

Then he went and knelt before the donkey, saying 'So you were telling me the truth after all. God bless you! I have wronged you, and I won't beat you again!' And he said to her again 'See how the foolish boy and his mother tricked me. May God put them in our way again!' 'Amen' said the donkey. *Kurungus kan kusu.* It wasn't because of Spider that I made it up – I was making it up in any case.*

———

The Old Woman and the Chief † [^I/₁₆₀]

There was once an old woman who used to go begging. Thus she collected some money and bought a calf. And she kept him tied up till he was quite big and grown into a bull.

Just then Spider was walking by and came to the old woman's compound. He peeped in and saw a great ox tied there. Then he ran off to the chief of the town and told him that he had some news 'I've seen a great ox in an old woman's compound.' So the chief sent some men to bring it. When they got to the old woman's

* Cf. I/156.
† Cf. TR. No. 4 and M. No. 38.

compound, they tried to loose the ox, but it refused to be loosed. Then Spider said 'Beat the old woman' and they beat her. And the old woman began to sing thus 'Be loosed, loosed from your tether-ing-post, princely yearling, for they are greedy and think nothing of taking you to the court and before the chief.'

So he let them loose him, but refused to move. So Spider told them to beat the old woman, and they beat her. Then said she 'Go, go from your tethering-post, princely yearling, for they are greedy and think nothing of taking you to the court and before the chief.'

Then he went with them and they reached the chief, together with the old woman. The chief told his men to slaughter the ox, but he wouldn't be slaughtered. Then Spider said 'Beat the old woman.' They beat her, and she said 'Be slaughtered, slaughtered at your tethering-post, princely yearling, for they are greedy, and think nothing of taking you to the court and before the chief.' Then he was slaughtered and skinned.

Then the old woman ran up to the chief and asked to be given the intestines, the stomach, liver, kidneys, heart, bowels, lungs and fat. 'Let her have them' said the chief.

The old woman collected them all together and took them home. And putting them all into a pot, she covered it and left them for ten days or so. Then she uncovered the pot and saw that the intestines had turned into children. And so the old woman began to go out to get food for them.

A little later Spider was out walking and returning to the old woman's compound, made formal salutation. She returned it and he asked for water to drink. Then the old woman told one of her daughters 'From-Stomach, take out some water and give it to the visitor who is outside.' Then From-Stomach said 'Where's From-Liver?' And From-Liver said 'Where's From-Heart?' And From-Heart said 'Where's From-Kidneys?' And From-Kidneys said 'Where's From-Bowels?' And From-Bowels said 'Where's From-Fat?' Then From-Fat got up and took out some water and gave it to Spider. And Spider gazed and gazed at the girl till the calabash fell from his hand.

Then he ran off to the chief and, having made formal salutation, said 'How many ears have you?'* 'Two' said the chief. 'Well' said

* A standard formula intimating that you have news worth hearing.

Spider 'here's news that is for you and me alone.' 'What did you say?' said the chief. 'Well' said Spider 'it's for you and your sons alone.' 'That's better' said the chief. 'Now let's have your news.' 'I've just seen a beautiful girl' said Spider. 'And in all my life I've never seen such a beautiful one.'

So the chief sent his people to the home of the old woman to tell her that he wanted her daughter, who was called From-Fat. 'Well well' said the old woman 'what can *I* do? When a thing gets beyond you, you just have to wait and see I suppose.'

So the chief's people settled the marriage and took away the girl. But the old woman said to them 'I give you solemn warning, for God's sake don't let From-Fat get close to a fire. And don't leave her out in the sun. You tell the chief this, for fellow-wives are no good!' And the chief's people assured her that they understood and would do so. Then they returned to the chief, and the feast was held and that was that.

A little later the chief made ready to go to war, and setting out left his bride at home with her fellow-wives. He was away for two months in the bush.

Whereupon the other wives made the girl go to the fire-place to prepare the *tuwo*. She went over and sitting down began to make up the fire, when she melted away on the ground. When the other wives saw that, they began to make a great wailing, saying 'What shall we do? Here's the chief's bride melted away.'

Then the chief's head slave sent off many horsemen to bring news to the chief of what his wives had done while he was away.

But a little bird got to the chief before them, and alighting on a tree in the house where the chief was, began to sing 'Chief, chief, take the army back, From-Fat has melted and become a river.'

And so the army set off and returned home. When the chief got home he asked 'Who was it put From-Fat to cooking?' And they answered 'It was your chief wife.' 'Send for the old woman' said he. The old woman came and she said 'At the time I gave my daughter to the chief, I said that she wasn't to do any cooking.'

Then she went to where From-Fat had melted away, and carefully swept up and collected what was left and put it in a pot. Then she poured water on to it and covered it up with a calabash. Next morning she uncovered it, and there was From-Fat a beautiful maiden again.

Kungurus kan kusu. It wasn't because of Spider that I made it up – I was making it up in any case.*

The Malam† [II/12]

Here's another. Spider went to a malam and asked him to teach him to be cunning, and the malam said 'Go and get an elephant's tusk.' 'O.K.' said Spider. 'Go and get a lion's tears.' 'O.K.' 'And the skin off a hyena's forehead.' 'O.K.' 'And the milk of a bush-cow.' 'O.K.' said Spider.

So Spider set off and went into the bush and there he saw a bush-cow. Says he 'Bush-cow, we've been having an argument about that baobab tree, and some of us said that if you butted it, your horns wouldn't pierce it.' 'Which baobab?' asked the bush-cow. 'That one there' said Spider. So the bush-cow went full tilt at the baobab, butted it and her horns went right in. Then, though the bush-cow pulled and pulled, her horns wouldn't come out. Says Spider 'Let me just milk you. Perhaps if I sprinkle a little on them, they may come out.' So he milked her and sprinkled a little – quite uselessly – on her horns. The bush-cow pulled again, but they still wouldn't come out. Whereupon Spider went off, saying that he would fetch an axe.

Next he went to the elephant and said to her 'Elephant, I have heard that there's going to be a hunt in this part of the bush tomorrow – so I thought I would come and tell you, and take you to somewhere where I can hide you. But you'll have to stand quite silent and not move.' 'Very well' answered the elephant. 'But, Spider, where shall I go to?' 'They said' replied Spider 'that they wouldn't go to the fetish-place.' 'Right, then take me there.' So Spider took the elephant along there and said 'Now, elephant I must fasten you to this tree and tie you up.' 'All right' said the elephant. 'Just a minute while I strip some bark off this *kalgo*' says Spider. Then he went and did so and came back to the elephant and lashed her

* I/156.
† Cf. I/34, III/58. Also J. p.12 and D. No. 90

tusk to the tree. Says he 'Try moving it to see if it's tight.' She moved it a little and said 'Tighter', so Spider tightened it. Then she tried again and said 'Now, that's tight, Spider.'

Then off went Spider and tightened the skin on his drum. Then, next morning when it was light, he took the drum and went towards the fetish-place, beating it and saying 'All meet at the fetish-place, all meet at the fetish-place.' Whereupon the elephant gave a violent start and left her tusk where it was. Then Spider came and took the tusk away and hid it, and went and found the elephant lying down with her mouth swollen. Says he 'Well!! People! Oh mighty one of the bush, people nowadays are too prone to change their minds and what they say in the morning gets reversed before the evening and vice versa.'

Then off went Spider and told the lion about it. 'Lion' says he 'you should know that the elephant is sick. All the beasts of the bush have gone to see her but you haven't heard about it. So I thought I would come and tell you.' 'Where is she, Spider?' said the lion. 'Over there, lying down' he replied. 'Take me to her, let's go' said the lion and so they went.

When they got there, the lion began to cry, and Spider took out a gourd, saying 'We mustn't let the tears of the great fall to the ground.' And he caught the tears in the gourd and then said 'Let me take it and make a hole and bury it.'

But Spider turned aside and went and told the hyena, saying 'Hey, hyena – the elephant has had a tooth knocked out and everyone has gone to rejoice. Why haven't you gone too?' So the hyena quickly reached the scene. 'Very nice! So our big brother has had a tooth knocked out! Very nice!' At which the lion became angry.

And when the hyena got near, Spider said 'For shame, hyena, when others are crying, for you to come and laugh and sing about it!' Then the lion sprang at the hyena and, knocking her down, killed her.

'Oh dear, oh dear' said Spider. 'Mighty one of the bush, I think I'd better drag her away some distance. For if she is left here, you'll be offended by the stink.' 'Then drag her away' said the lion. So Spider dragged her away, some distance off, and then took off the skin of her forehead.

Then he took the lion's tears, and the elephant's tusk, and the bush-cow's milk and went to the malam and said 'Malam, here you are. I've brought them.' 'Very well, Spider' said he. 'Considering the tricks you've used to get all these, what cunning is there that anyone could presume to teach you? No, Spider, the cunning you've used to get hold of these will suffice for the ordinary run of things. Be off with you and stop bothering me!' *Kungurus kan kusu.* If it hadn't been for Spider, would I have been making it all up?

The Chief's Daughter [$^{II}/_{23}$]

There was once a chief who had a daughter. And the girl refused to marry anyone save only the man who could excrete without grunting. But all who came and tried, grunted.

Then along came Spider. When he got there he said 'Now, when the others are squatting, they have bits of corn-stalk in their hands – right?' And they told him that was so. 'O.K.' said he. 'As for me, I'll grip whole lengths of guinea-corn.'

So, when his turn came, he gripped a length of guinea-corn and said 'O-oh! What a huge stalk this guinea-corn has!'* and did his business and got up. And everyone said 'Well! Spider excreted and didn't grunt!' And the chief's daughter said 'He's the one I'll marry.' So she and Spider were married. That's all. *Kungurus kan kusu.*

The Old Woman† [$^{II}/_{30}$]

Once Spider bought ten cowries' worth of *tafasa*‡ leaves from an old woman. Next he went to a shea-butter tree and climbed it. And

---

* Concealing his grunt by pretending it was one of admiration?
† Cf. TR. No. 78.   ‡ *cassia tora* for soup making.

the tree fell over and Spider with it. Says Spider 'Shea-butter tree, feller of Spider; Spider that owes the old woman ten cowries' and addressing the tree 'You must share my debt of ten cowries, owed to the old woman' and Spider went off leaving the shea-butter tree there.

Up comes a maiden and when she gets to the spot, she sees that the shea-butter nuts are ripe and have fallen to the ground. So she helped herself and ate some. Then said the tree 'Shea-butter tree, feller of Spider; Spider that owes the old woman ten cowries. Spider said I must share his debt of ten cowries, owed to the old woman. Well, you can share it too, maiden.' 'Very well' said she and passed on.

Presently, as she went along, she stumbled. Then said she 'Tree-stump, that made the maid fall; maiden that ate the shea nuts; shea-butter tree, feller of Spider; Spider, debtor to the old woman. Tree-stump, you can share the debt.' And the maiden went on.

Presently the tree-stump put forth leaves, and along came a goat and ate the tree-stump's leaves. Says the tree-stump 'Goat, that eats my leaves; I'm the tree-stump that made the maiden fall; the maiden that ate the shea-nuts; from the shea-butter tree, that felled Spider; who owes the old woman ten cowries.' And he said to the goat 'You can share the debt.'

So the goat went on, and coming to where there was corn spread out to dry, made free with it. A slave-girl belonging to the chief's wife comes up and hits the goat, and the goat says 'Slave-girl of the chief's wife, that beat the goat; that ate off the tree-stump; that made the maiden fall; who ate the shea-nuts; from the shea-butter tree that felled Spider; who's in debt to the old woman. You can share the debt.'

So when the chief's wife hit her slave-girl, the girl said 'Chief's wife that hit the slave-girl; that hit the goat; that ate off the tree-stump; that made the maiden fall; who ate the shea-nuts; from the shea-butter tree that felled Spider; who owes the old woman ten cowries.' And she said to the chief's wife 'You can share the debt.'

Then came the chief and upbraided his wife in anger, and she said 'Chief that upbraids his wife; who beat the slave-girl; who hit the goat; that ate off the tree-stump; that made the maiden fall; who ate the shea-nuts; from the shea-butter tree that felled Spider; who owes the old woman ten cowries. Chief, you can share the debt with us.' 'What's all this about?' asked the chief, but he agreed and fetching the ten cowries gave them to his wife. She gave them to her slave-girl, who gave them to the goat; who gave them to the tree-stump; which gave them to the maiden; who gave them to the shea-butter tree; which gave them to Spider; who took them to the old woman.

'Well' said Spider to himself, 'if I hadn't done that, I should have had trouble raising those ten cowries.' That's all. *Kungurus kan kusu.*

Mrs. Spider [$^{II}/_{65}$]

Here's another tale. Spider set off for a stroll, and coming to another town there found the young men gathered together. For it seemed that a beautiful girl there had had a piece of land cleared as a farm for her, and had had it sown. Now she said that she would marry any man who could hoe it all without taking a drink of water. 'Really?' said Spider. 'Yes.' 'Well, I'll just go home and fetch my little hoe, and then I'll come back and do that bit of hoeing.' And the people said 'Ho-ho! There's a damned, good-for-nothing liar for you.' But others said 'No, he's not lying. He can do it.'

So Spider went home and fetched his quiver, and took some arrowheads and some shafts, and then he got some water and poured it into his quiver, and taking the shafts he put them in on top. Then he went back and said that he was ready to start hoeing. 'Where are the limits of the farm?' he asked. They showed him, and the girl herself came to keep an eye on this fellow who was to hoe her farm. Off went Spider and bent to the work and began to hoe. At length the sun grew hot, and Spider was beset by thirst.

So he said that he had trodden on a thorn. 'Then take it out' said the girl. So he went to where his quiver was, and taking a shaft, pulled it out. And the girl saw that it had no head to it. 'Bother' said Spider, 'the head's come off', and putting his mouth to the quiver, drank the water till his thirst was quenched. Then he poked about at his foot, to make a deliberate show, and went back to hoeing, and so finished it. Then the girl said that she had found a husband. So they were married, and what is more the day's work that he had put in hoeing from start to finish without a drink–that was counted as the bridegroom's customary present to the bride! And so the girl was brought to his compound. And presently she became pregnant and produced a daughter.

And Spider went and set up a loom.* Now the baby girl began to cry, and so Spider started to sing and this is what he sang 'Tricky baby with a tricky father – for I married your mother by the water in the quiver. Quietly, quietly, tricky baby, for I married your mother by the water in the quiver.' But the mother heard it and began to be very angry, saying 'So! You had water in the quiver, when you did the hoeing. Well, I'm not staying married to you.' 'No, no, you have it wrong' said he. 'It was one of the Tuareg's slaves, on his camel that was singing "Tricky baby with a tricky father – for I married your mother by the water in the quiver". And what's more his camel had trousers† on. I heard him singing that.' 'You're lying' said she.

And she rose and went off back to her parents' compound. And there she told them how she had discovered that Spider's hoeing had been done with water in his quiver.

Spider got up and went off and made a pair of trousers to fit a camel's backside. Next he went off to some little, black ants, and said 'Little black ant, I have a request. My wife has run off and left me, and I want you to suck my mouth, to take the sour taste (?yami) away.' So the little black ant sucked Spider's mouth.

From there he went on to one of the Tuareg's slaves and said 'I want you to lend me a camel, to put trousers on and take to the market.' The other fetched a camel and gave it to him; and Spider put the trousers on to it, and himself got on.

Then he went round by the compound of his wife's parents, singing as he went 'Tricky baby with a tricky father – for I married your mother by the water in the quiver. Quietly, quietly, tricky baby, don't cry, tricky baby, for I married your mother by the water in the quiver.' 'Hello!!' said the girl's parents, 'Hey, look, girl – it *is* one of the Tuareg's slaves singing that song. There he is, and on his camel. And the camel's got trousers! Get up, and go

* 'Weaving-of spider' is a cobweb in Hausa.
† Cf. II/98.

back to your home!' So Spider went on to the market singing like that. Then he hit the camel into a gallop, and went and returned it to the Tuareg's slave.

From there he went to the little black ant, and she again sucked his mouth for him and the sour taste returned. Then back home, and he jumped up on to the loom and began singing 'Tricky baby with a tricky father – for I married your mother by the water in the quiver. Quietly, quietly, tricky baby, don't cry.' When who should come along but his wife, home again. And there she found him, sitting at his loom, weaving away and singing. 'Well' said he, 'you've found that I was telling the truth, haven't you? I *told* you, but you said I was lying.' So that was that and they settled down together again. *Kungurus kan kusu.*

The Black-hooded Cobra
and the Chief's Son [$^{III}/_8$]

Here's another tale. There was a snake had a bull. And he took his bull and began walking through the town, saying 'Where shall I find a man who will seize my bull and slaughter him and eat him – so that then I can get inside him and make my home there?' He continued saying this, until he had been right round the town – and found no one to accept.

Then up comes Spider. 'Hullo!' says he, 'cobra, where are you off to with a bull?' 'Nowhere' answered the cobra, 'it's selling him that I am.' 'What have you been offered for him?' asked Spider. 'Oh no' said the cobra, 'it's not that sort of sale. The idea is for someone to seize my bull, slaughter him and eat him, and then I'll get inside him and make my home there.' 'Pooh' said Spider, 'is that all? Here, give him to me.' So the cobra gave the bull to Spider.

Then said Spider 'O.K., cobra. How many days will you allow me?' 'One week' said the cobra. 'No' said Spider, 'you can give me two. For you know how it is with a bull – it takes days to eat through all his meat.' 'O.K.' said the cobra, 'get going. I give you fourteen days.' And the cobra departed.

Spider slaughtered the bull. And then he ate and ate, and Mrs. Spider too, she ate and ate, until the fourteen days were up.

Then said Spider to his wife 'I'm going to get in under the bed. If the cobra comes, tell him that I've gone into the country, and I'll not be back for seven days.' 'O.K.' said Mrs. Spider. So he got in under the bed, and Mrs. Spider fetched a mat and covered in the front of the bed.

Along comes the cobra. Getting there, he makes salutation, and 'Welcome' says Mrs. Spider. 'Where's your husband?' says the cobra. 'He's gone into the country' says Mrs. Spider, 'and he said to tell you, when you came, that he would be back in seven days.' 'Very well" said the cobra, and going off again, returned home.

When the seven days were up, Spider got back in under the bed. Along comes the cobra. 'Peace be upon you' says he. 'Welcome' says Mrs. Spider. 'Where's Spider?' says he. 'He said to tell you' she answered, 'that he came back, but went off again to another town.' The snake was vexed, and went off again.

But as he was going he met a hornbill. Says she 'Where are you off to, cobra?' 'Hornbill' says he, and then he told her all that had occurred between Spider and himself. So she flew down to the ground. 'Come on' said she, 'get on my back, and coil yourself round.' 'O.K.' said the cobra and did just that. Away flew the hornbill, and went and alighted just outside Spider's hut.

'*Chilin chilin*'* went the hornbill, 'wherever can my peck-pecking have brought me – it's Spider's compound.' To which Spider replied 'That's right. Greetings, little sister. But I'm avoiding an earth thing. That's the cobra.'

Then the hornbill flew up on to the top of the hut, and said '*Chilin chilin*. Wherever can my pecking have brought me, me, hornbill (*chilikowwa*) – it's Spider's compound.' To which Spider replied 'That's right. Greetings, little sister. But I'm avoiding an earth thing. That's the cobra.'

But just as he was going out, the hornbill alighted right at the entrance to the hut; and when he emerged from it, the cobra uncoiled himself from the hornbill's back. Says Spider 'Yes, yes. I wasn't here, for I had gone out into the country. I'm just back –

* Presumably onomatopoeic.

29

I haven't even had a drink of water.' 'In you go' said the cobra, 'and have a drink of water. I've waited a long time for this meeting!'

Spider went into the hut, and picking up a wooden bowl, concealed it within the folds of his gown. Then he says 'Cobra, just let me take a message for the people here.' Says the cobra, 'I'll come along too, Spider.'

So Spider found that wherever he went, the cobra said 'I will come along too.' So he returned home.

Next the cobra swarmed into Spider's stomach, and when Spider got up, his stomach was bulging. Then said he to his wife 'Give me your cloths and your headcloth, and all your ornaments.' And he took all her things and put them on his own body.

Then he set off and walked along, soliciting like a prostitute. And coming to another town, he lighted on the son of a chief sitting there. 'Hey' says the latter, 'see that girl there. Seize her and take her to the compound for me!' So they seized Spider and took him to the chief's son's compound.

Then said Spider 'I'll not stay, unless I get a calabash full of honey.' And at once one was brought to him.

Night fell, and they went into the hut. And Spider took some honey and smeared it on his anus*; and some more, and did the same to the chief's son. Then he moved his close to the other's. And the cobra licked the honey off Spider and so on to the chief's son. Next the cobra emerged and went right in, into the stomach of the chief's son. Whereupon Spider got up and ran off with the calabash of honey. The other started up and found his stomach bulging. Spider went off home, and malams were gathered to make medicine for the chief's son.

Next Spider got himself a gourd waterbottle, a little calabash and a short loincloth, and putting these on, once again set off for the town where the chief's son lived.

Word went round that another pious man had arrived. All the fine malams were scornful, saying that where they had failed this one would not succeed. But someone else said that he should be brought anyway. So they brought along Spider. And he put out his hand and felt the stomach of the son of the chief.

'Fetch me some honey' said Spider. Immediately there were brought some hundred calabashes of honey. 'Bring me a goatskin

* For the trick, cf. III/7.

30

water-carrier' said Spider, and immediately some fifty of them were brought. Then he poured honey into the goatskin, shook it and turned it over. Next he took more honey and smeared it on the anus of the chief's son; and took the goatskin and put it by the chief's son's anus.

Presently the cobra put out his head and began licking the honey – and so into the goatskin. Spider stood there watching, until the cobra had gone right into the goatskin. Then he grabbed the mouth of the goatskin and held it. Says he 'Get seven hefty fellows. Now, tie up the mouth of this goatskin.' They did so, and he said 'Carry it away outside, and get some wood and give this bag a good beating.' And so they beat the goatskin, until the snake was dead. Then said Spider 'Undo the mouth of the goat-skin' and again 'Shake out what's in it.' And so they did, and there was the cobra, little black bastard. 'Well!!' said everyone, 'So *that's* what was the matter with the chief's son.'

And the boy's father had horses brought, and cattle and goats and sheep. Spider said that he didn't want horses – just cattle. So he was given cattle. And he drove off his cattle and his goats and his sheep.

And when he got home, he said to his wife 'Look what I've got. As for that cobra, I tricked him out of his bull; and I killed him into the bargain. Just look what I've got.' That's all. *Kungurus kan kusu.*

The Louse and the Chief* [$^{III}/_{24}$]

Spider was out for a walk one day, when he came upon a well, that was brimful with water, so much so that it was flooding over all around.

So he went and sowed beans there, and the beans grew, and

* Cf. M. No. 31.

had large pods on them. Says Spider 'Who shall I ask to guard these beans?'

Then a louse said 'Give me the job, Spider.' So Spider gave the louse the job of guarding his beans, taking her to a tree and putting her up on it.

There as she sat, presently along came some slave-girls of the chief to draw water. They broke off some beans, and the louse went 'Kuru-ru-ru-ru! Who's eating those beans? Those beans belong to mighty Spider, Mrs. Spider's lord, the specific for [naughty] little boys.' And the chief's slave-girls began dancing and couldn't stop.

And while they were dancing, along came some slave-lads from the chief's compound to gather grass, and they too broke off some beans. Says the louse 'Kuru-ru-ru-ru! Who's eating those beans? Those beans belong to mighty Spider, Mrs. Spider's lord, the specific for [naughty] little boys.' And the chief's slave-lads started dancing, and danced and danced.

Next the chief sent people to fetch them home. But the guards who came to fetch the slave-girls of the chief who had come to draw water and the slave-lads of the chief who had come to gather grass, all of whom were dancing – the guards too fell to dancing, as the louse sang.

Well, the chief waited for a long while, and when they didn't come ordered his horse saddled. It was done, and he and the town judge both mounted and went to the well. There they saw the guards, and the chief's slave-girls and his slave-lads, all a-dancing.

Up comes the chief, and the judge and 'Kuru-ru-ru-ru' says the louse. 'Who's eating those beans? Those beans belong to mighty Spider, Mrs. Spider's lord, the specific for [naughty] little boys' – and the chief and the judge fell to dancing.

The chief had them search for the louse, but they couldn't find her. At last they found her up the tree, and the chief made them take her off and put her in a little box; and so they all ceased dancing. And they took her away. That's all. *Kungurus kan kusu.*

The Sheep and the Goat* [$^{III}/_{26}$]

Here's a tale, how once Spider went to the home of a mother goat and a mother sheep. When he got there, he said 'I want you to give me a sheep to come as my travelling student.' 'Good. Fine' they said. 'Someone to teach our children to read the Book is what we've been looking for. And now – Allah has sent someone along!'

So they gave him a sheep, and went and told him to teach her to read.

He went off and made himself a satchel, and threw into it a verse or two of the Koran. Then he went and made himself a wooden writing-board and some ink. And he set off along the road, accompanied by the sheep. But when they drew near a town, he dropped his spoon and ladle.

They reached the town and went and found somewhere to stay. *Fura* was brought to them, and he said 'Look, sheep – see, we must have dropped our ladle on the road. Run back and fetch it. then we can drink our *fura*.' So the sheep ran back along the road.

Then Spider went and took the *fura*, and drank it all up before the sheep got back. When she got back, the sheep said to Spider 'Malam, here's the ladle. I've brought it.' Says he 'Tch tch, you've played us a scurvy trick. For, when you didn't bring back the ladle speedily, in the end a dog came along and drank up the *fura*. So you get none to drink, and I haven't had any to drink. And so, you see, we shall go to bed hungry.'

So they sat there till it was evening, and *tuwo* was brought to them. Then said he 'Sheep, get up, and go back and get our spoon. Then, when you get back, we'll eat the *tuwo*.' 'Right' said the sheep and off she went. And before she got back, Spider had eaten up the *tuwo*.

When she got back, Spider began to upbraid her violently, and she answered 'But, malam, you know it's a long way to the spot.' 'Well' said he, 'just see the scurvy trick you've played on us again. A dog's been and eaten up all the *tuwo*; and neither I, nor you get

* Cf. J. p. 14, TR. No. 24, and D. No. 122.

33

anything to eat.' So they went to sleep, the sheep gnawed by hunger. So two days passed.

And so in every town they came to, he treated her in the same way as he had there.

Next they again went into the bush and came to the bank of a river. And he took a roughening-stone* and put it in his bag.

Then Spider said 'Now, sheep, let us go and get wood to light a fire.' 'Very well' said the sheep, and they fetched wood and returned and lit a fire.

He picked up the stone, and said 'Look sheep, I'm going to climb right up to the top of this tree; and then I'm going to jump into the water. When you hear the splash, you jump into the fire. Understand?' 'O.K.' said the sheep.

And Spider climbed right up to the top of the tree with his roughening-stone; and he took it and tossed it down; and it made a splash. Whereupon the sheep jumped into the fire, and squirmed and squirmed until she was quite roasted.

Then Spider climbed down and found that the sheep was done to a turn. And taking her out, he ate and ate until he had quite eaten her up. Then he rose and went home.

Next he went to the sheep's home and told her mother. Said he to her mother and father 'Alas, the sheep's life has ended. Had I known what would happen, I wouldn't have asked to have her to teach her to read, but would have held my peace and said nothing.' 'As for that' said her mother, 'here's a goat. Come and take her.'

So they set off back along the same road, this time Mr. Spider having the goat with him. Presently he said 'Look, goat – throw away the ladle and spoon. When we get to a town we'll get others from the townspeople.' 'Very well' said she, and taking them, tucked them away under her tail.

So they came to a town and found lodging, and *fura* was brought them. Says Spider 'Look, goat, they've brought us *fura* and we've no ladle. Go back and fetch our ladle.' 'O.K.' said the goat.

But she returned as soon as she had left the compound, saying 'Malam, here's the ladle.' Says Spider 'You take the *fura*, and drink it. I won't. For the sheep was a fine girl; and fine people never

* For grind stones.

34

seem to live long. That's why she died.' So the goat finished up the *fura*.

They set off and came to another town, and the same happened, and the goat drank all the *fura*.

At the third place, Spider said 'For shame, goat! It's now two days that you've drunk all the *fura*. Won't you leave some for me today?' So she left Spider a little, and he took it and drank it.

Next day they again entered the bush and travelled till they came to the bank of the river. There he found himself a roughening-stone, and said 'Goat, let's go and fetch wood.' 'O.K.' said the goat.

So they fetched a lot of wood and brought it back and threw it down, and lit a fire. And the fire burnt up, red-hot.

The Spider said 'Now, goat, I'm going to climb up this tree, right to the top, to jump into the water. And when you hear the splash, then you jump into the fire and roll about.' 'Right' said the goat.

And Spider went and climbed the tree, right up to the top. And taking the stone, he tossed it into the river, and it made a great splash.

Then the goat took some shoes and tossed them into the fire, but she herself got right into Spider's satchel where he kept his readings from the Koran.

Down came Spider, and went and found the shoes, all stiffened. He picked them up and said 'Oh! God's curse on the goat! So her meat is tough is it! The sheep had better, more tender meat than this – but all the same I'll eat it.'

And Spider ate and ate at the shoes, until he had consumed them. At which the goat began to sing 'Mr. Spider's a fool, he ate the shoes.' Says Spider 'Holy writ in my little bag, how well you sing!'

And he began to dance, and danced till he reached the goat's mother, who was also the sheep's mother. He approached lamenting loudly. Says he 'Alas for the goat too, her life has ended.'

But as he said this, the goat lept right out of Spider's bag, and there she was, fat as butter!

Whereupon Spider fell down and turned into a many-legged insect. And that is what he still is. *Kungurus kan kusu.*

The Beasts of the Bush* [$^{III}/_{38}$]

Spider fell ill, and became so ill that he was like to die, so that he could only lift himself with difficulty and some assistance. Says he 'Mrs. Spider I have a craving – how can I get hold of some meat?' But he continued 'I know a scheme that'll do.'

He went and told the elephant and the bush-cow that there was to be a gathering of friends to help with his work; and he told the giraffe the same, and the roan antelope, and the lion, and the leopard – in fact all the beasts of the bush. Spider went and told them that there was to be a general gathering to assist him on his farm.

And they all gathered, but Spider went and hid in the leaves and began to yell. And the beasts of the bush took fright and ran away, killing the small ones as they did so. In this way the hare was killed, and the gazelle, and the duiker, and the western cob, and the reed-buck, and the western water-buck.

While the elephant, wherever she went, she killed bush-cow, roan antelope and Senegal hartebeeste. Then along comes Spider and sees the beasts of the bush, lying about in great numbers.

So he went and called Mrs. Spider, and the two of them returned and removed all the meat and took it home. They collected it all in their compound, and ate and ate, Spider and his wife, Mrs. Spider – until he was strong again. That's all. *Kungurus kan kusu.*

The Hyena, the Monkey, the Ground-squirrel and the Lion [$^{III}/_{61}$]

Another tale. The hyena came across some calves and said to them 'Hallo, calves! So it's here you are!' 'Yes, hyena, here we are'

* Cf. I/94 etc.

they answered. Says she 'I'll be along in the evening for a long chat.'
'Fine' said they.

The hyena went home and lay down watching the sun, until it got
low in the sky. Then she said to her children 'I'm going out for
an evening chat', and off she went.

Meanwhile the calves had sent the smallest ones home, leaving
only the big ones, whose horns had begun to grow.

Along comes the hyena, and the calves said 'Is that you, hyena?'
'Yes, it's me' she answered, 'I've come along for our chat.' But the
calves said 'We are thirsty. Let's go, and you can give us water to
drink. There's a well over there.' 'Very well' she said.

She went and picked up a big bucket and let it down into the
well. And when it filled with water, she began to pull it up. Says
the hyena to the calves 'Come and help me pull the bucket up. It's
got a lot of water in, and when we get it up, it'll be enough for you
all.' The calves came over, but when they got there they put their
horns to the hyena's anus, and pushed her into the well. Then
away they went at a gallop, leaving the hyena there in the well.

Presently along comes the monkey to draw water for the ants of
all sorts – and there the insects were following behind the monkey.
The monkey picked up the bucket and let it down into the well,
whereupon the hyena took hold of it. The monkey pulled, but he
could feel that something had hold of the bucket. So he said
'Whatever's in the water, let go of my bucket, so that I may water
my stock. When I have done that I'll get him out.'* So the hyena
let go of the bucket and the monkey poured the water out for the
insects, and they all drank until they had had enough. Then he
let the bucket down again and got the hyena out.

But when the hyena saw the monkey, she said 'What insolence!
It was my father's slave, and you refused to get me out till just
now, when you had finished watering the others! Very well then,
bend down! For I am going to get on your back and stay there till
I am dry.' So the monkey bent down, and the hyena climbed up,
and spread herself out until she was dry. Then the monkey said 'All
right, hyena, you're dry now.' But she answered 'No, no – my
anus isn't dry.'

After a while the monkey said again 'Now your anus is dry,
hyena, so now you can get down.' 'My ears aren't dry' said the

* For the exchange, cf. III/17.

hyena. After a while the monkey said 'Get down now, hyena, for your ears are dry.' 'Oh no' she answered, 'for my mouth isn't dry'. 'But, hyena' said the monkey, 'that mouth of yours never dries, and you know it.'

Then the hyena got down, and took hold of the monkey's leg. Says she 'You must give me meat, before I let you go. And if you don't give me some meat, I'll eat you up.' Then the monkey said 'Let me go, and then I'll fetch some meat for you.' 'Oh no' she replied, 'I'm not letting you go. Right there where you are you must give me some meat. Then I'll let you go.'

Just then a ground-squirrel came out of his hole. Says he 'Hey, monkey, how did you get involved with this mighty beast that hunts at night?' And the monkey told the ground-squirrel what had occurred between him and the hyena. And the ground-squirrel began to abuse the monkey* violently, and then said to the hyena 'Let the monkey go so that he may bring you some meat.' 'All right' said the hyena, and let go the monkey's leg.

Says the ground-squirrel 'Monkey, *dal!*† Ground-squirrel, hole! ' Again he said 'Monkey, do you twig?' But the the monkey didn't, so the other said again, 'Don't you understand what I'm saying, monkey? I said to you "Monkey, *dal*! Ground-squirrel, hole!" ' Then the monkey understood.

He gave a leap and up into a tree, grimacing at the hyena as he did so. As for the ground-squirrel, he slipped into his hole. The hyena looked from one to the other, and then began to dig up the ground-squirrel's hole.

But the ground-squirrel was digging away down there, and presently emerged, and up on to a black horse, wearing a black gown and black trousers and a black turban, and having a club in his hand.

Then he came up to the hyena and said 'Hey, what are you doing here?' 'Oh' said she, 'I'm digging out a gwound-squiwwel.' And the ground-squirrel took a good look at her ear, and lifting his club, struck her and down she went. Then he changed back into a ground-squirrel.

When she got up she recognised him. 'Well' said she, 'so it was

* In prefence.

† Perhaps 'whoosh' would render this. It usually describes the movement of a projectile? He is telling the monkey covertly to move fast, upwards.

the gwound-squiwwel who gave me such a wallop (?)*' Down into the hole went the ground-squirrel and started to dig again, and the hyena went back to digging out his hole.

Out popped the ground-squirrel again, and this time he was up on to a white horse, with a white gown, white trousers and a white turban, and a club in his hand. He went up to the hyena and says 'Hey, what are you doing here?' Says she 'I'm digging out a ground-squirrel.' Again he aimed with his club at her ear and fetched her a blow and down she went.

Back he changed into his proper shape. Up gets the hyena and sees the ground-squirrel at the mouth of his hole. Then in he went again into the hole and started digging again. And she, getting to her feet, started hers again too.

Presently the lion too came along. Says he to the hyena 'What are you digging?' 'Mightiest of beasts' she answered, 'I'm digging out a gwound-squiwwel.' 'Let me come and help you' said the lion. And he went and joined in.

Then the hyena saw the lion's testicles swinging, and grabbed them and ran off. Down went the lion.

She made her way home. There she flayed the testicles and ate the meat; while with the skin she made a little drum, which she began to beat, singing 'Other than me, hunter of the night, who could make a drum from a lion's testicles? Other than me, Amina†, who could make a drum from a lion's testicles?' Spider heard this and went off into the bush, looking for a lion. He walked till he eventually found him. Then said Spider to him 'For shame, mighty one of the bush! A mighty one like you – however were you caught off your guard to the extent that the hyena took off your testicles? And now she has gone and made a drum and is bringing your name into her song for all the beasts of the bush to hear.' 'What shall I do to catch the hyena?' asked the lion. 'Go and get some meat' said Spider.

So the lion went off and made a kill and brought it. Next great strips of meat were cut off, and Spider covered the lion quite over with the meat; and taking one of the strips, made for the hyena's home. When he got there, he made formal salutation. 'Is the hyena

* From the italics *yayata* would seem to be another piece of hyena-ese, but unlike *kwiyege* it is not obvious what she was trying to say.

† Standard epithet of the hyena.

there?' he asked, and her youngest child answered 'She's not here.'
'Well, of all the — !' said Spider, 'See this meat – well, I came to
invite the hyena – and now she's not at home.' 'Hey'* said the
hyena, 'Here I am. It's false. I *am* at home. It was on account of the
lion that I told them, if anyone came to say that I wasn't at home.'
And out she came.

They set off along the road, and as they went, the hyena said
'Say, Spider, I suppose it's not by any chance to the lion that you
are taking me?' 'Oh no' says Spider, 'Look, here's another piece of
meat; let me give it to you to eat'; and he took another strip from
his bag and gave it to the hyena to eat.

On they went till they came to the meat. As soon as they got
there, the hyena set to, taking the meat and putting it into a pile;
at length she reached the piece that was on the lion's back.

Then the lion took a firm hold of the hyena, and gouged out
one of her eyes. He cut off an ear and took out all her intestines.
Then he let her go, and she went off and died. *Kungurus kan kusu.*

The Lion and the Monkey [III/96]

The lion and Spider were walking along the path through the
bush one day, when they saw the monkey. 'Monkey, come here'
said the lion, and the other came over and they began to wrestle.
First the lion threw the monkey, then the monkey threw the lion.

After they had struggled for a while they got themselves into a
thicket, which concealed a hole in the ground. Next they tumbled
into the hole. And all the while Spider was beating his drum. The
lion killed the monkey there in the hole, and getting a piece of
higher ground managed to get out of the hole, back into the thicket.
Then he dug,† and presently emerged from the thicket. Says the
lion 'Spider, go in and eat meat, for I have killed the monkey.'
'O.K.' said Spider, and going in, ate some meat; then came out

* Cf. III/48.
† Why?

40

again and went and told Mrs. Spider, and she too went in and began to eat.

Next Spider went to the elephant and said 'Hey, elephant, look, you're the biggest in the bush, yet today the lion belittled you and abused you. In fact there was nothing he didn't say about you!' 'Is that so?' said the elephant. 'Yes' said Spider, and off went the elephant looking for the lion.

From there Spider went to the lion and said 'Look, lion, the elephant has been abusing you – there's nothing she hasn't said about you.' 'Right' said the lion.

And he too set off. Presently he espied the elephant, and went and hid. Then when the elephant came up and was about to pass by, he sprang on to her back. She put out her trunk and the lion seized it and broke it. So the lion killed the elephant very quickly.

Meanwhile Spider had gone off to the giraffe, and said 'Giraffe, the lion abused you shamefully in public, slandering you and saying that you are nothing but a long neck, skimpy buttocks and eyes in the middle of your head.' Then Spider beat a retreat.

Off went the giraffe looking for the lion, and when he found him, he caught him a swinging blow with his neck and killed him.

Off went Spider and led Mrs. Spider back to the spot. And when they got back, they set about carrying all the meat home, and then ate and ate and ate. That's all. *Kungurus kan kusu.*

Bareɓare* [II/72]

Spider was at home one day with Mrs. Spider and their two children. Says Mrs. Spider 'Husband, won't you go and cultivate a farm for us, so that we are not left watching others eat, but haveing nothing to eat ourselves?'

So he rose, saying that she must cook some bulrush-millet, add salt and oil, and take it along to him at the farm. And Mrs. Spider put some water on to boil; cooked some bulrush millet, added salt

* Cf. next tale and TR. No. 15 (where the second part occurs as a separate story). Also D. No. 89.

and oil, and picking it up went off to the farm with it, for him.

When she got there, he says 'Put it down in the shade over there.' 'Very well' said she, and did as he had told her. 'Good' said he, 'Now you can go off home, while I sow the farm.' And she went off home. But he went and sat down, ate up all the millet, and then went home.

Next morning when it was light, he said to her 'My dear, make an early start with pounding the guinea-corn; then cook some and add salt and oil, so that I can take it with me to the farm, when I go to sow.' 'Certainly' said she.

So she got up very early, pounded guinea-corn, cooked it and added salt and oil. She mixed it all up well, and he picked it up and off he went to the farm. There he sat himself down, and having eaten all the guinea-corn up, spent the day there. Evening came and he returned home.

Again he told his wife to cook some beans and add salt and oil, so that next morning he might take it to the farm, where he was going to sow, to ensure a really good crop. And the beans were duly cooked for him, and he took them and so off to the farm again. Then in the evening he returned home once more. Says he 'My dear, shell some groundnuts and fry them, for in the morning I'll be off to the farm again, to sow.' And he took the groundnuts to the farm, and once again just sat there and ate them. And in due course rose and went home. There he said 'My dear, you'll have to be up betimes tomorrow, for Bambarra groundnuts take a lot of preparing as you know. When they are nearly cooked, take them off, scooping them out for me, into a smaller pot, frying them and continually turning them over.' 'All right' said she.

So next day when it was light she fetched all the Bambarra groundnuts and prepared them exactly as Spider had said. Well, the time came when the bulrush-millet was ripe in the fields, and Mrs. Spider said 'Husband, please bring us some of the new crop to eat ' 'O.K.' said he.

Well, there was a woman had a farm there, and she had cut her crop and tied up the bundles of heads. Her name was Barebare*; she had only one leg and one arm, and her head was like half a cola-nut. And Spider would go to her farm and steal her corn,

* TR. speaks of 'half people' (p. 123)

stealing some twenty bundles and taking them home, where he hid them.

Next his wife said 'Husband, please bring us some beans to eat.' 'O.K.' said he and went off to Barebare's farm and stole some beans. And these he brought home and they ate them. But soon after Mrs. Spider again said 'Husband, couldn't you bring us home some Bambarra groundnuts. Everyone else is eating theirs, and we – it's as if we hadn't farmed any.' 'O.K.' said he, and again went to Barebare's farm and stole some Bambarra groundnuts. And they cooked and ate them.

But presently his wife said 'Husband, tomorrow I'm coming along to take a look at our farm.' 'Oh no, my dear' said he, 'Women can't come.' 'Oh, very well' she answered, 'But I had thought that if I went and took a look at the farm, I might lift some groundnuts and bring them home to cook.' Spider jumped up and said 'My dear, did you say that you wanted some groundnuts? Well, I'll go right off and lift some.' 'Good' said she. And again he went to Barebare's farm, and lifted some of her groundnuts and brought them home.

Now, no one had ever seen this Barebare, until at length one day she paid a visit to her farm, and there she saw that someone had helped himself to some twenty bundles of bulrush-millet; and beans; and Bambarra groundnuts; and groundnuts. So she went and made a maiden of sticky gum, saying to herself 'I'll catch whoever's stealing from me thus.'

Along comes Spider and sees the maiden, sees her breasts. Says he 'Aha! Maiden, little maiden, may I touch your breast?' and stretching out his hand, he touched one – and his hand stuck. Says he 'Oh well! I've got another hand. I may as well touch it with that.' And so he did, and that hand too stuck. 'Well, well'! said he, 'Maiden, little maiden, may I touch you with my foot?' And he moved his foot forward, and that stuck too. Again he said 'Oh, well! I've another foot' and touched her with that. And that foot stuck too. Then he said 'Hey girl, let me go! I was only in fun, and here you go seizing every bit of me and holding on. Let go, before I get angry!' And he began to complain bitterly.

Presently along comes Barebare, and says to him 'So Allah has caught you, you cursed rascal!' But he said to her 'Not so! For I was just coming along, taking a little walk out to my farm, to lift some beans and groundnuts and Bambarra groundnuts, to take home. And when I got here, I saw her and thought I would have a little fun with her. But she got hold of me, all over, and hung on.' So Barebare pulled him off the maiden of sticky gum, and said to him 'Then go and take your beans, and Bambarra groundnuts, and groundnuts, and be off home. But I warn you, that if you tell anyone that you have seen me, you'll be hearing from me again, you will!' 'Of course not' said he, 'For who should I want to tell?' And Spider went and took his Bambarra groundnuts and beans and groundnuts, and went off home.

Night fell, and he was lying on his bed. Says he 'Well, today I saw Bare—'* 'What sort?' asked Mrs. Spider. 'A Bambarra groundnut' said he. But presently he could keep silence no longer and again started 'You know, today I saw Bare—' 'Tch tch' said Mrs. Spider, 'What sort?' 'Oh, er – a bean' he answered. And presently he burst out again 'You know, today I saw a *bare*, such as no one else has ever seen.' 'What sort was that?' she asked. 'Oh, er – a – er – cola-nut.' And finally he said again 'You know, today I saw someone with a *barebare*.'† 'Is that some woman?' asked Mrs. Spider. 'Yes' he answered. And then they went into their hut, and so to bed.

Presently Spider said to his eldest son 'Open the door for me to go and relieve myself'. His son got up and groped round the hut, but found no entrance. So he returned. 'Dad' said he 'I can't find the entrance.' For – though Spider didn't know it – Barebare had come along and blocked up the entrance. Then Spider said to his younger son that he was to get up and open the door for him so that he could go and relieve himself. And his son got up and went and groped round the hut, but returned, not finding the door. 'Dad' said he, 'I felt all round the hut, but I didn't find the entrance.' 'You're both lying' said Spider, and then to his wife 'You get up and go and open the door for me, so that I may go and relieve myself. For that leaves only you – go and do what your sons were doing.' So she got up and groped round the hut, but couldn't find the door. And returning she said 'Husband, I felt, but I couldn't find the entrance.' He answered 'Good-for-nothing

* Which also means a single nut or bean out of its shell or pod.
† I.e. he still avoided saying it directly as a name.

slut, are you just as bad as the boys? Are you just going to repeat*
what they said?'

Next day when it was light, they heard people talking, and these
began knocking, for they too couldn't find the entrance.

And suddenly there was Barebare in the middle of the hut.
Says she to Spider 'You damned rascal! Don't say I didn't tell
you! I said to you, I warned you that if you told anyone that you
had seen me, you would surely be hearing from me again.' 'Oh'
said he 'I never said that I had seen you, Barebare. I just said to my
wife that I had seen the *bare* of a Bambarra groundnut, and of a
bean, and of a cola-nut. That was all I told her.' But she answered
'Oh no, Spider! This is the reckoning between you and me. Cook
one of your sons for me.' And Mrs. Spider did so, and she ate
him up. And when they looked for her, she had vanished. But next
day she returned, saying 'Cook another of your sons for me to eat.'
Again they did so, and again she ate him up. And as she was going
she said 'Spider, you and your wife – the two of you – before I
get back, one of you must cook the other.' 'Very well' said Spider
and Mrs. Spider, and off she went.

Up they jumped and lifted a cooking-pot on to the fire. Then
Spider and Mrs. Spider fell to struggling. She picked him up and
was about to tip him into the pot, when he cried out 'For shame, my
dear! Consider the respect due to a spouse!' repeating this several
times. Whereupon, having lifted him up, she put him down; and
then went to one side and sat down. Presently she lay down.
Spider waited until she had relaxed her guard, and then went over,
picked her up and forced her into the pot, while she in her turn
began to cry out 'For shame, Spider! Consider the respect due to
your spouse!' 'Oh no, my dear!' says he, 'You're not my spouse
any more, for our marriage has ended today.' And he cooked her.

Presently along comes Barebare, and picking up Mrs. Spider,
eats her. Then as she departed again she said 'Now, Spider – before
I get back, you cook yourself.' 'O.K.' said Spider.

He picked up a cooking-pot, put it on the fire, which he lit,
fetched water and filled the pot. When the water boiled, he dipped
the end of his finger into it, and immediately scalded it. He withdrew his hand, howling and saying 'Surely no man could ever

* Emending *ki* to *bi* tentatively.

cook himself – except on Barebare's orders. Only Barebare could be so heartless!'

Just then he saw that a tortoise had come out into the centre of the hut. Says he 'Hey, Spider, if I do you a good turn (give you day*) now, I know that you'll immediately do me a bad one (give you night*).' He went on 'Get into the hole here' and Spider went in. He had just got in, when Barebare returned. The tortoise tumbled into the hole and closed the entrance to it. And so the tortoise saved Spider.

Then said Spider 'Tortoise, come on out, so that we may say goodbye to each other' and the tortoise did so. Then Spider struck him down, saying 'That was a rotten lie, tortoise. I'm afraid that you're just meat to me' and he bent and picked him up, and went and ate him up. That's all. *Kungurus kan kusu.*

The Hyena† [^{III}/108]

Spider and Mrs. Spider were once living in a town, where people grew nothing but groundnuts.

Well, one day the rainy season started and everyone went off and began planting groundnuts. Says Mrs. Spider 'Husband, you see the rains have begun, but you don't farm. You know, you ought to plant some groundnuts.' 'Mrs. Spider' he answered, 'you know I was intending to do so myself.' 'Fine' said she.

So Spider gave his wife three thousand cowries and told her to go and buy some groundnut seed. 'O.K.' she said and went off, bought it and brought it home. 'Fry it' said Spider. 'But, Spider' she protested, 'Whoever heard of frying seed groundnuts?' 'Don't ask stupid questions, my dear' said Spider! 'Just do what I

* A metaphor that occurs several times in TATS, e.g. at the end of I/3.

† Cf. last tale; also M. No. 40. See J., p. 8. There is another version of this popular tale in LND which has a chief as the one setting the trap; and the monkey the one tricked by Spider into taking his place. But the orange-headed male lizard reports this to the chief. However, Spider tricks the monkey and the lizard in the end (LND, p. 111).

told you.' So Mrs. Spider fried the groundnuts. 'Now' said Spider, 'Put them all in the mortar and pound them up and add pepper and salt.' 'Very well' she said, and poured them all into the mortar and pounded them; then adding pepper and salt, she made groundnut paste.

Spider took it and picked up his little grubber and went off into the fields, taking his water in a goatskin bag. There he selected some thick, cool shade, and lay himself down. He ate steadily at the groundnut paste until the evening came. Then he got up, rolled on the ground,* and went off home.

'Welcome home' said Mrs. Spider, at which he turned on her rudely and said 'What are you burbling about? Get me some hot water to wash with.' She brought it for him and he washed. Then she said 'Greetings, Spider' and he acknowledged them.

Time passed, and hoeing began. Says Mrs. Spider to her husband 'Look, people have started hoeing. When are you going along to do some?' But he answered 'Look wife – groundnuts grow bigger and more plentiful, if you leave the ground undisturbed.' 'I see' said she.

Again time passed, and Mrs. Spider saw people bringing home the new groundnuts. Says she 'Spider, look, people have started lifting their groundnuts.' 'Very well' he replied.

So he set off and went to the farm of a Fulani, helped himself to a large calabash full of groundnuts and brought them home. Says Mrs. Spider 'Well, Spider, these *are* fine ground-nuts, fine big ones.' And Spider went back to the Fulani's farm to spy out the land, found no one there, and came home. Says he to his wife 'Come, my dear, let us go and take a walk round.' 'Very well' she said, and they went off to the Fulani's farm.

Says he 'Look, from here eastwards is all mine; from here westwards is all mine; from here north is all mine; and from here south is all mine too.' 'Husband' said Mrs. Spider, 'you have indeed done a great deal of work! All this great area!' And so they returned home, and more time went by.

Presently Mrs. Spider said 'Husband, you must start building storage bins, for this year we have indeed got a supply of food!' Then Spider built seven storage bins. Groundnut-lifting began in earnest, and Mrs. Spider said 'Husband, you must get your ground-

* To give verisimilitude to the idea of having worked.

nuts up and bring them home, and we'll fill our bins with them. 'Very well' said Spider, and they went and began bringing the groundnuts home.

The Fulani would go and take some, and then Spider would go along and take some more, until he had filled four bins, leaving three bins that had no groundnuts in.

But one day the Fulani said 'What can it be that comes when we've just taken some groundnuts, and then when we come again we find that more have been taken?' So they went and made a maiden of sticky gum and set her up in the farm. And they fetched *tuwo* and *fura* and left them with her – and fried meat too; setting them down in front of her.

Presently along comes Spider and says 'Ah, little maiden, little maiden! So you've got this tasty food all to yourself, have you?' And he grabbed it and ate the meat and the *tuwo* and drank the *fura*. 'And now' said he, 'just let me touch your breast – that's all I want.' So Spider touched the breast of the gum-maiden – and there his hand stuck!

'Now, now, little maiden' says he reproachfully, 'Let me go. I was only playing,' and he touched her with the other hand – and that one stuck too. 'Let me go' said he, 'or I'll use my knee on you.' He did so – and his knee stuck too.

'This left foot of mine is no trifler' he said, 'Let go, or I'll use it on you – and it won't be a laughing matter.' And he applied his left foot to her – and that stuck too.

'Let me go at once' said he, 'or I'll knock you down with my chest, and you'll get hurt. Let me go.' But she wouldn't. So he pushed his chest against her – and Spider's chest stuck too.

'Little maiden, little maiden' said he. 'Let me go, or I'll butt you and knock all your teeth out.' He butted her – and his head stuck.

Presently along came the Fulani and saw Spider stuck to the gum-maiden. Said they 'Spider, Allah has caught you.' They went on 'Spider or not, even if you were an elephant, today you're getting a flogging.' And they went off into the bush to fetch switches.

Up comes the hyena. 'Hullo!' says she, 'You here, Spider?' 'Yes indeed. I've – er – stopped for a bit.' The hyena saw the rest of the meat. 'Spider, whose is that?' she asked. 'Look' he answered, 'Some Fulani stopped me here, and brought me meat and *tuwo* and *fura*, and I have eaten until I'm satisfied. See the rest? Well, help yourself, eat it! But they've gone off to fetch a big bull for me – a real fat one with so much meat on him that he can scarcely walk.' 'Will you leave some for me?' asked the hyena. 'Yes' said Spider, 'But if you want me to keep a little for you, detach me so that I may go and relieve myself and be back before they return. But I mustn't go off unless you are sitting here, for fear they come back and, not finding me here, take the bull away again. Just come here and put your body as I have had mine. Do you understand?' 'Yes' says she.

So the hyena detached Spider from the gum-maiden, and stuck herself there in his place. Says Spider 'But, listen, hyena. I don't want to come back and find that you've eaten it all up and not kept a share for me.' Says the hyena 'Fancy suggesting such a thing! Spider, whether you come back or not, if they bring the bull, your share will be here for you.' 'Good' said Spider, 'That's dandy, hyena.' And he went off some way from the farm, found a tree and climbed up it, and squatted there waiting.

Along came the Fulani and saw the hyena. 'Hullo!' they said, 'Look! Spider has become a hyena.' They went on 'You bastard! Hyena or not, even if you turn into an elephant, today you're getting a flogging.' And they took hold of the hyena and flogged her and flogged her, until at last she escaped and ran away. She came to the foot of the tree, up which Spider was, and said 'Just as sure as I'm a hyena, if I can find that Spider, I'll eat him. I won't leave even the blood – if I can find him.'

Just then Spider broke off a branch and threw it down. The hyena lifted her head and saw Spider, and said 'Come on down and I'll eat you up!' 'O.K.' said Spider.

But he came down very slowly, step by step, and when he got near he said 'What? Oh, leave her to me, I'm just catching her.' 'Spider, who are you talking to?' asked the hyena. 'Oh' he answered, 'just some Fulani.' But the hyena didn't wait any longer, but ran off as fast as she could.

The Spider came down and went off home, and, having no trade, he began to weave. One day he was busy weaving, when along comes the hyena and finds Spider. Says she 'Spider, today your lies are at an end – you damned rascal!' 'What's that?' he said [not talking to her]. 'Who are you talking to?' she asked. 'Oh, I wasn't talking to you' he said, 'it's some Fulani who've come looking for you.' And off ran the hyena and escaped. And Spider went on with his weaving.

On another day Spider went into the bush to collect firewood so that he might weave late into the night*. The hyena caught him there and said 'Well, well, Spider. And what will you do now? For now I am going to eat you up.' He answered 'Yes – but, hyena, surely one doesn't eat a person when his bowels and his bladder are both full? Let me go and empty my bowels.' But the hyena wouldn't let him. 'Very well. Then let me go and relieve myself, hyena.' 'All right, you may go and do that' said the hyena.

So Spider went aside and going a little way squatted down. Then he began to make loud noises as if talking. Says the hyena 'Spider, who are you talking to?' He ignored her and went on talking, ending by saying 'Yes, there she is. You go round by the east.' When the hyena heard that, she started up and ran away. And that was that, for he saw no more of her.

And that is why Spider, being afraid, turned himself into an insect, for fear the hyena should eat him up. *Kungurus kan kusu.*

The Monkey, the Camel, the Hyena, and the Lion† [III/ 117]

The monkey set off and climbed a shea tree and began to eat [the nuts]. Along comes the camel and says 'Hey, monkey! Throw me down two nuts to eat.' 'Catch hold!' said the monkey, and picked them and gave them to him. Says the monkey 'But they're not ripe, you know.' Says the camel 'Hey, monkey, give me some more. Bloody young rascal.' Says the monkey 'Well!! Camel! Damned bastard with a long neck and a little anus!' Then the camel stuck out his neck and seized the monkey and pulled him down; put him

* By the light of the fire.   † Cf. T.R. No. 26.

on his back and tied him up with *kalgo* bark. And he tied him up really tight, so that he couldn't escape.

He set off and travelled for a while. Presently he met the hyena. Says she 'Hey, monkey, what brings you and the mighty one of the bush, our big brother, together?' 'You must ask the camel' said the monkey. But the camel said to the hyena 'Ask the monkey.' The hyena asked the monkey, saying 'Hey monkey what brought you and our big brother together?' 'We-ell' said the monkey, 'It was like this. I was up my shea tree, enjoying a feed, when along comes the camel and asks me to give him two. I gave them, telling him they weren't ripe. But when he had eaten them, he called me a bloody young rascal, a sharp fellow.* So I called him a bastard with a long neck and a little anus. Whereupon he seized me, took off some *kalgo* bark and tied me tight on to his back.'

Then the hyena said 'Bend down, camel, so the monkey can get down and I give judgement for you both. So the monkey got down. But when he was down, he caught the hyena a blow in front and mounted her. And that is why the hyena's front is up and her anus is down.

The camel lay down and began to graze, whereupon the monkey gave a jump and so up into a tree; and so, jumping from one tree to another, escaped. Then the camel said to the hyena 'You must get my monkey for me.'

While they were talking, up comes Spider with his drum. When he arrived, he asked the camel, and the camel told him what had happened between him and the hyena. And Spider beat his drum and chanted 'Oh, hyena, you're a meddlesome creature. What made you involve yourself in judgement with the long-necked one?' The camel was diverted exceedingly by the drumming and began to dance there in the bush. Whereupon Spider said to the hyena 'Get running, you damned good-for-nothing creature; and if you stop, the camel will come and kill you – you'll be for the next world for sure.' And the hyena ran off as fast as she could.†

Back comes the camel to Spider, still dancing. Says he 'Hey, Spider, where's the hyena?' 'The hyena's run off' said Spider. Whereupon the camel made after the hyena as fast as he could. And the hyena, seeing the camel was after her, would run for a

* Lit. 'a see-er of the sky', a phrase often applied to the monkey.
† Cf. II/57.

little, then lie down for a little, and then run on again, and so she escaped the camel.

The camel came back to Spider, and said 'Right, Spider, you can give me back the hyena.' Says Spider 'Camel, reward me for the drumming that I did for you. Mind you, my drum cost me two million cowries to buy. If you reward me for the drumming that I performed for you, in my turn I'll catch the hyena and bring her back to you.' And the camel said 'Very well, Spider, come along and I'll give you one thousand,* and you can fetch the drum for me'.†

They set off along the road together. Spider called Mrs. Spider. Then they went and set about fetching the money. They had nearly finished doing this, and Spider had given the camel the drum, when up comes the lion. Now Spider was the lion's drummer.

Says the lion 'Hey, Spider, what are you doing with this fellow?' 'Well, lion' said Spider, and he told him all that had passed between him and the camel.' 'But' said the lion, 'that drum – the drum – the skin of that drum belonged to two of your brothers, camel. Yes, they were sewn up to make that drum.' And the lion killed the camel, divided him into two, and giving Spider half took half for himself.

Spider went off home with a million cowries and his drum, and moreover he had got some meat – half a camel. So he and his wife lived happily. That's all. *Kungurus kan kusu*. I ate the rat, not the rat me.

The Hyena, When They Went to Take a Present to the Chief ‡ [^{III}/₉₉]

Spider filled his gourd water-bottle with honey, and the hyena

* Probably 'thousand' has been omitted, in view of the other two references.

† Conjecturally emending *kama ganga* ('seize the drum') to *kawo mana ganga* ('bring us . . .').

‡ Cf. next tale, TR. No. 34 and M. No. 44. In D. No. 93 it is the hyena and the monkey who go to the chief.

filled hers with watery faeces,* and they went off to see the chief.
There they were given lodging, and Spider's gourd was accepted
and found to contain honey; and the hyena's gourd was accepted
and found to contain faeces.

Bedding was brought them, plaited palm-leaf mats and skin mats.
Says the hyena 'Good. You can have the plaited ones, Spider; me –
the skin ones 'll do me.' Then they lay down for a while until night
fell. [They hyena kept fidgeting] and each time she moved, she
caught the skin mat and tore it. 'Hey!' said Spider, 'what goes on?'
'There are mice here' the hyena answered, 'they're troubling me.'
And by the time it was morning, there were no skin mats left, for
she had eaten them all. Word was brought them that they should
get up and go outside the compound and sit and wait, until a
dismissal present was brought them.

A hide was plaited into a rope and tied to a billy-goat; and cotton
thread treated similarly and fastened to a bull, and the announce-
ment that each should grab one of the ropes as soon as they
appeared. Then they were thrown towards them.

The hyena darted forward, knocking over Spider, and, reaching
it first took the hide rope. So when Spider got there, he took the
cotton one. Then the word was given to pull. The hyena pulled
first and pulled in the billy, while Spider pulled in the bull. Says the
hyena 'O.K., Spider, God willed you should have it. Let's go.'
And they set off along the road.

The hyena grabbed her billy-goat and gobbled it up, leaving the
liver, which she kept aside and gave to Spider. And on they went.
But Spider didn't eat the liver. At length when they had gone a long
way, the hyena said 'Give me my liver that I gave you, since you refuse
to slaughter your bull.' 'It's all yours' he answered and she took it,
but then she returned it to Spider, saying 'I was only pulling your
leg!'

They reached the edge of some water, and the hyena said 'Well,
Spider, let's have a bathe.' 'O.K.' said he and got down from his
bull. But while they were bathing, she said 'Let's play the diving
game!' 'O.K.' he said, and they dived under.

But the hyena came out very quickly and snatched up the liver
she had given Spider and ate it up; then she got back into the water
and submerged again. Up comes Spider, then, after a long pause,

* Hyenas are proverbially loose-stooled.

up comes the hyena. Says she 'So I can stay under longer than you, it seems, Spider. Well, let's be getting along,' and off they went again.

Then said the hyena 'And now, Spider, give me my liver, if you please; moreover I'm not joking now.' Spider looked in the place he had put the liver. No liver! For while they were under the water, the hyena had stolen it and eaten it. 'Hey, you, hyena' said he, 'You've eaten your liver.' 'That's a lie – before God!' she answered, 'And now you can slaughter that bull of yours right away.' 'Very well' he agreed, and got off and slaughtered the bull.

Then he said to the hyena 'Go and fetch some fire – look, there's some there!' It was the ball of the sun he had seen! Off ran the hyena, departing after the sun. Spider flayed his bull and set up a shelter for himself. Then he got all the meat and put it up on top of the shelter, and climbed up himself.

A storm came on, and the hyena turned back. But before she reached him, the rain had started. She reached the spot where Spider's shelter was, with some difficulty; but it was dark and she couldn't see in any direction.

And at every flash of lightning, Spider would pick up a bone and throw it at her forehead. Said she 'Today, Allah is raining bones' – and took up the bone and ate it.

Eventually she realised what was happening and saw Spider up on the shelter 'Oho!' she thought, 'So it's you, is it, Spider? Very well, then. I'll play the same trick on you as you've played on me.' And she went off and summoned the ostrich.

Spider made a rope. The hyena came back with the ostrich and said to her 'Look, you've got a long neck. Stretch it out and grab Spider for me.' The ostrich stretched out her neck, but Spider took his rope and throwing it over her neck, pulled it tight. And the ostrich began to dance wildly around, with her tail-end on the ground.

Next the hyena, annoyed, called out 'Spider, come a little closer; come much closer, Spider and we'll eat the eggs – three for you and two for me.' The ostrich nearly died, but managed to escape from the hands of Spider. Off goes the hyena, with the ostrich after her, flat out, and they ran and they ran. The hyena just escaped and got into her hole. There she turned and began looking out from the mouth of the lair. While the ostrich squatted there, guarding her.

Presently the ostrich grew tired of sitting at the mouth of the hyena's lair, so pulled out one of her feathers, stuck it in the ground and went her way. The hyena didn't come out for twenty days and grew very hungry. But a wind got up and blew away the feather. Then the hyena came out, very thin.

Presently as she walked along she saw Spider. 'My word!' said he, 'What's the matter with you, hyena?' She answered 'Spare me any more*! Today is the finish of your lying.' 'No, no' he answered, 'For the ostrich sent me here – I'm not alone.' 'You're lying' she said. Then Spider said 'Hullo!! And there comes the ostrich too!' and, pretending to address someone else. 'You cut off that way, while I block this one!' At which the hyena made off fast, and that was the last Spider saw of her. *Kunkurus kan kusu.*

A Variant [III/ 146]

The hyena said to Spider 'Let's go and collect honey for the chief.' They collected honey and each one filled his gourd bottle. Then the hyena said to Spider again 'Let us excrete, and take that to the chief' and she filled a gourd bottle with excrement, but Spider didn't. And they took [their presents] to the chief.

They were told to call along a fly, an honest one. Along came an honest fly, went into the hyena's bottle and came out very quickly; then he went into Spider's bottle and didn't come out for a long time. He was told 'Surely it's time you came out?' and out he came.

Orders were given for them to be given things to sit on. They were given an oval, plaited mat and a skin, and the hyena was told to choose one. 'Well' she answered, 'you know my family's in-herited tastes,' and she was given the skin, while Spider took the mat.

Night came and they were going to settle down, when the hyena asked whether there weren't by any chance rats in the hut. She was

* Reading a full-stop after *dai*.

told there weren't any. But in the night she tore up her skin mat, and swallowed it. 'I think there *are* rats in the hut' she said, and again she was assured that there weren't.

Morning came, and they were given a billy-goat and a bull, and the hyena was told to choose one of them. 'Well' said she, 'You know my family's inherited tastes' she said, and took the goat.

As they went along, the goat began to bleat. 'Is your foot hurting?' asked the hyena – and took off one of them. With the pain of this the goat bleated again – and the hyena took another of its feet, and eventually ate the goat up on the road.

Spider was on his bull, with a skin-bag. Says the hyena 'Spider, here's a strip of meat for you' and gave him one, which he put in the bag. Later it fell out, and the hyena ate it.

When they got home the hyena asked 'Spider, where's my strip of meat?' and he answered 'It fell out – but I'll kill my bull and give you a strip of that.'

Two nights went by, and on the third day the hyena said 'Spider, let me have your bull and I'll wash him'. Then she went to the washing place by the river with the bull and heaped a lot of earth on his back*. 'Look, here's a beast, Spider' said she.

Then Spider shot his bull. 'Oh, Spider' she said, 'I said "Look, here's your bull" – however could you bear to shoot him?' 'Hm, I see, hyena' said Spider. 'But, no matter,' and Spider proceeded to cut up its flesh, separating the meat and the bones. Then he climbed a tree and took the meat up there.

When Spider saw that the sun was setting, he said to the hyena 'Look, there's some fire, go and get it.' Off she ran, but [naturally] didn't overtake the fire. Then, when morning came she returned and said to Spider 'I didn't catch up with that fire.' 'Very well' he said, 'but sit you down a while.' Then he knocked a bone down to her, and she remarked 'God is causing it to rain bones!'

The bone was disposed of and she called over the ostrich. 'Ostrich' says she, 'this is your big day.' Spider shrank back, hiding, and the ostrich began eating the meat, passing some to the hyena. Then Spider grasped the ostrich's neck firmly, and the hyena said 'Harder, Spider – harder! One for me, one for you' – for the eggs were coming out! Then the ostrich got away, and chased the

* ? So that he looked like some other beast and she might trick Spider into shooting him?

56

hyena all the way to her lair. There she pulled out a feather and set it up by the entrance.

Whenever the hyena peeped out, she would see the feather and say 'I see you!' But, staying in her den, she got very thin and eventually died there. That's the end of that one.

2

HARE

────────

The Hyena's Children* [$^I/_5$]

One day the hare was sick. When he got up, he found himself short of meat to eat. He set off walking and entered the hyena's hut. There he found the hyena's children, ten of them. Said he 'Peace be upon you'. Said they to the hare 'Here! Where do you come from?' Said he 'From outside, hyena has borne me.' Said they to the hare 'What's your name?' and he answered 'My name is All-of-Us.' And they said 'O.K., sit down there' and the hare sat down at the edge of the lair of the hyena's children.

He was just inside the lair, when along comes the hyena with meat. Says her eldest son to her 'All of us, mother?' and she says 'Yes.' Then said the hare 'Did you hear that? 'Twas me she said to give the meat to.' So they gave him the meat, and he ate it without giving them any. And again the hyena brought meat and put it in the lair. And they said 'All of us?' Says she 'Of course – all of you.' And again the hare took the meat and ate it without giving them any. And the hyena's children grew thin, there was no fat on them.

Then came the hyena and said 'My children, come out that I may see you.' Out they came and she looked them over and said 'You – what's the matter with you, that you're not fat?' And they said 'When you bring meat, All-of-Us takes it.' Says she 'And who is All-of-Us?' And they answered 'Oh, he's just here, inside the lair.' Says the hyena 'All-of-Us, come out and let me see you!' And the hare put his ears together and stuck them through the mouth of the lair. Then the hyena seized the hare by the ear and flung him far away in anger.

The hare ran off. As he was running he met the dog, and the dog said 'Hullo, where are you from, looking so fat?' Says hare 'Oh, I've been to the hyena's lair.' Says the dog 'Won't you please take

* Cf. TR. No. 18 and S. p. 73. See J. p. 39.

me?' and the hare answered 'When you get to the mouth of the lair, say that your name is All-of-Us.' 'Right' says the dog.

And as he went along he kept saying to himself 'All-of-Us, All-of-Us' so as not to forget. But when he came close to the mouth of the lair, he forget the name that the hare had told him. So he stopped still and debated with himself 'Was it Hamizga*, or was it All-of-Us?' and finally plumped for 'Hamizga.' Then he entered the hyena's lair and said to the children of the hyena 'Peace be upon you' and they said 'Where do you come from?' and he replied 'Outside there I was born. I was told to come and stay with you.' And the hyena's children said 'Stay, sit down there' and the dog sat down between the hyena's children.

Then came the hyena with meat and put it in the lair. And they said 'Mother, shall we give Hamizga meat?' 'Who's Hamizga?' says the hyena. 'Let him come out so I can see him!' Then the dog came out and stood in front of the hyena, and the hyena seized him and pinned him down and said to her children 'Hold him, while I get fire and wood and grill him for you to eat!' But when the hyena had gone to get fire, the dog knocked down one of the hyena's children and ran off.

As he was running, he met the hare. Says he 'You there, hare, is that how you treat me, sending me to the hyena's place for her to eat me? Well, it's my turn now and I get my own back by eating you' and the dog set out in pursuit of the hare. As they were running, the hare met the hyena, and said to her 'Your meat is just behind me. Seize him when he comes!' When the hyena saw the dog, she seized him and took him along to her children. And they ate him up. Then everyone relaxed again.

The Elephant and the Giraffe† [I/20]

Once the hare suggested to the elephant that they should farm

* A name with, apparently, no special meaning.

† See J. No. 17. Cf. III/149 and S. p. 191, where camel (*rakumi*) is substituted for giraffe (*rakumin daji*).

together. Said he 'You go and clear the trees, while I burn off the area.' So the elephant went off and cleared the trees.

Then the hare went along to the giraffe and suggested that they should farm together. Said he 'You go and burn off the area, for I've cleared the trees.' So both the elephant and the giraffe were ignorant of the truth.

When enough rain had fallen for sowing, up comes the hare and says to the elephant 'You go and sow. I'll do the hoeing.' And again the hare went also to the giraffe and said 'I'll sow – you go off and hoe. And I'll do the reaping.' When the giraffe had hoed and the corn was ripe, then he went to the elephant and said to her 'Hey, elephant, you go and reap! I'll cut the heads off and collect them.'

Then he went and said to the giraffe 'I've done the reaping. You go and cut the heads off and collect them!' Next he went and said to the elephant 'Well, elephant, I've collected the heads. Tomorrow let's go and tie them in bundles!' and he added 'But there's something called a giraffe keeps coming and taking our corn away.' And the elephant answered 'What! Is a giraffe something to worry about? Off you go! Just let tomorrow come!'

And the hare went back to the giraffe and said to him 'Hey, giraffe, there's something called an elephant keeps coming and taking away our corn'. And the giraffe answered 'What! Is an elephant something to worry about? Just let tomorrow come!'

The giraffe made the earlier start, and went to the farm where the corn was collected. He stopped, waiting for the elephant. Then he asked the hare 'Where's the elephant you said would come to take away our corn?' And the hare answered 'Just wait a bit! You'll be seeing her.'

After a while the elephant appeared, and the hare said to the giraffe 'There you are – there! There's the elephant coming.' Says the giraffe 'Where? Somewhere by that hill?' and the hare answered 'Oh no! That's not a hill! That's the elephant.' And the giraffe said 'No, hare! I'm no match for that.' And the hare replied 'In that case, you lie down here, but keep your neck sticking out'. And the giraffe lay down, leaving his neck sticking out.

Up comes the elephant. Says she to the hare 'Hey, hare, where's the giraffe you said would be coming to take away all our corn?' And the hare answered 'Oh, he's been here since this morning and he was waiting for you, but you never came. His wee guitar (*molo*) is there on the ground. He's gone off for a bathe.' Then said the elephant 'Oh, hare! I'm no match for something big enough to handle that guitar.' And the hare said 'O.K. If you're no match for him, run away, elephant!' And she ran off eastwards.

Then said the hare 'Righto, giraffe – get up and run, before the elephant comes back and finds you!' And the giraffe went running off westwards. So the corn fell to the lot of the hare, for his sole enjoyment. Then the hare stowed the corn away in his burrow and settled peacefully down. That's all.

The Sheep* [$^{I}/_{156}$]

There was once a sheep that was left tied in the bush. She was pregnant and had a son, which grew and would go off grazing.

Time passed and the hare, as he was out walking, saw the sheep tied up. So he went and told the chief of the town, saying 'How many ears have you?'† 'Two' said the chief. 'Then get two more and listen to this tale!' 'Right.' 'When I was walking along I saw a sheep at such-and-such a place. Give me twenty men and we'll go and catch her and bring her here.' So the chief gave him the men.

They got to the sheep and freed her. But while they were doing this, she began to sing thus 'A host is carrying me away, Zanzabariya, a host from the town.' When her son heard that he set off at once. Now he had servants, the birds and the wind, and they used to follow him. When he came to where the people were, he too began to sing 'I've killed a thousand men – and think nothing of a hundred, I Zanzabariya.' And the birds squawked 'My eggs! My eggs!' and flying up, they beat against the men with their wings. And the wind too helped. And Zanzabariya himself was butting men with his horns, killing them. And they killed all of those men, except for two, and the hare, making three. And these returned home.

* Cf. TR. No. 66.   † Cf. I/6c

The hare said to the chief 'The men were too many for us. Give us some more horsemen and footmen, say forty.' And Zanzabariya killed them too, except for five who returned, and the hare, making six.

The hare said to the chief 'Give us some more men.' So seventy men were sent – and only ten returned, and the hare, making eleven.

Then the hare came back to the chief and said 'This matter is more than we can handle, you'll have to do it yourself.' So the chief prepared himself for war and had swords and long spears and guns brought forth, and they set out.

When they got there, the hare stopped a little way off and said 'There's the place.' Then when they reached Zanzabariya's mother she began to sing thus 'There's a host on the way, Zanzabariya, a host from the town, Zanzabariya.' When her son heard this, he set off with his servants, and the birds began squawking 'My eggs, my eggs' and fluttering with their wings against the men, and the wind too was helping. And Zanzabariya himself was singing 'I've killed a thousand men, and think nothing of a hundred, I Zanzabariya.' And they and the chief's men fought fiercely, killing each other, until at length Zanzabariya and his servants were all killed.

Then they took his mother home, and catching the ram of the [chief's] mother, mated him with Zanzabariya's mother. And they are still producing young ones to this day. *Kurungus kan kusu.* It wasn't because of Spider that I made it up – I was making it up in any case.*

The Lion and The Hyena† [III/48]

Here's another fable. The lion and the hyena quarrelled. The lion was on his way home, when he saw the hare. Up comes the latter, and the lion says to him 'How can I find someone who will bring me the hyena?' Says the hare 'I'll bring you* the hyena, lion, right to your home – but you must do one thing for me.' 'All right' said the lion, 'What's that, hare?' 'Meat' said the hare. 'You must go and get some meat for me. For you know how greedy the hyena is.' 'Right' said the lion.

And he went off and got some meat.‡ The hare took the meat and set it down, and got the lion to hide just near.

Next the hare took some skins and made holes in them, all except one. That one he spread over the lion, and then heaped the other ones with the holes, on top. And there, underneath them all, lay the lion. Then off went the hare to the home of the hyena.

Now the hyena had given her children orders that if anyone came they were to say she wasn't there. So when the hare reached her compound, he made formal greeting, and the hyena's children said 'Hyena's not here.' 'Well, well!' said the hare, 'we've slaughtered some cattle in our encampment, and I came to invite the hyena to come and share the meat.' 'Here I am, I'm at home' said the hyena, 'the damned rascals are lying.' Out she comes and 'Let's go' says she.

The hare led the way. 'Here' said the hyena, 'You don't travel fast enough. Get on my back.' So the hare got up on the hyena's back.

On they went, and presently the hare said 'Here! hyena, your hair's sticking into me.' 'Pick some leaves' the hyena answered, 'and spread them on my back.' He did so, and so they came to the place where the meat was.

The hare dismounted and said 'There you are, hyena – this is the meat you're invited to share.‡ 'Good' said the hyena.

She went on triumphantly to claim the meat by chanting all her epithets in full. Then she took the whole lot for herself and put it into a goatskin.

She was just going, when the hare said 'Oh, hyena – the youngest one said to take him home some shoes.' 'That's right' she answered, 'I forgot, you know.'

The hare went on 'Look, there are some skins there. Go and take a skin that'll make some shoes for the youngest.' She went and picked the top one. 'This skin's full of holes' said she. The same with the next one, and the same with the next one. At last she reached the

---

* *Ki* must be a slip for *ka*.

† Cf. III/61.   ‡ Deleting the comma.

skin that was not full of holes, and as she lifted that – the lion took a hold of her foot.

Now the lion had three sticks that he had taken from a thicket. Says the hyena to the lion 'I want to go and relieve myself.' 'Do it here' said he. Again she said 'I feel the need to excrete.' 'Do it here' said he.

Then the lion took a stick and thrust it up the hyena's anus, and stripped out all her intestines, liver and bowels – the lot – and pulled them all out. And taking some earth began pushing it in a little at a time, until he had stuffed her full of earth. Finally he took some fat and plugged up the hyena's anus with that. Then he let her go.

When she got home she said 'You damned rascals, good-for-nothing children – didn't I tell you, that whoever came here, you must tell them I wasn't at home? Now, see, you've been the cause of my going and catching a packet of trouble.'

The time came for the first prayer of the afternoon. 'Time to get up and say my prayers' said she. She got up and began her prayers, and the youngest child came close to her. Then, as she bent forward, the child saw the fat. 'Ha' said he to himself 'Mother's been with some others, eating meat until the fat started coming out of her anus.' And he pulled it out and ate it. And the earth ran out from inside the hyena, and ran and ran, and she fell down and died.

Then all the young ones said 'Well, just look! Mother's dead. Come on, let's go find a malam and question him!' And they went off to a malam.

'Malam' said they, 'if a man's mother dies, may she be eaten?' 'No' he said. So they left him, saying 'This malam is on her side, he's not a proper malam.'

And they went on till they came to another malam. They asked him 'Malam, if a man's mother dies, may she be eaten? Or not?' 'She may' he answered. 'There!!' they said, 'there's a proper malam, who has inherited his learning from several generations of malams, all learned; he is surely a learned man!'

Home they went, and skinned their mother, and ate her up, except for three bones and three strips of meat. They went back to the malam's compound, but found him asleep, his cap fallen off. So they put the bones in the cap, and going out went home again.

Some days later the malam saw them and said 'Hey there, children! After you came to me and asked me and got your answer

64

– did you eat her up?' 'Yes, we did' they answered. 'And your share was there in your cap where we put it, when we came and found you asleep.' The malam went and looked and found it. And they went their way. *Kungurus kan kusu.*

How the Beasts of the Bush had a Farm* [$^{III}/_{44}$]

The beasts of the bush had a meeting. It was the elephant who summoned them. She said 'Come along every single one of you, and we'll have a farm.' 'Very well' they said, and the elephant went on 'And you can stay there for a week, until you have cleared the farm.' 'Right' said they. And the hyena was among those clearing the farm.

They worked away and presently the week was up. Says the elephant 'Let me go along and see how much land you have cleared for the farm.' But when she got there she saw that the farm wasn't very big – if you started walking over it, before the sun was very high you were out of it.

This vexed her and she grew angry. And going in she set to, knocking trees down on all sides – until she had cleared enough trees for the farm to extend for a day's journey.

Came the day when the sowing rains fell, and they went along and made the holes for sowing. But the mouse† kept falling in and couldn't get out; and he kept saying 'You in front there, stop digging holes for the ones behind to fall into.'

But they went on with their work and finished sowing the whole farm. Then they returned home and settled back there. Came the time for hoeing and forth they went again and hoed, and hoed the whole of the farm. In due course the corn ripened, and they went along once more, and felled it and took off the heads. Next they made corn-bins, and covers for them, and put the covers on.

* Cf. next tale, also Uncle Remus, No. XVII, Mr. Rabbit Nibbles up the Butter. Also see J. p. 43.
† Or 'rat'.

Then said the elephant 'Now, come here and let me tell you all something. See here – let us go now and eat from the trees. As for our corn, we'll keep that till the hot season before the rains.' 'O.K.' said they, and all set off to journey in the bush.

Then said the hare 'Just let me go into the undergrowth* for a minute.' And he went into the undergrowth and lay low. All the other beasts went on.

Then the hare went back and got into the corn-bin and began to eat the corn. Next he went and collected some of the hyena's excrement and took it and threw it into the corn-bin.

This he continued to do, until the time came and all the beasts of the bush returned from their dry-season travels. Then they all gathered – except the hare. He was just by, hiding in the undergrowth.

And when they called him, saying 'Hey, hare!' he delayed his answer, and all the beasts said 'The hare *has* been a long way off. Just hear how he answers when we call him.' For when they called 'Hey, hare!' he took his time about answering.

Then he leapt up and came dashing in, spattering them with earth and dust, and they saw that his tongue was out and he was panting.

Says the elephant 'Who shall be made to get our corn out for us to eat?' Says the lion 'Well, how about the hare?' 'No' said the hare, 'there's the hyena. She's just the right build to go into a corn-bin. Her backside is low and her front is high.'

So the hyena put her paws on the corn-bin – and saw there was nothing in it, except only her own excrement. She exclaimed loudly and incoherently and retired to squat on one side.

At which the elephant became angry, and going to open the corn-bin, knocked a piece out of it. 'I swear to God it was not me' said the hyena. 'Hm' said the elephant, 'I'll catch the one who did this, whoever it was.' She went on 'Let's all go and fetch wood.'

So they went and fetched wood. 'Bring some fire here' said the elephant. Someone fetched fire and they took all the wood and put it on the fire. And the fire caught and burnt.

Then the elephant crossed over it, and said 'Whoever fails to cross over this fire – he's the guilty one.' And the beasts of the bush crossed it, one after the other – until only the hare was left. Then he set off very fast, jumping – and went round the side of the

* To be exact, 'bushes grown again, whose tops have been slashed back'.

66

fire. Then, as he got close to them, he kicked up earth and dust in their* faces, and by the time they could see him, he was already with them.

Then said the elephant 'Very well. Beasts of the bush, let each go his own way. For I won't feed with any other, save only my son or my brother. Let each go his own, separate way.'

And that is why among the beast of the bush, none feeds with any other kind, but only his own kin. So that, when you are in the bush, if you see the beasts, you will only see them with their own kind – not with any other. Nor will they allow any other kind to come amongst them – and this is still true today. *Kungurus kan kusu.*

A Variant [III/150]

All the beasts of the bush, both small and great, worked a farm and filled one large corn-bin. Then they went off on trading journeys, closing up the corn.

But the hare kept going and eating the corn, putting in hyena droppings. This continued for two years – until the hare had eaten up all the corn.

Two years they were away trading. Then, in the third, the elephant said 'Let's go and take a look at our corn.' And they came to the bin.

But the hare hid. They began calling him and he answered from where he was hidden. Again they called him and he answered and came along. Says the elephant 'Have all the beasts of the bush gathered?' and the camel answered that they had.

The hare was told to look in the corn-bin, but the hyena said that she would. She looked in and said 'By God, it wasn't me.' 'What's the matter?' they asked, and she answered that she swore by God that it wasn't her. So they told the hare to get up on the corn-bin and see what it was. He did so and saw the hyena's droppings. Says

* Reading *su* for *sa*.

67

he 'There's nothing but hyena's droppings in the bin.' '*Whose* droppings?' said the elephant. 'The hyena's' answered the hare. 'Gather round and kill her' said the elephant. So they gathered round and began beating her, but the elephant saw that she would be killed and, feeling pity, said 'Let her be.'

Then she ordered 'Let everyone go and make themselves a loin-cloth.' Then everyone else made one from hemp fibre, but the hyena made hers from earth. The hare made a beautiful one and went in front of the hyena, frisking about. Says the hyena 'Some people have all the luck', and again 'Won't you give it me?' 'There it is' said the hare. So the hyena gave him the earth one and took the fine one.

Then the word was given to make up the fire – which was done – and for everyone to cross it. If anyone got burnt – it was he who had eaten the corn. The elephant crossed, the giraffe crossed, the bush-cow crossed, the hare crossed – all of them.

But as the hyena crossed, her loin-cloth caught fire. 'Beat her' they said. The elephant stamped on her backside and it sagged down. Again the word was given to let her be. Next they said 'Let everyone lie down. Whoever's head the moon falls on to, he's the one.' Then the hare lay down close by the hyena, and the moon fell on his head. 'Won't you let me have it?' said the hyena. 'But I've only just got it from the sky.' But the hyena persisted 'For God's sake give it to me.' Then he handed it to her, and said to the others 'You can get up now, there's the moon with the hyena.' So they seized her and debated whether to kill her. Says the giraffe 'Let her be crushed'. So they stamped on her. And that is why her backside is so near the ground. That's all.

3

JACKAL
also called Malam Dan Ba'ura

The Lion [$^{I}/_{13}$]

The jackal went out for a walk when he met the dog. Says the dog 'Where are you off to?' Says the jackal 'For a walk.' Says the dog 'May I come too?' Says the jackal 'Of course, come along!'

They were going along together when they met the crow. Said the crow to the jackal 'Where are you two off to?' Said the jackal to the crow 'The dog and I are taking a little walk.' Says the crow 'May I come too?' Says the jackal 'Of course, come along!' and the crow joined the jackal and the dog as they went.

As they were going along they met the hunter, and he said 'May I come too, jackal?' and the jackal answered 'Of course, come along, hunter!'

And as they were going along together, they met the monkey. He saw the jackal. Said the jackal to the monkey 'Hey, monkey! Where are you off to?' and the monkey answered 'I'm taking a walk.' And the jackal said to him 'Come and join us!'

They were going along, when they met the wart-hog. Said he to the jackal 'Where are you off to?' and the jackal said 'I'm taking a stroll.' And the wart-hog said 'May I come along with you?' Says the jackal 'Of course, come along!' And there they were walking along, five of them, with the jackal, the sixth, in charge.

As they went along, they met the lion, who was playing draughts. Then the jackal said to the lion 'Peace be upon you', and the lion said to the jackal 'Where are you off to?' The jackal answered 'We're taking a stroll.' Says the lion 'Come and play draughts', but the jackal answered 'I couldn't play draughts with you, for you are our great lord.' Then said the lion to the jackal 'Right – if you don't play draughts with me, I'll seize your fellow-travellers and eat them up.' So the jackal sat down.

69

He and the lion played for a while, then the jackal said to the lion 'For my part, I'm weary, let me send the crow off to bring some meat for us to eat.' Says the lion 'O.K., O.K., send her by all means!' Says the jackal 'Hey, crow! Off with you quickly and bring us some meat from home.' But he added 'If you get there, don't come back!' The crow went flying off, nor did she return though a long time passed.

Says the jackal 'The crow's been a long while – monkey, be off with you, after her!' And off went the monkey after the crow, nor did he return, though a long time passed.

Then said the jackal 'The monkey's been a long while! Hey, dog – be off with you after the monkey.' And off went the dog after the monkey, and the dog also was a long time and still didn't return.

Then said the jackal 'The dog's been a long time! Hey, hunter, be off with you, after him!' And off went the hunter after the dog, nor did he return though a long time passed.

Then said the jackal 'Hey, wart-hog, you usually blow* a furrow through the earth. – Go on, get blowing* as fast as you can! Off you go!' and he added 'If you get there, don't come back!' The wart-hog put his nose down to the ground and off he went.

That left the jackal and the lion sitting there, the two of them, and the jackal said to the lion 'Do you see? Those I've sent off to fetch meat, they're refusing to come back.' And again he says 'I'd better be after them myself' and was into the trench dug by the wart-hog and off he went.

†The lion looked about and could see no one. He got up and tried to get into the trench but couldn't. So he set about digging it bigger. And there he was, crouching down to it, with his penis hanging out behind, when along comes the hyena. She picked up a long corn-stalk and poked him with it. He swung round, saw her and struck her on the backside. And *that* is why the hyena's backside is so near the ground.

----

* I think it probable that *huda* in Arabic script was misread as *hura*. In which case, not 'blow' but 'dig up' – which seems much more likely – should be read.

† Cf. III/133.

The Dog* [$^I/_{85}$]

The jackal was once going along when he met the domestic dog. Says the jackal 'Dog, what have you gained from living with human beings?' Says the dog 'I've acquired twelve tricks. Each one of them will help you to get out of a tight place.' 'You're a lucky dog' replied the jackal. 'Maybe' says the dog. 'Dog' says the jackal again 'Let's visit a malam and get him to tell our fortunes and what's happening in the world.' 'O.K., let's go' says the dog and off they went.

So they went along, till they came to some thick jungle, and entering it they squeezed their way through till they came to a clearer place and emerged into it, and there they saw the entrance-hut to a compound, with nothing in it but small packets of writing-paper. The malam was in his compound beyond. Says the jackal 'Let's sit and wait till he comes out.' So they sat down.

Then out came a puppy† and said 'Oh, has the malam got guests?' and sat down. Then another puppy appeared and he sat down too, saying 'Well! Has the malam got guests?' And another, and he sat down, and before long there were some twenty puppies all lying down there, packed tightly against each other and on top of each other and against the dog. Then the malam came out of his compound and saw his guests. 'You are very welcome' says he, and going back into the compound, he brought out skins and bade them sit on them. This they did.

Then the jackal said to the dog 'What trick do we use now?' and the dog answered 'There are two possible ones: howling and being frightened, for today I have seen a hyena‡ and she has seen me and I am shaking with fright.' Says the jackal to the malam 'Malam, we've come for you to tell our fortunes.' 'Very well' says he, and smoothing the ground he began drawing on it. And when he had finished drawing, he said to them 'Here's the news that I have seen.' 'What's that?' says the jackal. 'I see a way in, but no way out.' 'Have another look' says the jackal.

* Cf. D. No. 82.
† Johnston suggests these are hyena puppies (pp. 32–34).
‡ Meaning the malam?

71

Again the malam drew on the ground and again he said 'Here's the news that I see.' 'Ah' says the jackal 'What is it?' 'I see sudden death.' Then said the jackal to the dog 'Remember what I said to you? If you had – we should have got a proper answer now. 'What's that?' says the malam. 'Nothing' said the jackal, 'Just the goats that we've brought you, thirty of them, I said to bring them in, but the dog said not yet.' 'Where are they?' says the malam. 'Over there, grazing on the jujube tree.' 'Bring them now' says the malam and the jackal told the dog to go and get them. 'Right-o' says the dog.

And as soon as the dog was away out in the open, he slunk stealthily for a while and then ran off as hard as he could. After a while, the malam said 'The dog's a long time.' 'That's true' says the jackal. 'You go after him,' and the malam set off after him. The jackal waited a few minutes, then he too set off, taking a different road. He met up with the dog, and asked him 'How are your tricks?' Says the dog 'Me? I've no tricks – *you*'re the one with tricks' and the jackal answered 'Only the one!' And then the dog was ashamed. *Kurungus kan kusu.*

The Dog [1/ 86]

Here's another one.* The dog, it was, who went out for a walk and met the jackal. Says the jackal to the dog 'Where are you off to?' Says the dog 'I'm off to look for food.' 'Will you take me' said the jackal. 'Surely I'll take you' said the dog. The jackal asked the dog 'How many tricks have you got?' and he answered 'Two' and added 'How about you?' 'Oh, I haven't tricks' says the jackal. 'I see' says the dog. 'Come on, let's go!' and off they went.

As they went along, they came to a compound, which had a very small entrance. They went through this and found something covered up. The dog uncovered it, and they saw, on one side,

* The Hausa begins with the stock formula for beginning tales; often shortened to simply *ga ta nan*. Cf. III/199 and D. No. 94

daddawa, and on the other side, palm oil. Then they began to drink the palm oil. After they had drunk a little, the jackal would leave off and go to the entrance and measure it against his stomach, before going back to start drinking again. He did this several times. But the dog just drank, thinking that the jackal was only going to relieve himself. Finally the jackal measured his stomach and found that it fitted the entrance. Then he stopped drinking. But the dog drank and drank until his stomach was quite full, and only then did he go to the entrance meaning to pass through. But his stomach wouldn't let him get through it. The jackal had gone through and from outside saw that the dog couldn't get through.

Says the jackal 'Dog, where are your tricks?' and the dog answered 'Jackal, today I fear I have no tricks at all.' 'Well, isn't that too bad' says the jackal. 'Then today, dog, let me show you a trick.' 'Yes, please' says the dog and the jackal told him to lie down and sham dead. 'Even if they hit you, don't move!' 'Very well' said the dog.

Off went the jackal, and then the people heard the movement, and getting up, made the fire bright, thinking it was a rat eating the *daddawa.* Then they saw the dog lying there, and one woman, picking up a stick, hit him, saying 'The bastard has drunk up our oil.' Then, seeing that he didn't move, she added 'Hullo! He's dead.'

When it was light, the entrance was opened and he was carried out and thrown on to the dung-heap. Another woman pinched his ear, saying 'The so-and-so's drunk up all our oil and now he's dead' and, letting it go she went away. All the while the jackal was hiding nearby, till he saw that there was no one there, and the dog still hadn't got up. Then he went up to him and said 'Get up and run away!' whereupon he rose and went off. That's all. *Kungurus kan kusu.*

The Hyena and the Trap [$^{I}/_{92}$]

The jackal was out walking one day, when he came upon a piece of shade and lying there a hunk of meat and some cool water.

Said the jackal 'There's something wrong with this place', and going away he walked on till he met with the hyena. Then he said to the hyena 'Hyena, the head butcher owes me money and won't pay. I've asked and I've asked but still he won't pay. And when I speak to him, he won't even answer me.' Says the hyena 'Lead me to him!' and the jackal said '*You* ask him – perhaps he'll pay you' and off they went.

When they approached the place, the jackal drew back some way off and said 'There he is, go on up to him!' The hyena went on and said 'Head butcher.' No reply. 'Head butcher.' No reply. Then she said 'Do you want some meat?' and the jackal said 'Yes' and she sprang into the shade to grab the hunk of meat, when a trap closed on her. Up it lifted her and down to the ground it dashed her. Off went the jackal, laughing, leaving her there held fast in the trap. *Kungurus kan kusu*. I ate the rat, not the rat me.

The Dog, The Monkey, The Hyena and The Cat [I/119]

This is a fable about the dog and the monkey and the hyena and the cat. Here's the dog hopes to grab the monkey. Here's the hyena hopes to grab the dog. Here's the dog hopes to grab the cat. There they all were and the situation was a confused one. Each feared the other, and no one could hope to escape from the other.

So there they were when along came the jackal. 'Hullo!' says he 'What's up here?' Says the monkey 'It's the dog, he's going to grab me.' Says the dog 'But I'm afraid the hyena's going to grab me.' 'Stop a minute while I judge your case' and then to the monkey 'Giddup!' and to the dog 'Giddaway with you!' and to the cat 'Psst, be off with you!' Then the malam of the bush popped into a hole, and when the hyena turned round, they were gone!

The Hyena [$^I/_{129}$]

The hyena was appointed chief, and the jackal was the *imam*. There was a river between them, and the jackal would come over and lead the prayers for the hyena, before returning home. Now the mosque was on the bank of the river at the foot of a tree.

This went on for a while, but there came a day when the hyena's children and the jackal's children quarrelled, and the young jackals beat up the young hyenas. The hyena heard about it and sent her servants to go and beat up the jackal's children. The jackal was in ignorance of this, and when the time of prayer came he went to the mosque, and he and the hyena said the prayers together. When they had finished, the hyena accompanied the jackal down to the river and then went home.

As soon as she got home she called one of her followers and said 'Quick – follow the *imam* to his home, secretly, and hear what he says there'. When the jackal got home, his children said to him 'Just see – the hyena sent her children to come and beat us up today.' And he answered 'You haven't any sense. If you weren't crazy, you wouldn't go fighting a chief's children. I'm very glad she sent her servants to beat you up. You'll not do that again!' And the hyena's follower went back and told her what the *imam* had said. She was very pleased and said no more about it.

Now the jackal had a billy-goat, that he had fattened up, and he said to his children 'Catch the billy-goat, let's take it to the bush and slaughter it.' So they caught the billy-goat, and the jackal led the way and they followed. They passed the entrance to the hyena's compound, and found her there, all her retainers having gone elsewhere, alone. '*Imam*' said she, 'where are you going to?' 'We're going to slaughter a billy-goat and perform the fetish for our home with it' says he. 'Come on, let's go' said she. 'Oh no!' said he. Just for some meat am I to take the chief away into the bush?' 'No matter, let's go' said she. 'Very well' said the jackal, and led on, the hyena following, till they came to the place where the billy-goat was to be slaughtered. And they slaughtered it.

But previously the jackal had said to his children 'When the billy-goat is slaughtered, take the liver out secretly and hide it.

Even if I talk as if I am going to kill you, don't you produce it!'

So he said to them 'Give me the liver, I'll grill that first for the chief, while you are finishing the skinning', and they answered 'Oh, there's no liver,' 'Here!' said he, 'are you crazy? How can you have a billy goat without a liver?' But they insisted 'We've looked and couldn't find one.' Then the jackal said 'I see. Well, since you insist that you could not find one, if I find someone has taken that liver, I'll kill him.'

Then he took hold of his eldest son and threw him down and tied him up. He took a one-edged knife and put the blunt side to his neck. 'Well, since this knife won't cut you' said he, 'it's not you. Get up!' The young jackal got up, and he took hold of his next son, and did the same to him, and so on till he had reached the end of all his children.

When only the hyena was left, she said 'I think I should lie down too, for you to see if you can cut me, so that you don't think that I stole the liver.' 'No, no' protested the jackal, 'I couldn't play tricks with the chief.' 'No, come on' said she, 'I'll lie down and you try to kill me, so that you don't think that it's me.'

Then the jackal tied the hyena up very tightly, and turning the knife so that he was using the sharp edge, he cut her throat, saying 'You bloody rascal, I'm killing you for having my children beaten up.'

Ever since then the hyena has no truck with the jackal, and even today if he hears her coming, he runs away.

The Jackal and the Same-Day-Corpses* [II/54]

The lion and the hyena and the leopard and the snake went and built themselves one compound. Now the lion said he didn't like dust being raised. And the leopard said she didn't like being stared at. And the hyena said that she didn't like a lot of questions. And the snake said he didn't like having his tail trodden on. And there they all lived, when along comes Malam Dan Ba'ura – that's

* Cf. next tale and M. No. 33

76

the name for the jackal – and he says 'Greetings to you, Same-Day-Corpses.' And then he went a little way aside.

Then said the hyena 'Humpf! Just like the jackal to pass us by! Are you coming to see our compound?' 'No' says he, 'thank you. I can see very well from here what goes on inside your compound.' And passing by, he went on and left them.

And presently the hyena went out for a stroll, and when she returned, the leopard said 'Well! The hyena is speedy. There and back already? Or is it that the place you went wasn't far?' 'Leopard' she answered, 'I'm looking at you. Yes, and I'm even pointing a finger at you.'

They sprang at each other and began fighting, raising the dust in such quantities that you couldn't see the ground. At which the lion leapt at them and knocked both the hyena and leopard down. But as he was making his spring at them he trod on the snake's back – which broke, and the snake bit the lion. The lion killed the hyena and the leopard. The lion died, and the snake died to.

So when the jackal got back, he said 'Just so. I knew this is how it would end. For haven't you all died? For none of you cared to preserve any of the others; so now you're all dead.' That's all. *Kungurus kan kusu.*

The Hyena, the Leopard, the Lion and the Snake* [$^{I}/_{147}$]

Here's a tale of the jackal. Once he came upon the hyena, the leopard, the lion and the snake. Says he 'My greetings to you, you four corpses' and he went on. But the lion called out to him 'Who's a corpse?' 'You are, all of you' says he. 'Why so?' 'Because the hyena is too fond of looking at others. Because you, leopard, don't like people looking at you. Because you, lion, don't like dust. And because you, snake, don't like being trodden on.' And he passed by and went his way.

* Cf. last tale and M. No. 33.

77

Presently the hyena started looking at the leopard, and the leopard up and grabbed hold of her. This covered the lion with dust and he became angry. He made for them – and trod on the snake. Then the snake bit the lion, and the hyena died, the leopard died and the snake died.

The Loan* [I/ 159]

Here's a tale of the jackal, the malam of the bush and his children once when they lacked food. He went off to the town to get a loan, to buy something to eat. He went to the home of the rooster and made formal greetings. The rooster came out and they enquired after each other's health. Says the jackal 'I've come seeking a loan. I want you to lend me ten thousand cowries, so I can feed my children. If you come on the second of the month I'll pay you.' So the rooster brought the ten thousand and gave it to him.

On he went, and called on the cat. Says he 'I've come seeking a loan of ten thousand from you, so I can feed my children, till the second of the month.' And he agreed.

He passed on to the dog's and called on him. 'I've come for a loan' he said 'of ten thousand. I want you to let me have it, till the second of the month.' And he agreed.

He passed on to the hyena's and said to her 'I've come to ask you to let me have a loan of ten thousand till the second of the month.' And she agreed.

On he went to the leopard's and called on her. 'I've come to you for a loan' said he, 'of ten thousand till the second of the month.' And she too agreed.

He went on to the lion's and called on him, saying 'I've come to you for a loan of ten thousand, till the second of the month.' And he agreed.

Then he passed on to the hunter's and called on him. 'I've come to you for a loan of ten thousand till the second of the month' said he. And taking the money, he spent it.

* Cf. I/151 and I/94. See J. p. 30.

Time passed and the second of the month came. The jackal cleared the space in front of his home so that anyone coming out would be seen; then erected a booth and made a little hole in the compound fence at the back. Then along comes the rooster and after formal salutation they enquire after each other's health.

As they were sitting there, up comes the cat. 'Isn't there a back way out in this compound?' said the rooster. 'Well' says the jackal, 'there's a little hole the children have made, but you have to pay twenty thousand to use that.' 'Look' says the rooster, 'when I get home, you come along and I'll give you the other ten thousand.'

He was sitting there with the cat, when up comes the dog. 'Isn't there a back way out of this compound?' says the cat. 'There's a hole the children have made, but you have to pay twenty thousand to use that' said the jackal. 'Look' said she, 'when I get home, you come along and I'll give you the other ten thousand.' And she slipped away.

Then the hyena came along, in her turn. And when the dog espied her he said to the jackal 'Isn't there a back way out of this compound?' 'There is' said the jackal. 'But it costs twenty thousand to use it.' And the dog said 'When I get home you come along and I'll give you the other ten thousand.'

And while they were sitting there, up comes the leopard. Then the hyena said to the jackal 'Isn't there some little back way out of this compound?' 'There is' answered the Jackal. 'But it costs twenty thousand to use it.' 'When I get home' said the hyena, 'you come along and I'll give you the other ten thousand.'

Presently along came the lion, and the leopard said to the jackal 'Isn't there a little back way out of this compound?' 'There is' answered the jackal. 'But it costs twenty thousand to use it.' 'Look' said she, 'when I get home, you come along and I'll give you the other ten thousand.'

He was there with the lion when up comes the hunter 'Hullo!' said the lion 'Were *you* expecting the hunter to come this way?' 'No' said the jackal. 'I expect he saw you and followed you.' 'Hm' said the lion. 'Jackal, where can I hide?' 'Let me see' said the jackal. 'Here, get inside the booth and hide until he goes.' And the lion did so. Then the hunter said to the jackal 'Here I am. Now give me my money.' 'Just sit down for a minute' the jackal answered, 'while I count it out.'

But while they were sitting there, the jackal stealthily drew the hunter's attention to notice the lion. Whereupon he crouched ready and aimed his bow, and shooting the lion, killed him. And they ate their fill of the meat. That's all. *Kungurus.*

The Dog, the Beasts of the Bush and the Hyena [II/ 89]

The dog and the jackal set forth on their travels to learn the ways of the world. And the jackal left the track for a moment and found the beasts of the bush gathered – the lion, the elephant, the roan antelope, the bush-cow, the giraffe, the senegal hartebeeste, the western waterbuck, the hyena, the gazelle, the reed buck, the wild dog, the field rat, the hare, the duiker, the fennec, the monkey, the hyrax – all the beasts of the bush, and they were all there. And the jackal, and the dog too, joined them. Then *tuwo* was prepared, and someone said 'Well, who'll take his *tuwo* to the lion?'

Now, before, the dog and the jackal had got hold of some honey. The dog had eaten his, but the jackal had hidden his carefully away. Says he 'Well, now – the *tuwo* for the mighty one of the bush – dog! Pick up the mighty one's *tuwo* and take it to him.' So the dog picked up the *tuwo* to take to the lion, who was a little way off, apart, lying down. But to get to him the dog had to pass close where the hyena was lying. And just a little on the other side of his way lay the leopard!* And the dog would have to pass them to reach the lion as he lay. The dog came abreast of the hyena, and the hyena looked at him; at which the dog fell to the ground, howling, and the wooden bowl of *tuwo* was broken. 'Hey!' said the elephant, 'who ever caused the dog to fall down when he was carrying the

---

*The Hausa equivalent of 'betwixt the Devil and the deep' is variations on the situation depicted here.

chief's *tuwo*?' 'Well, now! Who can it—' began the jackal, and then 'Where's the hyena?' 'Over there near where the dog fell' someone answered. 'I see' said the jackal, 'she glared at the dog: he was frightened of her and fell; and the chief's bowl was broken.' 'Well, Malam Son-of-Ba'ura' said the elephant, 'What can be done to sew up the chief's bowl now it's broken?' 'Well, now' said the jackal, 'What we must have to sew up this wooden bowl, so that you'll be able to fill it with *tuwo*, and then pour on soup, and none of it will leak out – we must get the sinews of a hyena, and when they are brought to me, I'll put them into medicine and give them to the mighty one of the bush to chew and return to me. Then I'll sew up the bowl.' So the hyena was seized and told to produce some sinew with which to sew up the chief's bowl, for, they said, it was she who had glared at the dog, whose fall had broken the chief's bowl; so let her produce some sinew. So she pulled some out and gave it to them and they passed it to the jackal; and he, taking it, dipped it in the honey. Then they passed it to the lion, saying 'Mighty one of the bush, please to chew this and return it, so that your wooden bowl may be sewn up.' But when he had put it into his mouth, he swallowed it, and said to the jackal 'Malam of the bush, as I was turning it over in my mouth, it just slipped down my gullet', and then to the hyena 'Hey, give us another.' So she produced another and passed it over, and it was handed to the jackal, who put it in the honey and then, taking it out, gave it to the lion, saying 'Now, mighty one, turn it over carefully, so that it doesn't slip down like the last one.' 'Very well' said the lion and took it. But as he was turning it over, that one too slipped past his gullet, and he said 'Jackal, that bit of sinew slipped past too' and then, to the hyena 'Hey, give us another.' And the hyena ran off, yelling.

And then all the other beasts gathered there also ran off, the large ones trampling on the smaller. The dog too made tracks for home as fast as he could, saying that he wouldn't even make a journey as far as the compound entrance from now on, unless he was with a man. As for the hyena, she swore that henceforward she would eat every dog she could – and jackal too. And that is why if the jackal howls in one part, he'll run off in the opposite direction; and then again run off somewhere else – all for fear lest the hyena come and find him.

And people say that when the hyena howls, she is saying 'Domestic dog and I are relatives'.* And the dog answers 'Now when? Now when?' *Kungurus kan kusu.*

———

The Two Chiefs [$^{III}/_{42}$]

The beasts of the bush gathered and appointed the lion as their chief. But the jackals went and had their own gathering, just themselves altogether, with no other beasts there, just them.

Now, among the jackals there had been born a pair of twins, Lu and La. And they began to discuss which of these two twins should be appointed as their chief.

Finally they chose Lu and made him chief, and he became the chief of all the jackals.

Presently Lu, as their chief, ordered them to go into the bush and catch grasshoppers and bring them home. And off they went and did as they were told.

'Good' said Lu, 'each of you give me a grasshopper', and they did so. Then he gave them permission to take the rest and eat them themselves.

So the day came when they expelled Lu, saying that he was always taking one grasshopper from each of them. And they put La in his place, making him chief.

But when La became chief, he said to them 'Now, jackals, let everyone catch a grasshopper and bring it to me.'

And then, when they went and caught grasshoppers and brought them, he would take the lot, and then say 'And now be off and search again for grasshoppers for yourselves to eat.'

So they got together and made a plan to go and get Lu back. For La caused them hardship, not allowing them food for themselves.

And even now you will hear jackals, after the sun has gone down,

* Doubtless the sound of the word *zumu* (relative) played as large a part in its selection, as its meaning.

howling, and what they are doing is trying to get their old chief to come back, so that they may reinstate him, for La has been a burdensome chief to them. That's all. *Kungurus kan kusu.*

The Malam* [$^{III}/_{58}$]

The jackal went to see a malam and asked him to request God to give him more cunning. Says the malam 'Jackal, that's easy. Go and get one of the large calabashes used for milk by the Fulani.' 'Consider it done, malam' said the jackal.

Away went the jackal, and along the road, and there he lay down† and waited, baring (?) his teeth. Along comes a Fulani woman and says 'Hullo! Here's a beast that has died.' And on she went.

Up gets the jackal and taking a roundabout way, gets in front and lies down again. Up comes the woman and says 'Well! What a lot of beasts are dying like this! Let me put my calabash down and go and fetch that other one, and then take them both to those who will eat them, to eat.' And she went back to fetch the jackal.

Up gets the jackal and drinks his fill of the sour milk. Then he poured away the rest and picking up the calabash, took it to the malam. 'Fine' said the latter. 'Now, jackal, go and get me some bush-cow's milk and bring that.'‡ 'O.K.' said the jackal.

Away goes the jackal again, and as he goes along he keeps saying 'Of course it'll penetrate! Of course it won't penetrate.' And he went on saying this as he went along until he saw the bush-cow.§

'Bush-cow' said he, 'what you heard us arguing about was that baobab tree over there – whether or not your horns would penetrate it.' 'Well' said she, 'let's go and see.' So he took her to the tree, and pointed it out to her – a whopping great baobab too.

Back goes the bush-cow and starts off running at it. Then butts the baobab with all her force. And her horns went right into the tree, all the way to her hair. So the jackal milked the bush-cow,

* See J. p. 28 † Cf. III/3. ‡ Cf. I/34. § Cf. II/12.

and went off, leaving her there, and took the milk to the malam.

'Good' said the malam. 'That leaves one more task for you, jackal.' 'What's that?' asked the jackal. 'A black-hooded cobra' – and the jackal answered 'Consider it done.'

Away went the jackal and sewed up a goatskin bag, and then went to the cobra's hole. As he went along he kept saying 'Of course he'll fill it' and again 'He won't fill it', over and over, till he reached the cobra's hole.

Then he said to the cobra 'The argument you heard us having was whether or not you would fill this bag.' 'Well' said the cobra, 'let me see', and he went and got himself into the bag. Then the jackal tied up the mouth, lifted it up and took it off to the malam.

Says the malam 'Well, jackal – today's your day for learning cunning', and again 'Jackal, get into this big calabash.'* 'O.K.' said the jackal, and picked up the calabash and put it on a stump. The malam picked up a stone. The jackal hid, and then saw the malam pick up a huge stone and throw it at the calabash.

'Tut tut, malam' says the jackal, 'is that your cunning – to kill me?' 'All right, jackal' said the malam, 'but if you were to get any more cunning than you already have, you'd be a real nuisance to the rest of the world. Be satisfied with what you've got – it's sufficient.' That's all. *Kungurus kan kusu.*

———————

The Camel, the She-Goat† [III/132]

The camel married a goat. After a time she became pregnant and bore two children. And she would go to market and bring home her purchases.

One day when she was at the market, the jackal came and found the camel at home. Says he to the camel 'You fool! For who would live with meat, fat meat and not eat it up, except a fool!'

This happened regularly, until one day the camel said 'Very well,

* Cf. III/136.

† Cf. II/13. I am unable to say why the jackal is called *Ballo* on several occasions in the Hausa version of this story.

today when she comes back from the market, I'll knock her down, kill her and we'll eat her up.' 'O.K.' said the jackal. 'Just let me get in under the bed.' 'Fine' said the camel, and the jackal got in under the bed. The camel went into the middle of the hut and knelt down, saying 'Now, if I frown (?), you're not to speak, jackal.' For the camel was angry.

It chanced that the goat's children heard what the jackal was saying, and the camel's answers. So they went out on to the road and played until their mother turned up. Then they said 'Hey, mother! Listen to what the jackal is always saying, and today Dad has got angry, and when you get home they're going to eat you up.' 'So' said the goat, 'that bastard has found where our home is, has he? Very well, go on playing here, until I get back.'

Then the goat went back to the market and bought some *alewa* made from honey. Then she came back and reaching her children, said to them 'Let's go home.' They said 'Mother, we're afraid that they'll eat you up.' 'No fear, come along' she said, and they went off home.

She went into the hut. The camel was kneeling there with his lips all loose. She said something but he ignored her. She spoke again and again he ignored her. She gave him the things she had bought in the market and he refused them. Then she took the *alewa* made from honey and put it to his lips. And when he tasted the sweetness, he said 'My, oh my! Where did you get that?' And she answered 'Well, you haven't much sense; I'm always telling you you should come to the market, and you refuse. And now look – today every man who came to the market got some of this. At market today a lot of jackals had been caught; and every man who caught one would tear him open and enjoy the sweetness. And you were just lying uselessly at home here!' 'But you – but we' said the camel, 'We've got a jackal under the bed here.' 'He's where?' said the goat. 'Right here' said the camel. 'Block up the entrance.'

Then the camel leapt at the jackal, and the jackal started up. 'You're a liar' said the camel, 'And this sweet stuff that you've got in your belly, today we're going to enjoy it; right now we're going to.' Away went the jackal, but the camel cut him off. So he got back under the bed. 'Goat' said the camel, 'since you're small, get under the bed and butt him,' and the goat got under the bed and butted the jackal with her horns.

Away went the jackal, making for the entrance, but the camel cut him off again and grabbed him, the jackal saying the while 'By God, I don't have any sweet stuff.' But the goat kept saying 'Lying is what he is, he's got the sweet stuff.' 'But it's not my sweet stuff' protested the jackal. 'Just let me take you where there is some.' But the goat said to the camel 'Don't you. He's got it all right; for today they caught a lot of his brothers, and ate up all that they had.'

Then the camel tore him open and said to the goat 'Where's the sweet stuff?' And she took the rest of the *alewa* and put it in the jackal's ribs. 'There it is' she said, 'lick it – you'll taste it.' So he licked it. 'Mm' he said, 'it *is* sweet' and he went on tearing it apart. Wherever he tore, there she put *alewa*, saying 'Lick – you'll taste it,' and he would lick and say 'Mm! Goat, you're right – they must have had a sweet feed in the market today.' 'Yes' she said, 'They caught a lot of them.'

So the jackal was killed, and the goat went on living quietly with her husband, the camel. And still, today, the jackal doesn't love the goat. And this is how they came to be enemies.

———

The Lord God* [III/ 136]

The jackal told the Lord God that he wished for more cunning. But the Lord said 'No jackal. What you have is enough for your needs.' But the jackal persisted that he should be given more. 'Very well' said the Lord, 'Get a large calabash, jackal, and fill it with water and get inside it.' 'O.K.' said the other.

And the jackal got a large calabash and went and filled it with water, got into it and lay down. Then there came thunder, but before the sky fell, the jackal made a hole, and (getting out) crouched just by the calabash. Then the sky fell and that was the end of the calabash.

But the jackal said 'Well! Just as well I was hiding here to one

* Cf. III/58 (end part).

86

side of the calabash', and he went off at a run, off into the bush, and settled down again. That's all. *Kungurus kan kusu.* I ate the rat, not the rat me.

The Hyena [$^{III}/_{151}$]

Says the jackal to the hyena 'Let's go and catch fish by putting a dam across the stream.' They did so, and caught fish, two large calabashes full. Says the jackal to the hyena 'Here are two calabashes full. You eat them. I'll get four tomorrow.'

And on the next day, when he saw four calabashes full there, he said to the hyena again 'Here you are, you eat four, but tomorrow I'll have six.' And the hyena wouldn't, saying he could eat the four, and she would wait for the six. So the jackal ate up the four calabashes.

Next day when he saw six there, he said 'Here are six, you eat them; but tomorrow I'll eat seven.' And again the hyena refused, saying he could have the six and that she would wait for the seven. So he ate up the six calabashes.

Again, when he saw seven, he offered them to her, saying that he would get eight next day. Again she refused, saying he could have the seven and she would wait to eat the eight.

Next day there were the eight, and he told her to help herself, adding that he would have nine to eat next day. But the hyena said 'No, you eat the eight, I'll get nine tomorrow.' And he ate up the eight calabashes full.

On the morrow they caught the nine, and he offered them to her in the same way. She refused, and so he ate them up.

Again, on the next day they caught ten, and he told her to eat them, while he would wait and get eleven calabashes full next day. 'No, you have them' she said, 'I'll wait for the eleven tomorrow.'

The next day the same, and the next day – when they caught twelve large calabashes full – the same. He said he would wait for the thirteen they would catch on the morrow.

But at this point the hyena [got sick of it] and collected the fish-dam [and moved off]. People [laughed at her] saying 'Look at the hyena with the fish-dam!' and she said 'Never again!' and went on saying it till she got to where the chief butcher was [where she could get meat]. And so, seeing there was no profit in fish-dams, she set light to it and burnt it. That's the end of that one.

4

LION

The Duck and the Donkey and the Horse and the Camel and the Man* [$^{I}/_{18}$]

One day the duck was walking through the bush and she came upon the lion-cub in a kraal, jumping up and down. When he saw that the duck was running, he asked her 'Hi, duck, what are you running away from?' and she answered 'I'm running away from man.' Says the lion-cub 'What sort of thing is that?' and the duck said 'The man has two legs and more intelligence than any other of God's creation' and she added 'In the short time you and I have been together here, a man would have managed to bring about your death'. But the lion-cub said 'What, duck! Do you think there is anything greater than I? Here, sit down beside me and don't move away. Whatever comes along this way, you'll see, I'll have the answer to it.' And she agreed.

As they sat there, up comes the donkey, and the lion-cub says 'Hi, donkey, what are you running away from?' And he answered 'I'm running away from man. Look at me! Among men I was born, among men I grew up, but I've never prospered. If a journey is to be made, they drive me in, lift up a thing called a pack-pad and put it on my back. Then they lift another thing, a different pad, and put that on top. After that they pile on a load that is too much for me, so that I can barely walk. Then, when they see that I don't walk fast, they lay into me with a stick. And that's my lot till the day I die!' Then said the lion-cub to him 'Right, sit down here! Nothing will harm you while you're with me'. But the donkey answered 'No sir! Don't you believe it, I'm going on!' and he passed by and went on, leaving the lion and the duck sitting there.

They were still there when the horse came running up. And he

* Cf. next tale See J. p. 4.

didn't stop running till he came to where the lion-cub was. Says the lion-cub 'Hi, horse, what are you running away from?' and he answered 'I'm running away from man' and he added 'And I think that a man is coming along right close behind me – because I ran away!' And again the horse said to the lion-cub 'Yes, here am I, a horse. If a journey's to be made, they put a thing called a halter on me, on my head, and then they bring another thing called a bit and put it in my mouth. Then they bring a thing called a saddle-cloth and put it on my back, and then they bring a thing called a saddle and put it on and tie me round the belly, tight so that I can scarcely breathe. Then they mount me and make me go – I know not where. If I won't go, then they prick me with a piece of metal, called a spur, so that I give a start and off I go willy-nilly. When we get back, they tether my foot to a post and tie my front leg to my hind leg, so that I can't go off anywhere. It's all this ill-treatment that has made me run away. What's more, I'm not staying either, I'm off!' And off went the horse.

They sat on for a while when up came the camel. He was in a hurry as he came up to the lion-cub. Says the lion-cub 'Hi camel! What are you running away from?' and the camel replied 'Lion-cub I'm running away from man. And the reason I'm running away from him – everyone runs away from him – is that – for all my greatness, I'm just a beast of burden to him. Among men I grew up, but even water to drink I only get once in seven days. As for the loads that I have to carry, only the earth is able to bear them, so heavy are they. And when I'm loaded up, they put a thing called a head-rope on me and lead me – so that I don't run away, they say. Well, when I got the chance I ran away – and now, are you saying that I should stop? Oh no, I'm not stopping. Maybe a man is right behind me, following me.' And passing by, off went the camel, leaving the lion-cub and the duck.

And they sat on for quite some time, when up comes a man. He gets into the kraal and comes up to the lion-cub. And the lion-cub says 'Hey ,what's this?' and he answered 'It's me.' Then said the lion-cub 'Hi there, are you a man?' and he said 'No' and again 'Lion-cub, look – you're the son of the greatest of us all, how come that you're in this wretched house?' Says the lion cub 'Where shall I get another?' and he answered 'Let me devise something that you'll be able to go into.' 'Good' says the lion-cub.

So the man cut four broad pieces of wood and put them together like a box, and made a little door. Then said he 'There you are, lion-cub, there's a fine abode!' And in went the lion-cub.

When he was inside, the man brought a piece of wood that fitted the doorway and closed it tight, and said 'Something unpleasant has happened to you today, lion-cub. I am man! Hitherto you've been saying there was no one greater than you.' Then he kindled a fire and lifting the box with the lion in it, put it on the fire, and the fire consumed the lion and he died.

But when the duck saw this, she up and went off, and alighted on an island in the middle of a big river and there she stopped, for, said she, here there are no men.

And there she dwelt, until one day a great canoe came by the island, full of people. And they cried 'Look, there's a duck – don't let her get away!' And off went the duck. As she took off, some threw their sticks at her, some shot at her, some threw stones, and they were too much for her and caught her. Then said she 'However swift or cunning you may be, you'll not escape man! And knowing that, I have the laugh of the lion-cub.'

The Duck and the Man* [^{I}/$_{95}$]

The duck and the lion were arguing. The duck said 'God is to be feared, and man is to be feared.' 'No' retorted the lion 'why do you say that, duck? God is to be feared, and *I* am to be feared.' 'Is that so?' said the duck. 'Yes, it is' said the lion. 'Do you really not know the nature of man? He kills you before you even know it.' And the duck went on 'Man looks for a long spit, which he calls a "shaft" and a pointed piece of metal which he calls an "arrowhead"; and then he gets something he calls "poison" which he smears on the arrow; then he looks for a piece of wood which he bends – he calls this "bow" – and then some cord which he calls "bowstring" and he ties that on to the bow, and he is ready and he sets out with these.

* Cf. last tale.

If he spies you in the distance, he hides. Then he takes the arrow and fits it against the bow, and shoots it at you. If it gets you in a vital spot, you won't see the next day, you'll be dead!' 'Ridiculous' said the lion. 'You're a stupid creature, duck! How could man devise such a contraption so as to kill me – and without my even seeing him!' 'All right' says the duck, 'One day, when we're together you and I, you'll see!'

Time passed for them and there came a day when the lion and the duck were feeding in a wooded spot. And it chanced that a man was hiding in ambush there, and they didn't see him. Till he drew an arrow from his quiver, fitted it to his bow and shot the lion's wife, and she fell, kicking. Then said the lion to the duck 'Did you see that spit that came from somewhere and pierced my wife so that she fell and lies there kicking?' The duck looked and saw an arrow sticking in the lioness's body, while the poison had almost finished her off. 'Yes' said the duck. 'This is what I told you of one day. You see! This is man's work' and before her words were ended, the lion's wife was dead. Then said the duck to the lion 'And you too, if you don't run away from here at once, you too will get shot, and die.'

And off went the duck, leaving the lion standing there, amazed at what had befallen his wife. Next moment there was another arrow in front of him, which had been shot but missed him. He jumped and leapt to one side. Then he went off at a gallop, and didn't stop till he got home. When he got home, he said 'God is to be feared and man is to be feared,' and from that day on he never again said 'God is to be feared and *I* am to be feared.'

The Donkey and the Hyena [$^{II}/6$]

This is the tale of how the donkey set off with his sister* and wife to spend the dry season travelling away from home. Off they went, and as they journeyed, they came suddenly upon the lion's home.

* Strictly 'elder sister' but could be 'daughter'. Edgar's orthography does not distinguish *'ya* from *ya*.

'Well, this is a nice surprise!' said the lion. 'A hearty welcome, stranger!' The donkey answered 'Oh mightiest of the beasts, truly I had heard of your name and came that I might see you with my eyes.' 'Well, isn't that fine?' said the lion. 'What's your name?' 'My name is Masu' said the donkey. 'I see' said the lion.

Up got the lion and quickly set about cutting grass, with the donkey, and they made a grass booth for the donkey to stay in. And he and his sister and his wife moved in. Now the lion had a wife and children, and the donkey said to his wife 'Here! Whatever you do, don't let the lion's wife touch your head.' 'O.K.' said she 'I understand'.

Then the lion came and said to the donkey 'Donkey,* keep an eye on the house, I'm going to kill some meat for us and bring it home.' 'Sure' said the donkey.

The lion went off, made his kill and brought it home. 'Where's Masu?' said he. 'May the chief's life be prolonged'† says the donkey, coming forward. 'Come and divide up this meat into equal parts. You take a portion and I'll take a portion.' This happened regularly, until the donkey waxed fat.

And whenever the donkey began to bray, he would say 'Sharp point for piercing, sharp edge for cutting.'‡ When up comes the hyena and says to the lion 'Lion, where did you get hold of hyena's *tubani*?'§ 'What do you mean, hyena?' said the lion. 'Which is the hyena's *tubani*? Oh, him? He's called "Masu" ' 'Mighty one of the bush' she answered, 'he's lying. That's the donkey. Just leave him to me, and you'll see, I'll gobble him up right away.' 'Oh no, hyena' said the lion, 'you're the one that's lying.' 'Very well' said she, 'oh mighty one of the bush – I apologise. But may I tell you something?' 'Go ahead and tell' said the lion. 'Then you have him go and kill some meat and bring it here, so that you can see if he brings you anything.' 'Right' said the lion. 'Where's Masu?' 'Here I am, may the chief's life be prolonged' answered the donkey. 'Here' said the lion, 'off you go and kill some meat and bring it back to us.' 'Certainly' said the donkey.

* A slip by the story-teller? The lion wasn't meant to know.

† This honorific, obligatory in modern Hausa speech to one of high status, is noticeably rare in TATS.

‡ ? I.e. this life suits me exactly.

§ A food made from bean-flour.

So off went the donkey and entered the bush. There he came to a river at a point where the beasts of the bush used to drink, and went into a thicket and waited. Presently along came the beasts of the bush and began to drink. Then they moved on and some lay down, while others remained standing and began to play. Then the donkey brayed. And the beasts of the bush stampeded, and those like the elephants, the bush-cows, the roan-antelopes and the giraffes trod on the gazelles, the duikers, the hares, the western cobs and the western waterbucks. And there were beasts of the bush lying all over the place in large numbers, dead. And the donkey picked up a little duiker and slung it on his back, and so home.

When the hyena spied the donkey coming, she said 'Mighty one of the bush, look at this rascal of yours. He's killed nothing. Look at the wretched little thing he's brought!' 'Greetings, Masu' said the lion. 'And to you, mighty one of the bush' the donkey replied, and went on 'We must go and bring home the meat.' 'Right' said the lion, 'Come on out, hyena. Let's go!'

So off they went and travelled until they came to where they found the beasts of the bush lying about in large numbers. And they set about shifting them and bringing them home. And then the hyena ate meat and ate meat until she was full.

But the donkey, from the moment he had set eyes on the hyena had been troubled, and he was afraid. So he told the lion he wanted to visit his home, but would return afterwards.

Then the donkey took the meat his wife had fried and strapped it on to her, and on to his sister, and then took some himself. Then he made them start off in front, and the lion came with him a long way, to see him on his journey. Then said the lion 'Well, Masu, give my regards to those at home and to all your people.' 'Thanks, I will' said the donkey, and they parted, but the lion went and hid himself.

Meanwhile the hyena had made her way by a roundabout route and came and intercepted the donkey. Whereupon the donkey stopped his wife and sister, and, braying, rushed at the hyena, and 'crack' went his hooves as he kicked her head. Down she went. Now the lion, as soon as he heard the donkey's bray, came galloping up. And just as the hyena was trying to get up, coming up he threw her down again.

Then said the lion to Masu 'Well, now you can come back. Let's go home.' Said the donkey 'I was afraid of her even before, for she had been driven out of our home. And then she came and found me at your place and came and spoilt our pleasant existence there.' 'It's all right, Masu – I've killed her' said the lion. 'That's so' said the donkey. 'Then let's go back and carry on as we were.' And they went and did just that.

And men say – or so I've heard – that that is the reason that the lion won't kill the donkey. *Kungurus kan kusu.*

The Hyena and Her Slave [$^{II}/_{52}$]

There was once a hyena who had a slave, and every day she made him go and steal a goat and bring it to her. Then she would enter her hut and eat it, but would give the slave none. The slave's name was Arzikin-baba.*

Daily this continued, and he went and stole a goat and brought it and gave it to her; and she would go into her hut, close the entrance and eat the goat's flesh. Then getting on to her bed she would begin to sing 'I've played a trick on you, Arzikin-baba.'

And so it went on – he would fetch the goat and bring it, and she would eat it and then get on to her bed and start singing. But at last Arzikin-baba set off and went to see the lion. And when he got there, he said to the lion 'May your days be prolonged!' and then spoke thus 'Lion, the hyena is in the habit of insulting you. For I am always buying meat for her, but when I tell her to leave some for you, she says that she won't.' Says the lion 'Let's go – lead me to her!' and 'O.K.' says the other.

So he brought the lion along and right into the hyena's hut, and stationed him under the bed. Then Arzikin-baba went out again and off to steal a goat. When he brought it back for the hyena, there she was back at home again. He gave her the goat and went out. She closed the entrance of the hut and fell to eating the goat. When she had finished it up completely, she got on to the bed and lay

* Meaning 'Dad's good fortune'.

down, and then began her 'I've played a trick on you, Arzikin-baba' which she repeated again and again.

Then Arzikin-baba called out to her 'Oh yes! But have a look at your bed and you'll learn that there are tricks to beat tricks.' Again she chanted 'I've played a trick on you Arzikin-baba.' Again he answered 'Oh yes! But just take a look at your bed and you'll learn that there are tricks to beat tricks.'

At this point the lion stuck his claws through and pinched the hyena. Says she 'Hullo, this bed's beginning to get bugs!' and again 'I think I'll take off this top mat; that's the buggy one.' So she took it off and putting it to one side, got back on to the bed. Then the lion scratched her. 'Ow!' says she, 'this hut must have rats; they're even scratching me.'

So she lifted up the bed – and there she saw the lion. She made for the door, but found no way out; and her bowels were loosed for fear of the lion. But the lion was angry and reaching her, struck her down and killed her. That's all. *Kungurus kan kusu.*

96

5

CAT

The Chicken [$^{I}/_{46}$]

Here's a shocking tale! 'Who's there?' 'Only me' says the cat, 'a-playing with my little sister.' 'For shame' says the chicken, 'what sort of playing is that, with my whole head in your mouth?' So the chicken was saved and recovered.

Malam Cat and the Chicken* [$^{I}/_{75}$]

It is said that a cat was once ill, and when he recovered, he tried to get some meat,† but failed. So he turned into a malam and set off travelling, giving out cures for barrenness.

After some while, he came to a large compound, full of chickens. Among these was one chicken which, since coming to the compound, had never laid. When the malam reached the house, he was given a place to sleep just where this chicken roosted.

Later, in the dead of night, the chicken said 'Alas and alack! Could I but get someone to give me a cure for my barrenness, whatever he asked for – just so long as I could have a chick – I'd pay him.' Now the malam was lying there as if asleep. When he got up, he said to the chicken 'You there, that wants the cure!' 'Yes' says she. 'I have a cure for barrenness, but it's a difficult one.' Says she 'What's difficult about it?' And the malam said 'You must pluck the whole of your body and wash yourself, and then I'll give you some ointment to rub on.' 'Very well' says the chicken.

When it was light, she had herself completely plucked and washed

* In TR. No. 21, no reference is made to the cat's turning into a malam.
† Cf. I/5, I/6, etc. passim.

herself. Meanwhile the malam collected all sorts of pepper and spices,* and mixing them together, ground them up. Then he wrapped up the powder and put it aside.

Then the chicken came along and said to the malam 'Here I am.' Says he 'Good! Have you washed?' 'Yes' says she. 'Right – then into the hut with you!' And obediently she went into the hut, and he opened the bundle of spices and said to the chicken 'Here you are! Take this medicine and rub it all over your body, till you've finished it all up.' 'Very well' says she, and taking out all the medicine she rubbed it over the whole of her body. Meanwhile he lit a fire and built it up with logs. When it was really hot, he said 'Now, go round this fire twelve times, saying "I chicken, I've had medicine, I'm going to have a chick." Go on saying that till you've been round twelve times.' 'Right' says she.

And so the chicken started going round the fire, saying 'Today, I chicken I've had medicine, I'm going to have a chick.' But as she went round saying this, before the twelve times were completed, the heat of the fire added to giddiness overcame her and, falling into the fire, she died. Then the malam turned into a cat, and taking the chicken went into a corner, ate her up and went on his way. *Kungurus kan kusu.*

The Rooster† [I/132]

The rooster was going along when he met the cat. Says the cat 'Rooster, whither away?' Says the rooster 'I'm going to pay a call of condolence on some relatives who have had a loss.' 'Just fancy, now there'll be two' said the cat. 'Maybe two, and may be three' said the rooster, 'for I've got the dog here, he's accompanying me.' Then said the cat 'Rooster, you're a humorist, you make a fellow laugh, till he rolls off the road and into the spear-grass.'

---

* They are itemised in the Hausa.
† Cf. TR. No. 20. See J. p. 440; O. p. 260.

The Mouse* [$^I/_{78}$]

It is said that a cat once felt a craving for meat. So she went into her hut and lay down flat on her back, her mouth open, with the flies going in and out, as if she were dead.

Just then a mouse popped out of his hole to forage, but when he saw the cat lying there, he went back into it again quickly. He told his mates about it. Says he 'What will you give for good news?' and they answered 'Cola-nuts.'† And he said 'Give me cola-nuts and I'll give you a fine piece of news.' 'Tell us, we'll give them to you.' Then he said 'Today the cat's dead. The world is a pleasant place, there's nothing to worry us.' Then said the chief mouse 'We ought to send out cola-nuts to all our friends and relatives and tell them to come so that we may celebrate the fact that the cat is dead.' Then their chief sent round cola-nuts far and wide and all the mice gathered for a celebration.

They had their gathering close to where the cat was and began dancing. Each one as he began to dance chanted 'Today's a happy day, a joyful day, for the cat is dead.' Then he danced and whipped her with his tail, and resumed his place. Another came out and danced, chanting 'Today's a happy day, a joyful day, for the cat is dead and we are free' and he whipped her with his tail.

So they danced until it was their chief's turn and he came forward to do his dance, saying 'I, chief mouse, let me dance, let me pirouette for joy, for the cat is dead.' And he did his dance and was going to whip her with his tail, when she pounced and pinned him down. Then she seized him and picked him up and took him into her den.

Then the rest of them scattered, each to his hole, and they all hid themselves. And it wasn't for some ten days that they began venturing out again. And from that day, even if a mouse saw that the cat had died, he wouldn't trust her, but would circle round at a distance first. *Kungurus kan kusu.*

---

* Cf. D. No. 101 which adds a long tale on to the end.
† A standard question and answer.

6

GOAT

The Dog and the Hyenas* [$^{I}/88$]

Here's another. There was a dog, and a kid, and they went to collect custard-apples. Some they ate, some they threaded on to spits. Then they lost their way and night came upon them, the sun setting while they were still in the bush. But they saw firelight and went towards it. Now this was the compound of a hyena, where she lived with her husband and ten children.

When they got there, they made salutation and the hyena made reply and invited them in. So they went in and saw the young hyenas blowing up the fire. Said the kid to the dog 'Take over the bellows.' So the dog took over the bellows and as he fanned, he said 'My front is drip-dripping ,my arse is drip-dripping.'† 'Give them here' said the kid. 'You can't do it.' He gave him the bellows and the kid took over fanning, saying as he did so, over and over 'We've eaten nine hyenas, it's the tenth we're after; we've eaten nine hyenas, it's the tenth we're after.' Then he said to the dog 'Fetch those lions' testicles, let's grill them.' Then the dog fetched him the custard-apples on the spits and gave them to him; and he set them up by the fire, still saying 'We've eaten nine hyenas, it's the tenth we're after.'

Then he said 'Hyena, give us some water to drink.' And the hyena said to the youngest hyena 'Go and get them some water,' adding 'And when you get there, don't come back!' Off he went, and didn't come back. Again the hyena said to the next bigger one 'Go and get them some water,' and added 'You too, when you get there, don't come back.' And he said to another 'Off you go! And don't be too long!' 'Righto' says he and off he goes, and he doesn't come back. Then he said to the next biggest 'Up you

* Cf. III/104, III/142 and II/33.

† In fear?, or just a meaningless jingle to accompany the movement?

get, and be off with you, you too,' and added 'And when you get there, don't come back.'

This went on till all the ten young ones had gone, and hadn't come back. Then the hyena said to his wife 'You too, get up and be off with you! And when you get there, don't come back; and then all you have to do, is sit and wait, you stupid creature!'* 'Right' said she and off she went, and didn't return. Then the hyena began to say 'What a useless lot!' and continued grumbling like this for some time. Then he said 'Just let me go and get it for you, me too.' So up he gets and away he goes to where he found his children and his wife. 'Well' says he, 'we can congratulate ourselves. My word! Did you see the lions' testicles! I never knew they had so much fat on!' Then he called together his children and wife and they went and hid.

Then the kid and the dog went right into the compound and drank their fill of water, and looked into the corn-bins. The kid saw a bin full of beans, and the dog a bin full of dried meat, and each one got inside and started to eat. The kid scratched up the beans and got right into them, leaving only his beard showing on top.

After a while the hyenas returned to their home, very pleased with themselves. Then the father said to his youngest son 'Son, get up and go and get some beans out for us, to cook and eat' and to the one next to him in age 'Up you get, you too, and get us out some dried meat to eat, while the beans are cooking.' Both of them obeyed.

They got up and climbed into the corn-bins. The one who entered the bin with the beans saw the kid's beard and called 'Hey, dad! Here's a goat's beard belonging to one of your ancestors!'†

'Bring it here' said his father, so he grasped the kid's beard and pulled. 'Me-e' said the kid, and he let go. Out came the kid at the run, and out came the dog running too, and they left the hyenas to their own house.

---

* The Hausa seems a little obscure here; perhaps addressed *sotto voce* to the kid.

† Obscure. The Hausa seems to be jocularly vulgar. But see p. 105.

The Lion and the Hyena* [^{II}/$_{13}$]

Here's another. The lion married the goat, and they had a son, who grew to years of discretion.

Then one day along came the hyena. Now the goat had gone off to market. When the hyena saw the goat's droppings, she said 'Mighty one of the bush, where has the one that left these droppings gone to?' 'What the – ! Those droppings are my wife's' said the lion. Says the hyena 'Mighty one of the bush, how come you married a goat?' and again 'Yes, it's a goat that you married, and goats have got very tasty meat.' 'Is that so?' said the lion. 'Yes' said the hyena. 'Very well' said the lion. 'Wait till she gets back. I'll kill her and we can eat her.' 'O.K.' said the hyena.

But the youngster heard them, and went off, taking the road to the market. There he said to his mother 'Hey mother, the hyena came and told Dad that your flesh was tasty. And, when you get home, you'll be killed so they can eat up your flesh.' 'I see' said she, 'Very well. Go home now.' And she went on into the market and finished her business. Then she bought some *alewa*†, and went off home with it. Meanwhile the lion, was waiting, ready for her.

When she reached the space in front of the compound, the lion sprang at her and knocked her over. But she escaped the full force of his spring, although all her purchases were spilt. 'Tut, tut, my lord!' said she 'Not so much of that. I've got something for you from a friend of yours.' 'Where is it? Give it me' said he. 'Here you are' said she, 'your friend gave it to me, the one who squashes hyenas, until they produce excrement, which he takes to the market. And, in fact, people were crowding round him, so that it was with difficulty that he gave me this, so that you shouldn't go without.' 'Hush' said he 'There's a hyena in the compound.'

They entered the compound, and there was the hyena in a hut and she said 'Mighty one of the bush, the goat is here.' But he took no notice, only going up to the hyena and taking hold of her, he squeezed her. Whereupon she excreted and the flies came buzzing up.

Then said the goat 'That isn't the sort of excrement that it was'

* Cf. III/132.   † For the stratagem, cf. I/87.

and continued 'She's despising you – that's why she hasn't done that other sort.' So the lion squeezed the hyena again, but she was by now quite empty.

Next the goat said 'Look at her, my lord. It's because of that friend of yours who catches hyenas and squeezes them, and then takes the excrement they produce to market – she's run away from him to hide here. You'd better let her go.' So the lion released the hyena, and she made off. But, just as she was going, the goat said 'Oh – my lord, she should clear away the excrement that she produced.' So back came the hyena, cleared up her own excrement, and then went on her way.

But the goat moved into the town. And that was how the goat first came to live in the town.

The Hyena* [$^{II}/_{33}$]

Here's another. The goat had a son, and she set off for a walk with him once, and as they went, they chanced on the hyena's compound. 'Well!' said the hyena, 'Welcome, strangers! Twice welcome!' 'Thank you kindly' says the goat.

Up got the hyena and went to fetch corn. But fear seized the goat's son, that the hyena would eat him up.

The hyena began to grind the corn, and the goat said to her 'Here, hyena, let me relieve you.' 'Oh no!' says the hyena, 'For who would dream of making a guest grind corn.' 'Not so' said the other, 'for women don't expect treatment as guests,' and she took over the grinding, and her son came over and sat close by her.

Then said the goat 'I'm going to start singing, and you must sing the refrains.' 'O.K.' said her son. So she began singing 'I broke the elephant's bones, I broke the lion's, I broke the leopard's. Yours will be easy, you rascally hyena!' 'Sh!' Not so loud, mother' said the kid, 'Or the hyena will hear and run away.'†

* Cf. TR. No. 23, III/104, III/142 and I/88.

† Said in *Zanranci* using the –lle suffix attached to words, so that a third party has difficulty in understanding.

But the goat went on singing as she worked, until the hyena said to her young ones 'Look, children! We've been rejoicing at getting meat – but it looks as though we are going to be the meat.' Then she added, louder, 'Come here, children, I want you to go and fetch some hot ashes; for you see, we have guests,' and, more softly 'And when you're gone, don't come back!' And they went off and didn't return.

Then said the hyena 'Guest, I sent the young ones to fetch some fire, and they haven't come back, so I must go after them.' And off went the hyena, and she didn't come back either; and she and her young ones ran away, leaving the goat, and her son, in their compound.

And the goat finished her grinding, picked up the corn and pushing her son before her, set off again. That's all. *Kungurus kan kusu.*

The Dog [$^{III}/_{30}$]

A young goat and a dog disagreed over their diet. So the dog took his skin bag, filled it with bran and tied it up.

And they went down to the edge of the river. Now at the edge of the river there was fresh grass, *gurugu.†* And the young goat began to eat the *gurugu.* And after eating some, he would go and take a drink of water.

But the dog, he took a little bran and tipped it into the river, and putting his mouth down began to drink. But the bran was all scattered and carried away in the water, and the dog became very hungry, for he had nowhere to get food and his provisions were finished.

Says the billy-goat 'Hey, dog, look over there – there are some butchers at work. Get up and go over to them and tell them to give you some meat, enough to eat and be satisfied. If they ask you who

† probably *burugu,* i.e. *panicnm stagninum.*

said so, you say "The goat's senior offspring." ' 'O.K.' said the dog.

And he went over to them. 'Hey' says he, 'I'm to ask you to give me meat, enough for me to eat and be satisfied.' 'Who says so?' asked the men. 'The goat's senior offspring' says he. At which they took some of the meat and gave it to the dog, and he ate until he was satisfied. Then he went away back and drank some water.

This happened regularly until the hyena came along and saw the dog's footprints. 'What's this' she asked sharply. 'Where did the owner of these footprints go?' 'Oh' they said, 'he comes here regularly. He told us to give him meat to eat, on the authority of the senior offspring of the goat.' 'Well!!!!' said the hyena, 'there is no God save Allah! Why – she's been a slave since the days of our grandfather's grandfather! And as for the one that said he was the goat's senior offspring, he's one of our slaves born in slavery of slave parents.'

So she went and dug a hole on the road that the dog used to follow when he was coming to receive his meat. And getting into it, she kept her eyes just level with the edge of the hole.

But the dog heard about it, and when the billy-goat said to him 'Dog, you should be getting along now to get your meat,' the dog said to him 'But, billy-goat I have heard that the hyena is there.' 'Pooh' said the other, 'just take a spear, and when you get there thrust it into the ground, and tell them to give you meat before the eyes that are in the ground get a stabbing.' So the dog took a spear and went off, feeling fearful.

Well, he got there and stuck the spear in the ground and said 'Come on! Give me meat, before the eyes in the ground get a stabbing.' Well, it chanced that when he stuck the spear in the ground he got the hyena in the eye!

Out comes the hyena and runs off fast; and the people who saw it all ran off too. And the dog proceeded to eat meat till he was full.

Next he went back to the billy-goat and told him. The billy came along too, and the two of them followed the tracks of the hyena and came upon her lying down.

Then they cut off her feet and pulling out their spear, departed.

As they went along, they fell into the hyena's home, and the hyena was there working at the anvil. Says the young goat 'Dog, take over the bellows.' And the dog did so and started pumping.

And as he did so he recited 'We want to run away, we've fear in our hearts; we want to run away, we've fear in our hearts.' 'Hey' said the young goat, 'Dog, you're good for nothing, and always have been.'

'Here, give them to me' he went on, and he began to recite 'We've eaten nine hyenas, and here's the tenth.' Next the young goat said 'Fetch those feet along and let's grill them.' And the dog brought the hyena's feet.

The hyena that was at the anvil saw that they had produced the feet of a hyena – and ran off. Says the young goat 'Dog, come on. Let's get back to the town.' And back they went to the town and there they stayed. That's all. *Kungurus kan kusu.*

The Dog and the Hyenas* [$^{III}/_{104}$]

There were once a billy-goat and a dog. Said the former 'Dog, let's go for a walk in the bush.' 'O.K.' said the dog. Now the goat had a sword, and he said 'Dog, look – if we meet the hyena, I'll save you from her.' But the dog said 'More likely I'll save you from the hyena, billy-goat.'

Away they went, and presently coming to the top of a hill, espied hyenas a-plenty – about a hundred. Says the dog 'Hey there, hyenas! Your mother and your father!† Yes, and your grand-parents' grandparents too!' And he and goat quickly took refuge in a hole.

The hyenas came racing up. One large male one outstripped the others, and reached the hole where the two were, first. The goat drew his sword, and when the hyena stuck his head in cut it off. Then another of them stuck his head in, and again the goat took his sword and cut that off; and so for all the hyenas, the goat took off the heads of every one of them.

Next the goat took a goatskin bag, and they piled all the heads

* Cf. II/33, III/142, and I/88.

† Used thus directly, these words constitute gross abuse in Hausa (cf. Arabic *ummak*) – perhaps by some significant ellipsis?

into it, and having filled it, tied it up. And the dog filled another bag with more; and each of them lifted one bag on to his head and set off.

Presently as they walked, they came to the smiths' quarter of the hyenas.* There they sat down with the hyenas, who were overjoyed that here was some meat for them.

Presently the goat said 'Get up, dog, and take over the bellows from these people and work them.' Up gets the dog, takes over the bellows and starts pumping, reciting as he does so 'I want to run away, but there's no room to escape; I want to run away, but there's no room; the fire's just in front of me.' 'For shame!' says the goat, 'Dog, you're a useless sort of fellow to have around,' and he took over the bellows and went on pumping, until the metal was red-hot.

Then the goat took up a hammer and began helping the hyena smiths to shape the metal. Meanwhile all the smiths' people, children, women and adults had gathered.

Then the goat said to the dog 'Pass me over that bag, so that I may see whether there is anything to grill in it.' And the dog did so. And the goat took out the head of the huge male hyena and put it by the fire.

The rest of the hyenas, when they saw that, began running away and scattering. Presently they reassembled away in the bush and began to congratulate each other on their escape from one who consumed hyenas. And it was a long time before the hyenas ventured back from there.

But at length they said 'Now! Let's select some strong, young hyenas.' And they chose out three such. Then their elders said to them 'Go back there stealthily and have a look. If you find that those people are still there, tell us and we'll run further off. But if they spot you and come after you, don't come back in our direction. For if you do that, when they get here, they'll gobble up your younger brothers; so make your way into the bush, but don't come back to us.' 'O.K.' they said.

They got back to the place and found the goat and the dog very busy counting hyenas' heads. When they saw this, the three went back and told their parents that the people they had run away from were still there and were counting hyenas' heads; and that

* Cf. I/88.

there were a hundred of them! So the hyenas made off as fast as they could from there into the bush.

But presently the goat and the dog were overtaken by hunger. So the goat took four hyenas' heads; and the dog too took four, and they hung them over their shoulders.

Then, as they walked along, they came to the home of another male hyena, whose wife had prepared *fura* for him; he hadn't yet drunk it. Just then he saw the goat, and the dog, both of them carrying hyenas' heads. At this the hyena ran off fast, and his wife too. So the dog and the goat drank up all the *fura*, and then set off on their way again.

After a while, they came upon a little hamlet of hyenas. The latter saw the dog and the goat with their burdens of hyenas' heads. And then that lot too, from the hamlet, scattered in all directions, leaving their hamlet. Whereupon the dog and the goat promptly entered it, went through it, helped themselves to food, and coming out again, went home.

And *that's* the reason that the dog and the goat don't quarrel *Kungurus kan kusu*. I ate the rat, he didn't eat me.

The Dog and the Hyenas* [III/142]

The dog and the billy-goat were arguing. The dog said – didn't you, dog? – 'I'll save you from the hyena.' And the billy-goat said – what did you say, billy? – 'No, I'll save *you*.' Then the goat gave the dog – didn't you, goat?† – a skin bag to sling over his shoulder.

Off they went to the bush, and there they saw seven hyenas. Then the goat told the dog to go and tell them that they were worthless creatures.‡ At which they came running up to the dog to grab him. But when each of them came to a hole in the ground she

* Cf. I/88, II/33, and III/104.

† This second person address (quite common in small doses throughout these stories, but which I have not hitherto attempted to render) runs right through this tale.

‡ Reading '*yar* for *jar*.

would fall in, and the dog would take off her head and put it in the bag; one after the other – into the bag – until he had got all seven hyenas.

Then they went on, till they came upon more hyenas in an entrance-hut, busy smithing. The dog was put to blow the bellows. And as he worked he began saying 'I want to run away, my anus is dripping and my heart is fluttering.' But the goat took up the song, saying 'I've eaten seven hyenas, and the ninth* is here.'

Well, they had taken the metal from the fire and were beating it out, when the goat took out a hyena's head, and began hammering with that. At which the hyenas scattered. [Later] they said [to one of their number] 'Go and take a little look for us to see if they've left.' She went and looked and reported 'I saw them taking out hyena's heads – seven in all.' And they all agreed that they couldn't trust themselves in that place again. That's the end of that one.

---

* Sic.

7

HYENA

All the Other Beasts of the Bush* [$^{I}/_{118}$]

The beasts of the bush gathered and decided that the bush had been
spoilt. Then said they 'On Friday, let us all meet together and
decide who has spoilt the bush' and this was agreed to.

Next Friday all the beasts of the bush met together. But when
they were come together, and all were present, the hyena alone was
not there. So they waited and waited, but she never came. So they
all dispersed.

After this the jackal met her and said to her 'We were waiting
for you just now, but we never saw you.' The hyena answered
'When I didn't come, who did they grab?' Says the jackal 'They
didn't grab anyone.' 'I thought so' said the hyena 'I'm the bad
one – it was me they were waiting to grab. O.K. – I'm certainly
not coming.' And ever since then the hyena has known her own
wickedness.

The Monkey and the Old Woman† [$^{II}/_{I}$]

Here's the tale of the hyena and the monkey. The hyena found a
spot and said to herself 'This is just the place for me to build a
hut, God willing.'

Well, the monkey came on the same spot and said 'This is just the
place for me to build a hut, God willing.'

* Cf. TR. No. 35; O. p. 260.
† Cf. D. No. 96 where the donkey replaces the monkey.

So the hyena went and rallied all her friends to help, and they came and erected the hut.

Thus when the monkey brought his friends along to help, and arrived at the place, he exclaimed 'Well, I am a lucky monkey! God must like me. For look, I find a spot where I want to build a hut – and, when I return to it, I find the hut built! Now I must put the thatch on it'.

And when the hyena came back, she arrived and found that the hut had had its roof put on. Then she exclaimed 'Well, I am a lucky hyena! God must like me. I come and build a hut, and then someone else comes and puts a roof on it for me.' Then she up and made a grass booth inside the hut.

Next along comes an old woman, who has been to market and is on her way home. A storm breaks, and the old woman goes into the hut, sees the booth and climbing up on top of it, seats herself.

Very soon the monkey comes running along, into the hut, and with a jump up he gets on to the booth. There he turns and faces the doorway of the hut.

Along comes the hyena with a goat she's killed, and coming up to the hut, she throws it in. Then she tears off a leg and brandishes it. Whereupon the monkey takes it and thrusts it behind him. The old woman takes it and puts it with her bundle of things.

The hyena tears off another leg and brandishes it, and the monkey gets it and thrusts it behind him and the old woman takes it and puts it with her bundle of things – and so on until the hyena had taken off all four legs and thrown them up; the monkey had taken them and thrust them behind him, and the old woman had collected them and put them in her bundle.

Whereupon the old woman said to herself 'Well! This fellow has been kind to me!' adding 'Let me do something for him in return.' So she took the shoot of a deleb-palm nut* and thrust it into the monkey's anus. The monkey leapt into the air and landed on the back of the hyena. And the hyena shot off outside at full speed.

She ran and ran and ran, saying to herself 'My, oh my – but I've had some running today.' Whereat the monkey said 'Is it you who feels the running, or me?' and the hyena looked behind her, and she looked to the right and to the left, and then she looked in front of her, but saw no one. She just heard a voice speaking – so off she

* Which monkeys proverbially like to eat.

went again at full speed, and ran until she was tired out. Then she reached a big tree and said to herself. 'Oh dear! What a long way I've run today!' Then the monkey gave a leap and shinned up the tree. And the hyena lifted her head and, looking up, saw that it was the monkey. And then she fell down dead. *Kurungus kan kusu.*

The Donkey [II/2]

The donkey had eaten the cornstalks and he had eaten guinea-corn and he was replete, when the hyena saw him and said 'Hey, donkey! Let's play the biting game!' 'Oh no' said the donkey, 'I can't bite, but I can kick with my hind legs.' 'O.K.' said she, 'I agree, but let's make it tomorrow,' and went on 'You go home, and I'll go on with my round.'

So the donkey went off, and he got them to strip off *kalgo* bark and then he came along and they bound it round and round his body. Then he went to some mud and rolled in it, and coming out, lay in the sun to dry. The mud caked hard on the bark. Then he went again and, lying down, rolled in the mud. Then he went off home.

Well, along comes the hyena. 'Where's the donkey?' says she. 'Here I am' says he. 'Good, come on out!' But, when he came out and she saw him, she exclaimed 'Oh, donkey – you're a sight to inspire fear.' 'Why, what do you see?' says he. 'I see you've put some powerful medicine on yourself' she answered. 'Oh that' said he, 'but surely you know all donkeys can't resist rolling in ash, when they see it.' 'Oh, I see. Then let's begin' said the hyena. 'O.K.' said he.

'How many goes shall we have?' asked the hyena. 'Whatever you say' he answered. 'Let's have ten each then,' she said. 'O.K.' said he.

Then the hyena drew back a way, and springing forward, seized the donkey and bit him, but got only mud. Again she withdrew, again sprang forward, again bit him and again got mud. The same happened to the hyena ten times. Then she said to him 'Now it's your turn, go ahead.'

The donkey drew back a way, brayed, then galloped up, took a good look at the hyena and kicked her on the head. 'Ow!' she exclaimed 'That's five you've had.' 'Oh no, hyena' said everyone, 'that makes one.' 'No, you people' said the hyena, 'he's had five turns.' 'Oh no, hyena' they said, 'that makes one.' 'All right. Very well' said she. And the donkey galloped back a way, and returning, caught the hyena a terrific kick on the head. Whereat she had diarrhoea. 'Twenty' said she. But the people said 'Oh, no, hyena. That makes two.' 'No, no' she said 'I'll swear it's twenty.' 'No, hyena' they said 'that makes two.' 'Oh, very well, you people' she said, 'I'll take your word for it.'

The donkey drew back a way. Then he came galloping forward and took a good look at the hyena, and let fly another terrific kick at her head. But the hyena didn't wait. She set off at full gallop, with the donkey after her, and so escaped. Then the donkey returned home. *Kurungus kan kusu.*

The She-Ass and How They Married [II/40]

One day the hyena said to the she-ass 'Donkey'. 'Yes' she replied. 'Let's change ourselves into humans and go into the town and get married.' 'Oh no, hyena' said the donkey, 'for I am prone to break wind.' 'I'll give you a cure for that' said the hyena, 'To stick in your anus.' To this the donkey agreed, and the hyena fetched the round earthen head of a spindle and put that up her anus. And then they both turned into human beings, beautiful women.

They went off into the town, and the hyena married a man who had four thousand cattle, and the donkey married one with three thousand cattle.* And both their husbands made them go regularly to the corrals to milk the cattle.

Well, whenever the hyena went, she would take a fat cow and

* Originally, perhaps a Fulani tale. It is not noteworthy how often in TATS *dukiya* 'wealth' = 'beasts'.

consume it, leaving only the head. The she would do her milking and return home.

But as for the donkey, she would just go, do her milking and then return home.

This went on, day after day, until one day their husbands thought that they would go to the corrals to see how the cattle were. And first they went to the corral of the donkey's husband's cattle, and they found them greatly increased, with calves beyond number. Then said the hyena's husband to the other 'Your herd's grown. That woman brings good luck!'

And the donkey's husband replied 'Let's go over to your herd.' So they went to the herd of the hyena's husband, and as they approached it they espied a huge pile of heads. Then said the donkey's husband to the hyena's husband 'Well – it seems that your cattle too have increased – look at all that! That's all cattle.' But when they got to the corral, they saw that the cattle were few, and that what they had espied was just heads. And the hyena's husband expressed his surprise and disappointment, and they returned home.

Then the hyena's husband cut himself a stick from a tamarind tree, and went and said to his wife 'You're not to go to the corral again.' 'Very well' she replied. But after three days had passed, she said that she was going to the corral, and 'Oh no' said he. Then in the evening, he told his neighbours that when he started beating his wife, none of them need come, and they agreed not to.

Night came, and he picked up the stick and taking hold of his wife began to beat her. 'Help! Ow! Ow!' she cried – but he just went on beating her. But presently she grew sick of being beaten and started to howl like a hyena; and rushing out she vanished into the bush.

But when evening came round again, the hyena came near the compound of the donkey and began to howl in animal language that she wanted her spindle-head back. And presently the donkey's husband asked her what it was that kept on like that. She answered 'It's the hyena. For she's complaining about the spindle-head I borrowed, when mine broke.' 'Well, fancy that!' said her husband.

Well, one day the hyena was back as usual, but when she started to talk, the donkey's husband picked up a stick and ran out after her, and she fled.

But one day the hyena changed herself back into a woman again and returned to the donkey's home. And she found the donkey bending over a pot, washing it. And the hyena went up to her and pulled the spindle-head out of her anus, and away she went again. And the donkey went after her, breaking wind continuously, 'Bur bur bur.' 'Well fancy that' said the donkey's husband, 'It seems that both of us married wives who – you a hyena, and I a donkey.' 'Where are they?' asked the hyena's husband. 'Over there – look, they're off! Can't you hear my wife breaking wind?' 'No, I can't' said the other. So the hyena and the donkey departed, and that was that. *Kungurus kan kusu.*

The Donkey[II/81]

One day the donkey had been loaded up and was being driven along. And as he was beaten, he tried to move his quarters to the side, grunting and hastening along. Now while this was going on, the hyena saw it and came and said to him 'Donkey, can it really be that I see them beating you as you go along, for all that you're laden with stuff?' The donkey answered 'Oh, I'm having a very pleasant time.' 'Really?' she asked. 'Yes' he replied, 'for whenever you see them hit me, they give me a piece of *kilishi*.' 'Donkey' said the hyena, 'won't you let me come with you, and take over your work tomorrow?' 'All right' he answered. 'Good' said she. 'Then tomorrow, we'll go off together, and they can load me up. O.K.?' 'O.K.' said he.

So they duly set off, and the hyena was loaded up. Then, as they went along, the hyena stopped, refusing to go on, so they would hit her and give her *kilishi*. And they beat her, whereupon she turned her head, expecting to see *kilishi* being offered her. But there was no such thing to be seen. So on went the hyena, and on they went beating her. At first she paid no attention, but at last began to say 'Mos kilis',* and each time they hit her she would say 'Mos kilis.'

* Some reference to *kilishi* in hyena language presumably.

And she kept at it all the way to their destination. From there she ran away as fast as she could. Then she said 'So! *That's* the way the donkey treats me, is it? Fine! Well, if I see the donkey, when there's no man near, I'll eat him up.'

And people say that that was how the enmity between the hyena and the donkey began. And when you hear her howling in the night, that's her still asking for the *kilishi*. That's the end of that one.

The Scorpion* [$^{III}/_4$]

Here's a fable of the hyena. She was walking along one night when she trod on a frog. She turned her head and said 'Here's profit for my foot', and gobbled it up.

On she went and saw the scorpion. Says she 'And you – what about you? What's your name?' 'Who – me?' said the scorpion. 'Yes, you' said the hyena. Says the scorpion 'My name is Shorty-With-The-Bow.' 'Is that so?' said the hyena. 'Yes' said the scorpion, and the hyena went on.

After that, whenever the hyena saw the scorpion, she would say to her 'Shorty-With-The-Bow.'

But the hyena tired of this and went to the scorpion and said 'Look. You said you'd got a bow, but I still haven't seen you kill any game.' Says the Scorpion, 'Hyena, go along, and when you find a place that the beasts collect, come back and I'll come along with you.' 'What sort of beasts?' asks the hyena. And the scorpion answered her 'Oh, elephants and the like, and such as bush-cows and roan antelopes.' And she repeated 'Any beasts of the bush, big and small – get along and find where they gather. Then come back and tell me, and I'll come along with you.' So the hyena went off to a lake where the beasts of the bush would all drink water. And there they were: they had drunk water and were lying around, resting.

Whereupon the hyena ran off fast and returned to get the

* See J. p. 46. Cf. M. No. 32.

scorpion. Says she 'Shorty-With-The-Bow, come along. There they are, they are gathered.' And the hyena led the way, and the scorpion followed, right in among the beasts of the bush, close up against the elephant.

Says the scorpion 'Hyena, put your nose down and massage my anus, so that I may tighten my bow-string (?).' The Hyena came closer, and the scorpion said again 'Brace yourself, hyena, so that the draught from the bow doesn't knock you down.' 'O.K.' she answered, and put her nose right on the scorpion's sting. The scorpion took careful aim at the hyena's nose and let fly with her sting. The hyena shrieked.

The beasts of the bush took fright, leapt up and stampeded away. And the ones like the elephant and the bush cow and the roan antelope and the giraffe trampled on the hare and the gazelle, and the duiker and the western cob.

But as for the jackal, he had been away at some distance from the others. And there was the hyena, lying unconscious. Presently she came to her senses, got up and looked eastwards – and saw nothing but meat lying all over the place. She looked west, she looked north, she looked south – just the same. 'My word!' said she, 'Shorty-With-The-Bow is some shot!'

People say 'However dark the night, the hyena sees where she is putting her foot, for she still fears the scorpion.' That's all, that's the end of that tale.

The Ram, the Billy-Goat and the Dog [III/ 16]

The ram and the billy-goat and the dog set off to fish the hyena's lake. When they were in it, the ram said 'Look, billy-goat, your name is First-To-Run-Away; and, dog, your name is Escaper; as for me, mine is Thunderbolt.'

So they went on fishing in the lake for a while, when up comes the hyena. 'Hey' she exclaimed, 'what the –! What are you doing in my lake – for you're all my meat, billy-goat, dog and ram.'

Says the ram 'Well, well. It seems that you don't know who we are. This one here is First-To-Run-Away; and this one is called Escaper, and as for me, my name is Thunderbolt.' 'Is that so?' she answered, 'Then just catch some fish for me.'

Says the billy-goat 'Wow! I touched a big fish then. Just let me go and get some medicine to catch him with.' And the billy-goat got out, and went a little way. And when he was some way off, he set off at the run. The hyena pursued him until she saw that he had got into the town.

Then she returned and found the dog and the ram. Says she 'Well, come on, catch some fish for me. For I said that you were my meat, but you contradicted me.' Presently the dog said 'Wow! I touched a big fish then. Just let me go and get some medicine, then I'll come back and catch him.' So the dog got out, and when he saw he was well clear of the hyena, slunk away, and then running off, reached the town safely.

Back comes the hyena again to the ram. Says the ram 'Wow! I touched a big fish then. Let me fetch some medicine with which to catch him.' And the ram came out and lay down in some fine gravel, then shook himself. Some of the gravel hit the hyena, who said 'Well, it seems you really are a thunderbolt.'

Then the ram went and fetched the medicine and going back into the water, caught a big fish and threw it to the hyena. She took it and ate it up.

Out comes the ram again and rolls in the gravel. Then he set off along the path home. Presently he saw a dead tree by the roadside. Taking a jump, he butted it and smashed it to pieces. Says the hyena 'Oh-oh! By God, he's a thunderbolt!'

The ram went on, and when he got close to the town, he saw a tree-stump. And taking a jump, he butted it – and over went the tree-stump. Says the hyena 'Well! By God, he's a thunderbolt!' And so the ram went on into the town, and the hyena went back to the bush. That's all. *Kungurus kan kusu.*

The Bitch and the Filani* [$^{III}/_{31}$]

There was once a bitch, which climbed up a tree, and getting into a hole in it, had a litter. Then she got a rope and fastened it on, and said 'If you hear me say *"Sur,*† my children", then let down the rope to me, so that I can climb up.' 'Very well' they said.

So it continued for some time, until the hyena observed what was happening. Then she waited till the bitch had gone off, and going up, said 'Sur, my children', and they let the rope down to her. She took hold of it, and they started to pull the hyena up. But when they had her quite close, they saw that it wasn't their mother. Whereupon they let her go and she fell on her head; and her head went right into the ground.

Presently the bitch returned from getting her food, and saw the hyena, with her head stuck in the ground. Says the bitch 'Sur, my children', and they threw the rope down to her, and she went up.

When she got there, she said to her children 'How did that one come here?' And her children answered 'She came here and said to us "Sur, my children". So we threw the rope down to her, and pulled her up. But when we saw that she wasn't you, and saw that she was a hyena, we let her go, down to the ground, and she fell on her head. And her head went right into the ground.'

Says the bitch 'Well, we've gotten a mortar for pounding' – and proceeded to use the hyena's anus for her pounding.

Presently the bitch saw a Filani come along. He said that he wanted a mortar to pound a ball of *fura*. 'There's one there' said the bitch, 'You can pound in that.' 'Thanks' said he.

So he started to pound, but presently said 'Bitch, give me a long pin.' She fetched one and gave it to him, and the young Filani began pulling out thorns. Says the bitch 'Take care not to prick the eyes of my mortar.' 'O.K.' said he. But then he stabbed the hyena's eye, when he noticed that the bitch's gaze was turned away. Up jumped the hyena, and away she ran.

* Cf. TR. No. 84, p. 402, for the hyena trying to get up the tree, and S. p. 113 for the type of the tale.

† An open sesame.

And so that is how the hyena came to produce white excrement, for she still produces the Filani's lump of *fura*, whenever she excretes. She still does it, she hasn't left off. That's all. *Kungurus kan kusu.*

The Sky-People and the Kite Hawk [^{III}/ $_{47}$]

Another fable. Word was sent to the hyena from the sky telling her there was a party on there. 'Oh dear' she said, 'who can take me up into the sky? I shan't be able to get to this party.' But they said to her 'If you'll come to the place that we point out to you and beat your little drum, we'll know that you've come, and we'll let a rope down to you. You can tie that on to your backside and we'll pull you up to the party.'

Then they took the hyena and showed her the place. Off she went straight away to get her little drum.

When she got back, she beat the drum, and the sky-people said 'Hey! The hyena's come.' And they fetched a rope and let it down to her. Then the hyena tied it on to her backside. Then the sky-people began to heave away at the hyena, like men pulling up a leather bucket. Up she came and the sky opened.

In went the hyena, and the entrance shut tight again. 'Hey!' said the hyena, 'Look – the door's shut!' 'Never fear' they answered. 'Sit you down and join in the party. When you want to go again, you'll see – the door will open.'

So the hyena enjoyed the party until evening. Then she said 'I'm off home.' 'But, hyena' they said, 'the party hasn't begun yet; the girl's* parents haven't come yet. They won't be here until to-morrow.' 'Very well then' said the hyena and there she spent the night.

In the morning the girl's parents came, bringing cattle. These were slaughtered, and the hyena got some meat – two goatskins full. And so the party came to an end.

* I.e. the bride's?

Says the hyena 'I'm off home now', and the sky-people said 'Just a minute, hyena – let's have a properly drawn up agreement. Take the rope and tie it on to your backside. Now, when you reach the ground, beat your little drum, and we shall know that you have reached there.' 'Very well' said the hyena.

Then they picked up the hyena and started to lower her down to the ground, like a leather bucket going down into a well.

But the hyena wasn't half way down when she saw a kite-hawk with some meat. Says she 'Kite-hawk, won't you give me that meat?' 'Hyena' answered the kite-hawk, 'drum out my special rhythm for me.' 'Oh no' said the hyena, 'for I have made an agreement with the sky-people. They told me not to start drumming till I reach the ground. But look – I'll sing your praise-song instead, kite-hawk.' But the kite-hawk answered 'You won't get any meat, until you drum out my special theme.'

So the hyena turned and grasping her little drum, began to beat it. Whereupon the sky-people said 'The hyena has reached the ground' – and they let her go. By the time the hyena reached the ground she was dead, and when she hit it, she burst.

Then up comes the kite-hawk and begins to tear at her flesh – and the meat she was carrying too.

So now people say 'He who doesn't swallow his greed will be swallowed by his greed' and 'If any man is not content with a little, he will lose all' and 'Any man who fails to subdue his greed will suffer.' That's all. *Kungurus kan kusu.*

The Dog and the Rooster† [III/113]

The cat and the hyena went and made farms for themselves by the road. One passed the cat's before coming to the hyena's.

Well, the rooster and the dog set off for a walk. As they walked along the road, the rooster said 'Dog.' 'Uh?' said the dog. 'Let me teach you a stratagem, dog' said the rooster. 'O.K.' said the dog, and

† Cf. F. p. 97.

the other continued 'Look – it's the cat's farm that we get to first. So you put me in a grass bag, and draw me along, until we are past the cat's farm. Then, when we reach the hyena's farm, you get into the bag, and I'll pull you along, until we are passed the hyena's farm.' 'O.K.' said the dog, and the rooster got into the bag.

And when they got close to the cat's farm, the dog began dragging the bag, until they were past the farm. Then, when they drew near to the hyena's farm, the rooster said 'Now then, dog, you get in and I'll pull you along'. In gets the dog, the rooster begins pulling him along, and so they came to the middle of the hyena's farm.

The hyena saw the rooster dragging a grass bag. Says she 'Hey, rooster, what are you pulling there?' And the rooster whispered to her that it was the dog. Again she asked the rooster what he was pulling along. Again he whispered to her that it was the dog. And the dog, there in the bag, began saying to himself 'God in heaven!' Then the hyena came up, and the rooster ran off.

The hyena picked up the dog, still in the bag, and took him to her children. Says she 'Here's a dog. Guard him well, while I go and fetch some wood.' 'Very well' said her children.

But when the hyena had gone, one young hyena said 'My! But mother's dog is a fine one.' Says the dog 'How can you see how fine I am, when you haven't even seen me outside the bag?' 'Then come on out and let me see you.' So the dog came out and the young one said 'Good. I've seen. Now you can go back.' But another of the young hyenas said 'My, my! He surely is a fine one!' And the dog said 'How can you see how fine I am, when you haven't even told me to walk a little?' And the young hyena said 'Walk a little so that I may see.' So the dog began to move, and then the young hyena said 'Come back now, and get into the bag.' But another of them said 'Mother's dog can really travel!'* And the dog said 'But have you seen me running?' and the young hyena said 'Run fast for me to see.' And the dog ran off fast, and when they said 'Come back now,' he wouldn't.

But as the dog was running along, he met the hyena, who grabbed at him. 'Bow wow' said the dog. 'Little bastard' she said, 'you belong to me, you're my property.' And when she reached her children, she asked them about the dog, and they said 'Oh, he ran away.'

* I have altered the original question mark to an exclamation mark.

As for the dog, he went and got right into a heap of chaff. The hyena followed his tracks right up to the chaff – and then she saw his eyes. 'Oh-oh!' said she, 'those look like the dog's eyes,' and the dog said 'No, it's not him.' 'But –!' she said, 'those are the dog's eyes.' 'No' said he again, 'it's not him.' 'Well' said she, 'if it is the dog, I'll see,' and she began to move a little closer to the dog. The dog didn't stir, just went on lying there. Again she said 'The eyes are like the dog's eyes.' 'No' said the dog, 'it's not him.' And the hyena moved back farther away from the dog.

Then the dog emerged from the chaff and ran off fast in the direction of the town. The hyena followed him. And as the dog reached the moat of the wall, the hyena made a desperate grab at him. But the dog escaped into the town.

And that's how the dog came to move into the town. Long, long ago he lived in the bush, but from fear of being eaten by the hyena, he moved into the town. That's all. *Kungurus kan kusu.* I ate the rat, not the rat me.

The Elephant and the Bull [$^{III}/_{121}$]

The bull and the elephant had a dispute, and said 'Very well, we'll meet on Thursday and have a wrestling match, and whichever throws the other, let him kill him.' Now the elephant's drummel was the hyena, and the bull's was the cat.

Thursday came and they met. The hyena was drumming for the elephant, thus 'He-man, bull-elephant, let's eat the stomach and the bones.' And the cat was drumming for the bull, thus 'He-man, white one, with the black horns.' And so they clashed, the bull and the elephant. The elephant knocked the bull to the ground. And when he fell, he died. And they ate up the meat.

Now the bull had had a son. And this young one would come every day and place his hoof in his father's footprints* – until he saw that his foot was the same size as his father's had been, no

* Cf. S. p. 86.

bigger and no smaller. Then he sent word, saying that the elephant should be told that he was going to take revenge for his father; and that they should meet on Thursday in the same place where the elephant and his father had wrestled.

The elephant sent for her drummer, the hyena; and the bull sent for his, the cat. So they met, the hyena with her 'He-man, bull-elephant, let's eat the stomach and the bones,' and the cat with his 'He-man, white one with the black horns, take revenge for your father.'

And so they clashed together, the bull and the elephant. The bull sprang, aiming at the elephant's chest, and put his horn right into her neck, and the horn pierced it, and the elephant fell down dead.

Says the hyena 'I've nowhere to run to – if I had, I'd run there. I've no one to protect me but God.' The bull made after the hyena, and the hyena said 'Bull, be patient – for how is the drummer concerned?' The bull agreed to be patient and went away. And so they all went home. That's all. *Kungurus kan kusu.*

The Lion* [III/ 133]

The lion's children had fever. The jackal came along and said he had medicine for it. 'Fine' said the lion, 'Give me some.' The other said he must go and pull up some *tsada†* roots. So the lion went and bent down and started digging up the roots.

Along comes the hyena. 'Mighty one of the bush' says she, 'what goes on here?' 'What?' said he, 'oh, I'm getting out some medicine.' 'Medicine for what?' she asked. 'Medicine for the children's stomach trouble' he said. 'I see' says she, and retires behind him and stands there for a while.

The lion's testicles were swinging in front of the hyena's eyes, and presently she cre-ept up and plucked off the lion's testicles and

* Cf. III/48 and also I/13.   † *Ximenia Americana,* presuming *tsada = tswada.*

ran off fast. The lion collapsed, but after a while got up and went home. There he said to the jackal 'Look what the hyena has done to me.' 'Leave it to me' said the jackal, 'I'll get revenge for you.'

So he set off and went to the hyena's home, and having found where it was, went back again. 'Lion' said he, 'go and kill some meat.' So the lion went off and killed a huge bull, returned and said to the jackal 'I've killed some meat.' And the jackal had the meat taken and put in a hut. Then he went back to the hyena. 'Bother you!' he said, 'You're too slippery a customer. I came here and didn't find you. There's a ceremony on at my home, and I've told them not to touch the meat – any of them – till you come. Come on, let's go.'

Off they went, and presently drew near the compound. Says the jackal 'Let me go ahead and send the people packing from my compound.' And going in, he called the lion, saying 'Go into the hut where the meat is' and the lion did so. The jackal followed him and said to the lion 'Lie down' and the lion did so. Then the jackal took the bull's flesh and heaped it up on top of the lion, covering him completely.

Then he went back to the hyena and said to her 'Come along with me' and they came in. Says the hyena 'Jackal, I suppose the lion hasn't by any chance come to this party has he?' 'Oh no' says he, 'you see, we've had a quarrel.' Then the hyena went on in to the hut, and saw meat a-plenty. Says she 'Look, jackal, I – if you don't close up the hut, I shan't be able to make a proper job of dividing up this meat for you.' So the jackal went to the door and shut the hut. 'Close it really tight' said the hyena. 'Very well' said the hyena and did so.

The hyena put out her paw and touched the meat and was just putting her mouth to it and starting to eat, pulling it aside, when she saw the lion's eyes. 'Hey, jackal' said she, 'open up the hut.' But the jackal wouldn't. The lion grabbed at the hyena, who pushed the door to get out. Then he walloped her on the backside.

And that is why her rear end is so low down – the blow he gave it; and even now her rump hasn't straightened out. That's the end of that story.

The Donkey and the Cattle-Fulani* [^{III}/$_{134}$]

The hyena went and found some Fulani and then began coming and taking their beasts. They set a trap; but when she reached it, she saw it, and wouldn't go near it.

But as the donkey was strolling along he came upon the Fulani and found them talking, saying how the hyena was causing them loss. Says the donkey 'If I catch the hyena and bring her to you, what will you give me?' The Fulani answered 'Donkey, we – look, if you bring us the hyena, we'll let you off all domestic work, we certainly won't put loads on you, and we'll give you corn-stalks and guinea-corn, and you can eat until you're full'. 'Really?' said the donkey. 'Yes' said the Fulani. 'And I' said the donkey. 'Will bring you the hyena right to your compound.' 'Really?' said they and he answered 'Yes.' 'Righto' they said, 'go and bring her to us.'

As for the hyena, she had said that if anyone came looking for her, her children were not to admit that she was there, but to say she was out.

The donkey arrived at the hyena's compound and made formal greeting, but the young ones said 'Oh, she's not here.' 'Oh really? Well, she's out of luck.' At which the hyena said 'It's not true. Hey! Here I am.' And the donkey said 'Hullo – look, there's a lot of meat over there. No one's eating it, so that it's nearly rotting.' 'Is that so?' she said. 'The birds are there, eating' the donkey added. 'The vulture, the griffon and the crow. Come on – get on my back. I'll take you there in a minute – for you're a very slow traveller. But if you get on my back, I'll gallop with you and take you right there and put you down.'

The donkey galloped a bit and the hyena nearly fell off. Then she said 'Hey, donkey, stop a bit, while I fix something – I'm nearly falling off.' And she got her young ones to strip off some *kalgo* bark, and they tied her on the donkey. She moved a bit and said 'Here, just here it's not properly tied; they must tighten it up.' So they lashed the hyena really tightly on to the donkey.

Then the donkey started to go slowly, and the hyena said 'Hey, go fast. You said you were going to gallop – and now you won't.

* Cf III 48.

126

If you don't gallop, I'll bite you.' 'Really?' said the donkey. 'Yes' said the hyena, but the donkey still went along slowly. Then the hyena dug her teeth into the donkey's mane. And when the donkey felt the pain, then he really got started and galloped all out, not stopping till he was among the Fulani.

Then the Fulani put irons into the fire and taking the hyena, branded her all over with them. The hyena screamed until she was tired. No one came to rescue her. And so they made the hyena suffer.

Now, people say that those black marks on the hyena's body are the Fulani's branding. Then the hyena passed out, and not until it was night, did the pain ease and she got up and, crawling, made her way home.

Then the Fulani brought corn-stalks and guinea-corn and gave them to the donkey, saying 'We Fulani will never sell you, donkey, nor will we enslave you.' But of course, those Fulani were cattle-Fulani. They made a promise to the donkey, and that's why cattle-Fulani don't keep donkeys.

But the hyena, when she recovered, said that she, whenever she saw a donkey would eat him up. And that's how the hyena and the donkey came to be at enmity. If the hyena sees a donkey, he runs away. For if he doesn't, she'll eat him up. And the enmity goes on to this day. That's all. *Rungurus kan kusu.*

Ears and Eyes [III/ 143]

The hyena set off for a walk which took her by the outside of a compound fence. Just then a husband and wife were quarrelling, and the husband said 'Now I'd like to take you and throw you out of the compound, and a hyena get you and eat you up!' And the hyena said, standing there 'Some things a fellow hears with his ears, but his eyes won't see them!'

The Beasts of the Bush [$^{III}/_{176}$]

All the beasts of the bush gathered and made a kill. But they said 'Let us all fast today. Let no one speak until sunset. Then we'll break(our)fast* with this meat.' So they fasted till the evening, and they said 'Let the younger ones do the flaying,' and these set to work.

But as for the hyena, greed would not allow her to be patient, and speaking in her throat, said to her son 'Take some intestines and run off.' 'Ha!' said the others, 'the hyena spoke.' 'Did I open my mouth?' asked the hyena. 'But as you're taking that line, we may as well scramble for it.'

And that is why it is said 'If you have a greedy man for a partner in anything, he can't be patient.'

The Jackal [$^{III}/_{177}$]

The hyena and the jackal were walking along and came to a town. They were given lodging close to the river. And the townspeople said 'Since we have guests, let us take meat to them. They took them a goat, saying 'Here's a present to welcome you, a goat. Let anyone who has performed the ritual ablutions, slaughter it for you and you'll be able to eat it.'

The hyena jumped up in great haste and went and sprang into the river. Out she came again, saying 'Unless of course you dislike me personally, a bath is more effective than any ritual ablutions.' Says the jackal 'God's curse on you. But go and slaughter it and skin it.' 'And that' said the hyena, 'is why I like your company when I am out for a walk.'†

---

* Lit. 'open mouth'.   † Because he wasn't fussy?

8

A MISCELLANY

The Poor Man, the Dog, the Jackal, the Hyena and the Lion* [I/ 151]

There was once a poor young fellow who had nothing, so that it was with difficulty that he even managed to marry. But he did and his wife bore a child.

Then he went to the dog and borrowed five thousand cowries. And he went to the jackal and borrowed another five thousand, and to the hyena and borrowed another five thousand, and to the lion and borrowed another five thousand. And he said 'In seven days time, come and get your money.'

Seven days passed and the dog was the first on the scene. The young man took him to a shelter and brought him food. But while they were eating, the jackal arrived and made formal salutation. 'Who's there?' said the dog. 'It's the jackal.' Says the dog 'If only I could find a hole in the compound fence, I'd be off.' 'Oh' said the man, 'there's only the hole that my mother uses and to go through that costs five thousand.' 'Keep the five thousand you owe me and let me go through there' said the dog, and away he went.

Then the jackal came into the shelter, and as they were eating, the hyena made formal salutation. 'Who's that?' said the jackal. 'It's the hyena' he said. 'If only I could find a hole in the compound fence, I'd be off.' 'Well' said the man 'there's the hole my mother uses, but that costs five thousand.' Says the jackal 'I'll let you off the five thousand you owe me' and he too went out of the compound.

The hyena entered the shelter and began to eat. Whereupon the lion arrived and made formal salutation. 'Who's at the entrance?' said the hyena. 'It's the lion' said the man. 'Oh' said she, 'if only I could find a little hole, I would slip through it.' 'Well' said he,

* Cf. I/159.

'there's the little hole my mother uses, but it costs five thousand to go through that.' 'I'll let you off the five thousand' said she and he opened the hole for her and away she went.

Then the lion came into the shelter, and the young man used cunning and killed him. And so he enjoyed the use of his money, for his creditors were no more.

The Old Woman who had Sheep, the Male Hyena and the Lion* [$^I/_{154}$]

There was once an old woman who had a flock of many sheep.

Presently there came a male hyena to her and told her he wanted some goat dung. 'Go on in and help yourself' said she. So he would go in, wring a sheep's neck, put it in a large calabash, and heaping sheep dung on top would pick it up and depart. This went on day after day until the sheep were all finished, and there remained just one ram.

Next the old woman, wailing and screaming, went off to the bush. Well, the lion heard the din she was making and came up to the old woman. 'What's the matter with you?' says he. 'I had a flock of many sheep' said she, 'and the hyena has finished them all up.'

Then said the lion to the old woman 'Go home. I'll be along in the evening. When I come, put me where the sheep are and tie me up, but take the ram out and put him in a corner of your hut. Then light a fire and lie down just in the doorway.' The old woman did just as the lion had told her.

When night came, the male hyena came to the old woman and said 'I've come to take some sheep dung.' 'Very well' she answered, 'go and help yourself, but don't take my ram.' 'Of course not' said he, 'what should I want with your ram?' But when he went in, he seized the lion and held him; then he gave him to his son.

Well, the hyena's son was delighted. 'My' says he, 'today we

* Cf. TR. No. 16 and S. p. 75.

have got a large beast.' And he felt the lion and stroked his body. He felt the stiff hair, the shining coat, and he saw the lion's eye like a red-hot coal. Then he said 'This thing that you've given me to hold, this is what chases you in the bush.' 'You're lying' says the hyena. Now the young hyena's name was Kwaďin Kwarďo,* and he said 'Here, Dad, it's all yours.'

And the youngster ran off home to his mother, and said to her 'Dad has caught the thing that chases you in the bush.' 'Get on with you, little liar!' said his mother. But he refused to stir. Then she took a stirring-stick and hit him and he went out of the hut and squatted down. He heard his father coming. Then his mother came out, very pleased, and going up to the male hyena, began to stroke the thing that he had captured.

The lion turned his head and saw her foot, and chopped it off. Then she ran as fast as she could, saying 'This sheep isn't like the earlier ones.' When the male hyena saw this, he put down what he was carrying, in great fear. Then the lion chopped off his foot just like his wife's, and the hyena made off fast.

After this the lion returned to the old woman's compound and said to her 'I've paid the hyena out for what he did to you.' 'Thank-you' said she, 'may God enable me to pay you back!' 'Amen' said the lion, and again 'The hyena won't come back to your home after today. Well, I must be off. Goodbye.'

A while later the hyena said to his son 'Please make me a little shelter, so that I can rest my leg till it is better.' 'O.K.' said the youngster, and when he had finished it, the hyena went in and lay groaning. Then he said to his son again 'Heat some water and give me a fomentation.' When the water was hot, he said 'Dad, come on out!' But the hyena couldn't.

Whereupon Kwaďin Kwarďo began to yell and said 'Hey, Dad, the thing that chopped off Mum's foot, and killed her – look! It's coming here.' Then the hyena burst through the back of the shelter and made off fast, while his son stood there laughing. *Kurungus kan kusu.* It wasn't because of Spider that I made it up – I was making it up in any case!

---

* 'Frogs of a frog', if one letter is deleted.

The Bull-Calf and the Elephant-Calf* [$^{II}/_4$]

When the bull-calf and elephant-calf were boys they used to graze together. Whenever the bull-calf was let loose from the compound, he would go off to the bush to meet the elephant-calf. This would occur regularly, until they grew up.

Then one dry season, the bull-calf said 'Elephant-calf, let's dig a well.' But the elephant-calf answered 'Not me – I'm not digging one.' And the bull-calf said 'Very well – I'll dig one myself, so that I have somewhere to come and drink.'

So the bull-calf went and dug a well, and would come there to drink water; and the elephant-calf also would come to drink. And when he drank, he made the water foul. And when the bull-calf came along he exclaimed 'Well! Who's been drinking the water here?' and he went on 'Whatever has been done, it's the elephant-calf's doing.'

Next day the bull-calf came straight from his compound, not stopping till he reached the well. Then he entered a thicket and hid. Presently the elephant-calf came along and drank the water, fouling it. Then the bull-calf said 'Hey there, elephant-calf! I asked you to come and dig a well with me, and you said you wouldn't. So why have you come and drunk the water and fouled it?' And the elephant-calf answered 'Well, bull-calf, what would you like me to do?' Whereupon the bull-calf answered 'We'll meet in the clearing.' 'O.K.' said the elephant-calf 'We'll meet tomorrow in the clearing.'

The elephant-calf went off and told the elephants. He told the bush-cows. He told the lions. He told the roan antelopes. He told the West African hartebeestes. He told the Senegal hartebeestes. He told the western cobs. He told the western waterbucks. He told the hyenas. He told the gazelles.

And the bull-calf went off and told the cattle. But they said they weren't fighting elephants. He told the horse. And he said he wasn't fighting elephants. He told the donkey. And he said he wasn't fighting elephants. He told the ram. And he said he wasn't fighting elephants. He told the billy-goat. And he said he wasn't

* Cf. next tale.

132

fighting elephants. All the animals in the compound, one by one, the bull-calf went and told them. And they said they weren't fighting elephants. 'Very well' said he, 'but I'm going. The elephant-calf shan't say I was frightened, even if he kills me.' So he set off and went along.

Then along comes the dove and says 'Bull-calf, there's a general gathering, and are you going along all on your own?' 'Yes' said he, 'I'm going on my own.' 'May I get on your back?' says the dove. 'Surely, jump up' said he.

Then says the bustard 'Bull-calf, are you going all on your own to the big gathering? Aren't you frightened?' 'No' said he. 'Then let me ride on your back with the dove.' 'O.K.' said he, and up the bustard got.

Then the bustard began to call out 'Nine killed, you've killed nine and you've nine more to come.' And the dove began a noisy chant about a conquering cock-dove*.

Meanwhile, in the elephant-calf's ranks, the hyena was drumming away, chanting 'Today we'll eat intestines and stomachs, we'll gobble him up.' Then she heard the words of the bustard 'Nine killed, you've killed nine and you've nine more to come.' Then said she 'Hey, fellows, listen! There's a big party of them coming.' Whereupon she resumed her drum very vigorously. But presently it began to get slower, and she said 'Now, what did they say? "Nine killed, you've killed nine and you've nine more to come"' and presently 'We – we're among the ones to come, that's where we are. I'm not waiting to be one of those that get killed.'

By then the bull-calf was quite close, and the dove's noisy chant about the conquering cock-dove could be heard, and again the bustard said 'Nine killed, you've killed nine and you've nine more to come.'

Then the hyena threw away her drum and ran away at full speed. Then the rest of the beasts of the bush ran off after her, leaving the elephant-calf standing there on his own to await the bull-calf. 'Well' said he, when they appeared, 'so it was a dove and a bustard and the bull-calf that scattered my band of supporters.'

Said the bull-calf 'Peace be upon you, elephant-calf.' 'And upon you be peace' said the other.

* A guess. The Hausa is clearly onomatopoeic.

And the elephant-calf rushed at the bull-calf, and the bustard and the dove took off; and the bustard beat against the elephant-calf's eyes; and the dove beat against the elephant-calf's eyes. The bull-calf took a good look at the elephant-calf and applied his horns to him. And the bustard beat against the elephant-calf's eyes; and the dove beat against the elephant-calf's eyes. Then the bull-calf struck hard with his horns and they went in. This happened again and again, until the bull-calf found the elephant-calf's heart, and gored him there, and the elephant-calf fell to the ground. Then the bustard and the dove flew down, and alighting, pecked out his eyes. Then they went on their way and returned home.

After that, the hyena said to herself 'Let's pay a visit to the battlefield.' And when she got there, there lying before her was the elephant-calf, dead. 'There' said she 'What did I tell you? He who starts a fight, will find it comes back on him at the end. Let me settle down to eat some meat, and then tie some on my back and on my head, when I go home.' *Kurungus kan bera.* I ate the rat, he didn't eat me.

The Rooster and the Elephant* [II/9]

Here we go again. Here's a tale of the rooster, the billy-goat, the dog and the vulture, beasts of the home; and also the elephant, the lion, the hyena, the bush-cow, the roan antelope, the monkey, the leopard, the gazelle and the hare, all beasts of the bush.

All these met and decided to have a wrestling match. 'Let the beasts of the home make up a team and come along, and we, beasts of the bush, we'll do the same and all meet at the wrestling place.'

The beasts of the bush gathered straight away. Now, in the bush, the elephant is in charge of games; in the compound, it is the rooster.

The rooster went and got ready a gourd, and mixed red earth and water in it and filled it up. Another gourd he filled with plain

* Cf. TR. No. 22, last tale, M. No. 43, D. No. 95. and O. p. 266, line 9 et seq.

water, another with whitewash, and another with cotton thread –
all in preparation for the contest.

Well, the dog set off and was first to arrive at the place where the
contest was to be held, together with his drummer. And as he went
along, he chanted 'His head is shaven, his eyes are clear* and he
can't be overthrown.' And his praise-singer was going along singing 'Swift of glance, shaven of head, clear of eye, never overthrown.'

So the dog reached the scene, and everyone said 'Here's the
dog. Who's to be his opponent?' Says the elephant 'Let him and
the monkey wrestle.' So the dog and the monkey wrestled, and the
dog picked up the monkey and threw him to the ground. Then the
monkey excreted, and the elephant ordered the dog to pick up the
excrement and eat it. And the dog did so, and set off making for
home.

As he went he met the vulture, who asked him 'Where are you
going, dog? Is the match over?' 'No, it's not over' he answered,
'But when I got there I was matched with the monkey. I threw him,
and then he excreted. Then the elephant told me to pick it up and
eat it.' 'Is that all?' said the vulture, 'Turn back and I'll come too.'

And as the vulture went along, he too had his praises shouted –
'Behold the emir's slave, whose head never wears a cap!'

And when they reached the scene, everyone said 'Here's the
dog back again.' 'Where's the monkey?' said the elephant –
'Come on – here's the dog.' And the monkey came forward and
they started wrestling, and the dog threw the monkey, and the
monkey again excreted. Then said the elephant 'Dog, pick up that
excrement and eat it!' Then the dog looked at the vulture, and all
he said was 'Pick it up and eat it.'

Again the dog set off, making for home, and fell in with the
billy-goat. 'Where are you going, dog?' said the billy, 'is the match
over?' 'No' he answered, 'I went first, and was matched with the
monkey, and threw him, and then he excreted. The elephant told me
to pick up the excrement and eat it. I picked it up and ate it and set
off home. Then I met the vulture. I told him about it and he said to
go back. So I went back and was again matched with the monkey.

* Presuming *kanzo na talili* = 'the dried mucus from his eyelids is on the
cotton-wool'. It might also be 'whose charms are scraps from the bottom of the
pot'. Or possibly *Talili* is a female nickname.

I threw him, and then he excreted again. The elephant told me to pick it up and eat it. Then I looked at the vulture, and the vulture said "Go on, pick it up and eat it." So I picked it up and ate it.' Then said the billy 'Here, you come back with me and I'll see this fellow that makes you eat excrement.'

The billy had a drummer and an oboe player, and the drum was saying 'Great male of the goats, penis-licking lord, with a rank and fetid smell!' And at the same time the oboe was saying 'Billy, lord of the nanny-goats!' And they continued to do so till they reached the place of the contest, while the dog's drummer went on chanting 'Shaven of head, clear of eye,* never thrown, swift of glance.'

Then everyone said 'Look, here's the dog back again!' 'Where's the monkey?' said the elephant, 'Come on – here's the dog.' The monkey came forward and started wrestling with the dog. The dog threw the monkey, and the monkey excreted. Said the elephant 'Dog, eat up that excrement!' The dog looked at the billy, but he said 'Better pick it up and eat it.' So the dog picked it up and ate it, and setting off, made for home.

On his way he met the rooster, coming along with his oboe-players. And they were chanting 'One man, but two shields and a superb crest!' and again 'One man, but he has routed a thousand!' When he met the dog, he asked 'Where are you going, dog? Is the match over?' 'No' said the dog 'But I've been three times and each time I've thrown the monkey, and each time he excreted and each time they made me eat it.' 'Well, dog' said the rooster 'Now that I've come, no son of a good-for-nothing mother is going to make you eat excrement. Come on, let's go back together!' and back they went.

When they got there, everyone said 'Here's the dog back again, here's the dog!' 'Where's the monkey?' said the elephant, 'Come on – here's the dog.' The monkey came forward and started wrestling with the dog. The dog threw the monkey to the ground and the monkey excreted. Then said the elephant 'Dog, pick up that excrement and eat it up.' Then the dog looked at the rooster, and the rooster said 'Hey, dog – you there – son of a good-for-nothing – don't you eat that excrement. Come back here, and let me have a look at the fellow who told you to eat it!'

* See note on previous page.

Then said the elephant 'Now then, rooster! Your playing a risky game!' 'Hey, elephant!' said the rooster, 'of all the people gathered here you're the one I want to wrestle with.' 'Who, me?' said the elephant. 'Yes, you.' 'You're joking, rooster' said she. 'You'll see, come on!' he answered, and she came out and they joined battle.

As she rushed at him, the rooster moved to one side and used his talons, and pecked at her. Then picking up his gourd of water, he smashed it over her, saying 'Ugh, you brute! the minute we start fighting, you pour your sweat all over me.' The elephant wiped it away and said 'By God – so it is – sweat!' Says the rooster 'You go back and have it wiped off you, and then come back and we'll wrestle.' So she went and had the sweat wiped off her. The rooster stood in the middle of the arena and called '*Kikirikiyi*' until the elephant returned and they started again.

Again the rooster side-stepped, tearing at her with his talons and pecking at her. Then, taking the gourd of red ink, he smashed it against her and said 'Ugh! You've bled all over me!' The elephant wiped some off and said 'By God it is blood.' And the rooster said 'Go and get it wiped off. Then come back and we'll wrestle.' And the rooster stood in the middle of the arena and called *Kikirikiyi*

Back came the elephant and again they started wrestling. The rooster side-stepped and again tore at her with his talons and beak. Then he took the gourd of whitewash and, aiming at her head, smashed it against her and said 'Ugh! Blast you! Just a little game like this and your brain starts to come out!' adding 'Off you go and have it wiped off. Then come back and we'll wrestle.' Away went the elephant, and the rooster stood in the middle of the arena, calling *Kikiriki yi*.

Back came the elephant. They started wrestling and the rooster side-stepped and tore and pecked at her. Then he took the gourd of cotton thread and threw it all over her backside, saying 'Here! Just a little game like this and you start to come to bits. Ugh! Look – here are your intestines coming out!' The elephant drew back and saw it – and then fled, and the whole gathering dispersed. The rooster followed, but the elephant escaped. *Kungurus kan kusu.* I ate the rat, he didn't eat me.

The Hunter, the Jackal and the Lioness* [II/ ₅]

There was a hunter lived with his wife, and he used to say that if ever his wife became pregnant, he would have a lion-cub for the naming ceremony.† People would ask him what sort of wonderful child he thought he would have, but he would just reply that he had made a promise to do what he said.

Well, his wife became pregnant and in the due course the child was born. On the day before the naming ceremony, he set off, while everyone was saying how he had made a promise that, if his wife had a child, he would provide a lion-cub for the naming ceremony.

Meanwhile he had made his way into the bush, and finding two lion-cubs, he picked them up and brought them home. But while he was still on the road, he met the jackal, and the jackal said to him 'Young man, throw a present behind you, that you may come across it in front of you!' And taking one of the cubs, the young fellow gave it to the jackal, who took it.

Then, taking the other cub, he went on home, and everyone said 'He's fulfilled his promise,' and they duly had a lion-cub for the naming ceremony.

But the mother lioness got back and found her cubs gone, and she determined to be revenged on whoever had done this to her. So she turned herself into a beautiful woman.

And coming in,‡ she found a group of them playing draughts; and they said to each other 'There's a pretty woman!' And each one said that he would marry her, but the young man who had taken her cubs didn't even lift his head to look at her. Then said she 'The one that hasn't lifted his head to look at me – he's the one I'll marry.' 'Do you mean me?' said he. 'Yes' said she. 'Done' said he.

So he went and told his father. 'Right. Very good' said his father. 'Let them be married.' And so they were married, and returned to his hut. There the first thing that met her eyes was the skin of the

* See J. p. 66.   † Instead of the usual ram.
‡ For a similar incident, see II/7.

lion-cub. But she said nothing, till during the night, when they were lying down. Then said she 'Husband, what sort of skin is this?' and he answered 'It's the skin of a lion-cub. When my wife produced her child I said that I would have nothing but a lion-cub for the naming ceremony. 'Ah' said she, 'he was someone's darling. How could you take someone else's child and use him for a naming ceremony?' Then she left the subject – until he had forgotten about it. Then one day she said to him 'Husband, I want you to take me to my home, so that they may see you and so that I may get some calabashes to bring back here.' 'Certainly' said he and went and told his father, who readily gave him permission.

*As soon as it was light, he took his quiver. But she said to him 'Where are you off to with a quiver? When you get there, are you going to shoot my family?' 'Very well' said he and put it down, back in its place. Then he picked up some charms. 'What!' said she, 'when we get into the bush, are you going to make yourself invisible and vanish from me?' 'Oh no' said he and put them down, back in their place.

So away they went. But it chanced that his senior wife had risen early and gone down to the stream to get water, and she met them. Surprised, she asked 'Hullo! Where are you off to? Are you making a journey?' 'Yes' he answered. 'Where's your quiver? Where are your charms?' she asked. 'They're all at home' he answered. 'What!' she exclaimed, 'how dare you be so wickedly heedless. Here you are, off to some town you don't know, and you set off like that, without even a staff in your hand.' Then she went and got his quiver and charms and knife and axe and brought them along. 'Here you are! Take them!' she said. But his bride became angry and said 'Well! We mustn't fail to do what the senior wife says must we? As for a mere bride, like me, I'm not to be listened to am I? Are you only going to pay attention to you senior wife?'

So they set off, and they journeyed for a while till they came into some dense bush, and she brought him to the spot where he had taken the lion-cubs. Then she asked him 'Do you know this place?' 'Yes' he answered, 'it was here I got those two lion-cubs.' Whereupon she threw off her cloths, fell to the ground and rolling

* Cf. TR. No. 95 and M. No. 21; also Dupins Yakouba, A. *Les Gows ou Chasseurs du Niger*. Paris 1911, p. 191.

there, turned back into a lioness. Then she roared, and along came all the beasts of the bush.

The young man put his bow ready leaning against him, and the hyena came up and said 'Just look! Here's the fellow who ate up our children – isn't it?' and went on 'Well! What are we waiting for? Let's eat him up!' But one of them objected 'But the jackal isn't here.' Another suggested that he be sent for. So they went off to look for the jackal. When he arrived, he came up and said 'Just look – isn't this the fellow who ate up our children?' 'Yes' said the hyena, 'it's him.' 'I see' said the jackal, 'Well, just let me ask him some questions and find out what made him come and take our children.' 'All right' said the others, 'ask him!' Then said the jackal to him 'Young man, string* your words taut, fit your words to the string, send them to the speaker, and all the rest of the matter will disperse straight away.' 'Eh?' said the young man. 'Young man' said the jackal, 'listen to what I am saying. Give me your attention, for I am speaking to you.' 'Very well' answered the other, 'say on – I'm listening.' Then the jackal repeated 'String your words taut, fit your words to the string, send them to the speaker, and all the rest of the matter will disperse straight away.'

Then the young man tightened his bowstring, took out an arrow, fitted it, and drew his bow, looking at the lioness. 'This is for you' said he. The lioness began to rise and then fell with a roar. Then the rest of the beasts of the bush scattered and ran off. And drawing his knife, he slaughtered the lioness and skinned her. Then he tied up the meat and putting it on his head, went off home.

And when he got home he said 'Wife, I give thanks to God and to you. Had it not been for you, I should have died – for you and the jackal.' Then he went and took some of the meat and, returning to the bush, took it to the jackal. *Kungurus kan kusu.* I ate the rat, he didn't eat me.

---

* Cf. his similar advice in II/83.

The Hen and the Elephant [$^{II}/_{10}$]

Here's another. The hen and the elephant had a dispute. Said the elephant 'Hen, I'm a bigger eater than you.' 'No' said the hen, 'I'm a bigger eater than you, elephant.' 'O.K.' said the other, 'let's go for a walk together.'

So off they went and spent the morning grazing together. At noon the elephant looked for the hen and said to her 'Come on! Let's go and drink!' So they went to the water and drank, and then looked for some shade and lay down.

Presently the hen got up and started pecking around, while the elephant still lay there. The hen espied a tick close beside the elephant's eye and, running quickly up to it, pecked hard at it. Up leapt the elephant and went running off. 'Hen' says she 'You can't be quite normal. With all the grazing that we've done, you're still not replete, but must needs start in on my eye!' and she galloped away into the bush.

And I've heard tell that is why people say 'If an elephant hears a rooster crow, she'll run off into the bush.' *Kungurus kan kusu.*

The Hen and the Frog* [$^{II}/_{20}$]

Here's another. The hen and the frog once met. There was a storm coming and the hen said 'Frog, let's make a hut.' 'No' said the frog, 'I'm not making a hut. Here's a hole – I'm going to get into that.' 'Very well' said she and went and made herself a hut, with a bed in it. And going inside, she lit a fire. The storm broke and down came the rain, filling the hole which the frog had gone into.

Out comes the frog and hop, hop, hop up to the hen's hut. 'Hen, hen' says he, 'may I come into your hut?' 'No' said she, 'when I

* Cf. TR. No. 39.

asked you to come and help me make a hut, you refused.' 'Cat!' said he, 'Come and eat hen!' 'For shame, you scamp!' said she, but added, 'come on in!' So in he went and said 'Hen, may I warm myself by the fire?' 'No' said she, so he said 'Then I'll call the cat to you, the cat that eats little chickens.' 'Warm yourself then, you scamp' said she. And he warmed himself.

Then he said 'Hen, may I lie on your bed?' 'No' said she. 'Then I'll call the cat to you, the cat that eats little chickens' said he. 'Lie on it, you scamp' said she. And he lay on her bed.

Then said he 'Hen, hen, may I touch your waist?' 'No, you scamp' said she. But he said 'Then I'll call the cat to you, the cat that eats little chickens' and she said 'Touch it then, you scamp.' And he touched it.

Then she said to him 'Hey, you scamp, climb on to the roof of the hut and fetch us some pumpkins, to cook and eat.' 'O.K.' said he, and up he went on to the roof.

As it happened, a hawk spied him from a distance and came and transfixed him. 'Hen' said he, 'I'm being carried off.'

Then said the hen 'Take the little so-and-so away: I'd had more than enough of him – little tough-buttocks!' So, that was that – the hawk took the frog away and the hen could relax again. *Kungurus kan kusu.*

The Youth, the Maiden and the Beasts of the Bush* [$^{II}/_{57}$]

Here's another. Once there was a maiden and a young man, and the girl lived as it might be in Argungu, while her young man lived as far away as, say Bubuche. From there he would come in to the town where she lived and take her back with him.

This went on for some time, and between their two towns – just as between Argungu and Bubuche – there was bush. Now in this bush, there was a date-tree growing in the middle of a thicket, and

* Cf. TR. No. 53.

all the beasts of the bush would come and rest at its foot. At dawn they would all depart, not to return till evening. Then back they would come and spend the night there.

Well, one day, the young chap went and fetched the girl and was bringing her back. But when they reached the date-tree, she said to him 'Let's go over to that date-tree, and you climb it and shake the branches for me. For we're early today.' 'Sure, let's go' said he. So in they went and forced their way under the branches of the trees till they came to the date-tree. And the lad climbed it, and shook it and the dates came tumbling to the ground. And the girl began picking them up and filling her cloth with them. But she heard a drumming as of galloping hooves, and looking out through the branches, she saw that the beasts of the bush had arrived. Whereupon she squeezed through the undergrowth until she reached the open, and then lay low for a minute before running off at top speed. But she hadn't told the young man. The first he knew of it was seeing her in the distance, running towards her home-town.

The beasts of the bush came and settled down round the foot of the date-tree, each one quarrelling with the others about a space to lie down in. Then said the hyena 'I can smell* something.' Says the elephant 'Far-seer, you have a look.' And the monkey lifted up his head and said 'She's right, there's a man – look he's up there.' 'Really?' said the elephant. 'Yes' said the hyena.

Now the lad had a flute and he began to play, and this is what he played: 'E-elephants are gre-eat da-ancers, laa-di-daa. Li-ions are gre-eat da-ancers, laa-di-daa; roan a-antelopes are gre-eat da-ancers, laa-di-daa; bush co-ows are gre-eat da-ancers laa-di-daa; gira-affes are gre-eat da-ancers laa-di-daa; le-eopards are gre-eat da-ancers laa-di-daa.' Thus he played to all the beasts of the bush.

Says the elephant 'We'll leave the hedgehog to watch him, while we dance, away from here† and back again.' And they danced away as far as Bubuche is from here.

Presently the hedgehog said 'Man, play for me too a little.' So he began 'Awa-ay from here before the big chaps get back; awa-ay awa-ay before the big chaps get back' and soon the hedgehog too was carried away with her dancing, rattling her quills. But when

* Presuming that *wayi* is hyena-ese for *wari*.
† *Wowan* eludes me but the general sense seems clear.

she heard the big fellows coming back, she ran quickly back and lay down on guard. But they would stop and call from where they were 'Man, play for us.' So he started fluting again: 'E-elephants are gre-eat da-ancers, laa-di-daa' and so on right through* all the beasts of the bush, playing the tune for each one.

And away they all went again dancing for all they were worth. They got about as far off as from here to Katami, and the hedgehog said 'Man, play for me a little.' So he played again 'Awa-ay from here before the big chaps get back.' Off she went with a rattle of quills and danced away about as far as from here to Bubuche. Then the lad climbed down and ran off fast and so escaped.† Whereupon back came the hedgehog and lay down on guard.

And the elephant and the others came back and stood some way off, saying 'Man, play for us.' No answer. So they came closer and repeated 'Man, play for us.' No answer. So they came right under the date-tree, and the elephant said 'Far-seer, take a look.' The monkey looked and said 'Oh, there's no one there.' Says the elephant 'Hey, hedgehog, where did you go off to?' 'Nowhere' says she, 'why, ever since you went off, I've been here. I haven't been anywhere.' Then the elephant picked up the hedgehog and threw her against the tree and she burst. That's all. *Kungurus kan kusu.*

———————

The Man, the Crocodile and the Jackal‡ [II/84]

There was once a man on journey, walking along. Now the path he was following was through water in one place, and travellers had to pass through this water. But in it there was a crocodile, so that anyone who came by was in some danger. Well this man passed through the water and put his load down at the edge of it; and stepping back into it began to wash. Whereupon the crocodile crept up and seized hold of the man. Then began a tug-of-war,

* The Hausa has the mixture as before, with the addition of the hyena.
† For a similar escape see III/117.
‡ Cf. III/109.

ending with the man's pulling the crocodile out of the water, or at least his head was out.

This was their situation when along comes Malam dan Ba'ura (the jackal) to have a drink. Says he to the man 'Hey, man, is all well?' 'That's a stupid question!' said the man. 'How can all be well, when a crocodile is holding my leg.' 'Hm' said the jackal, 'Crocodile – and you too, man – come before me and I'll judge your case.' And as he said this, he moved a little away from the water. The crocodile released the man and they both came out and close to the jackal. But the jackal mistrusted this and moved away again, increasing his distance from them. 'O.K., stop there' said he, 'And, you, man, strip some bark off a *kalgo*, and bring it.' The man went and did as he was told, obediently. Whereupon the jackal launched an angry tirade at the man, saying 'There you are, entering other people's homes and treading on them – why shouldn't he arrest you? So now, man, you can bring that bark that you've got; and you, crocodile, you stand quietly and let the man put the bark on your body.' 'O.K.' said the crocodile, and the man tied him up.

Then said the jackal to the man 'Go on, man, pick him up and take him off back to your town; or don't they eat meat in your compound? He's a plague that you've rid us of today; for we too, when we come to drink, have been in fear of him, but now you've freed us from him. Pick him up and take him home!' So the man bent, picked up the crocodile, and went off home. *Kungurus kan kusu.*

The Farmer, the Snake and the Heron* [III/]₇

There was once a man hoeing away on his farm, when along came some people chasing a snake, meaning to kill it. And the snake came up to the farmer.

Says the snake 'Farmer, please hide me.' 'Where shall I hide you?'

* LND (p. 56) has a bowdlerised (it would seem) version of this, under the heading 'Ingratitude'. It substitutes weaver for farmer and mouth for anus (perhaps because it was meant as a school reader). See also J. p. 48. Cf. M. No. 10. Also D. Nos. 103, 104.

said the farmer, and the snake said 'All I ask is that you save my life.' The farmer couldn't think where to put the snake, and at last bent down and opened his anus, and the snake entered.

Presently the snake's pursuers arrived and said to the farmer 'Hey, there! Where's the snake we were chasing and intend to kill? As we followed him, he came in your direction.' Says the farmer 'I haven't seen him.' And the people went back again.

Then the farmer said to the snake 'Righto – come out now. They've gone.' 'Oh no' said the snake, 'I've got me a home.' And there was the farmer, with his stomach all swollen, for all the world like a pregnant woman!

And the farmer set off, and presently, as he passed, he saw a heron. They put their heads together and whispered, and the heron said to the farmer 'Go and excrete. Then, when you have finished, move forward a little, but don't get up. Stay squatting, with your head down and your buttocks up, until I come.'

So the man went off and did just exactly as the heron had told him, everything. And the snake put out his head and began to catch flies. Then the heron struck and seized the snake's head. Then he pulled and he pulled until he had got him out, and the man tumbled over. And the heron finished off the snake with his beak.

The man rose and went over to the heron. 'Heron' says he 'You've got the snake out for me, now please give me some medicine to drink, for the poison where he was lying.'

Says the heron 'Go and find yourself some white fowls, six of them. Cook them and eat them – they are the medicine.' 'Oho' said the man, 'White fowl? But that's you' and he grabbed the heron and tied it up and went off home. There he took him into a hut and hung him up, the heron lamenting the while.

Then the man's wife said 'Oh, husband! The bird did you a kindness. He saved your life, by getting the trouble out of your stomach for you. And now you seize him and say that you are going to slaughter him!'

So the man's wife loosed the heron, but as he was going out, he pecked out one of her eyes. And so passed out and went his way. That's all. For so it always has been – if you see the dust [of a fight] rising, you will know that a kindness is being repaid! That's all. That story's finished.

The Land-Monitor and the Scorpion [^{III}/$_{120}$]

The land-monitor and the scorpion met and joined forces; and they set off to commit robbery on the road. The land-monitor had as his drummer the millipede, while the scorpion had the dauber-wasp. So they went along and took up their positions beside the road.

Presently along came some traders. The millipede started to drum her song 'He-man, Jatau, red of eye (?), whose associate is the red sorrel.' While she was doing that, the monitor said 'That sort of drumming will soon make people tremble.'

Then the monitor went up to the trader who was at the head, and struck him hard with his tail three times. And the trader never even knew he was being hit!

Whereupon the scorpion said 'Ha, monitor! So your size is useless is it!' Then the wasp began drumming out the scorpion's song 'Mighty one, wicked poison, your only antidote is to get out of your way.'

And the scorpion went up to the same man, the leading trader, and stung him. At which he gave a yell, and the rest of the people began flinging down their loads and running away.

The scorpion, the monitor and their drummers helped themselves to the wealth and returned home. And when they got there, they settled down to enjoying their possessions. That's all. *Kungurus kan kusu.* I ate the rat, he didn't eat me.

The Husband, his Wife and the Beasts* [^{III}/$_{125}$]

There was once a husband and wife, and for as long as they had been married, she had never been sated with meat. Says she 'Husband, when will you give me enough meat to eat and be satisfied –

* Cf. next tale, I/94, etc., etc.

enough to leave some over, to feed my eyes on too?' And he answered 'I must seek for some – for he who seeks will find.'

Then he got to his feet and went to a dung-beetle and said 'Dung-beetle, won't you come to my compound and spend the day with us, chatting about things in general?' The dung-beetle answered 'Me come to your compound and spend the day there – doesn't the rooster wander in there?' 'Oh no' said the man, 'the rooster doesn't come into my compound.' And the dung-beetle said 'If the rooster doesn't come, I'll come and spend the day with you.'

The man went on from the dung-beetle to the rooster. Says he 'Rooster, won't you come to my compound and spend the day with us – just you and me – chatting about things in general?' Says the rooster 'Well, man, I'm not refusing to come to your compound, but I fancy the cat tends to wander into your compound.' 'Oh no, rooster' said the man, 'The cat doesn't come into my compound.' 'Then I'll come' said the rooster. 'O.K.' said the man.

And he passed on and went to the cat. 'Cat' said the man, 'when will your stroll take you in my direction?' 'Well, man' said the cat, 'it's fearful of coming to your compound that I am, for I fear that if I go there, I'll meet the dog – and then we might start an unfortunate scene in your compound. For the dog is my great-great grandfather's slave; and all of us cats, whenever we see a dog, spit out water on to a rope, and tie him up; for he is our slave, by inherited right.' So the man said 'The dog doesn't come to my compound.' 'O.K.' said the cat, 'I'll come to your compound, and we'll spend the day, talking about things in general.'

From there the man passed on to the dog. 'Dog' said he, 'Won't you come to my compound, so we can have a good, long chat?' But the dog answered 'Oh no, man, I can't come to your house at night. I might meet the hyena, and she'll kill me.' 'All right, dog' said the man, 'go in the daytime, when eye sees eye.' 'Very well, man' said the dog, 'then I'll come, and we'll spend some days together.' 'Good dog' said the man, 'if you'll do that for me, I shall be very pleased.' 'I will, man' said the dog.

Then the man passed on and went to the hyena, and said 'Hyena, won't you come and spend the day with me, so we can discuss things in general?' 'Is that all, man?' asked the hyena. 'Yes' said the man. 'But, man' she objected, 'I suppose the leopard doesn't come to your compound?' 'No' said the man, 'the leopard doesn't come to my compound.' 'Very well then' said the hyena.

On went the man, and so to the leopard. Said he 'Leopard, I sit all alone with no one to talk to during the day. Won't you come and spend the day with me and chat about things in general?' But the leopard answered 'I'm frightened, man, that the lion might come to your place.' 'What a terrible thought!' said the man, 'Leopard, if the lion were in the habit of coming to my compound, of course I shouldn't have invited you.' 'O.K.' said the other, 'off you go. I'll be coming.'

And the man went on and came to the lion and said 'Mighty one of the bush, there you are – I should be very glad if you would come and take to spending the day in my compound, so that we may discuss things in general.' Says the lion 'Very well, I'll start coming to your compound for the day, so that we may discuss things in general.' Then the man went home.

On the day the dung-beetle arrived, he stuck his spear in the ground and said 'Here I am, man, for us to spend the day together.' And the man gave the dung-beetle a warm welcome.

Next came the rooster. Up he comes and makes formal greeting, and the man replies. 'Man' said the rooster, 'whose is this spear?' 'The dung-beetle' said the man. 'the spear belongs to him.' 'And where is he?' asked the other. 'Just there in the grass.' And the rooster went into the grass, found the dung-beetle, killed him and ate him up.

Then the rooster lay down, put his head under his wing and began to scratch himself. Presently up comes the cat and makes formal greeting. 'Welcome' says the man. 'Who stuck his spear here?' asked the cat. 'It's the dung-beetle's spear' answered the man, 'But the rooster killed him and ate him up.' 'And where is the rooster?' asked the cat. 'The rooster is in the grass.' And the cat went in and found the rooster and seizing his head, bit it off.

Then he lay down and was eating the rooster, when up comes the dog and greets the man formally. 'Welcome, dog' said the man. 'Whose is the spear?' asked the dog. 'It's the dung-beetle's spear' said the man, 'but the rooster ate him up; and the rooster too has been eaten up by the cat.' 'Man' said the dog, 'where's the cat?' 'The cat's in the grass.' Then the dog went into the grass and found the cat eating the rooster, and the dog sprang and caught the cat's throat and bit through it.

He lay down and was eating the cat, when up comes the hyena. She made formal greeting. 'Ah' said the man, 'Welcome, hyena.' 'Who stuck the spear here?' asked the hyena, and the man answered 'It's the dung-beetle's spear, but the rooster ate him up; and the rooster was eaten up by the cat; and the cat was eaten up by the dog.' 'Where's the dog? asked the hyena. And the man answered 'The dog's just there in the grass.' And there he was lying there, eating the cat. Then the hyena sprang, seized the dog's neck and killed him; then lay down and began eating him.

Next up came the leopard. 'Peace be upon you, man' she said, 'Who stuck this spear here?', and the man answered 'It's the dung-beetle's spear, but the rooster ate him up; and the rooster was eaten up by the cat; and the cat was eaten up by the dog; and the dog's been eaten up by the hyena.' Says the leopard 'Man, where's the hyena?' 'There's the hyena in the grass' said the man. Then the leopard went into the grass, found the hyena and killed her.

She was lying there eating the hyena, when up comes the lion and makes formal greeting. The man welcomed the lion, and the lion said 'Who stuck that spear there?' It's the dung-beetle's spear' answered the man, 'but the rooster killed him; and the rooster was killed by the cat; and the cat was killed by the dog; and the dog was killed by the hyena; and she was killed by the leopard.' Then the lion asked 'Man, where's the leopard?' And he answered 'She's there in the grass.'

Then the lion went into the grass, grabbed the leopard and began to wrestle with her. And the man took a club, came up to them and aimed at the lion's head and fetched him a wallop; and at the leopard's, and fetched her one, saying as he did so 'For shame, great leaders! They don't heed requests to stop, they just do what they feel like! For shame! Be patient! Desist! Lion! Leopard! Give over, both of you!' And all the while he was bashing them on the head, saying 'Great leaders, they don't heed requests to stop! Lion, desist! Leopard, desist!' And finally the man killed both the lion and the leopard.

Now the leopard hadn't finished eating the hyena when the lion came; nor had the hyena finished eating the dog when the leopard came; nor had the dog finished eating the cat when the hyena came;

nor had the cat finished eating the rooster when the dog came; nor had the rooster finished eating the dung-beetle when the cat came.

Then the man called his wife, and they set to, carrying the meat and taking it to the woman's prepared slab* and collecting it there. And even before they got there, the man's wife was already sated with meat,† and all she could do was gaze at it. And they dried it. Says she to her husband 'Today, I have had my fill of meat, and, see, all I can do is gaze at it, and I've put some to dry in the sun.' 'Have I done what you wanted?' asked the man. 'Yes, you certainly have, husband' she answered.

So that was that, the man settled down again with his wife, and she never troubled him with the matter again. *Kungurus kan kusu.* I ate the rat, not the rat me.

———————

A Variant‡ [^{III}/145]

This is about a wife and her husband; she had fever and said to her husband 'Could you get meat for me – enough to give me a satisfying feed?' 'Surely I can' he answered.

So he gave an invitation to the beasts of the bush. First he told the dung-beetle and he said 'I suppose you haven't told the rooster?' And he went and told the rooster, and the rooster said 'I suppose you haven't told the cat?' He went and told the cat, and the cat said 'No dog, I hope?' He went and told the dog, and he said 'No, hyena, I presume?' He went and told the hyena, and she said 'Without the leopard, I trust?' He went and told the leopard, and the leopard said 'Without the lion?' Then he went and told the lion. And lastly he fetched his stick.

On the day of the gathering, the dung-beetle stuck his spear in the ground, and when the rooster came, he asked 'Whose is the spear?' He was told it was the dung-beetle's, and going after him, he ate him up.

* Specially pounded floor.
† Reading *ga shi* for *gashi*, and inserting a comma before it.
‡ Cf. last tale, I/6, etc.

The cat came, and asked 'Whose is the spear?' and was told it was the dung-beetle's. 'Where's the dung-beetle?' 'The rooster has eaten him up.' 'Where's the rooster?' 'There he is.' And the cat went after the rooster and ate him up.

Along comes the dog. Says he 'Whose is the spear?' and is told it's the dung-beetle's. 'Where's the dung-beetle?' 'The rooster's eaten him up.' 'Where's the rooster?' 'The cat's eaten him up.' 'Where's the cat?' He was pointed out, and the dog ate him up.

The hyena came, and asked 'Whose is the spear?' 'The dung-beetle's.' 'Where's the dung-beetle?' 'The rooster's eaten him up.' 'Where's the rooster?' 'The cat's eaten him up.' 'Where's the cat?' 'The dog's eaten him up.' 'Where's the dog' and she was told. Whereupon the hyena ate up the dog.

The leopard came and said 'Whose is the spear?' 'The dung-beetle's.' 'Where's the dung-beetle?' 'The rooster's eaten him up.' 'Where's the rooster?' 'The cat's eaten him up.' 'Where's the cat?' 'The dog's eaten him up.' 'Where's the dog?' 'The hyena's eaten him up.' 'Where's the hyena?', and, being told, the leopard killed her and ate her up.

The lion came along and asked 'Whose is the spear?' 'The dung-beetle's.' 'Where's the dung-beetle?' 'The rooster ate him up.' 'Where's the rooster?' 'The cat ate him up.' 'Where's the cat?' 'The dog ate him up.' 'Where's the dog?' 'The hyena ate him up.' 'Where's the hyena?' 'The leopard ate her up.' 'Where's the leopard?' 'There she is – in the thatching-grass.'

The man took his stick, and as the lion and leopard fought, he lifted it and began beating them saying 'Leave off, lion! Leave off, leopard! These great ones pay no heed to my "Leave off!"' and he killed them, both of them. The he gave his wife the lion, and took the leopard for himself. That's all.

The Nile Perch ('Water Elephant'), the Elephant ('Land Elephant') and the Big One of the Bush* [^{III}/$_{149}$]

The wart-hog told the Nile perch to come and help him clear a farm next day. He said the same to the elephant, but for the day after.

So next day the Nile perch came along and did her share of the work. And on the next day, the wart-hog said to the elephant 'Off you go and do your share of the work. See, I've done mine.' So the elephant went off and did her share.

The first rain fell and it was time to sow. Says he to the Nile perch 'You sow your bit today, and tomorrow I'll do mine,' and she did so. Next day he told the elephant 'Off you go and sow your bit. I've done mine.' And she did so.

When the corn was big enough to hoe, he told the Nile perch to go off and do her share of the hoeing one day, and that he would do his next day. Then he went along and said to the elephant 'Come and do your share of the hoeing. I've done mine.'

The corn ripened and he said to the Nile perch 'You go and cut down your share today.' And she went and did so. Next day he said to the elephant 'You go and cut down your share. I've done mine.' Next day he said to the Nile perch 'Go and gather your corn together; and the day after tomorrow I'll come and collect mine.' But two days later, he said to the elephant 'Go and gather your corn together. I've gathered mine.'

Two more days passed, and on the third day he said to the elephant that she should come and collect her corn.† And so she gathered all her corn in one place. Another night passed, and on the next day, he said to the Nile perch 'Come along tomorrow and we'll divide the corn.' And he said exactly the same to the elephant.

The Nile perch arrived first. Then came the elephant, and when she found the former by the corn, she thought it was a thief. The

* Cf. I/20. The wart-hog is usually *mugun dawa*, or 'bad one of the bush'. *Manyan dawa* is usually an honorific for the lion.

† This seems redundant, and is probably a slip.

wart-hog (big-one-of-the-bush) hid there, watching them fighting. And the elephant killed – didn't you, elephant? – the Nile perch, and when she had killed her, out came the wart-hog. Says the elephant 'I found a thief at our corn.' 'Did you drive her away?' he asked. 'I didn't drive her away – I killed her' she replied. And so the wart-hog and the elephant divided the corn, and each one filled its corn-bin.

PART II

CARICATURES

———

Ethnic and other stereotypes, as seen through Hausa
eyes.

I

THE MAGUJE*

This is the Hausa who is still pagan, living mainly in communities in Kano and Katsina provinces. In Edgar's day, and before, such must have been much more plentiful. The origin of the word is probably the Arabic *majūs* (fire-worshipper, Zoroastrian). The normal word for a pagan is *arne* (plural *arna*). Trimingham† suggests that the use of the word *Bamaguje* was to find a formula by which irreconcilable Hausa pagans could be included in the administration, and pay tax – rather than be treated as enemies to be warred upon. In TATS there is often some confusion in the use of the two terms. It is, however, noteworthy that the Maguje occurs frequently and in the role of a shrewd though simple countryman, whose proceedings often show up the quackery and hypocrisy of the malam. He is especially good at word play (*karin magana*).

See also J. H. Greenberg's *Influence of Islam on a Sudanese Religion* (American Linguistic Society Monograph No. 10, 1946).

———

The Butchers‡ [^{I}/$_{12}$]

One day a Maguje set out to market, first lifting his son and putting him on a pack-ox.

He drove him along till he came to the gate of the town. There he stopped and went into the market with his ox. The butchers called to him 'Hey – you with the ox – stop!' and the Maguje stopped. Said the butchers 'Say, is that ox for sale?' and he answered 'It's for sale.' Whereupon they bought it, he agreeing to the price. And the butchers took hold of the ox.

Then said the Maguje 'Stop a minute while I lift my son off,' but they said 'Oh no, we bought it including the son.' 'All right, all

* Hausa *Bamaguje*, plural *Maguzawa*. † *Islam in West Africa*, 1965, p. 39.
‡ Cf. III/73.

right, off you go!' says he, and the butchers led off the ox with the Maguje's son on top of it. Thus they swindled him of his son.

The Maguje went off home. Nor did he return again till a year had gone by. Then, at length, he visited the town again.

He entered the town and came to the market. As he stood there, he noticed that an ox had been slaughtered and he called to the butchers 'I want the head.' When they had finished slaughtering it, they said to the Maguje 'Hi there! Here's the ox head you asked for' and he answered the butchers 'No, no – I didn't say I wanted an *ox* head, but the head of a man.' Said the butchers 'There's a madman for you! Where've you ever seen them selling a man's head?' And the Maguje, in his turn, answered 'Here are madmen for you! Where've you ever seen an ox sold including its rider?'

Their argument grew, and they took it to the judge. The judge asked 'What has happened?' and the butchers replied 'Well, this Maguje came and found that we'd slaughtered an ox. He asked us to give him the head. And when we had finished slaughtering, he was given the head, but he said "No, no – I didn't say I wanted an *ox* head, but the head of a man".'

And the judge said 'Maguje, where have you ever seen them selling a man's head?' and the Maguje said to the judge 'Where've you ever seen an ox sold including its rider?'

Then the judge said to the butchers 'Give him his son! But he must release your lad to you!' Then the butchers gave the Maguje his son, and he gave the butchers their son.*

And he went home, but from that day he never returned to that town.

The Malam [^{I}/₁₉]

One day a malam came to the home of a Maguje, seeking alms. Said the Maguje to the malam 'Hey, malam, you're too fond of being useless. You're always coming around begging for alms and

* ? a *lapsus calami* for lad (i.e. apprentice) though in fact, it is nowhere actually said that the Maguje had taken him.

never do any work. Well – come on, I'll ask you a lesson. If you perceive the meaning of it, then I'll give you alms. But if not, I'll never give you any again.'

And the malam answered 'O.K., tell it me then!' And the Maguje said 'When the hot weather before the rains comes, you put down your satchel (*gafaka*) and take up your *gafaga*, but when the dry season comes again, you put down your *gafaga*, and take up your satchel (*gafaka*).' Says the malam 'I don't know that sort of lesson. What's *gafaga*? What's *gafaka*?' And the Maguje answered 'As for *gafaga*, well – take "broad-bladed hoe" (*galma*) and "hoe" (*fartanya*) and also "axe" (*gatari*). There you are, there are the farming tools, I've said them. As for *gafaka* – it's what you put your book in. Call yourself a malam – you know nothing! Off with you, to work in the fields and cease begging!'

The Malam and the Maguje [$^{\mathrm{I}}/_{43}$]

It is said that it was once a time of hunger and a certain malam set out on a journey. And during his journey, he stopped at the house of a Maguje. Said the Maguje 'Welcome, malam' and they exchanged greetings. And his host slaughtered a dog and made soup from it; and adding *tuwo*, he brought it to the malam.

The malam was eating the *tuwo*, when the Maguje came up and sat down close to him. Said he 'Malam, don't eat my dog (*kada ka ci kàrénà*)' and the malam answered 'Oh no, indeed I don't despise it', misunderstanding him.* And the Maguje said several times 'Malam, don't eat my dog!' and each time the malam answered as before.

So it came as a surprise to him to learn that he had been eating dog, and when he had finished his *tuwo* and the other said to him 'Malam, you've eaten dog', he spat. But he had already eaten the dog meat.

---

* Thinking he had said ' . . . *ci, kà rĕnà*'.

The Malam [^{I}/₄₉]

A Maguje and a malam were once wrestling. The pagan threw the malam. But when the malam found himself underneath, getting the worst of it, he spat in the pagan's eye. The pagan became blind. Whereupon he let the malam get up and he went off home. Then the pagan went off to seek a cure, and – after some difficulty – recovered.

Time passed and the pagan happened to see a mate of his also wrestling with a malam. Then he called out 'Have you thrown that malam?' 'Yes' says the other, 'I've thrown him.' 'Then' says the first, 'Be careful of what he's got in his mouth – don't let him spit on you! He did it to me and I lost the use of my eyes.' So the other got up, and the first pagan went on 'From today, don't have any more fights with malams!'

———

The Maguje and the Jackal* [^{III}/₃]

Here's another tale. A Maguje was carrying some chickens and walking along. A jackal saw him and ran off and went in front of him and lay down on the road.

Up comes the Maguje and says 'Well I'll be—whatever killed this beast?' And, catching hold of the jackal's foot, he turned it over, but couldn't see any wound on its body, nor had it swelled at all. 'Well, well' said the Maguje, 'but I must hurry along,' and on he went, leaving the jackal.

Up gets the jackal, cuts across the bush at full gallop and again reaches the road. He got on to it and lay down, opening his jaws.

Presently up comes the Maguje 'Oh-oh!' says he, 'whatever can be killing these beasts like this?' He went on 'Just let me put my

* See J. p. 28. Cf. Uncle Remus, No. XV, Mr. Fox Goes A-Hunting. Also III/58.

chickens down here, and go back for that other one – then I'll have the both, and that'll be *some* meat.'

Off went the Maguje, but when he got there – no jackal! And by the time he got back again, the jackal had vanished, taking his chickens, off into the bush. So when the Maguje got there, he couldn't find either his chickens, or the jackal.

Says he 'Today I've caught bandicoots like Baidu.'† And he returned, walking back along the road till he reached his home. That's all for that story.

His Son and the Owner of the Ox [^{I}/$_{1/80}$]

There was once a Maguje and his son, whom he was training in the ways of the world.

One day they stole an ox, and he and the boy slaughtered it. They hid the meat away, eating it as they needed it. The son was outside the compound one day with a piece of cornstalk, swotting grasshoppers and catching them, when the owner of the ox came by, searching for it in the town. He reached where the boy was catching grasshoppers beside the fence of his compound, and he stopped.

'Hey, lad!' said he. 'Yes' said the boy. 'Have you by any chance seen an ox around here' and he described it. 'Yes' said the boy 'That's the one we stole the other day and slaughtered.' It happened that his father, inside the compound, heard them, and, pretending that it was his son's name called out 'Here! Change!' 'Yes' says the boy. Now he had called him 'Change' meaning that he should alter what he had said, so that they shouldn't be found out. His son twigged what he meant and when his father said to him 'Who did I hear you talking with there outside?', he answered 'I'm talking to a madman. He says, he imagines that we have slaughtered an ox and eaten it! One who ate an ox one day, would he turn to and catch grasshoppers the next?!' Then the man went on, saying to himself 'That boy knew nothing of it after all.'

† See I/124.

When his son entered the compound, his father said to him 'Well, now you see that the sort of tricky ways I've been trying to teach you and you've been refusing to learn – now they've come in useful!'

———————

Who Married his own Daughter [I/ 100]

There was once a Maguje who lived with his wife away on their farm, and the wife had a daughter.

Time passed and the girl grew up and reached the age of marriage. At this time her mother died, leaving the girl. So there they were, the Maguje and his daughter. Then one day he set off and went to the compound of a leading malam. And he asked him, saying 'Malam, imagine that you had a mare, and the mare had a daughter, and the daughter was old enough to ride. Now, if your mare died, where would you put your saddle?' The malam answered 'On the daughter of course.' So the pagan went off and married his daughter.

They lived thus for a while on their farm, when news reached the judge that the Maguje had committed a great crime and married his own daughter. Then he ordered his guards to arrest him and bring him before him. Then the judge asked the Maguje, saying 'Well – what is the cause of your breaking the law and marrying your own daughter?' And the pagan answered 'Oh, no! I don't lay my own eggs, if there's no rooster. I didn't marry my daughter lightly without thought. First I asked a leading malam, and he said that it would be good to go and do it. Then I did it.' The judge asked the Maguje 'What malam is that?' and the Maguje pointed out his compound.

So the malam was sent for. The judge said to him 'Why did you tell the Maguje that he might marry his daughter?' 'I didn't say so' said the malam. 'Pardon me, malam, but you did' said the Maguje. 'When I came to your home and asked you, saying that if you had a mare and she had a daughter and the daughter was old enough to ride, if the mare died, where would you put your saddle. And what did you say to me?' 'I said to put the saddle on the daughter' said the malam, and the Maguje said to the judge 'There! That's my excuse.' Then the judge said to them 'You are both right. But you, pagan, you didn't tell the malam that it was your wife that had died and left a daughter, you said it was a mare. And you, malam, you didn't perceive the meaning of his words, not enquiring of him whether it was a mare or a human being he spoke of.' He went on 'You may get up and go now, but you, Maguje, you must divorce your daughter and marry her to someone else.' 'Right' said the pagan 'I understand. I'll do it – and I won't commit this offence again.'

———

A Variant* [^{I}/$_{150}$]

Here's a tale of a Maguje who went to the judge and said to him 'If a man has a mare, and the mare has a daughter, and the mother dies, leaving the daugher – if the daughter is of age to take a saddle, should he saddle her, or not?' Then the judge said 'She may be saddled.' Three times the Maguje asked his question and three times the judge gave him the same answer.

Then the Maguje returned home, and taking his daughter, put her in his hut and slept with her. Later she became pregnant.

News of this reached the chief of the town, and the Maguje was summoned before the judge and asked 'For what reason have you done this wicked thing?' 'I've done nothing wicked' said the Maguje 'For I came to the judge on such-and-such a date, at such-and-such a time, and I asked him whether, if a man has a mare, and she has a daughter, and the mother dies, and the daughter is old enough to saddle, he may saddle her. And the judge said that he

* Cf. last tale.

may. I asked him three times and he gave me the same answer. So I went home and took her into my hut.'

Then the judge drove him out, saying 'Get away out of here, you good-for-nothing fellow!'

The Trader and the Youth* [$^I/_{162}$]

A trader once said to a lad 'I want you to come with me to Gwanja. When we get back, you'll get something to get† meat with.' 'Righto' said the youth and off they went. When they got back, the trader bought a knife for a hundred cowries (½d.) and gave it to the boy. The boy took the knife and began to cry. Then he went to the judge and complained.

The trader was sent for and he was asked what had passed between him and the lad. And the trader told exactly what had been said. Then the judge was at a loss how to give judgement.

Just then they saw a Maguje and called him in. Says he to the judge 'What's the matter with you that you're all gathered together thus?' 'We were hearing a case' said the judge' 'but we've found it impossible to adjudicate between this trader and the boy here.' So the Maguje heard both their stories.

Then the Maguje took out two hundred cowries and told them to go and buy him a knife and bring it to him with some meat. Then, taking up the knife he put it on the meat, and said to the knife 'Eat the meat.' The knife showed no sign of doing so.

Next the Maguje said to the judge 'Only teeth can eat meat' and again 'Have the teeth in the boy's mouth counted and their value estimated. Then let the trader pay the boy.' And that concluded the case.

---

* Cf. I/98.

† Lit. to eat (the verb *ci* has innumerable idiomatic uses in Hausa).

The Quarreller [III/ 34]

In the days of old there was a Maguje lived in the land of Kano who kept a dog. And he went to market and bought a goat, and when he got back he said 'This goat belongs to the dog. I bought her for him, so that he may get a regular supply of milk.' And so the goat suckled the dog for a period during which she produced four kids.

Then the dog died, leaving the goat and her four kids, five in all.

Off goes the Maguje and makes his way to a malam. 'Malam' says he, 'I had a dog, and I went and bought a goat for him; now the goat has produced four kids, which makes five including her. But now the dog has died. Who inherits from the dog?'

Says the malam 'Go to the market and sit down. Then when you see two men quarrelling, and one adjures the other in the name of Allah and His Prophet, and the other refuses – that's the man you must call, and give him the goats. For he is a dog.' 'I see' said the Maguje.

And he went off to market and seated himself there.

Presently as he sat, two people started to quarrel. Others came and separated them, saying 'For God's sake, and for the sake of His Messenger, stop quarrelling, for it is profitless.' And one of them said 'I abjure quarrelling, for the sake of God and of His Messenger. I forbear.' But the other one went on with his shouting and abusing.

Up gets the Maguje saying 'For shame, friend! Will you not forbear?' and he went on 'Come with me, for your brother has died. Come along so that we may give you your inheritance.'

And the Maguje drew the man away, and took him and showed him the goats, five of them. 'These are the goats of your deceased brother' said he. But the man answered him 'It's a lie. These aren't my brother's goats, for they are more than these.'

Again the Maguje took the fellow by the hand, and this time took him to the malam. Says he 'Malam, you see this man. I showed him the goats, the five of them, but he says it's not true; they aren't his brother's goats.' 'Let me question him, Maguje' said the malam.

'My boy' said he turning to the other, 'Tell me now – which

of your brothers has died?' The other thought for a moment and then said 'None of them, malam. There isn't one of my brothers that has died.'

And the malam said 'Very well. It is no great matter. A dog died and the goats were his. The Maguje asked me who should inherit from the dog. Then I told him to go to the market and sit there; and if he saw people quarrelling, when someone came up and adjured them by Allah and His Messenger, if one of the two showed forbearance and the other refused to do so – then the latter should inherit from the dog; for he is the same as a dog. If they begin a fight, and are asked to desist in the name of Allah and His Messenger, whichever refuses to, is related to the dog, and in the next world shall have the same dwelling.'

And so the man expressed repentance and promised not to err thus again, and went his way. That's all. This with peace.

His Accusers* [III/ 53]

One day a Maguje set off and as he walked along, saw a farm of sugar-cane, with the farmer in it. The Maguje went over to him, bought some sugar-cane and began chewing it. Presently he met a woman with a baby on her back, of an age almost to cease being carried. The child began to hold his hand out to the Maguje. Says the latter 'Young fellow, what do you want?' His mother answered the Maguje 'He wants you to break a section (*gaba*) off for him.' At which the Maguje took hold of the boy's arm and broke the joint (*gaba*). Then on he went, chewing his sugar-cane. And the young mother followed him.

As he walked along he met a malam on a mare, which had recently given birth to a foal. The foal was following her along. Says the malam 'Hey you walking there, hit the foal along for me.' The Maguje took his axe and struck the foal, which gave one leap and fell to the ground. Then the man on the mare also began to follow the Maguje.

* Cf. next tale.

On walked the Maguje and presently saw a lot of people hoeing; and an old woman by a cooking-fire with a large pot on it. The Maguje went up to them, to light his smoke at the fire. And the men hoeing called to him 'When you get there push up* the fire for the old woman (*or* push the fire on to the old woman).' The Maguje lit his pipe from an ember, and then picked up the old old woman and pushed her into the fire. Then on he went again. And her companions began to follow him.

The Maguje reached a town and found himself a lodging where he put up. There they took him to the hut in which there were chickens. Says he to the people there 'I am on my way to' and he named the town, 'What time must I start to reach that town?' 'When the cock crows you must start'† they said. 'Right' said he. Night fell and the Maguje went into the hut and to sleep.

Before dawn the cock started to crow. Up gets the Maguje and seized the cock and wrung its neck, and departed – with the cock. Its owners followed the Maguje to the next town, where there was a judge. And they took a complaint against the Maguje before the judge.

The woman with the child comes along, and the judge asks the Maguje 'How did you get involved with this woman, so that you even broke the joint of her son's arm?' 'Well, judge' answered the Maguje, 'I had a good reason.' 'And that is just what I want to hear' said the judge.

'Very well' said the Maguje. 'I was chewing sugar-cane, when I met her. The boy held his arm out to me. Then, as I was passing, his mother said "You there! The boy wants you to break off a section (*or* break a joint) for him." So, judge, I broke the joint for him. For she never said "section (joint) *of sugar-cane*".' 'Very well' said the judge to the Maguje, 'I have heard your side of it.'

Then he asked the woman 'Is that how it was? Did you tell him to break off a section (joint)?' 'Yes' says the woman, and the judge continued 'The Maguje is more accurate than you. It was you caused your son's arm joint to be broken. Get up and be off with you, for you have brought a baseless complaint.'

Next the judge had the malam with the mare called. 'Here I am, learned sir' says the malam. 'Come forward and give your version of

* I.e. 'push the smouldering ends into the centre to burn.'
† Or, 'you must cause him to rise'.

what passed between you and the Maguje' said the judge. And the malam gave it. 'Very well, malam, I've heard your account' said the judge. 'Remains the Maguje's.'

And he turned to the Maguje and asked him, in his turn, for his. 'Surely, learned sir' answered the Maguje. 'I met the malam, when I was chewing sugar-cane. He was riding his mare, which had a foal following her. We had already passed each other, when I heard the malam say "Hey you walking there, hit that foal for me." So I did so, and it gave one leap and fell to the ground. But he never said anything about *driving* on the foal.'

'Well, malam' asked the judge, 'was that what you said to him? Did you tell him to *hit* the foal along?' 'Yes' answered the malam. 'Malam' said the judge 'Your complaint is baseless. The Maguje is more accurate than you. Get up and be off.' And the malam departed.

Next the judge called those who were complaining about the old woman and they came forward. 'Come here' said the judge, 'let us hear what you have to say.' So they told their story. 'Very well' said the judge, 'I've heard your story.'

Then he turned to the Maguje. 'Is that what happened?' he asked. 'Yes, that's how it was' the Maguje answered, and went on 'But judge, when I got there I felt a longing for tobacco, but had no fire for a light. That was when I saw these people hoeing. They had lit a fire and put a large pot on to boil. So I went over to them and asked if I might go and get a light for my smoke from the fire over yonder. They said to go over, and when I had lit up, to push the fire on to the old woman (*or* push up the fire for the old woman). So, judge, I went and lit up, and then I picked up the old woman and pushed her into the fire. For they never said anything about *stoking* up the fire.'*

The judge turned to the old woman's people 'Is that so?' he asked, 'Did you in fact not tell him to *stoke* up the fire?' 'Yes' they answered, 'We just told him to push up the fire for the old woman.' 'Then' said the judge, 'Your complaint is baseless, and the Maguje more accurate than you. Get up and be off with you!'

Next the judge turned to the owners of the cock and they duly came forward. 'Come and tell your story too' said the judge, and

* The point being that *tura* is a general word, *iza* is used more particularly for fires.

they told him all that had occurred. The judge heard them through and then addressed the Maguje. 'Here I am, judge' said the latter. 'Tell your version' said the judge.

'Well' he began, 'I went and lodged in their compound. The hut they gave me to sleep in proved to have chickens sleeping there too. I asked them what time I must start to reach the next town. They answered "At the first crow of the cock, cause him to rise."* That was all they said to me, so when the cock began to crow, I put an end to him. Had they but said to me "When the cock crows, *come out* and be off on your way" – but, well – they didn't say that to me.'

Then the judge said to them 'Well? Did you not use those last words to him?'; and they replied that they had not.

So the judge told them that their complaint was baseless, and that they had not spoken truly. 'You, all of you' he went on, 'Not one of you has been strictly accurate. The Maguje has shown you all to be wrong. And now be off with you, all of you!' And so the judge sent them all packing, for their inaccuracy. That's all. This with peace.

––––––

The Woman with a Son and the Man with the Mare† [^{I}/ 161]

There was once a woman walking along when she came across a Maguje, eating sugar-cane. She said to him 'Break off a piece for the little boy (*or equally* break one of the little boy's limbs).' 'O.K.' said he and coming up to her, took hold of her child's arm and broke it. Then the woman took hold of him and hauled him off to the chief.

And as they were going along they met a man riding a mare, with her foal alongside. Says the rider to the Maguje 'Hey, you there! Hit that mare along for me!' And the Maguje duly struck her a hard blow, killing her. Then the rider seized hold of him and was for taking him to the judge. 'Let's go' said the Maguje.

* Presumably idiomatic for 'do away with.'
† Cf. last tale.

When they got to the court, the woman with the child on he back told her tale. The judge heard her to the end and, turning to the Maguje, said 'Did you hear what she said?' 'Yes, I heard and I've got something to say too, judge.' 'Say on' said the judge. 'I fell in with this woman when I was eating sugar-cane. She asked me to break a *gaba** for her little boy, but she didn't say that it was a *gaba* of the sugar-cane she meant. So, thinking she meant "limb", I took the boy's arm and broke it. Whereupon she arrested me. After that, as we went along, I met the fellow with the mare. Her foal had stopped behind. He said to me "Hey you! Hit on that mare for me." "O.K." said I. 'And lifting my stick I hit the mare. Whereupon she fell down, dead. Then he arrested me. But he never asked me to *drive* her on for him.'

Then said the judge 'You can all get up and go now, and resign yourselves, for the Maguje speaks more truly than you do.'

The Chief† [III/73]

A malam and a pagan had set off on a journey together, when an army came and carried off the malam's daughter and the pagan's son. Neither the Maguje, nor the malam were at home. When the attack was over and many of the people of the town had been taken, those who had escaped began to go and ransom their children and their wives.

Back comes the Maguje and finds that his son has been carried off. Back comes the malam and finds that his daughter has been carried off. He asks how it happened and is told 'Well, malam, your daughter and the Maguje's son were both together in the one place.' Says the Maguje 'O.K., malam, when shall we go for our children?' But the malam answered 'Bah! Hurry up and get along! I'm not coming with you.' 'O.K.' said the other, and went off home and just stayed there.

The malam sought a propitious day and set off. The Maguje,

* A piece or limb.   † See J. p. 187.

seeing the malam set out, took up his things also, and followed behind him – at some distance – till they reached another town. There they spent the night. The malam found himself lodging and then went out begging to get food, and so in due course set off again. The Maguje kept out of sight until the malam had travelled for two days, then the malam saw him. Says the Maguje 'Hullo, malam! So you're here too!' 'Yes I'm here, Maguje' said the malam. 'Well, that's fine' said the Maguje.

They set off again and travelled for a while till they came to where there was a chief. Says the chief 'Welcome, malam! Today is a fortunate day for us, for I have a malam as a guest.' He went on 'What brings you here, malam?' 'May the chief's life be prolonged' answered the malam, 'This is what brings me: an army came to our town and carried off my daughter' and he described what she was like. 'So I have come after her.' Then said the chief 'I see.'

He turned to the Maguje. 'And how about you?' says he. 'Well' said the Maguje, 'An army came to our town and carried off my son' and he described him, adding that he had an umbilical hernia.* 'Just so, just so' said the chief.

Then said the chief 'Go into the compound and fetch food for the malam – the best food. As for the Maguje – give him something to eat in a piece of calabash.' So the malam was given of the best food to eat; while the Maguje had something on a piece of calabash. The malam ate his *tuwo*; while the Maguje got up and went outside to eat his.

The chief sent for some slave-girls from in the compound. 'Malam' says he, 'Look amongst these girls, and see if you recognise your daughter.' 'May the chief's life be prolonged' said the malam, 'I see her. There's my daughter.' 'Dad' exclaimed the girl, and the malam called out her name. Whereupon the girl burst into tears at the sight of her father.

Says the chief 'Look, malam, the usual ransom is two heads for every captive; but, seeing that you're a malam – well, you can – I'll reduce it to one head for you.' The malam thanked the chief profusely, and went off to the market at once, bought a slave-girl, paid the price, brought her back, and gave her to the chief.

Next the Maguje came to the chief, and the latter had some slave lads called. The Maguje saw his son. 'There's my son, chief' he

* Hardly very distinctive in Hausaland!

said. 'Dad' says the Maguje's son, and the Maguje answered him calling him by name.

Whereupon the chief said 'Very well, Maguje. Since you've seen your son, go and bring me two heads – a virgin and a youth – and let them be young ones. 'Well, I'll be —' said the Maguje, 'then, if I bring you two heads, chief, you'll give me my son?' 'Yes, Maguje' said the chief, 'if you bring me two heads – young ones – I'll give you your son.' 'But, chief—' protested the Maguje. 'By Allah' interrupted the chief, and then the Maguje said 'Very well, chief. I understand. And since I heard you mention this Allah that you people talk about, I know that you are in earnest.'

So the Maguje went off with his goatskin bag, along to the market, and there went to the butchers. When he got there, he found that a young billy-goat had just been slaughtered. Says he 'Hey, butchers! That young billy you've just slaughtered – I suppose he's not yet adult?' 'That's right' they answered, and he continued 'I want you to sell me the head. What has anyone offered for it?' And a young man answered 'Sixty (*lit.* three score) [cowries]'. At which the Maguje said 'I'll buy it for fifty.* If you agree, here's my money. I'll pay now. If not, I'll try somewhere else.' And another young man said 'O.K. Come on. Done.' And he went and counted out fifty cowries which he gave to them; and taking the kid's head he tossed it into the bag.

He† went on farther and found where a young female goat had been slaughtered. He bought the head of that for sixty cowries, paid, and taking the head, tossed it into his bag.

Next he went back to the chief's compound. 'Chief' says he, says he, 'Where's my son?' 'Here he is, Maguje' said the chief, 'Have you brought two heads?' 'Yes, I've brought them. May the chief's life be prolonged' said the Maguje. 'Where are they?' And the Maguje said 'Here they are.'

Then the Maguje asked the chief to send for his son. The chief did so and the boy came.

Then the Maguje said 'Did you really say that if I brought two heads you would give me my son, chief?' 'Yes, Maguje' said the chief, 'I said if you brought two heads, I would give you your son.' 'Oh, no, chief' says he, 'but I also heard you mentioning

---

* Yet another example of his shrewdness.   † From here on, cf. I/12.

that Allah of yours.' And the chief said 'Yes, Maguje. I said that I swore by Allah, that if you brought two heads, I would give you* your son.' Then the Maguje said 'Chiefs don't go back on their words.'

And he brought out of the bag the two goats' heads, and said 'Chief, here's the head of a young male goat; and here's the head of a young virgin female.'

The chief laughed and he laughed until he toppled over. And all his courtiers laughed too. Said they 'Chief, the Maguje speaks truly.' Then the chief said to the Maguje's son 'Take the heads with you. When you're in the bush, you can grill them to eat on the way.'

And that was that. The Maguje brought his son home, without paying a thing for him. And so back home and about his business. That's all. This with peace.

The Malam [^{III}/ 76]

Another story. A Maguje went and slaughtered a dog; then he slaughtered a monkey; and lastly he went and bought some beef. Then he threaded the meat on skewers for grilling; on one the dog's meat, on one the monkey's and on one the beef. Next he got his fire going and began puffing his wares, crying 'Come and eat meat. Here's bitch's ten cowries each, here's female monkey's, fifteen each, here's cow's for a score each *or, (with slightly altered tones and pronunciation*, these I am throwing away at ten cowries each; I'll let these go for fifteen each; I'll sell these for twenty each).'

Up comes a malam with his satchel slung over his shoulder and goes to the man with the meat and addresses him. 'Yes, malam' answers the other. 'How much each is the meat?' 'This is bitch's at ten cowries the piece, this is female monkey's at fifteen, and this is cow's at twenty. [Misunderstanding, as in the parenthesis] the malam said 'Give me some of that.' 'The bitch's here? (I'm

* Correcting the second *ba* to *ka*.

throwing away these)' 'Yes,' Again the Maguje asked the same question and got the same answer – three times in all. Lastly he said 'Well you're eating, knowing what you're doing, and he gave the malam the meat, and he ate it.

Then the malam said to the Maguje 'Give me one of those skewers too.' 'The female monkey's here, malam? (I'm letting these go)'. 'Yes' said the malam. Once again he asked him three times and getting the same reply, said 'Well you're eating, knowing what you're doing.' Then he took some of the meat and gave it to him and he ate it.

Then the malam asked how much the third lot was. 'The cow's meat here?' asked the Maguje. 'Yes' said the malam, and again was told three times. 'Give me one to take the taste of that one away' said the malam, and the Maguje took some meat and gave it to him.

'No. This meat's too expensive' said the malam, 'Here – take it back. I'm not buying it.' Then he paid the Maguje the cowries that he owed him, and getting to his feet, said 'Well, meat-seller, I must be getting along.' 'O.K.' said the Maguje.

The malam went to another place, and calling a meat-seller asked how much his meat was. 'This lot a hundred each' said he, 'This lot fifty each; this lot twenty each; and this lot two hundred each.' At which the malam said 'But? – that fellow over there's meat is very cheap.' And then the meat-seller told the malam that it was dog and monkey flesh that the other was selling. The malam expressed himself dumbfounded and horrified.

Up he gets and takes his complaint to the chief's compound. The chief ordered that they should be taken before the judge. The malam went to the judge's compound, and the Maguje was arrested quickly and brought there too.

The judge asked the malam how he had become involved with the other. 'He sold me dog meat and monkey meat, and I ate it' said the malam. The judge asked the malam three times, and the malam repeated his statement three times.

Then the judge asked the Maguje about it, and he replied 'Judge, the malam came and found that I had three lots of meat and asked me how much each lot was. I said "Malam, this one, this is bitch's meat, ten cowries each." When he asked about the next lot, I said "Do you mean this, female monkey's?"; and you said "Yes"', turning to the malam. ' "Fifteen each" I said. Again you asked me, and I said "The cow's meat here?" "Yes" you said. "Twenty each" said I. Three times you asked me and I told you; and you told me to give you some of the bitch's meat, the ten cowrie stuff. And I said "Very well, malam. You're eating, knowing what you're doing." '

The judge asked the malam if this is what had occurred, and the malam agreed that it had happened like that. 'Well, malam' said the judge, 'The Maguje is not at fault. He told you, and you still ate it.' He went on 'Malam, can't you tell meat that has been bought for money? A properly slaughtered beast's meat will never be sold cheaply. And any meat that you see is cheap has not been bought [from the butchers].' And turning to the Maguje he told him to be on his way, and announced that he had the right of it. That's all for that.

FULANI

―――――――

His Two Slaves [$^{I}/_{45}$]

A Fulani and his slave were travelling along through the bush. Says the slave to the Fulani 'Just wait a minute while I go aside and relieve myself.' 'Right' says the Fulani. But the slave, when he went aside to relieve himself, ran away. The Fulani waited and waited, till the next morning, but no sign of his slave. So he went home and carried on.

Time passed and the Fulani got some more money and bought another slave. And again he set off on a journey with this one, and as they travelled the Fulani said to his slave 'Just wait a minute while I go aside and relieve myself.' 'Right' says the slave and the Fulani goes aside to relieve himself. And thereupon he made his way home by a roundabout way, leaving the slave there. The slave waited and waited, and, not seeing the Fulani, returned home.

When he got home, he found the Fulani already there and said in surprise 'You left me there, sitting and waiting for you! And now I find you here at home!' 'Yes' says the Fulani. 'I was getting my own back for what your mate did to me. That's what happened when *he* said "Wait while I go and relieve myself" – he went off. That's why I've got my own back on you.' And the slave answered 'You, Fulani, you've no sense, you never realised that he ran away: I too thought of running away, but not all men are bad. Each character is different.'

―――――――

His Wife [$^{III}/_{75}$]

There was once a Fulani who from the day he was born, even when he had grown up, knew nothing of women – until he got married. Then when he came to sleep with his wife, he said 'Well, indeed to goodness!* Is this where you come each year?' 'Yes' she answered.

'Oh, you must eat some eggs' says he. 'But you haven't any guinea-fowls.' 'Oh' he answered, 'I'll keep stealing the neighbours' for you, and give them to you to eat.'

---

* Fun is made here of the Fulani's inability to pronounce *sh* and *c*; also to make distinctions of gender. The – presumably – sexual nuances behind the conversation, I regret, escape me; except that *ci*, 'eat' is also the normal word for 'copulate'. 'Eat beans' = 'become pregnant' and perhaps 'eat eggs' has some similar meaning. But it may just be the nonsense of a simpleton.

3

GWARI

These are the Hausa's other pagan neighbours to the South, who provided him with many of his slaves. The Gwari, in particular, had a reputation as a worker, the Hausa phrase for 'jack-of-all-trades' being 'Gwari's hoe'.

The Bassa [$^{I}/_{27}$]

It is said that a Gwari and a Bassa had a quarrel. The Gwari said to the Bassa 'I make a little meat go further with my *tuwo* than you do.' And Bassa replied 'On the contrary, I do it better than you.' Says the Bassa again 'Let me go first, you'll see!'

Then the Bassa broke the tail off a mouse and eating his *tuwo* with it, continued till he was satisfied. And there remained some of the mouse's tail. Then the Bassa said to the Gwari 'There you are! You see!' Then the Gwari answered 'You cursed rascal! That's nothing, all you can do is waste meat! I'll show you how to make meat go further! You'll see', 'Right' says the Bassa.

The Gwari picked up a piece of meat, fixed it on a skewer and stuck it in front of the fire. When the meat began to cook, the fat in it began to trickle down the skewer, drop by drop. Then the Gwari began breaking off little bits of *tuwo* and catching up the drops, put the whole in his mouth, continuing till he was satisfied. Then said the Bassa 'Well, it seems you can make meat go further than I can!'

The Bassa and the Gwari and How they Made a Little Meat Go a Long Way [I/61]

The Hausa people used to quarrel as whether the Bassa or the Gwari could make a little meat go further. Some said the Gwari made his go further, some the Bassa.

Then one day a Gwari cut off the tail of a mouse, and for three days used it to go with his *tuwo*. He was then told to make way, having shown what he could do, and the Bassa was summoned and told to do his stuff. Then the Bassa spitted a fat mouse and set it by the fire. Soon the fat began to trickle down the spit, and taking a piece of *tuwo* in his fingers, he ate it with the fat from the spit. He went on to eat all his *tuwo* thus, without touching the meat. Then it was agreed that the Bassa was the superior at eking out his meat.

Kundila* and his Slave Girl [I/63]

There was in Kano a very wealthy man, called Kundila. So wealthy was he that he didn't know how many slaves he had.

Then one day a Gwari woman cut wood and brought it to town. She was going along when she met a man in a dark-blue gown with his arms full of cloth for sale. She called to him and when he answered she told him to stop. He stopped and she said 'I have a question for you – where's Kundila's home?' and he answered 'Come with me and I'll take you to the house.'

He went ahead and she followed, till they came to the entrance to his house. And he went on into the house and sat down. Then he said to his *jekadiya* 'Go to the entrance and call here a Gwari woman you'll find standing there with a load of wood.' She went and called her. And she came in and knelt down and said 'Here I am.' Then he said 'I am Kundila.' 'Well I never!' says she. 'Then

* Cf. The proverb *abu ba na sayarwa ba, ya gagari Kundila a Kano*, 'unsaleable merchandise, even Kundila at Kano couldn't sell it'.

God does actually make a man who doesn't know all his own slaves! Well, well! I'm your slave, for though you may have forgotten me, I haven't forgotten you. God give you health!' Then he gave her two cloths, and she went home to her village. She was full of joy and told her fellow slaves of it.

The Rich Man and his Slave Girl* [I/64]

There was once a wealthy man, who had slaves and cattle and camels – everything in the world he had, but God had not granted that he should have children.

Then one day he went to the market, and walking through it came to where the slaves were sold. As he looked he saw a Gwari woman sitting there, and said to himself 'I wonder now, shall I buy that Gwari girl? Perhaps if I take her as a concubine, God will grant us children.' So he bought her and paid for her, and took her home as his concubine.

The months passed and God gave them a child, a son, and everyone rejoiced. The child grew and began to crawl.

Then there occurred a fire in the house. The Gwari woman took the boy, and putting him in a small grain bin, covered it. The master became worried when he didn't see his son and he said to the Gwari woman 'Hey, Gwari, where's the boy?' and she answered 'I've hidden him with my reserve store.' Then again, as the confusion of a fire spread round them, he asked her 'Gwari, where's my son?' and still she replied 'I've hidden him with my reserve store', for – you see – she'd put the boy in the little grain bin! The fire reached him and a pop was heard. The boy had swelled up and burst! Then the master said 'Curse you, Gwari, is that your reserve store – to burn up my son? Very well – get out and don't come back to my home! God preserve us from Gwari ways!' and he drove her out.

---

* Cf. TR. No. 45.

4

THE KANO MAN

This is the sharp fellow, the city slicker.

His Character [I/xxxi]

A Kano man puts on a dark-blue gown, and a white Nupe one, and a black-and-white one; then he wears Kano-style trousers, either white or black-and-white; puts on a length of muslin for a turban; hangs a book over his shoulder and off he goes to school to recite the Koran; he takes a staff, a little gourd water-bottle, and away he goes. When he has finished at school, he returns home. When it is time for market he goes to market. Returning from there, when it is night, he puts on a leather loincloth, picks up a rope-ladder, and off he goes to steal. Sometimes he gets shot or wounded with a sword, and sometimes dies, and sometimes gets better.

The Kano character is also, if a rich visitor arrives, to receive him joyfully, and give him a gown, or a turban or a length of cloth. Then they get together with one of the household where he is staying, and start bringing shoddy stuff to sell him. When the householder sees it, he praises its quality. They abuse his trust in them and trick him. But if the visitor is shrewd, he rejects all the stuff they bring him, saying 'I'm not buying it', and waits till he gets to the market and buys what he wants.

Trickery and fraud are Kano characteristics. Whoever you are, a Kano man will trick you – unless he thinks it can't be done. For there is no one so cowardly.

A City-Man and a Country-Man* [I/ 17]

There was once much argument whether a Kano city-man or a Kano country-man was the smarter. Some said one, some the other. This argument went on till the day when the city-man tied up his bundle and went off trading. And as he went, he travelled till he came to the gate of a certain town.

He put down his load and was resting, when a Kano country-man came up to him. 'Peace be upon you' says he, and the city-man replied 'And upon you be peace.' Then the country-man asked him where he was going, and he answered 'I'm going trading. I've put my load down to take a rest, for I'm tired – you know how it is with travellers.' And the country-man said 'Give me the load and let me carry it for you.' He agreed and gave him the load, and he picked it up.

The city-man went ahead and the other followed, and they travelled thus till they entered a town. When they came to their lodging place and the city-man would have taken the load, the country-man suddenly was struck dumb.† The city-man protested that the load was his and he said 'Good people! See this man – he took my load at the gate of the town as we were coming in – and now, it seems, he's struck dumb,' and beckoning to him, he took him to the house of the chief.

The chief asked the Kano city-man 'How did you and this dumb man come together?' and he answered 'I was travelling along with my load, and had put it down to rest, when I saw him come along. He offered to take it for me and carry it into the town. So I agreed and let him have the load. He took it up and we went along. But when we got into the town and I asked him to give me my load, he pretended to become dumb and said that the load was his.' The chief asked the people 'What shall we do in this case?' and the people said 'The dumb man should be asked, to hear what he has to say.' So the chief made signs with his hands to the dumb man, in the way that is done to such. Then the dumb man struck the ground and pointed to the heavens, indicating that the load was his. Then

* Cf. III/175   † *Lit.* deaf and dumb (the Hausa *bebe* connoting both).

the chief turned to the people and said 'Do you understand what the dumb man says?'

There was a pause, and then one man said 'Chief, do you see what this dumb man is doing? He is abusing you! And you don't realise it.' Then said the chief 'Is that so? Right!! Away with him and kill him!'

The guards seized him to kill him, and then he said 'God prolong your days, really I wasn't abusing you. It's not my load. I shammed dumb deliberately. I'm very sorry for what I've done!'

What Happens When You Throw Something up to Catch Again [I/54]

'If you throw a thing up, and don't dodge, it'll come down on your head.' The origin of this saying is the story of an old woman at Ruka. She would sell *tuwo* beside the road along which the traders came and went. Everyone who followed it, by day or by night, used to buy *tuwo* from her.

Then one day some men from Garko* arrived at night and put up in her compound. Said they 'Mother, get us some *tuwo* we'll pay for it.' She answered 'What, now, at night?' 'Yes' said they. 'Very well' said she 'where's your money?' and they took it out and gave it to her. Up she got, made the *tuwo* for them and took it to them in their hut. When they had eaten the *tuwo*, they wiped the calabash clean, then excreted into it, covered it up, and before it was dawn went away.

When it was light the old woman came to the hut where the guests had been to take away the calabash. But when she looked she saw excrement in it and said to herself 'Is that so? Is that how they've treated me? All right, I'll pay them back. If you throw a thing up and don't dodge, it'll come down on your head.'

So she took the excrement and left it on a flat rock in the open to

* A country town forty miles S.E. of Kano.

dry, till it was quite dry. Then she pounded it till it was like flour, wrapped it in a rag and put it aside.

Some time went by, maybe three months, and the Garko men returned from Gwanja.* They reached the home of the seller of *tuwo* and put up there. Said they 'We're back, mother!' 'Who are you?' says she and they answered 'We're the Garko men who came here once two months ago and bought *tuwo* from you at night.' Says she 'Well, well, so it's you' and they answered 'Yes, it's us', thinking that she had forgotten how they had excreted into her calabash. But she hadn't. Then she asked them 'If I make you some *tuwo*, will you buy it?' 'Go ahead, we'll buy it' they replied.

Then she got up and put a pot on the fire. When it had boiled, she put the first handful of flour in and then fetched the powdered excrement and poured it in. Then stirring the *tuwo*, she took it off and brought it to them. They ate it and wiped round the calabash. Then they sat back and began chatting (or, as Zaria people say, 'having a crack', *roka*).

Up comes the seller of *tuwo* to the Garko men and says 'Feeling better now? How's things?' 'Fine' say they. And she asked them whether they had eaten. 'Yes, indeed' they reply 'Eaten it all up and wiped the calabash clean.' 'Well, isn't that fine!' says she 'You rascals – it's your own excrement that you left for me in my calabash. I pounded it up and mixed it up for you to eat. Your intentions have come back upon you; you haven't harmed me, but yourselves. God's curse on the men of Garko!'

The Woman and the Slave [I/ 21]

Here's another. There was once a Gwari woman, whose town was on the trade route. She was used to Kano people and knew their character well. Then one day war came to her town and it was taken.

She was captured and taken to Kano where she became a slave.

* Ashanti region, whence they will have brought cola-nuts.

There came a day when the Gwari woman got hold of some meat when she was out in the town, and she asked the wives of her master to cook it for her. Now the women that cooked the meat conceived a strong desire for it, but, for their position's sake, were unwilling just to help themselves. So they said to each other 'Let's eat this meat. Then when the Gwari woman comes, we'll trick her.' Whereupon they took the meat from the pot and ate it up.

Then the Gwari woman returned from the town and said 'Where's my meat?' and they answered 'While it was cooking, it got burnt and only the gravy is left.' And the Gwari woman said 'I don't believe it! That's Kano talk, try again! Whoever heard of meat being burnt and leaving gravy!' Then the other women said 'Oh! She knows all about Kano talk does she? We'll have to buy some meat and pay her back.'

The Kano Man and the Katsina Man* [II/35]

There was a rascal, a Kano man and another rascal, a Katsina man. The Kano rascal went and stripped some bark off a baobab tree and took it to a dyepit. There he dyed the bark, and then went and bought some dry indigo and from there went to the place where clothes are beaten. Then, taking water in his mouth, he spurted it over the baobab bark and pounded it, adding the indigo; then he wrapped it in paper.

Meanwhile the Katsina rascal had gone and got himself a goat-skin bag, and picking up some gravel, poured it into the bag. Then he got two hundred cowries and poured them in on top of the bag. Next, tying it up, he set off for market – and fell in with the Kano chap. Says the latter 'Hullo, my friend! Where are you off to?' 'I'm going to market. What are you taking there?' 'A shiny, indigoed gown' says the Kano man. 'That's just what I was going to buy' said the Katsina man, 'for here's my money – twenty thousand.' 'Well, well, well' said the other, 'Here was I, taking a gown to sell; and you on your way to buy one!' and he went on,

* Cf. I/134, M. No. 17 & No. 18, D. No. 76. See J. p. 212.

'Give me the money, and I'll give you the gown.' 'Done' said the Katsina man. And he gave the Kano man his money, and the Kano man gave him the gown. And then they separated and each went his own way.

But when they had travelled a little way, each went aside from the road: the Kano man confident that he had done the Katsina man; and the Katsina man equally confident that he had done the Kano man. Then each opened his parcel and saw what was there. 'Well! So it was baobab bark that that Kano fellow dyed!' said the one. And the Kano man opened the mouth of the bag and saw the gravel with the cowries. He picked out the money and counted it, and made it two hundred. 'So' said he, 'That Katsina fellow filled the bag with gravel and then added two hundred cowries on top of the bag to fill it up.'

They set off again, and presently they met again. 'So' said the Kano man, 'It seems that you're a rascal, Katsina man.' 'Rascal yourself, Kano man' said the other. Whereupon they agreed that they were pretty equal as regards cunning, and had better team up and go off together to look for a bite to eat. So off they went, one behind the other, until they came to another town. There they found themselves water-bottle gourds, small calabashes and long sticks and again took the road.

They walked for a while and presently, in the middle of the bush, they saw where some traders were camped. And going up near, they hid themselves. But they didn't go right up to the traders until it was dark; then they approached them, with their eyes shut, pretending to the traders that they were blind. And they sat themselves down in the traders' camp. The traders went off to sleep whereupon the blind men opened their eyes and made a clean sweep of all the traders' goods; and taking them, they put them into a well.

Next morning when it was light, the traders got up and started lamenting the theft that they had suffered. And the blind men began saying 'Where are our water-bottles? I think somebody must have taken them.' 'Stupid idiots, you blind men' said the traders angrily, 'You see that our stuff has been stolen, and then you wonder whether perhaps someone has taken your waterbottles! Get away! We don't want you here!' But the blind men went on groping for their staves and water-bottles.

Soon the traders went on their way, bewailing the theft that they had suffered. Whereupon the blind men opened their eyes and went to the mouth of the well where they had thrown the goods. Says the Kano man 'In with you, Katsina man!' 'Oh no!' says the other, 'In with *you*, Kano man!' 'No no, Katsina man, it's you who must go in.' And the Katsina man went into the well and began tieing the things on to a rope, for the Kano man to draw out. And each time he took something out, he would carry it away a distance and put it down and bring back a stone and put it down by the mouth of the well.*

Then the Kano man called out 'Katsina man, when we come to the end of the goods, and you're going to tie yourself on, let me know so that I can pull you up carefully and don't bump you against the side of the well.' 'O.K.' said the other.

And he went on tying the things on and giving the word for the Kano man to pull them up. And he would pull them up, carry them some distance away and hide them; and then bring a stone back and put it down at the mouth of the well. The last load went up, and the Katsina man himself got into an oxhide and called out 'Kano man, here's a heavy one with the last four loads in it.' 'Righto' said the Kano man and pulled up the Katsina man inside the oxhide, without realising it. Then he picked him up and carried him over and put him down with the other loads. And, taking a stone, he returned and set about picking up all the stones and tumbling them into the well.

Out gets the Katsina man from inside the hide and sets about moving all the stuff into another hiding place. The Kano man went on filling in the well, and then made for the spot where he had left the goods. They were no longer there. Says he to himself, 'Damn it! Here am I busy finishing off the Katsina man down the well, and someone else comes along and takes all the stuff. But, whoever did it, if he hears a donkey bray, he'll come back to take the donkey to load the goods on to.'

So the Kano man went round behind a *geza* bush, and began to bray. Along comes the Katsina man, calling out 'Hey, Neddy, come along boy!' – and out pops the Kano man. Says he 'You're a rascal Katsina man.' 'Rascal yourself' says the Katsina man.

'Oh, all right' said the Kano man, 'Let's get to the goods.' So

* Cf. II/32.

they went and picked them all up and took them to the home of the Kano man.

Then said the Katsina man to the Kano man, 'I'm off to pay a visit to my home, but I'll be back in three months.' 'O.K.' said the Kano man, and off went the other.

Well, the Kano man waited for two months. Then he had a grave* dug for himself. And when he was in, he had them bring fragments of calabash, which they pierced and covered him with; and earth which they spread loosely on top of those. And there was the Kano man underneath that lot, in the hole.

Presently the Katsina man arrives and enquires at the home of the Kano man. And the Kano man's parents answered 'Oh, he's dead. He died four days ago.' 'It that so?' said the Katsina man. 'Yes' they answered. 'Then I want to be taken to see his grave.' So they took him there and he said 'God is ruler of all! So it's true – the Kano man's days have run their course' and he began to cry, saying. 'Now, you must cut some thorn branches and put them on top of his grave, so that a hyena doesn't come and dig him up.' And the people of the compound answered 'We'll get branches tomorrow.' Then said he 'Give me lodging for the night, and in the morning I'll go home.' To which they agreed.

They gave him somewhere to sleep and brought him *tuwo* and *fura*. But he couldn't eat, he said, for thinking of the death of his friend.

But when it was night, the Katsina man got up and went to the grave of the Kano man; and began to dig it up, making inarticulate sounds as he did so. Whereupon the Kano man began to scream 'Help, help, a hyena is going to eat me up!' 'Thank-you' said the Katsina man, 'Now you can come out.' And out came the Kano man. Then they went off and divided the goods between them. That's all. *Kungurus kan kusu.*

———

* For the stratagem cf. II/36 and III/21. Also in the story of Abdulbaki, Tanimuddarin Tureta (J. p. 146).

The Cunning Arab [I/66]

There was once an Arab at Kano who refused either to borrow or
lend money. If one of the Kano people came to borrow from him,
he would have a cat beside him and he would say to the Kano man
'Just a minute, I'll be right out again.' Then he would go into the
house and cut off a piece of lung or scrap of meat. When he came
out he would throw it to the cat. It would take the meat and move to
one side with the meat in its mouth, purring. Then he would say
to the Kano man 'Good – now get me that meat from the cat's
mouth!' The other would say to the Arab 'Oh no! That can't be
got away from it.' Then the Arab would say 'Is that so? Now, if I
had given you a loan, that's how it would be with us, with you in
the cat's place. Get out, be off with you!'

5

SOKOTO MEN

———————

Their Character [$^\text{I}$/ VIII]

The men of Sokoto are proud of their own importance but don't allow the importance of anyone else. They don't know how to pursue any useful occupation or work. As for getting the necessities of life – they expect to receive them for nothing.

A Sokoto man, if he comes up to you, even though he is a man of no position, certainly not of the ruling families, none the less will cover up his mouth and nose with his turban. And he'll go up to a rich man or one of the ruling families and say 'I've come to see you, so-and-so. For, look you, yesterday no one brought me anything to eat. God, man, just give me a couple of measures of corn – or five hundred cowries – or half a cola-nut. For tomorrow's Friday and then I can have *tuwo*. God, man, even a hundred to buy tobacco with would show what a big chap you are!'

But the men of Sokoto won't show anyone else respect, unless it is kicked into them. And yet if one in authority arrives at a town and the townspeople are told that he requires certain things, you'll hear them say 'Of course, of course, you shall have them right away.' But that's all that happens, they don't actually do anything about it – not unless someone gives them hell. Then, and only then will they do what they've been asked to. In all the world there's no one like the Sokoto people – they know nothing, but they expect everything to be given them.

If you are travelling in the bush and tired, being a long way from a town, and you meet a Sokoto man and you ask him 'Hey there! Are we getting near the town?' you'll hear him answer 'For goodness sake! Why, you've already reached it.' When actually in fact you're nowhere near! But if the traveller happens to know the nature of Sokoto people and says 'Hey, tell me the truth. If you don't I'll beat you up,' then you'll hear him answer 'Surely! Well, it's a wee way yet! You're quite near but you've a step yet.'

Then again, if Sokoto people see that a man has something, like a fine gown or trousers, they'll say 'That gown there – what sort of a gown is that now?' Then if you reply 'Oh, I bought it, it came from another town,' he'll say 'Would you give it me?' If, then, you ask him 'Why should I give it to you?' 'Well to be sure' he'll answer, 'because you've got it. We here we've nothing, we're a lazy lot. But you're always giving things away – so you'll give it to me won't you?'

The Men of Sokoto [II/XL]

I have noticed that the men of Sokoto have a practice which no one else follows. If a man has a *jekadiya*, she will live in his compound; and if he wishes to make someone a present, he will call her and tell her to fetch something for the purpose, and she will do so. But her master, whom she is serving as a *jekadiya* (messenger), will actually sleep with her regularly – for all that he has wives and concubines.

If a Sokoto man has a slave-girl, while she is still very young, he will deflower her. Everyone knows that's how it is in Sokoto. For no Sokoto girls keep their virginity till they are married – or very, very few. If a slave desires a particular slave-girl and brings along the payment for her, the Fulani of Sokoto will trick him. For they will take the money, and having done so, if they want her – even if the marriage has actually been made – when she comes to work in the compound, her master will have intercourse with her and then send her to her husband's compound. But, in fact, it is only the more scrupulous Sokoto men who act in this way. The others wait till two days after the marriage, when the slave-girl has come over from her husband's compound to do some work in her master's compound, and the latter will prevent her returning to her husband's compound, and sleep with her regularly. All the slave-girls in Sokoto have been seduced by their masters. This isn't just an idle tale or gossip – it is indeed so. The men of Sokoto act in this way.

And because they act like this, the men of Sokoto are all diseased, suffering from gonorrhoea, syphilis, soft chancre, piles and various venereal diseases. This is the reason that they are not prolific – though they have plenty of slaves. Sokoto people are great travellers, spreading over the country like gourds, spreading syphilis and gonorrhoea, through their excessive sexual immorality; the men of Sokoto are the guilty ones. Now Malam Shehu dan Fodio struggled against the practice of evil, for he was the servant of God and sinned against no man, but followed the Lord God, day and night. But the men of Sokoto who came after him, well, they'll swear by God and the Prophet and Shehu, and you'll find their words so much wind. In their oaths they will take in vain the name of Allah, that's certain. For we once had a Sokoto man who came and swore by Allah: he had a satchel in which he said there was a Koran – but in fact, it wasn't, just some odds-and-ends inside. He also said that, at Sokoto, any man might have intercourse with one of the slave-girls in his compound – such was not fornication, though it was sinful.* And he even went on to say that – if compelled to – a man could swear by Allah and the prophet and Shehu and the Koran, and swear falsely, and that no harm was done, no crime against God; that thus Sokoto people might swear falsely!

Yes, Sokoto men have some unique characteristics. For they won't wash; and even before saying their prayers, they will make the ablution with sand. They won't touch water for the whole of the cool part of the rains; nor for the whole of the cold period of the dry season. For if one of them does wash, he swells up all over.

Some of the Toronke clan, moreover, when their gown has been washed, will leave it in their hut to air for a whole month; for they say that only then will the water with which it was washed have completely dripped out. Then they are willing to take it and put it on!

The men of Sokoto transgress the laws of God. One of them will call on you in the name of Allah and of Shehu to spare him something to feed his household with. But he, if you do the same thing to him, will say 'For shame! 'Tis you upon whom God has bestowed it, and it is for me to seek from you. Please give me something, for the tomb of Shehu dan Fodio! Look at my gown and yours! Now,

* The meaning seems obscure for *farka*, practically by definition, is a *sabo*, yet – if my rendering is correct – the speaker excuses the act, as being *sabo*, though not so bad as to constitute *farka*.

if you were to give me that gown of yours, you'd find that by the grace of God and of Shehu, you'd obtain the money to buy another just like it.'

Then, too, Sokoto people are miserly, as if Zumbul* was their father; and as for their begging, they're like open palms only even they'd be ashamed to do it quite the way Sokoto men do it!

Now if Sokoto people set off to buy horses, they take to the road and travel east, a large number of them; some will make for Zaria, some for Katsina, some for Kano, some for Daura, some for Kazaure, some for Hadeja, some for Misau, some for Gombe, some for Katagum, some for Bauchi, and some will go to Adamawa. There they will be given slaves, and these they will fasten neck to neck with a leather thong, and come home with them. The good-looking women among them they will keep in their own compounds, so that they may have intercourse with them from time to time. The ugly ones will be taken out to their farms and shackled and there, in the farms, they will have to work day after day. The reason there are so many slaves at Sokoto is that they receive them from towns which control large territories. Katsina sends slaves to Sokoto; so does Daura and so does Kazaure; Kano sends slaves to Sokoto, and so does Zaria and Bauchi; so too do Hadeja, Misau, Shira and Gombe. As for Adamawa, every year they send to the Sultan for himself alone twelve hundred slaves. So now you know why there are more slaves than there are freemen in Sokoto; in fact, at Sokoto, if you were to add up all the slaves, you would find that there were more of them than all the natives of Sokoto. But most of them get taken out of the city. They shackle them and put them to work on the farms, clearing the land.

They tie them up, men and women, without exception; and they beat them mercilessly if they refuse to work. Moreover, if they are travelling with slaves across the bush, and one of them becomes exhausted, then they will draw sword and cut him down, killing him, and go on. And everyone knows that this is a true account, and that the men of Sokoto act in this way. That's all.

---

* A legendary miser.

6

KANURI

His Son who was a Bigger Liar* [^{I}/₆₉]

There was once a Kanuri who took his son in hand to teach him lying.

They set out and as they went, came to the edge of a river. They got into a canoe and were going along in that when the father said to the son 'Oh dear! My needle has fallen into the water.' The son answered 'Yes, bad luck, Dad! I heard the splash.' And his father said 'Now you can nearly tell lies.'

They went on, moving on in the canoe, and the father said 'I saw a fish rise, a big one' and the son answered 'I've got an oily taste in my mouth from it.' Then the father exclaimed 'Well! This boy is a bigger liar than I am. Here, let's turn back before you tell any more lies and we are taken and locked up.' So they went home, and he said 'I've taught my son to tell lies, and now he is a bigger liar than I am.' And people said 'He has inherited it from you.'

Two of Them and the Men of Paradise [^{II}/₄₆]

This is the tale of two Kanuris who were on a trading journey. They came to a well and drank water, and then took up their loads again.

But as they travelled, they missed their way, and meeting with another asked him the way. 'Go that way' he said, 'and cut through the cultivated land, and you'll find the road again.'

* Cf. I/70.

Now it chanced that a hole where matmakers work lay in their path. And as they travelled the one in front fell into the hole. And there he saw people. Says he 'People of paradise, will ten gowns and ten pairs of trousers see me back to earth?'* 'Yes' they said, 'Hand them over.' So he gave them ten gowns and ten pairs of trousers, and they showed him the way out.

When he got out, he ran off as fast as he could, and said to his friend 'Abba,† just imagine! I fell down a hole and there found the people of paradise, a lot of them. And I had to give them ten gowns and ten pairs of trousers, before they helped me get back to earth! And that's why I was running so fast!' That's the end of that story.

---

* The *-be* is the (common) Kanuri genitival suffix, added to his words here for verisimilitude.

† A very common Kanuri name.

7

TUAREG AND BUZU

The Buzu, slave of the Tuareg, is of a menial caste of which the Hausa saw more than of the Tuareg himself.

The Borrower* [$^{II}/_{36}$]

There was once a man who went to a Tuareg and borrowed money from him, five hundred thousand cowries, saying to the Tuareg 'This very month, if we both live, this very month you can come and get your money back.' The Tuareg agreed, went and fetched the money and gave it to him.

The days passed and the date for repayment came near. Then the debtor went out one day along the road that the Tuareg would have to follow when he came for his money, and cleared himself a farm by it.

The day came, and the debtor said to his wife 'Prepare cakes and *tuwo* and *fura*; kill a ram and fry the meat; prepare macaroni and wheaten cakes.' 'Very well' she answered.

So he set off on the road to the farm, but as he went he saw a ground-squirrel. He caught it and took it home and tied it up; then again took the road to the farm. And again he saw a ground-squirrel and he caught it too and took it to the farm and tied it up there. And presently as he worked there, along came the Tuareg. So, leaving his hoeing he went out to meet him and welcome him. 'Well' said he, 'I began to think you weren't coming, and I've had no food prepared. But all the same, that'll be easy to fix.'

And he went over and caught hold of the ground-squrrel, saying 'Nimble-fellow, I'm sending you off and I want you to get home as fast as you can and tell my wife that I've got guests; and that she's to prepare *tuwo* and *fura*, and cakes; and cook macaroni and make

* Cf. next tale See J. p. 219.

196

wheaten cakes quickly.' And he let the ground-squirrel go, as the
Tuareg watched; then he added 'And when you've told her that,
my wife is to catch you and tie you up – d'you hear?' Then he went
back to the Tuareg and sat down beside him, and they enquired
after each other's homes and families. Presently he said to the
Tuareg 'Come on, get up and we'll go home.'

So they got up and set off home. He took the Tuareg, and all his
people, to where he was to sleep; then returned to his own part of
the compound, and food was duly brought out and taken to the
Tuareg's lodging place. After a while the Tuareg asked his host
'Where's Nimble-fellow?' 'There he is tied up' said the other.
'Sell him to me' said the Tuareg. 'Oh no!' he replied, 'I couldn't
sell him. I paid money for him; and he comes with me to the farm,
and whenever I want anything I send him home, and don't have to
leave the farm myself.' 'How much did you pay for him?' 'I paid
good money for him. A million cowries was what I paid for him.'
'I'll buy him for a million' said the Tuareg. 'You owe me five
hundred thousand. I've another five hundred thousand here. I
can pay you right away.' 'O.K. I'll sell him to you' said the other.
And the Tuareg paid him the money.

The Tuareg then got up, saying he was off home, and the other
caught the ground-squirrel, brought it over and gave it to him.
The Tuareg set off on the road, putting the ground-squirrel on his
camel and tieing him there. He travelled on, and when he was only
three days from home, he said to Nimble-fellow 'Let me send you
on home. Go quickly and tell them that we are coming, and that
they are to prepare plenty of food so that there is enough for us.'
And the Tuareg released the ground-squirrel – which vanished
into the bush. But when the Tuareg and his party got home, no one
knew they had come. For his household had no news of him.

Says the Tuareg 'Where's the food you've got ready? It's three
days since I send word about it.' 'Who did you send?' asked his
household. And he answered 'I sent Nimble-fellow.' 'No' they
answered, 'We've seen no one.' 'You're lying' he said, 'for I
certainly sent him.' But they still denied knowledge, and a quarrel
started up between the Tuareg and his womenfolk; and people
nearby came along and besought them to be patient.

Then one day, the Tuareg set off to visit his camels, with his
slaves; and saw a ground-squirrel. Whereupon he began saying

'Hey, look, there's Nimble-fellow! When I sent him, he must have gone off into the bush.' And one of his slaves said 'But that's a ground-squirrel. He lives in the bush; he never comes into the town.' 'Is that right?' asked the Tuareg. 'Yes.' 'All right then I'm going back to that man who borrowed money from me and I'm going to get my money back from him.'

And the Tuareg went home determined to go back to the home of the other man. But the latter got news that the Tuareg was coming, and had a grave dug for himself,* deep and broad; and also had them collect fragments of calabash and broken bits of pots; and cut a long stick for him. And then he went and got into the hole.

Along comes the Tuareg and asks for the master of the house. 'Oh, he's dead' they said. 'Where's his grave?' asked the Tuareg. 'Over there,' they answered.

So he went over to it, and the man in the grave aimed a thrust at the bits of calabash with his stick, and as he struck them said 'I won't let you have my Tuareg!'; and then he lashed at the fragments of pottery and repeated 'I won't let you have my Tuareg.' 'Oh-oh!' said the Tuareg, 'He's fighting with the men of the other world on my behalf. I heard him say that he wouldn't let them have me' and he went on 'As God is my witness, I resign my claim to the money I lent you. For I can hear that you're fighting with the men of the other world on my behalf.' That's all. *Kungurus kan kusu.*

The Poor Man and the Buzu [III/27]

There was once a poor man who was in dire straits. And he went and borrowed five hundred cowries from a Buzu, saying to him 'Come back in this month a year from now, on the second of the month.' 'Right' said the other.

The creditor went off home and counted the months. At the beginning of the eleventh month he set about making ready his loads for the journey.

* Cf. II/35.

The twelfth month came, and on the second he set off, saying he was going to collect a debt.

He arrived, but before he did so, the poor man had been on his farm working and had caught two young hares.* One of these he tied up at home, but kept the other with him.

And he told his wife – the poor man – to prepare plenty of food, as he was expecting guests that day.

Then he went off to his farm. While he was there, the creditor arrived. 'Hallo there' said the poor man. 'Good day' said the other. Says the poor man 'Just let me send ahead a speedy youngster to go home and tell my wife to prepare plenty of food, by the time we get there.'

And he loosed the hare, which made off into the bush. 'Oh!' said the Buzu, 'But he's off into the bush—' 'Nonsense' replied the other, 'It's home he's gone.'

After a while, the poor man rose and, with his guest, went off home. And when they got there, they found food prepared a-plenty. And the poor man took it and lavished it on his guest.

'Man!' said the guest, 'Where's that speedy youngster of yours?' 'Here he is' said the poor man. 'Won't you give him to me?' said the other. 'Oh, he's worth a lot of money. I paid five hundred thousand cowries† for him.' 'Give him to me, and you've paid your debt.' 'Very well' said the poor man and went and took hold of the young hare and brought it and gave it to the Buzu.

The latter set off for home again, but when he was getting near his town, he let the young hare go, saying 'Go on home quickly and tell my wife that I'm on my way, and that she is to get food ready for me.' But when he let the hare go, it just went off as fast as it could into the bush.

So when he got home, he found his wife asleep. Says he 'Where's the speedy youngster that I sent on? I told him to tell you to get food ready for me.' She answered that she had seen no one. Says he 'You're lying', and he went off back again to visit the poor man.

Then the poor man had some red guinea-corn leaves brought him, and pounded them and soaked them in water. Says he to his wife 'When the Buzu arrives, I'll come and start beating you; you fall down; then I'll take a knife and make as if to cut your throat;

* Cf. II/36.

† Presumably 'thousand' is to be understood in line 2 of this story.

then if I hit you and tell you to get up, jump up quickly. Understand?' 'O.K.' said she.

Along comes the Buzu. Says he 'Peace be upon you!' He looked into the compound and saw the poor man assaulting his wife; so he went in to try to persuade him to desist.

There he saw the poor man knock his wife down, and take a knife and start to cut her throat. And taking the red dye, he spilt it down her front and her neck – and it was all bright red, as when a ram has been slaughtered.

Says the poor man to his wife 'Get up, you bastard!' And she got up.

'Man' says the other, 'Why did you attack your wife, even to cutting her throat?' 'She has behaved shamefully towards me' said the other, 'she is always slandering me.* That's why I cut her throat. But I revived her again – it's the knife. I'm always treating her like this.'

'Man' said the other, 'you must give me that knife.' So the poor man fetched the knife and gave it to the Buzu.

The latter went off home, and when he got there, went and attacked his wife; took hold of her and cut her throat. 'Get up' says he, but when he saw that she didn't do so he began to yell. And they came and took away his wife and buried her. Says he 'I must go back to that poor man.'

But now the poor man had had a grave dug for himself, and got into it together with fragments of calabash, pitchers, and cooking-pots.

Up comes the other and makes formal greeting. Then says he 'Where's your husband?' 'Oh, he's dead' said the wife.

'Well, come along' he said, 'you take me to his grave.' So she took him. And the poor man began to smash the pots.

Says the Buzu 'Man's there, fighting with Wanakiri.† There he is, hitting him.' So he returned to his home, and that was that, for he never came back again.

And the poor man came out and settled down again with his wife. That's all. *Kungurus kan kusu.*

---

* Or, perhaps 'quarrelling.' † Angel of Death.

Buzu and his Daughter* [$^{II}/_{98}$]

There was once a Buzu who had a beautiful daughter. Her mother died, and the girl took over preparing food for him. She was a girl with big, bouncing breasts, and he became enamoured of her, for all she was his daughter, and wanted to marry her. But he knew that if he did so, he would be bothered by what people would say.

So he made a pair of trousers† for his camel, and put the saddle on it. The market was in full swing and he mounted and rode to market; and everyone said 'Look, there's a camel with trousers on; look, there's a camel with trousers on.' And he was the centre of all attention, wherever he went, along the lines of the market, until he went home. He went back again another day, and again people said 'Look, there's the fellow with the camel that wears trousers.' They went on staring at him, as he went round the market. Fnally he left it and went off home. A week later, market day came round again, and again he went. A few people said 'Hullo! There's that fellow with the camel again,' but others said 'Oh, forget it! For we're long used to seeing him.' He heard what they said.

And when he got home, he said to himself '*Gala*!'‡ and went on 'So it only takes one month and ten days!' And he took his daughter and moved her into his hut, and she became his wife. And people had plenty to say about it, which was troublesome. But he heard it all, and ignored it. And he and his daughter just went on living together. And presently people stopped speaking to him about it. That's the end of that tale.

---

* Cf. I/100.   † Cf. II/65.

‡ This is one of two italicized words presumably Tuareg or pseudo-Tuareg, but I think that the sense is clear without them, this one first probably being an exclamation, in any case.

The Gobir Man [$^{III}/_{59}$]

A Tuareg arrived at a place and put up for the night, and was shown into a hut. Presently a Gobir man arrived and was brought to the same hut as the Tuareg. *Fura* was brought to them. They were both lying down, lying on their beds. Presently the Tuareg opened his eyes to see if the Gobir man had got up to uncover the *fura*, and saw that he hadn't

Next the Gobir man got up very quietly and went outside with a lighter,* struck a light and put it to the hut; then returned and, stealthily resuming his place, lay down. The fire took hold of the hut at the entrance. Then the Tuareg took a deep breath and bawled at the top of his voice.

Along came the people and gathered there and knocked the hut down. The Tuareg came running out, but it wasn't until they went inside that they found the Gobir man lying there. He wouldn't get up, and they had to lift him. That's all. That's the end of that tale.

----

* Flint, steel and tinder.

8

THE NUPE

———

The Thief and the Chief of Nupe [III/ XL]

A thief once set off from Kano – he was a famous thief, known everywhere – and made for Nupeland. Reaching there he came across the Chief of Nupe and went into his compound.

But while he was in there, word of this was brought to the Chief of Nupe. Someone told him 'A thief went into your compound – you must be careful.' 'Very well' said he, 'have a proclamation made. Say that there is a thief in this town; and that if anyone puts up a guest whom he doesn't know – he'll be sorry.'

Three days passed and the thief came along himself to where the chief was. 'Peace be upon you' said he. 'And upon you peace' came the reply. Said the thief to the chief 'I've come to say goodbye to you.' 'Who are you?' asked the chief. 'Oh, I'm the thief that you warned people to be careful of.' He went on 'And at the time that you were making that order, I was in your compound. Well, I looked through your compound – and that of your two chief title-holders (*lit.* chiefs). I looked right through all three of them, and found nothing. So now you know – know exactly what is in your compound, and the other two compounds. When you were making that order, I was in your compound – and there's nothing there, nothing. So I'm off home.'

Says the chief 'I see. Well, here's two hundred thousand cowries as provision for the road – but please, for God's sake, don't steal anything of mine.' The thief answered 'Look, if I was going to steal anything, you'd have known nothing and I should have been on my way having done it.' For, he said, he had looked through their compounds and there was nothing there.

———

9

STUPID COUNTRY FOLK

———

The Minstrel and the Dead Man* [$^I/_{72}$]

A minstrel (*dan kama*) was travelling from village to village and he came to a house where the women were gathered, wailing for the master who had died. The minstrel asked them why they were wailing, and an old woman answered him 'It is the master, who has died.' Says he 'Which hut is the body in?' And they showed him and took him to it.

He went into the hut and found the dead man lying there. Then, going out, he said to the women 'Stop crying; for he'll recover.' And they were silent. Then the minstrel said to them 'Prepare *tuwo* and *fura* and *gumba*,† and food of various sorts, and have it ready by the time I get back'. The women promised, and taking out guinea-corn, they husked it and ground it. They slaughtered chickens, and made *tuwo* and *fura* and *gumba*. They prepared a great deal of food, and collecting it together, put it aside till the minstrel should return.

When the minstrel returned, he asked the women if they had finished making ready the food. 'Yes' said they, 'we've finished. We've been waiting for you.' 'Good' says he and going into the dead man's hut, he said to them 'Bring all the food in here.' They obeyed him and heaped all the food up in front of the minstrel in the dead man's hut. Then said the minstrel. 'Very well! Now go out and leave me, and I will use my skill to make him rise.'

Out they went and the minstrel closed the door. Then he took *tuwo*, added the gravy and ate it. He mixed the *fura* with the milk and drank it. He stirred the *gumba* and drank that. He ate just what he wanted till he was full. Then he broke off a little bit of *tuwo* and took a little gravy and a little strip of meat, and, opening the dead man's mouth, put them in. And taking some *gumba* in a spoon‡, he put that

* Cf. M. No. 16   † Pounded bulrush millet and water
‡ A small gourd with stem, split lengthwise.

204

in his mouth too. So the dead man's mouth was all white with the *gumba*, as if he had eaten food.

Then the minstrel went out of the hut, wailing and crying. The women asked him 'How's this? You come out and you're crying! We thought, when you went into the hut, you were going to bring our master back to life and we rejoiced.' And the minstrel replied 'Well – what could I do? I gave him food. Then I gave him some more, and he refused to eat it. Indeed if you go into the hut now, you'll see traces of *gumba* on his mouth. And I ate too, when I saw that he wasn't eating. That's why I've come on out. I fear you'll just have to be patient and resign yourselves, God have mercy on him!'

Then said the women 'Well indeed! There's a rascal for you! That minstrel's just a scoundrel, it seems!' And he went out of the house playing his little drum and chanting 'No one but a foo-ool would swallow one about a dead man coming ba-ack' and he went off leaving them there.

10

THE MALAM

The Meaning of A-L-SH-Y-H* [I/ XLIII]

One shouldn't call a malam 'sheikh', unless he knows the meaning of the five letters of the Arabic title.

The first letter, *alif*, stands for knowing a thousand things,[1] and being known by a thousand: not knowledge of cattle, not knowledge in the sphere of frivolous things, but knowledge of learning or religion.

The second letter, *lam*, stands for mildness,[2] so that whatever is done to him, whether rude words or evil deeds, he will be patient.

The third letter, *shin*, stands for thankfulness[3] towards God. Whatever he receives, be it plentiful or scarce, he will give thanks and if he gets nothing, he can be patient, till God shall give it him.

The fourth letter, *ya*,[4] stands for training in good deeds and the forbidding of evil deeds.

The fifth letter, *kha*, stands for fearing[5] God and fearing what is in men's hearts, so that he avoids that which may make others grieved and surprised.

If a malam knows these meanings, one may call him 'sheikh.' If he doesn't know them, if he answers to the appelation, he is lying.

I got this in the town.

[1]Arabic *alf*, 'thousand'. [2]Arabic *lutf*. [3]Arabic *shukr*.
[4] Probably Arabic 'he' from the opening of a Hadith.
[5] Arabic *khauf* 'fear'.

---

* The Arabic consonants of *al sheikh*, 'the learned doctor'.

Who did a Shameful Deed* [^{I}/$_{102}$]

There was once a malam who set out to make a visit to his in-laws. He got on his mare and set off. Presently he met a boy and called out to him 'Hey, lad.' 'Yes' said the boy. 'Come and keep me company' said the malam, 'for I'm off to make a visit to my in-laws. You can hold my mare for me. Afterwards we'll come back here.' The boy agreed and followed the malam, till they reached the home of his in-laws.

When they arrived, the malam made formal salutation, and they made answer. Then they lodged them close to a hut where the food was cooked. Now three chickens had just been killed, for making soup. And the malam chanced to be watching when the women put on the pot to cook the chickens.

Then in the middle of the night the malam got up and, moving stealthily, went into the hut, lifted the lid of the soup pot, and took out the chickens. He dropped them into his bag and hung it on the pommel of his saddle. Then, as soon as it dawned he mounted his mare and went off, leaving the boy there asleep in the home of his in-laws.

The malam travelled till the sun rose fully as he reached the bank of a river, and getting off, he hitched the leading-rope of his mare to a tree. Then he went down to the river to make his ablutions before praying. He performed his ablutions, and was getting ready to pray, when the mare snapped her leading-rope and went off back to the home of his in-laws at a gallop, not stopping till she reached the post to which she had been tethered. 'Hullo!' said the women of the house 'Here's the malam's mare has run away from somewhere,' and, taking off her saddle, they gave her water to drink.

Meanwhile the malam had run after his mare, but before he reached the house he realised that the mare had got there before him. Then he crouched against the fence and heard the people of the house, saying 'Well, really, the malam was very wrong to do what he did. Fancy taking out chickens that were being prepared for you to eat! After doing such a shameful thing, I wonder how he'll set about getting hold of his mare.'

*Cf. TR. No. 5.

Just then it happened that the fence the malam was leaning against, being rotten, broke and precipitated the malam on his face in the compound. The people of the house saw him. Says he 'Truly I was pushed, from outside the house' and then he was ashamed. But they gave him his horse and he went off home. And as he went he talked nonsense,* saying 'That was a wicked lad that was, to make me act so shamefully at the home of my in-laws,' and he went on talking in this vein till he got home.

* Cf. proverb *tabarmar kunya da hauka kan naɗe ta*, 'the mat of shame gets rolled up with mad behaviour', i.e. covering one's shame by acting crazy. See I/112.

THE BARBER

———————————

The Merchant [$^I/_{55}$]

There was once a very wealthy man – slaves, cattle, camels, God had been exceedingly kind to him. Then one Friday he said to one of his slaves 'Go and call me a barber to shave my head.'* 'Right' says he and off he goes to the edge of the market. There he saw a clean barber. Returning he said 'Here you are, I've fetched you a barber.' 'Good' says his master, 'Let him come in'. Then, when the barber had come in, he said to him 'Come and shave me!'

The barber began wetting his head, all the time blowing his own trumpet: 'Me, I usually shave chiefs, and also rich merchants. When I've shaved them, some give me a gown, some a ram. I remember once I shaved a rich man – like you – *he* gave me a horse and trappings. In fact he wasn't as wealthy as you.'

When he had finished shaving him the rich man said to him 'Very well! Those people who usually give you wealth, even horses – off you go to them, let them give you some more! As for me, since you've said what you've said, I'll give you nothing. Get out of my sight! And if you don't I'll have you beaten. Bloody barbers, with their slanderous talk! God's curse on you!' and he gave him a hundred cowries, and he departed.

———————————

* Normal Hausa male hair style (now changing).

ALL HAUSAS

Character of All Hausas [^I/ XLII]

Let me tell you about the Hausa character – may God preserve us from it!

If there are two Hausas living together, and one sees that the other is wealthier* than he, he will try to bring misfortune upon him. If he succeeds he will go on laughing at him, saying 'Well, you see, anything that happens to So-and-So, it's his own nature has brought it on him.'

And if you observe that a Hausa enjoys fortune or position, and you pay him respect, he will treat you like dirt. Or, wherever a group of Hausas is gathered in conversation, all they do is run down their friends. If they see someone go into his house, paying no attention to anyone but just minding his own business, they will call him two-faced or swollen-headed. But if you join them and take part in the talk, when you have gone they will call you a liar, or a backbiter. Or if the Hausa see you trying to earn something to clothe yourself with, they will say that you are a thief or an embezzler.

Then if you see that a Hausa has been fortunate and greet him – he'll say it's because of his wealth that you come. But if you don't greet him, he'll say you are treating him contemptuously.

If a Hausa does an evil deed, he is anxious that no one should learn of it, but if his friend does it, he will continually strive to make it generally known. So that a man once said 'The Hausas would drive you to words – even if you were an egg.'

Then if a Hausa takes a dislike to you, he knows how to devise that you fall foul of the authorities and involve you in a crime that you have neither seen nor heard of. Then when the case is heard, and the authorities ask him how he came to see you do it, he will

* Or more fortunate.

say 'I have witnesses.' Then, told to bring them, he will call some good-for-nothing fellows and pay them to come and give false witness on his behalf, and even take a false oath. And he too will swear falsely – all to bring a man he dislikes into trouble. But they just laugh. That is what people do nowadays. In fact there are not many nowadays who don't do this – just one or two.

Again, if two Hausas are living together, with one master or one teacher, and their master consults one of them more than the other, the other will continually criticise his companion behind his back, so that their master turns him out and puts the other in his place.

If you see a group of Hausas gathered, busy slandering their neighbours, if you're wise, you won't join them. For if you do, even if you say nothing, they will maintain that you were one of them in all they did.

And whenever you hear a Hausa abusing his friend in front of you, remember that one day he'll do as much for you in front of someone else. A Hausa likes to take his friend into a situation which will destroy him.

May God protect us from the evil nature of the Hausa, amin!

PART III

MORALISING TALES

These usually end in an aphorism.

I

Women

It is worth noting that while most stories in Hausa compounds are told by the women, and the grandmothers in particular – witness the constant emphasis on the details of foods and other household activities – in general, in these moralising stories, we are enjoined not to trust women. There are one or two where women are shown in a favourable light (usually the men show up unfavourably in these), but these are very much in the minority.

The Chief's Daughter and the Calabash-Mender* [III/ 130]

There was once a chief had a beautiful daughter. Other chiefs and their sons would come, but whenever they did so, she would say 'Be off with you. I'm not marrying you. What would you give me?' And so, rejected, they would depart again.

But one day a very important chief got news of her and sent to her, but she wouldn't have him. Whereupon a calabash-mender went to this chief and said 'May the chief's life be prolonged.' And there he was – all ragged. 'Amen, calabash-mender' said the chief, and again 'Is all well with you, that you come now?' 'Very well indeed, may this chief's life be prolonged' said the other. 'Amen' said the chief. Then the calabash-mender went on 'Chief, here's why I've come to see you; now I hear you have sent to a certain girl, wanting to marry her, but she has refused you. Well, I've come to tell you that I can fix for you to marry her.' 'Really?' asked the chief. 'Yes' said the other. 'And how do you do that, calabash-mender?' 'Oh, I'll fix it all right' said the other. 'Calabash-

* A very humble craft. Cf. proverb *ban da tunin baya, g yartai ya sami sarauta,* ' "let's forget one past", as the calabash-mender said when he became chief'. Cf. next tale.

215

mender' said the chief, 'if you fix for me to marry that girl – anything that you ask me for, I'll give you.' 'Really, chief?' asked the other. 'Yes, that's what I said, calabash-mender' replied the chief.

Then the calabash-mender said 'Chief, I want you to give me four different things, each of them accompanied by five people that go with them.' 'Name the ones I am to give you, calabash-mender' said the chief, and the other answered 'Have five horses brought here and fully accoutred and produce five young men to ride them.' 'Very well, calabash-mender' said the chief, 'I have noted that one.'

The other continued 'Then I want you to give me five hide panniers of cola-nuts, together with five sturdy fellows to carry them.' 'Right, I've noted that – that's two' said the chief.

'Then' said the calabash-mender, 'give me five gourds of honey and men to carry them.' 'Very well – that makes three' said the chief.

'Next' said the calabash-mender, 'I want you to give me five loads of strips of woven cloth, each with a man to carry it.' 'Calabash-mender' said the chief, 'that makes four – that's the lot, and each with the people to go with it.'

So the chief had five horses and riders for them brought; five panniers of cola-nuts and men to carry them; five gourds of honey, and their bearers; and lastly five loads of strips of cloth, and men for them.

Then the calabash-mender said 'Me too, chief – have a horse equipped for me with fine accoutrement, and give me gowns and trousers and a turban, so that I may mount and set off, and go and get that woman for you to marry – the one who has rejected you.' But the chief said 'Calabash-mender, if you bring that woman as a bride, I'll give her to you; in fact anything you ask for, I'll give you, 'Really?' asked the other, and the chief confirmed it.

Then the calabash-mender rose and mounted the horse and set off along the road with all his people behind him. And reaching the other town, he alighted outside it. Then he said 'Go and tell the chief of this town that his master has arrived.' His man went and told the chief, who became very angry,* saying that he hadn't got a master.

Whereupon the calabash-mender sent another of his men, saying 'Go and tell the chief of this town that he must be crazy: here's

* Omitting the *shi kuma* after *tashi* which looks like diplography.

the son of his master arrived, and he refuses to come to him.' And the messenger went, and the chief duly mounted and came out, out of the town to the man there.

Then he turned to one of his 'servants', who was on horseback and said 'Hurry back and send those thousand horses back; for if they come and we stop at this town, we'll bring famine on them. And hurry too to those thousand horsemen whom we left in —' and he named a town – 'and tell them to stay the night there, and not to come on here.' And off went the man.

Then the fellow turned to the chief and said 'How is it that I sent two messengers and you wouldn't come?' and to his men 'Here, go and tie him up for insolence.' They rose to do so, but the chief said 'I'm very sorry, master, I won't do it again.' 'Very well then let him be' said the other.

Next the fellow said 'Hey, boys, go and give the horses water to drink.' And the chief of the town had water brought, but the horses wouldn't drink. Then the fellow said 'Oh, well – there's some of our town's water left. Give them that to drink.' So a large gourd of honey was fetched and poured into a big, brass basin and given to the horses, and they sucked up some of it. And the men said 'This water is beginning to smell, the horses have not drunk much.' And he answered 'Well, pour it away then.' But when they went to do so, the chief's courtiers jumped up and tumbled over each other in their eagerness to get some. Then the chief said 'This is indeed my master. He must be the son of the Sultan of Istambul.'

Next the calabash-mender asked 'Have the horses had their guinea-corn?' and was told that they had not. So the chief of the town had bundles of guinea-corn carried out and brought to them. 'What!' said the fellow, 'Will you give my horses chaff? You there! Go and get the rest of the guinea-corn from our town and give that to the horses to eat.' And they went and got a pannier of cola-nuts. 'Here's the rest of the guinea-corn' they said. Whereupon he said to one of his 'servants' 'Go back, and tell those hundred camelmen carrying water not to come on here; and tell the other hundred carrying guinea-corn for the horses to go back too, not to come on here. In the morning I'll come and join them.'

Then the chief sent word into the town, to his compound, telling his women to move out of one part, leaving a part for his master to lodge in. And to his son he sent word that he should make room n part of his compound for their master's servants to move in, for it was not fitting, he said 'For those who are members of our master's household to stay anywhere else but in our own compounds.'

Then the guest said to the chief 'Very well, let's go into your town. So they went on in, and when they got there went into the chief's compound, while the chief's son took the servants to his and put them up there.

When evening came, the man said 'Chief, this is why I've come to your town: it's your daughter. I've heard that, of my father's slaves,* every one he sends to you for her, is turned away by you. Well, it's because of her that I've come.' 'Oh, no' said the chief, 'I haven't a daughter.' 'What!!' exclaimed the man, 'I'll have you tied up here and now, and you can choose between your daughter and your life! Well, which is it to be?'

Then the chief sent someone to look for the girl. She came and greeted the man standing.† 'Your good-for-nothing slut' said he, 'I'll have you imprisoned here and now – you and your father. Or would you prefer that I killed you – and him too?' At which she dropped to the ground, saying repeatedly 'I'm very sorry. I won't do it again. Please restrain your anger.' Then he cooled down. So they went into the hut, he and she; and a hundred blankets were spread for him, and for her, fifty.

Her father said to him 'As far as I'm concerned, she's yours; I give her to you.' To which the fellow answered 'I don't travel with a woman. But when I travel, she can follow behind – but not by the same road as I. For my road will be all holes from the horses, and it will be too rough a journey for you; no, you must go this way, go round by this road and approach our town from the north entering by the northern gate. And the compound you must go to is a large one you'll come upon – that's my compound.'

So the chief of the town had the drum beaten and said that everyone within his domain, everyone was to go and accompany his daughter, when she set off to her husband's home.

Next morning when it was light, the fellow mounted and set off. When he got home, he went up to the chief of his own town and said 'I've arranged a marriage to that girl and she's coming.' 'Is that so?' said the chief. 'Yes.' 'Well' said the chief, 'Just like I said, if

* Amending *bayan* to *bayin*.   † Instead of kneeling courteously.

you did that for me, I would give her to you; and I also promised you that anything you asked for, I would give to you – except what I don't have!'

So the other said 'Chief, I want you to build me a large compound, half a morning's journey across.' 'Very well' said the chief, 'where do you want me to build it for you?' 'By the northern gate of the town.' So the chief had a compound built for him by the northern gate, large and wide. Everything in it was built four times the usual size.*

Then he said 'Chief, I want you to give me a thousand men to cut wood and bring it home for me.' And the chief supplied them and they brought the wood.

Next he said 'Chief I want you to have collected for me a hundred loads of cattle droppings; and a hundred loads of camel droppings; and a hundred loads of fowl droppings; and a hundred loads of sheep droppings; and a hundred loads of donkey droppings; and a hundred loads of mule droppings; and a hundred loads of rope; and a hundred loads of old rope that has snapped off; and a hundred loads of rags; and a hundred new gowns and cloths; and a hundred thousand cowries; and a hundred thousand loads of corn; and a hundred loads of cotton-seed cake.'† And the chief had the whole lot collected and taken to him.

Then the calabash-mender went and scattered the cattle dung in one place; and in another place the camel dung; and in another place the donkey droppings; and in another place the fowl dung; and in another place that of the mules; then back to where the cattle dung was, and scattered the sheep droppings by that. Then he went into the compound and proceeded to scatter, all over the place, corn and cotton-seed cake and money and rags, and the new gowns and the new cloths. Then he went round them all again putting fire to them and destroying them.

Then when he heard that his bride had arrived, he went and covered his body with dust and ashes, and going out on the road, sat down.

Now the girl's father had sent along fifty camels with loads of clothing; fifty pack-oxes with the same; fifty mules with the same; fifty donkeys with the same; a hundred milch-cows; a hundred

* Or, perhaps, 'everything was built with four extra rows.'
† Or possibly cotton-seed.

led horses; a hundred driven camels; twenty camels laden with gowns and trousers and turbans and burnouses – all for the personal use of her husband.

So they came and the people that led the way shouted 'Hey, get out of the way and let the wife of chiefs come by.' 'I won't get out of the way' he said.

Then the bride came up and thrust out her stirrup to kick him aside, when he said to her 'You good-for-nothing slut! Pauper! Now I really will kill you! Even before they said you were a pauper. See here, when I had visited you, my father seized me and tied me up. Women love lies!* For [he said] that I went after the slaves of our household had been and you had rejected them all; but when I went, you accepted me and I brought you home as wife. So he seized me and tied me up and took all that I had. Had what he did to me been done to your father, he would have died then and there, died of grief. And now I'm going to kill you.' 'No, no' she said, 'Just let me restore your possessions to you.' 'You're lying' he said, 'for if you include all the horses I had out around the country – which also my father took – there were three thousand.' 'But let us go and beg your father to restrain his anger.' But he said 'I swear that if anyone goes to beg the chief to restrain his anger, I'll order my horsemen that are around the country to go and burn the town,† and to kill the people in it.'

The girl ordered her horsemen into the compound and they saw the innumerable signs of destruction. They returned and told her and she entered the compound herself. When she came to the entrance, she spurred her horse forward and began to gallop, but before she reached the farther side of the compound, her horse became exhausted. And when she got back she gave some of her horsemen orders, saying 'Go quickly and tell my father what my husband has suffered for coming to seek me in marriage.'

Then her father sent riders, telling them to come and have a look. They reached the entrance [but before they covered the distance] from that one to the far one, one of the horses fell dead. Other horses were sent off at the gallop; but before they too reached the other gate, one of them failed from exhaustion.

The girl replaced the horses of her father's messengers and said

---

* See reference at the beginning of the story.   † Perhaps 'this town'.

'Go and tell my father to send a thousand men, to come and build up this compound; and two hundred cattle and two hundred camels, and two hundred each of everything else. And why I say this is because this chief's son has been treated in this way by his father because of me. And so I – since my father is a chief – that's why he must give these things, so that we can give my husband back his possessions; and even if we don't give him all of them, we can at least give him some.' And her father had all those beasts driven over, and with them the thousand builders too.

So they settled down there, and at once the girl became pregnant, and bore a child, a boy. Time passed and the boy grew.

One day he went to the market and saw a naked fellow with just a leather lioncloth. The boy struck him and the man said 'Ha! There's a shameless boy for you! Oho, your father was just the same as I – nothing but a leather loincloth. But just because he went and married your mother and your people made him rich, you think you can strike me. Yes indeed, your father was a calabash-mender, a stitcher of gourds.'

And the boy went and told his mother. And she called his father and asked him. And he said 'You crazy woman! How long – but we're already married, aren't we and we've got a child? So just let me fetch my tools for you, tools which everyone in the town knows are my trade'

Then he brought his large needle and cord and his little knife, and his loincloth and his rags and his little, round gourd.* Said he 'D'you see? These are the tools that everyone in the town knows are mine. You women, if anyone reveals the truth to you, you accord him no respect; but if someone tells lies to you, you're more likely to trust him.'

And now you know how it is that even now, women don't like the truth – just lies. That's all. *Kungurus kan kusu.*

---

* To hold water for keeping the cord damp.

Women-like-lies and his Wife* [^{I}/₂₆]

Once there was a man called Women-like-lies who set out to get a wife for himself. He hadn't any money, or a gown, or trousers – nothing to improve his appearance. All he had on was a loin-cloth, fastened round his waist and hitched over his shoulders. And his friend said to him 'Hey! How will you set about finding a wife, without any money? For you know, for someone to go seeking a wife without money is like someone who goes hunting a gazelle without a dog. Has he a hope of catching her?' 'No' he answered 'but I've an idea – you see, women like lies.'

And off he went to a village where he wasn't known, to see a certain rich man there. And he borrowed a gown, trousers, a turban and a horse. Also he said 'I want you to give me some cola-nuts, ten calabashes full, and a pot of honey – I'll borrow all these, and I'll bring them back to you before two days have passed.' The other agreed and collecting them all together gave them to Women-like-lies. And he took off his loin-cloth and left it there. Then, mounting the horse, he set off in search of a wife.

When he got to the house where he hoped to get one, he called out 'Peace be upon you.' And they answered 'And upon you be peace. Welcome, welcome!' He dismounted and was taken to where he was to stay, and they tied up his horse for him.

Then, when he came to his lodging-place, he exclaimed 'Here! Who told you to tie my horse up with *rope*?' And the boy replied 'I don't know.' Then the other said 'Well – here's what he is tied with' and he brought out a sword-sling made in Timbuctu and gave it to him, saying 'Tie him up with that! That's what we tie horses up with in our town.'

Well, the boy who tied his horse up for him was the younger brother of the girl he sought in marriage, and when he went home he told her. He said to her 'Here, I say! Do you know that stranger that has come seeking you in marriage, he's one of a chief's family!' And she asked 'Why, what did you see?' And he answered 'Well, even his horse isn't tied up with a rope tether, but a sword-

* Cf. last tale. See J. p. 176. For the cola-nuts and honey motif cf. O. p. 273, line 12 et seq.

sling.' Says she 'Let's go and see!' and they went to his lodging-place and she bade him welcome.

While they were exchanging greetings, his horse whinnied and Women-like-lies said 'Oh! I wonder if the horse wants grass. Here you, see that grass there, take some of that and throw it to him!' The boy looked and didn't see any grass. He said 'But I don't see any grass – just cola-nuts' and the other answered 'Cola-nuts? Oh, yes, that's what we give horses in our town' and he took some of the cola-nuts and gave them to the horse. The horse wouldn't eat them.

Then straight away the woman got up and went home, much amazed, and said to her parents 'Today I've seen a husband! He's the only one for me!' Her parents asked her what she saw in him, and she answered 'Well! Even his horse is fed, not on grass but cola-nuts; drinks, not water, but honey; and is tied up, not with a rope tether but with a sword-sling.' And her parents agreed with her and said 'You must be married and off with you both!' So she and Women-like-lies were married.

And they went to his town. When they got there, on the second day afterwards he returned what he had borrowed. Then he picked up his loin-cloth and, fastening it on, walked home. Then she asked him 'Where is your horse and all your things?' and he replied 'You haven't much sense! Didn't you hear my name, "Women-like-lies"? Other than lies, where did you ever hear of a horse being given cola-nuts to eat like grass? Or honey to drink like water? Or being tied with a sword-sling? If I hadn't done these, would I have got you to come along with me here?' And she answered 'No.' Then said he 'If you don't wish to be married to me, be off with you back home! Me – I've nothing, except this lioncloth I'm wearing.' *Kungurus kan kusu.*

The Hero, Dan Zuraidu, and the Jinns* [$^I/_{71}$]

There was once a warrior called Dan Zuraidu, chosen of God. In his time, he had no peer for mighty feats in time of battle. He was the son of an emir, and so jealous was he, that he didn't have his house in the town, but a long way outside, so that no man might come and see his wives. Of wives he had four, of concubines twenty, and none of them had ever borne a child.

One day he rode off to war. Whereupon an old woman took some *daddawa* and set out for his house, to sell it. She reached the gate of the compound and had put out her wares for sale, when the women of the house called out to her 'Come on in! The master is away.' She went in, and putting down the *daddawa*, sat herself down. Then the women of the house asked her 'Can you do hair?' and when she said she could, they combed out their hair and got her to plait it up for them. And as she worked she chatted with the woman whose hair she was doing. Says the latter 'Just look at us in this compound! In this whole crowd of us, there's not one has had a child from the master! We're seeking a cure for barrenness!' Says the old woman 'Oh, I've got one, but the ingredient is a difficult one to get.' Says the other 'How difficult?' 'Well' says the old woman, 'you need the head of the baby of a jinn.' 'Very well' said the women 'When the master returns, we'll tell him' and the old woman went off home.

When their lord returned from the war, his women gathered in front of him, and the chief one addressing him said 'After you went to the war the other day, an old woman from in the town came here. She did our hair, but also told us of a cure for our barrenness and said that when you came back from the war she would come and give it to us, but before she can do that, she said she needs the head of the baby of a jinn.' 'Oh, yes' says he, 'is that all? I'll get that right away.'

And he had his horse saddled, and, when it was midday he mounted and rode off into the bush. He travelled a long way, till he came to where the jinns were. There he found a female jinn who had lately had a child, with her son in her arms. And, drawing his

* Cf. III/64.

224

sword, he cut off the son's head and taking it, he went home with it.

But while he was still on his way and had not yet reached home, the jinns returned to their homes from their rounds, and saw that someone had cut off their child's head. Then said their chief 'Hey! What sort of creature has dared to cut off this baby's head? Even if he is twenty days' journey away, bring him here at once!'

So they sent one of the younger jinns after him and before Dan Zuraidu reached home, the jinn found him and seized him; and holding him with one hand, he brought him along, together with his horse. 'Here you are' says he, I've brought him.' Then they took him off his horse, and, taking a bush-cow, stripped the skin off it whole, and putting him inside it, they hung him up on a tree.

Forty years passed, and then two hunters happened to be hunting there in the bush. They saw what looked like a water-skin fixed to a tree, and taking it down tried to open it. But try as they would, they couldn't open it.

Then they took it to a stream and putting it in let it soak. Then they were able to open it and saw a man inside, but very far gone, very thin, mere skin and bones (bone and hair). They lifted him up and took him home, and gave him hot water to drink, and then gruel a little at a time, until he began to speak.

They shaved him and then they asked him about it. Said they 'Well now, what brought all this on you? And he told them the cause of the business, from the beginning to the end. Then, when they had heard it, they said 'Alas! You followed the advice of women – and look at the trouble that brought you to!' Then they left him, and settling in the town, he built himself a home there.

The Gazelle which Turned into a Woman*[I/81]

There was once a gazelle which turned into a woman and came into a town. As she was walking a farmer saw her, and called to her. She turned her head and he said 'Come here!' So she went over and

* Cf. next tale and TR. No. 58.

knelt in front of him, and he said 'I called you over because I want to marry you.' 'Yes' says she, 'I like you too.' So they were married and settled down together.

Time passed and he said to his wife 'Take a basket and a knife and go to the farm and cut some okra and bring them home. 'Certainly' says she and off she goes to the farm. When she got there she took off her cloth and threw it down, and her loincloth and threw that down; then she took off her headcloth and, rolling on the ground, turned into a gazelle. Then she collected her mates, the other gazelles, and they gathered. They ate up all the beans* completely. And when they had all gone, she rolled on the ground again and turned back into a woman, put on her clothes, took up her basket and went off home. There she told her husband that there were no beans as gazelles had eaten them all. And he had to agree.

This went on for some, until one day a friend of her husband got to the farm before her. He climbed up a tree and sat there till she arrived. Then, when she had got to the centre of the farm, she took off her cloths and lying down and rolling, turned into a gazelle. Then she gathered her mates and they came and set about eating the beans.

Her husband's friend came down from the tree and got home before her. There he said to her husband, his friend 'Do you know what! That wife of yours is a gazelle.' 'What have you seen?' said the husband. And he answered 'I went before her to the farm very early and climbing a tree waited for her to come. When she came she went into the centre of the farm and took off her clothes. Then she rolled on the ground and turned into a gazelle. Then she collected the other ones, and they ate up your beans.' And the husband said 'I see. Let us wait till she comes.'

When she returned, she put down the basket and said to her husband 'No beans! All eaten by the gazelles!' and he replied 'Very well, that's that! Go and sit yourself down!' And she did so.

And when it was evening she put the pot on the fire to make the *tuwo*, and as she bent down to blow up the fire, her headcloth fell down, so that you could see horns. And her husband saw them. She stood up and her cloth fell down, and she became a gazelle. When they saw her, the people yelled out 'Help! Help! Stop her! Stop

* Sic. cf. I/11.

her! There she is – don't let her escape!' And they caught her and killed her, and ate the meat. From that day he never again married a woman without ascertaining her origins. *Kurungus kan kusu.*

A Variant [$^{\mathrm{I}}/_{11}$]

It is said that a gazelle changed her form and became a beautiful woman. And she went into a town in search of a man to marry.

And a man saw her and took her in marriage. Then they were dwelling together, but he was in ignorance that she was a gazelle that had changed her form. Then she said to him 'I'm going out of town to collect some medicine' and he said 'O.K., off you go!' Then she made her way to her husband's farm – he had planted beans – and going in amongst the beans, threw off her cloth, rolled on the ground and turned into a gazelle.

She gathered together the gazelles on her husband's bean farm, and after they had eaten the beans, they ran off. As for her, she took up her cloth and fastened it on, became a woman again, and returning home, said to her husband 'I'm back.' And he said 'Where's the medicine that you collected?' she answered 'Oh, I couldn't get any.'

As it happened, at the time she had been transformed on the farm, a friend of her husband was up a tree and watched what she did. When he returned home, he said to him 'Terrible news! Your wife is a gazelle.' He answered 'Where did you see this?' and he answered 'I saw her on the farm, she rolled on the ground and turned into a gazelle. Then she collected the gazelles and they came and ate beans on your farm.' And the other said 'Tomorrow I'll come with you and see.'

In the morning, she came and said to him 'I'm going to the bush to collect some medicine' and he answered 'O.K., off you go!'

She went on the bean farm, threw off her cloth, rolled on the ground and turned into a gazelle. The she gathered together the gazelles and they came on to the farm and began eating the beans. Meanwhile her husband and his friend were up the tree watching them.

They returned home and waited till she came. But he said nothing to her, till evening came and she was sitting there. Then he came up to her and said 'Hey! Where were you today that you took so long?' and she answered 'I went to collect medicine.'

Then he began hitting her on the head with a stick, and suddenly horns appeared there. She got up – and she had four legs. He yelled for help and the neighbours gathered and, catching her, they slaughtered her and ate the meat. Then said he 'I'll never again marry a woman, when I don't know what home she comes from!'

The Hunter and his Friend [^{I}/ 126]

There was once a man who went hunting, but he caught nothing but four locusts.

He set out on his way home and met a friend of his. Says the friend 'Where are you from?' and he answered 'I've been hunting, but I didn't get anything except four locusts, 'Please give me one of them' said the other. 'No' said he, 'look – these four locusts are each needed for a particular purpose. This one – I've got to pay back a debt with it. This one I'm going to lend. This one is for myself, to eat. And the last I'm going to throw away. The one for settling a debt I'm going to give to my parents, who cared for me till I became a man: I'll recompense them with this one. As for the one that I'm going to lend, that is for my children, so that when they grow up, they'll have pity on me. As for the one that's for myself, to eat – well, charity begins at home.* And the one that I'm going to throw away, I'm going to give to my wife. For whatever you do for a woman, one day she'll turn against you and go to someone else. So whatever you do for her, you're throwing it away.'

And the other replied 'My word! What a fellow! You're too clever for me! Get along with your locusts, I don't want one.'

---

* *Lit.* all liking is liking, but liking oneself is best (proverb).

The Warrior, the Hunter and the Hunter's Wife* [$^{I}/_{149}$]

There was once a warrior, who desired to have the wife of a hunter. Said he to her 'What shall I do to kill your husband, that we may be married?' 'I'll think about it' said she.

They continued for a while in their profligacy, and there came a day when she said to the warrior 'Meet me at such-and-such a place on Friday.' On Thursday, in the evening, she made ready.

Early next morning the hunter said to her that she should get his food for him. 'Right' said she. But when he went out, she took his quiver and removing all the arrows, put them in her basket and, covering them up, took it and went off to where she was to meet the warrior.

A little later her husband returned and asked for her. The people told him 'We saw her carrying something, running away from here.' Then he went quickly into his hut and taking his quiver, slung it on his shoulder, and followed the way she had taken. As he was running, he saw her in the distance, and soon came up with her. When he did so he found her sitting with her paramour, the warrior. Then the hunter said to him 'Peace be upon you! On guard!' The warrior answered 'And upon you be peace.'

The hunter tightened his bowstring and moved his hand to take out an arrow, but found only a headless shaft. Again he felt and again he brought out a shaft. Then he turned his quiver up and found there was not a complete arrow in it, just shafts. Meanwhile the warrior had tightened his girth, mounted his horse and awaited him. Then he rode up to the hunter to cut him down, and the hunter prepared to die at his hands.

But then the warrior turned back and taking out his sword, struck the woman and killed her. Then said he to the hunter 'Let us be friends. Since she has treated you thus, if I were to kill you, she would have done the same to me. Any man who becomes involved with a woman will lose his life one day.'

---

* Cf. J. p. 173

The Chief and his Wife [$^{III}/_{41}$]

There was once a man who was exceedingly poor, and he went daily to the bush to cut wood and bring it in.

But one day, when he went out as usual, he saw an anthill. He began digging into it and found – a pot of gold. Getting it out, he took it home. He began selling the gold, and buying slaves and horses.

Now before, when he had no wealth, the people of the town hadn't liked him. But when they saw that he had money, he became more popular with them.

And, when the chief of the town died, they appointed him in his place. He had been chief for some time, when a prostitute* heard news of this chief. She went and sought out some thieves, and said to them 'I'm going to the home of this chief, this rich man, and when I get there I'm going to marry him. When I've done that, then you come along, and say that you are my elder brothers.' 'O.K.' said they.

Along went the woman and said 'Chief, your name has reached my ears, and I have come, for love of you, that we may be married, you and I.' 'Very well' said he and agreed. And so they were married, and she took up her residence in the chief's compound.

Then one day along came the thieves, four of them. They made formal greeting, and the chief asked them 'Hey there, boys – where are you from?' They answered 'May the chief's life be prolonged, we are the elder brothers of the women that you have married' and they gave her name. 'That's fine' said the chief, and to his people 'Take them in. There's a hut just close to the entrance-hut, just inside the compound. Let them stay there.' So they were taken there and put their things down there.

But the chief was still engaged with his courtiers, when the thieves had gone on into the compound, the woman made two of them go on out of the compound, while she and the other two set to, collecting together all the things there and passing them out, until they had stripped the compound. Then they climbed over the wall and so got out. And picking up the things, off they went.

* But for the connotations of *karuwa* See BABA p. 25.

Presently the chief rose and withdrew from the public gathering and going into his compound, found it stripped. he began to shout, and people asked each other 'Who's that shouting in the chief's compound?' And going in, they found that it was the chief.

They asked him what was the matter. Says the chief 'That woman conspired with thieves, and they came here and have robbed me. But now I want people to mount their horses and follow them and arrest them and bring them here. For they have taken all my things. They haven't even left me a mat.' So they were pursued, and the woman and two of the men caught. The other two men ran off into the bush and escaped.

So they brought her back to the chief with the two men, and all the things they had taken. The chief questioned her, but she denied ever having seen the two men before. They, however, refuted this, saying that she had brought them there.

So it was suggested that she should be taken to the judge. 'No' said the chief, 'for, people, you don't understand. Women are not persons of integrity. And if you deal with them honestly, they for their part will set a trap for you to try to kill you. No, I'm letting her go, to go where she will. I shan't do anything, for women are not persons of integrity. A hundred tricks a woman will play a man, and he won't spot a one of them. No, she can just return my things to me and then go – I don't want her.' That's all. *Kungurus kan kusu.*

The Hunter, his Wife
and the Guinea-fowl [^{III}/165]

A hunter went out shooting and came upon a guinea-fowl in the bush. He drew back the arrow to shoot her, when she said 'Stop. Don't shoot me. But tell me what in this world you would like, and I'll give it to you – be it high office, or learning, or wealth.' Said the hunter 'Very well, I won't shoot you. But give me your promise, while I go and consult my wife.' The guinea-fowl agreed.

He returned home, and his wife said 'Today you're back empty-handed. Haven't you shot anything?' 'I've got something to discuss' he answered. 'I found a guinea-fowl in the bush, but when I fitted an arrow to shoot her, she told me not to, but to tell her what I wanted most in the world and she would give it to me – high office, or learning, or wealth. So I came to consult you. What shall we choose?' 'Forget about all those' she answered, 'you go and tell her to give a slightly larger penis.'

He hurried back and, getting there, found the guinea-fowl and said to her 'The only thing I want – I only want you to make my penis bigger.'* Says the guinea-fowl 'Bring it here.' He held it out to her, and she took hold and said to him, 'Pull a little, and when you get it as you want it, tell me.' He pulled and moved back a long way. 'Do you want all that?' she asked. 'Yes' he said. So she bestowed it on him and he lifted it and coiled it round his body, with some even to spare. This he held in his hand and hurried off, back to his compound.

His wife saw it and said 'Phe-e-e-w! I don't like that. That's too much!' So he hurried back to where he had left the guinea-fowl, but he found her gone. He went home again, but his wife would have nothing to do with him.

And ever since then, anyone who aims at what a woman wants, comes to a bad end.

The Pious Man and his Wife† [III/₁₃₅]

There was once a pious man had an ugly wife. There was none in the whole town so ugly as she. Moreover they lacked food even for the day, let alone the morrow. The pious man had no gown, and his wife had no cloth to wear. And withal she was exceedingly plain.

But he went and built a hut, and said to his wife 'Look – I'm going into this hut, and I want you to block up the entrance, so that I may live as a hermit for forty days.' 'Very well' said she.

* Like a man, he got the details wrong, forgetting the 'slightly'!
† See J. p. 69.

Then the pious man went into the hut, and his wife closed up the entrance with earth. Thirty-nine days he spent, praying to God. Then on the fortieth day when he was sleeping, in the night, he had a dream, that if he prayed for three things, he would obtain them.

Next day when it was light, he said to his wife 'Hey there – open up the entrance so that I may get out. The time's up, for today I've been forty days in this hut.' Then his wife fetched a large adze and knocked an entrance, and he emerged. Says he to his wife 'Thirty-nine days I prayed to God, and on the fortieth, at night, I was shown in a dream that I would be granted three prayers – whatever I prayed for, it was said, God would give me'. 'Is that so?' said his wife. 'Yes' said he.

And she said 'Well! Look, husband, since I'm not beautiful, couldn't you pray for me to become beautiful? You know, in all this town there's none so ugly as I.'

So, when night fell, the pious man prayed to God. And next morning when it was light, there was his wife, a beauty, handsome without peer: if she waved to you, the marrow would flow out of your bones! News reached the chief's compound. 'Is this so?' asked the chief, and he was assured that it was. So the chief sent and had the woman taken into his compound.

Then the pious man's heart was very sore – his thoughts were very dark, and he said 'Now when I prayed to God, he said he would give me three prayers, and whatever I asked for I should get.' So the pious man prayed to God again, and the woman turned into a monkey, squatting there on the bed. At which the chief's women in the compound there, seeing it, went running off with all speed to the chief and told him. He rose and went into the compound, and into the hut, and saw that his bride had become a monkey. Then he called his slaves and said 'Come here and take this female monkey to the compound of the pious man, and leave her there.' And they did so. And the pious man sat for a while looking at the female monkey, and she at him.

Then at length he again prayed God, and his wife resumed her original form.

Then the pious man realised that he had the three prayers that had been granted him, and he had seen their results. And yet when he first began praying to God it was for food and something to clothe himself with and to give to others – these were why he had gone to pray, and he had been granted three prayers. But now, as it was, he had gone and prayed for something for a woman – and three times, so that all of them were gone on his wife, and now he could not pray for anything else.

Then the pious man said 'So it seems that anyone in this world who follows the advice of a woman, will be led by her to destruction.'

And that is how it is that still, unless a man has nothing to do with the advice of women, something will go wrong in the course of his life: things that he doesn't like will keep happening to him, nor will he have anyone he can trust. That's all. This with peace.

The Students [III/ 167]

There were four boys whose parents put them to school, and their teacher took them travelling round the country. This lasted for a long time, until they were advanced pupils.

One day they were chatting together, when their malam came and concealed himself to listen without their knowledge. One of them was saying 'If my father is still alive today, he's a pauper.' The next said 'If my father's still alive, he's a rich man.' The next said 'If my father is still alive, he's a cripple.' And the last said 'If my father's still alive, he's blind.' There their conversation ended, and none of them enquired of the others their reasons.

The malam got tired of standing there and went about his business. Next day when it was light, he called them over, and said 'Yesterday I came on you when you were talking, but I didn't hear the explanations for what you said. Now you said' turning to one of them, 'that if your father was alive, he would now be a pauper. What was your reason for that?' 'My father's characteristic' he answered, 'of never buying anything that isn't old.' 'How about you then? You said that if your father was alive he would be a rich man.' The next boy answered 'My father's characteristic of never buying anything that wasn't new.' 'And how about you, that said that if your father were still alive he would be a cripple. What was your reason?' And the boy answered 'It is in my father's character every year to clear a new piece of farmland. And I know that that won't have a healthy end.' 'And you that said that if your father was alive, he would be blind, what was your reason?' 'The circumstance of my father's farm being east of the town and a long way off. When he goes out in the morning, he has two hours of sun in his face; and when he finishes work to go home, every evening it is in his face too that the sun sets.'

Then he said to them 'The benefit of study is wisdom; and you have shown wisdom. Let each of you come and say what he would like, and I will pray for it from God.' The first said 'Pray that I may be fortunate in my wife.' The malam did so. The next said 'Pray for wisdom for me,' and the malam did so. The next said 'Pray for wealth for me,' and the malam did so. And the last said 'Pray for high office for me,' and the malam did so. Then he dismissed them and they went back to their parents' homes.

After this, God heard their teacher's prayer and each of them received that which he wished. Says the malam 'Just let me go and see my pupils.' So he travelled to where they were, and began asking after each one of them. Of one he was told 'Oh, he is a malam' and was given directions on how to find him. He went along and found him in his compound, with many other malams who were acquiring wisdom from him. The teacher stood at the door. 'Peace be upon you' said he; 'And upon you, peace' came the reply. Then he went in and his pupil saw him and, getting up from his sheepskin, embraced him with great joy. Then all the students went away, leaving him with his malam, and they spoke of matters concerning learning, until the day was far spent. Then they were brought a little *tuwo*, there in his old pupil's compound, and they ate. But neither teacher nor pupil ate their fill, for they were back to their talk of learning. Night came, and they lit a lamp. And only when the day came, did they say goodbye, and the malam rose to go.

Then he asked where the next of his pupils was. 'Oh' came the reply. 'He's a rich man now.' The direction to go was pointed out to him, and he made his way there and made formal greeting. Someone spoke with him and told him that his man had gone off to have a look at his young cattle. So the malam sat down and waited. Meanwhile his pupil inspected his young cattle and then went out and met the cows coming home. He returned with them and started milking them, and when the time for the night prayer came, he had still not had the chance to talk with his malam. Then, when he had finished all his tasks, he entered his compound, and was told 'There's been a guest here ever since it was day.' 'Where is he?' he asked, and they called his teacher in. He came in, and when the pupil saw him, he got up and embraced him, saying 'Welcome, malam!' He was delighted. Then plentiful food – worldly things – was brought; and the malam ate, and ate his fill. Next day when it was light, the malam said 'I'm going now.' And the other fetched out wealth a-plenty to give parting presents to his teacher with.

On he went and asked where the next pupil was. He was told that he was the chief. He was shown the way and he went there. But for a whole month he was unable to meet with the chief.

Then one day the chief came out to go to Friday mosque. The malam came out of the mosque before the chief and waited at the entrance. The chief turned his head – and saw him. Then he stopped and said 'There's my teacher.' And he clasped his hand,* pleased to see him.

They went into the compound, and all the courtiers dispersed. He and the chief chatted together, and then he told him that, if God brought the morrow, he would be off. And the chief showed him noble generosity. Then he took his leave of the chief, and was taken to his lodging, and there he passed the night.

Next day when it was light, he rose and set off, and as he went along he enquired where the last pupil lived. 'Oh' he was told, 'in all our country none has such a wife as he. Even the king of the world hasn't the like of her.' They showed him the way and going there, he made formal greeting, but was told that he was not at home.

The wife prepared delicious food and had it all ready. Her husband didn't get back until the evening. When he did so and found his teacher there, he embraced him with joy. Says he 'Let a mat be spread in the inner compound,' and it was brought, and the food at the same time. 'Did you hear that I was coming then?' asked the malam. But the other denied it. 'But this food has been prepared with special care.' 'That's the way my wife is.' 'Well' said the malam, 'God's blessing upon her.' Then he ate and was satisfied, and lay

* A rare privilege for a Hausa chief to accord someone.

down. Next morning when it was light, they took leave of each other, and the malam went his way.

Time passed and one day his courtiers said to the chief 'Just because you were a fellow-pupil of' and they named the other three, 'Is that why they show you discourtesy? Never since you have been chief have they come. Is it *their* country?'

So the chief sent to the learned one and had him summoned. When he came, the chief asked him why he had shown him discourtesy, but he denied having done so. Then the chief made him judge of the town.

Next he sent for the rich man, and he came. He asked him why he had shown him discourtesy, and he too denied it. 'Since I've been chief, have you ever come to call on me?' 'No, I haven't.' So he fined him a million cowries.

Then the chief sent to fetch the one with the wife. He got up to go, but his wife said 'We must go together.' 'You stay here' he said. 'Why?' she asked and then 'I won't let my husband go among crooks.' 'You're right' he said, 'Come, we'll go together.'

They came before the chief. Word was brought him that the man had come with his wife, who was without peer in the whole country. The chief coveted her, and said 'Yes, of course, for you know we were at school together.' And the chief lodged him in his compound. Then he sought out some hunters and brought them in and hid them in the compound. Now, the guest had a mare with him, and she was tied up at the entrance to his hut.

Midnight came and the chief made them loose a horse in his compound, saying to the hunters 'When the horse goes to that mare, and her owner comes out – shoot him!' 'Right' they said, and the chief went in and let the horse out. The horse rushed at the mare.

The woman's husband heard it and jumped up, but his wife clasped him and asked 'Where are you going?' Says he 'There's a horse got to the mare.' 'And what' she asked, 'do you expect a male to do to a female? Just relax,' and he did so. The horse mounted the mare. When it got down again, the two of them began eating grass together quietly, with no quarrelling.

After a little, the chief heard nothing, and thinking he had been killed, went out to go to the mare. The hunters saw him, and thinking he was her owner, shot him and killed him. Then, sure that they had done the task given them by the chief, they went out and departed.

Next day when it was light, there lay the chief dead in the hut. News came that a letter had been received telling of an attacking army on its way. The courtiers gathered at the entrance to the chief's home, but the chief failed to make his appearance.

His friend, the one with the wife, came out, and they said to him 'The chief hasn't appeared, and – look – there's news of an attacking army.' So he went in for the chief, and presently emerged wearing the chief's things. Says he 'The chief says that I am to lead you. He is not feeling well today. And now let us go and defend (our country) against this host.' And they went and checked the attackers and routed them.

Before they got back, the wife of the owner of the mare prepared food – worldly delights – and took it to the entrance of the chief's home. Then, when they got back, her husband dismounted and entered the compound; came out again and divided out the food. And while they ate, they were saying 'In all the time we've been in this town, we've never eaten such tasty food as this.' Then they enquired after the chief's health and he told them that he would come out in the early afternoon. And so they dispersed.

He went in and his wife gathered the chief's womenfolk. He took them and showed them the chief, dead, and said 'As for me, my friend is dead, but you – you have not lost your husband.' And he gave them lavish presents.

Then he took more wealth and carried it outside. The courtiers gathered, and he said 'The chief has told me to distribute presents to you.' And he gave them wealth lavishly, so that each one received more than he had ever before received. And they started to say 'May God leave this friend of the chief here. He's a good fellow. The chief never gave presents like this, before his arrival.'

Next day when it was light, he had the praise-singers sent for; made himself popular with them by giving them presents, and ordered them to play the chief's tune for him. They played it, and soon the whole town was astir with the news that the chief was better.

The chief's court was soon full and the coverings were spread out where he sat. Out comes the guest and takes his seat. They saw that it wasn't the chief, but greeted him. Then he ordered the commoners to depart. They did so, leaving him with the ruling men. He turned to one of them and asked him what his rank was. The other answered and was told that it had been increased twofold. All of them he treated in the same way. Then he said 'Your chief has killed himself.' They asked him how it was and he said 'He coveted my wife. He hid some hunters and let a horse out to my mare, intending that when I came out they should shoot me. I heard the noise the horse made and jumped up, but my wife clasped me, saying "Man, what do you expect a male to do to a female?" So I stayed there, and the horse mounted the mare. And when he got off, they began eating together quietly. The chief, hearing nothing, came out and the hunters shot him, thinking that it was me. Now, what I have to say to you is this – you are the chief men of this place. Do you want me for your chief? If you don't – I am still your chief. For I have given what I gave to you to the foot-soldiers too, and if you oppose me, I shall use them against you. If you accept my friendship, things will be better for you than they were before.' Then they all rose and held their hands out to him. Everyone gave him his fealty.

And that's why it was first said that if a man boasts a better mother than you, see if you can't get a better wife than he. End of tale.

2

POVERTY

The Son of the Emir of Katsina and the Poor Man* [¹/₁₄]

One day it is said the son of the Emir of Katsina went for a stroll. Said he to his servants 'What I want is to be shown poverty, clearly, so that I may see it.' And one said 'Really to be shown poverty?' And he answered 'Just so, show me some.'

And his people went off to the market, and, as they were walking along, they saw a man who had no gown and who was selling the leaves off corn stalks. He would collect a load of them and bring it in, sell it for forty cowries and buy food for himself to eat. And the Emir's son's people said to him 'Here you, seller of corn-stalk leaves, come here! The son of the Emir of Katsina wants to see you.' And he said 'You're – it can't be me, I'm a poor man, why should the son of the Emir send for me?' But they said 'You're the one he wants to see.'

And they took him to the Emir's son, and said 'Here's poverty, we've brought it for you to see.' He looked him over, and said to them 'This – is this poverty?' And they said 'This is it.'

Then said he 'Send for a barber to shave his head.' So a barber was sent for and he shaved his head. Then the Emir's son put a gown on him and trousers and gave him a horse and a compound. And he added thirty concubines and gave him ten goats, ten donkeys, ten mules and ten camels. Of all the things of the world he gave him ten each, and said 'Take him to live in the compound I have given him. All these things are his.'

And when he was brought to the compound, as he made to enter it, he fell down dead.

* Cf. TR. No. 28

And of him people said 'Whatever man may give you, if God is not the giver, your work is vain.' And the Emir's son said 'From now on I'll not ask for poverty to be brought me again – I thank God.'

A Poor Man* [^{I}/$_{32}$]

There was once a man who was very poor, so that he lacked food from day to day.

So he set off and went to the chief's home and said to him 'Chief, may your days be lengthened!' 'Amen' says the chief, and his retainers asked 'Here, you, what do you want?' He answered 'I've come to see the chief, I've something to say to him.' The chief said 'Let him be, let him say what he has to say!' Then he said 'Chief, I've come for you to kill me. My poverty is too much for me to bear. I've nothing to eat from day to day, nor do I possess anything but my leather loin-cloth.' 'Very well' says the chief, 'take him and kill him! Since he says that he can't bear his poverty, kill him, that he may be quit of his poverty.'

The guards seized him and took him away. They were on the point of killing him, when another man came up and said to them 'When you've killed him, I'd like you to give me his loin-cloth.' Then said the first 'Take me back to the chief, I've something to say to him.'

The guards took him back to the chief and the chief said 'What's this! Why have you brought back the man who asked to be killed because he couldn't bear his poverty?' And the man said to the chief 'The reason I asked to be brought back is that I have seen someone who is poorer than I am. Before I though I was the poorest, but when they took me to kill me in the market, another man came up and asked the guards to give him my loin-cloth, after they had killed me. So I asked to be brought back before you, since I had seen a poorer than I.' Then said the chief 'There! You

* Cf. TR. No. 9.

see? Where one man refuses to spend the day, another will willingly sleep. This loin-cloth of yours that you despised, so that you asked to be killed, here's someone else who hasn't even the like of that and says he wants it. So now, just thank God for what you have!'

A Variant* [^{I}/$_{33}$]

Another tale. There was once a man who was excessively poor so that he was at his wits' end and lacked for food from day to day. So poor was he that all he had was a leather loin-cloth.

So he set out and went to the chief's house. And he said to the chief 'God give you the victory! God lengthen your days! I've come before you to ask you to kill me. My poverty is more than I can bear.' 'Right' says the chief, and then to his guards 'Take him to the place of execution and kill him!'

The guards seized him and took him to the edge of the place of execution, and as they were about to kill him, another man said to them 'When you've killed him, give me his loin-cloth. I want it.' But the man who was to be killed heard this and exclaimed 'Take me back to the chief. I've got something to say to him.'

So the guards brought him before the chief. And the chief, when he saw that the guards had brought him back, said 'Why have you brought that man back?' and they replied 'He says he has something to say.' The chief said 'Very well, let him come forward and say it to me!' Then said he to the chief 'Let me be! I have seen a poorer man than I. He said they should give him my loin-cloth, when they had killed me. So now I say, thanks be to God and praise to the Prophet.' And the chief said 'Go about your business! God favoured you, for you might have been killed to no purpose.'

The Rich Man and the Poor Man [^{I}/₅₀]

There were once two brothers living together in the same compound. The younger of the two was wealthy, but the elder was poor, and they lived together.

One evening as they sat chatting, the elder of the two said 'Yesterday I saw a marvellous thing. I had left some *fura* in a calabash hanging from the ceiling, and a mouse got in and ate it.' And the others said 'A mouse get into a calabash hanging from the ceiling and eat *fura*? That must be a lie' and they accused him of lying – for he hadn't a penny (*lit.* a cowrie).

Time passed, and some ten days later, when this conversation was forgotten, again they were chatting in the evening, when the younger brother said 'Yesterday I saw a marvellous thing. I left a roughening stone* in a calabash hanging from the ceiling, and a mouse broke it all to bits.' And the others aid 'Just so! A mouse did it, you said? Just the sort of thing it would do!' Because he was wealthy, immediate agreement was given to his remarks.

And that explains why people say 'The remarks of a penniless man are in vain. Even when true, they become false.'

The Hungry Man and the Farmers [^{I}/₁₀₃]

A man was once walking along and he was hungry, exceedingly hungry.

Presently he came to a farm, where there were a lot of people at work hoeing. They had been brought their *fura*, and were drinking it. Coming up to them, he passed by, but the farmers called him and said 'Hey there, traveller!' 'Yes' said he. 'Come and have some *fura*.' But he refused, saying 'I thank God I am replete' and on he went.

He went on for a short while, and then returning said to the farmers 'Hey, you farmers there! Has that *fura* got tamarind in it?

* for grindstones.

Then they replied 'For pity's sake! What sort of a madman is this – when we invited you to come and drink *fura*, you didn't come, but now, now when you see that it's finished, you come back and talk about something having tamarind in it. Was it your blasted mother who prepared the *fura*? Get the hell out of here!' So he went on again, biting his lips and saying in great vexation 'Had I known, I'd have drunk the *fura* in the first place. I've brought this on myself.'

The Leper and his Servant [$^{III}/_9$]

There was once a leper who had money and beasts. People would borrow money from him. And he had a servant.

This leper would have *tuwo* prepared for him, and meat, and oil, a big wooden bowl full, and brought over to him. Then he would say 'Righto, boys, get up and come over and eat *tuwo* with me.' And they would jump up and come over and sit by him. And he, using his stump of a hand would stir the soup and the meat. His hand all covered with pustules! And he would say 'O.K. boys. Fall to, in the name of God!' And they would start forward and eat up the *tuwo*. Then he would fetch a calabash of gruel, again put in his stump of a hand, stir it, drink some, and pass it over to them. Next he would fetch cola-nuts and give them to them to eat. Then he would say 'Praise be to God. We thank God, and His Messenger too.' And then he would add 'May God preserve us from evil disease.'

This happened daily, until one day one of his servants said 'I – I'm going to ask the leper, how it is that he is always saying to us "May God preserve us from evil disease." For, is there a disease worse than the one that he has?' One of his fellows asked him 'Do you really dare say that to him?' 'Yes, indeed I dare' he answered. 'God spare us to see the morrow' he added. And so to bed.

Next day when it was light, *tuwo* and *fura* were brought. The leper did as he was accustomed, and then said 'May God preserve us from evil disease.' The rest added their 'Amen', and then sat

244

on for a while, before getting up to make their way home, bidding him a respectful farewell.

But this servant stayed on, sitting there. 'Hullo!' said the leper, 'have your friends gone and left you? Have you something to say to me?' 'Yes' he replied, 'I've something to say to you.' 'Very well, say it, for I'm listening.' 'I have a question for you. Every day, we are given *tuwo* and we eat it; gruel and we drink it; and then you give us cola-nuts and you say "May God preserve us from evil disease." Well – is there a disease worse than the one that you have?' 'Is that what you want me to tell you?' asked the leper. 'Yes.' 'Then go off home now. Tomorrow, when you come back, I'll tell you.' 'Very well' said the servant and went off home.

Next day when it was light, the servant came very early. The leper took the check gown that he was wearing off, and gave it to the other. Then he ordered him to go off to a particular town, 'For' said he, 'the chief there owes me five hundred thousand cowries. Not a cowrie of it must stay there any longer – when it has been paid to you, bring it back here.' 'Right' said the servant, and going, took the gown and put it on, and went off to the other town.

When he got there, he told the chief, who fetched the money, five hundred thousand cowries. It was poured into hide-bags, loaded on to oxen and donkeys, and they were driven off.

The servant returned and reaching the leper, said 'Here's your money, I've brought it.' 'Take it home' said the leper, 'to buy yourself soup with.' So the servant went home. So the night passed.

Next morning he took off the gown, covered it up and took it back to the leper, saying 'Here's the gown you gave me to go and collect that debt in.' Says the leper 'What shall I do with this gown? May God preserve me from wearing a gown that you have worn. Open the gown and have a look.' The other did so, and saw leprous pus on it.

Then said the leper 'Good fellow, in this world, poverty is the disease. Look – see my stumps of hands, all covered with pustules.' He continued 'Yet when *tuwo* is brought, and I put my hand into it and stir it, you come and eat together with me – yes, and scramble to do so. If you all had any money, you wouldn't let me treat you so. Poverty is the biggest disease.' That's all. That's the end of that story.

3

GRATITUDE AND INGRATITUDE

The Blind Man who wasn't Thankful [I/ 104]

There was once a blind man who was begging by the road to the market. It was nearly sunset and he was saying 'Who will give me the one or two cowries I need to buy some *tuwo*, for the sake of the Prophet?'

As he was saying this there came a man from the market. Night had caught him there, and he had sixteen hundred cowries bundled in his gown. Coming by where the blind man was, he heard him saying 'Who will give me the one or two cowries I need to buy some *tuwo*, for the sake of the Prophet?' Whereupon he turned out to him all the sixteen hundred cowries that he had, saying 'There you are, for the sake of the Prophet. Now be off home, night has come.' And he went on.

When he had gone on, the blind man moved on a little and again started saying 'Who will give me one or two cowries to buy *tuwo* with, for the sake of the Prophet?' But when the man heard this, he came back and said to the blind man 'Here! This begging talk of yours is lies. How can a man ask for one or two cowries, and then when he is given sixteen hundred go on asking for more?' and he went on 'Give me my money' and, taking his money back, took out two cowries and gave them to him, saying again 'Good-for-nothing blind men, who blaspheme against God, God curse you all!'

The Hen that Laid Golden Eggs [I/ 108]

Once there was a woman and her hen, and the hen would lay two eggs every day. When the eggs were broken, there was silver inside, and the shells turned to gold.

This went on for some time, when the woman took hold of the hen and cut open its stomach, thinking in her ingratitude that there were more eggs there that the hen was refusing to lay. So the hen died. And that is why people say that if a man doesn't give thanks for what he has received, he'll lose everything.

The Ungrateful Man who Refused to Give Alms and so Himself became Poor [I/ 145]

There was once a man eating his *tuwo*, just he and his wife, when there came a beggar, who begged that he might have some *tuwo*. And when he found that they were eating a whole chicken,* he begged them for some of that. And the husband went out and drove him away.

Time passed and they became very poor, till they had nothing. He became parted from his wife, and she married another. Then one day she was in her new husband's home when she heard a beggar. She got up to look, and saw that it was her first husband, from whom she had parted, and coming back she told her husband. He was sorry for him and told her to take some food to him. Then she took some and gave it to him, crying as she did so.

---

* Lit. 'a chicken that had been scorched to remove the feathers.

The Boy and the Dove [$^{III}/_{182}$]

There was once a fellow in the land of Gombe, called Gurama, whose father told him to go off to the farm to guard the corn from being eaten by the birds. So he went off to the farm, and when he got there climbed a tree, and began to drive away the birds. Up comes a dove and begins saying 'Gurama, break me off a ripe head of bulrush-millet, break me off a ripe head of bulrush-millet.'

So Gurama climbed down and went and broke off four heads of millet; then he went and lit a fire and rotated the heads, two of them and gave them to the dove. And she came and ate them; and he ate two himself. Then he rose and went and climbed back up the tree and began driving the birds off again.

Presently his father came to the farm, and saw where the fire had been and that millet heads had been roasted. 'Who has done this?' he asked. 'It was me' said Gurama. 'Come down here' said his father, and he did so. Then his father took hold of Gurama, and gave him a good beating. Over comes the dove, saying over and over 'Hit him on the neck! Hit him on the neck!'*

Then his father let him go and went off home.

Says Gurama 'So, it seems the world is an evil place. You dove there! You come here and finding me here, ask me to give you ripe millet heads. Then I take some off and give them to you. But when my father comes and, seeing it, gives me a good beating, you actually come along and say over and over that he should hit me on the neck! Well, now I'm going to get my own back on your body.'

And he picked up a stone, but the dove flew off and went away. Then Gurama said that from that day on he would make use of the enlightenment that the dove had given him. That's all. That's the end of that story.

---

* I imagine the Hausa is meant to sound onomatopoeic.

The Crocodile and the Hunter* [$^{III}/_{109}$]

A hunter once set off, out into the bush, and as he walked there, came upon a crocodile, right in the heart of the bush, where there was no water. Says the hunter 'Crocodile, if I pick you up now and take you to water, one day, if you see me, you'll grab me and eat me up.' But the crocodile answered 'Look, if you take me and put me in water, I'll – not only you, but any son you may have, and his son, until your grandson's grandson, I'll not sieze them; let alone you.' 'Really?' said the hunter. 'Yes' said the crocodile. 'Very well' said the hunter and rolled up a headpad and lifted the crocodile on to his head.

He walked until he came to a river. Then the hunter said 'Crocodile, let me put you down here, for I have brought you to a river.' 'No' said the crocodile, 'take me into the water first.' So the hunter went into the water with the crocodile, and when it was up to his knees, he said 'Now, let me put you down here, for we are in the water.' 'No, go farther' said the crocodile, and the hunter went on until the water was up to his thighs. 'Let me put you down here, crocodile' said he, 'For we are in the water, plenty of it.' 'No' said the crocodile, 'Take me farther in.' So the hunter went deeper into the water, until it reached his genitals. 'Crocodile' said he, 'let me put you down here, for we are right in the water.' 'No, hunter' said the crocodile, 'Take me farther in.' And the hunter went on still farther into the water, until it was up to his stomach. 'Let me put you down here, crocodile' says he. 'No, hunter, take me farther in before you put me down.' So they went on into the water, until it was up to the hunter's chest, and he said 'Crocodile, let me put you down here, for we are right into the water now.' But the crocodile said 'No, hunter, take me in where it's deep, and then let me down there.' So the hunter went on until the water was up to his neck.

Then the crocodile said 'Now, hunter, stand still with me still on your head, while I question three people to see what they say, before you put me down.'

So there was the crocodile on top of the hunter's head, when an old woman came down to get water from the river. Says the

* cf. II/84, M. No. 10, and also D. Nos. 103 and 104.

crocodile 'Old woman – you there, getting water! Don't draw water yet, but stand there on the bank and let me ask you something; if you don't do so, I'll kill you.' So the old woman stood on the bank, not drawing water. Then the crocodile said 'Now, old woman, if a man does a kindness to you, how will you repay him?' The old woman answered 'Crocodile, eat the hunter up – for God has given you meat.' Says the crocodile 'Hunter did you hear? That's the first to be asked.' 'Yes, I heard' said the hunter.

Presently, as they stood there, along came the elephant to drink water. Says the crocodile 'Elephant, stop there and let me ask you something. And if you refuse, when you come to drink water, I'll seize you.' So the elephant stood there and the crocodile said to her 'Elephant, if a man does a kindness to you, how will you repay him? 'And the elephant answered 'Pouf! Is that all? My good crocodile, you've got hold of some meat – eat it!' 'Hunter' said the crocodile, 'that's the second I've asked – did you hear?' 'Yes' said the hunter.

Then along came the jackal. Says the crocodile 'Hey, jackal, stop there on the bank while I ask you something, and then you can come and drink water.' 'No' said the jackal, 'I won't. I'll have my drink first, and then you can ask me.' So the jackal went and had his drink, until he was satisfied, and then went back up the bank.

Then the jackal said 'You, man, there – come on out; and you too, crocodile.' So the man come out of the water. 'Now' said the jackal, 'I'll not make a decision in your case, until you, hunter, go – and the crocodile too – back to the place where you picked him up.'

They set off back along the road until they came to the middle of the bush. There the hunter said 'Jackal, here's the place where I picked up the crocodile.' 'Right, I see' said the jackal, and he went on 'Now, hunter, pick the crocodile up again, and take him to your compound, to the entrance of your wife's hut, and there slaughter him and eat him.' So the hunter took the crocodile back to his compound, and to the entrance of his wife's hut and there slaughtered him.

And that's how it is – that's why anyone in this world that you do a kindness to, will, as soon as he has the chance, return evil to you. That's all.

4

THE WILL OF GOD

The Malam who told Fortunes [$^{I}/_{28}$]

Once there was a man who got up from where he was sitting and made his way to the house of a certain malam, to ask him to tell his fortune. The malam threw down some earth, spread it out and said 'Well, well – this man – your fate, I think will be a bush-cow!' And he answered 'Really?' Then said the malam 'If you hear a man reply to something said to him with "Really", it means he is going to argue. Off with you, home! Keep your eyes open for what comes! You'll see.' 'Right' says the other and goes off home, and settles down again.

Time passed, and he forgot what had been said, when one day the word went round 'There's a bush-cow in the farmland.' And everyone sallied forth to do war with the bush-cow. But he, realising that the malam had told him that his fate would be a bush-cow, refused to go out. He got into a corn-bin and sat there from morning until sunset, by which time the people had finished their war with the bush-cow. When it had been killed, one of the people of his household said he would like the head, and he was given the bush-cow's head. Then, picking it up he went home with it, and said to himself 'Let me put this bush-cow's head in the corn-bin and then tomorrow I'll skin it.'

He picked up the bush-cow's head and put it in the corn-bin where it fell on to the man who had been told by the malam that his fate would be a bush-cow. And the bush-cow's horn pierced his chest and he died.

Next day, when they came in to take out the bush-cow's head to skin it, they found the dead man in the corn-bin. And they asked each other 'However did he come by his death?' And his wife said 'Ah, you see, one day he told me that a malam had said to him that his fate would be a bush-cow. And now – there you are! He's died.'

And the people said 'What you will come by, and what will come upon you – all are ordained from the day of creation!'

The Blind Man and the Seeing Man [$^I/_{41}$]

Once upon a time a blind man and a seeing man dwelt together, taking their food and drink together.

They were thus for some while, when one day they were given a ram, and they slaughtered it. Next they skinned it, and the seeing man took the best meat and hid it, and gave the blind man the offal. The blind man took it, and they set about grilling their meat and eating it. But when the blind man tore open the intestines to eat them, liquid from inside squirted in his eye, and his eyes were opened and he looked and could see. And it was revealed to him that the seeing man had given him offal. Then said the blind man 'Very well! Do you see what you gave me? Do you realise what you had in mind – because you knew I couldn't see, when we were given a ram and had slaughtered it, you gave me nothing except offal! Just because you knew that I couldn't see! And now, you can see that the intestines you gave me have been the cause of my eyes being opened. Well, one day God will send a cause of blindness for you.'

Time passed, and the seeing man dried the rest of the meat. And he came to pick it up and saw a maggot in it. He took it meaning to kill it. But as he was squashing it, the blood of the maggot squirted into his eye and he became blind. And so he became the blind one, and the blind man became the seeing one.

And that explains why people say 'Whatever you sow, that will you reap.'

The Hyena, the Cat and the Lion [$^I/_{77}$]

One day the hyena was out walking when she met the cat who had caught a lizard and was taking it home to eat. The hyena snatched it away and made off with it. But she hadn't reached home when she met the lion. Then the lion, in his turn, snatched it away from the hyena and went off and ate it up. Then said the hyena 'My goodness me! Whatever you may seek in this world, if it's not your allotted portion, your wasting your time! The fruits of oppression are perishable, or if they do last, it won't be for the man who picked them!'

'The-Mouth-Which-God-Has-Cut' and the Rich Man [$^I/_{121}$]

There was once a man called 'The-Mouth-Which-God-Has-Cut' who had no other occupation but to go from place to place, getting his food from what people gave him.

One day he went off and walked on till he came to the compound of a rich man. Now this rich man had his in-laws on a visit to him and had slaughtered a ram and chickens. The pots were cooking and various sorts of food preparing, to be taken to the guests, when The-Mouth-Which-God-Has-Cut reached the entrance and made formal greeting. The rich man made reply and they exchanged courtesies. To the rich man's enquiring his name, he replied 'The Mouth-Which-God-Has-Cut.' 'Very well' said the rich man and, calling a servant told him to take him to a hut near where the in-laws were lodged. And there he was taken to lodge.

He sat there till sunset. By that time a large wooden bowl* had been prepared with *tuwo* and three chickens, and another with the meat of the ram. Then the rich man said to his servant 'Take the one with the chickens to the guests, and then come back for the other one.' The servant picked it up and took it to The-Mouth-Which-God-Has-Cut, saying 'Here you are – I was told to bring it to you." 'That's fine' said he, 'thank-you very much.' Away went the servant and brought the other bowl, and brought that too to The-Mouth-Which-God-Has-Cut, saying 'Here you are, I was told to bring it to you.' 'What!' says he 'Were you told to bring it all to *me*?' 'Yes' said the other. 'Well – thank you' said The-Mouth-

* But Bargery's dictionary prefers 'calabash'.

Which-God-Has-Cut. Presently the same fellow brought *fura*, two calabashes of it, one with honey and one with butter-milk, and both he gave to The-Mouth-Which-God-Has-Cut. 'No' said the latter. 'This is too much trouble – tomorrow morning I must come and express my thanks.'

And he ate the *tuwo* and drank the *fura*. But the in-laws went to bed hungry.

Next morning, while it was still very early The-Mouth-Which-God-Has-Cut came to the rich man's compound and said 'Thank you very much! May God increase your prosperity! May God give you a long life!' Says the merchant 'But I fear they didn't bring you any food yesterday?' And the other answered 'On the contrary, I had too much food yesterday, two large bowls of *tuwo* and two calabashes of *fura* – and all to myself!' Then the rich man called the servant who had taken the food and said 'Here! Where did you take that food yesterday?' The fellow replied 'You told me to take it to the guest, and I took it to him. And now look, here he is come to thank you.' Then the rich man said 'It is a true saying, the mouth which God has cut will not lack for food. For I treated you casually and forgot you, and I certainly didn't remember to send you any food. But, without any thought of it on my part, God provided it for you. Now be on your way!'

And that is why everyone knows that the mouth which God has cut will not lack for food.*

The Malam and the Wicked Man† [I/ 133]

When Abdullahi was Emir of Kano, there lived a malam who had no other means of livelihood. Each morning he would say ' 'Tis God who feeds his slave.' And he stayed in his hut, never going out.

This had gone on for some time, and God had always provided

* Proverb.

† In *LND*, the hero is an anonymous, pious man whose wife tells her lover of a pot of gold *dinari*. When he steals it, it turns into bees. When he returns it, it turns back into gold (LND p. 76). Cf. also TR. No. 38.

him with the means of food. Until one day a certain wicked fellow heard about him and said to himself 'Just leave him to me, this malam who's said to have no means of livelihood and who says it's God who feeds his slave. I know how to get rid of him, so that he won't both bother anyone any more.'

Up he got and away to the home of the snake-charmers. There he bought a hooded cobra, got hold of an old cooking-pot and put it inside, covered it with a potsherd and sealed it. Then, lifting it with difficulty, he took it to the malam's compound. 'Peace be upon you, malam' said he. 'Upon you be peace' he answered. Then, without even waiting to exchange greetings, as the malam stuck out his head, the wicked fellow pushed the pot into the hut, saying 'Here are alms in the name of the Prophet' and went off quickly, so that the malam should not recognise him.

When the pot broke – it was full to the brim with gold! And the malam gathered it up, saying 'Praise God! Indeed this is what I expected of God.' But when the wicked fellow heard the news, that the snake that he had taken to the malam to bite and kill him had turned into gold, he said 'Plague on it! That rascally malam has tricked me. Had I known that snake would turn into gold, I'd have stayed and joined him in scrambling for it.'

Then the others said 'What did you expect? A man who puts his trust in God will never fail. But "Had I known" has been the fate of many a malam and many a wizard.'

The Farmer and the Gazelle [^{III}/129]

There was once a man who was busy with the hoeing of his farm, and every day he would go and do it. One day when he finished work for the day he returned home. He was asked 'How's things? How goes the farming?' 'I' he began, '– tomorrow I'll finish doing the farm.' His friend said 'You mean, if God will?' 'No' he replied, 'even if God doesn't will it, tomorrow I'll finish doing my farm.' 'I see' said the other.

The night passed, and when morning came, he said he was off to the farm. 'Shall I bring you a ball of *fura*?' asked his wife. 'Don't trouble yourself' he answered, 'I'll be back right away. It's only a little, tiny bit of hoeing. Even if God doesn't will it, I'll finish it straight away.'

He picked up his little hoe and went off to the farm. He started to hoe and finished one ridge. He began another, but he hadn't finished it when a gazelle flashed by in front of him. Lifting the hoe he threw it at her. It caught in her neck, but she went on running, and he pursued her for the rest of the day. Then at last his hoe fell off, and he picked it up and went home. 'Hullo, there' they said, 'Have you finished?' 'No, I'm afraid I haven't finished' he answered. 'What prevented you from finishing?' 'A gazelle' he answered. 'I threw my hoe at her, but didn't kill her, but my hoe stuck and didn't fall off until the day was over.' Then his friend said to him 'There, you see – that's what prevented you finishing. And you said that even if God didn't will it, you would finish. Well, you see, He didn't will it.' 'Yes' said the other and expressed contrition, adding 'If God will, tomorrow I'll finish my hoeing; but if He doesn't so will, then whenever He does.'

So – whatever you're going to do, say 'If God will'.

5

MISCELLANEOUS MORALS

The Woman, the Malam
and the Bush-Cow* [I/34]

There was once a woman who set off and went to see a malam and after greeting him, said 'Malam! I want you to give me medicine, so that I may rule my husband' and he answered 'Very well, I'll give you some. But first you must get some bush-cow's milk.' And she said 'However shall I get bush-cow's milk?' He answered 'Well, you'll just have to devise a way to get hold of bush-cow's milk' and she expressed her agreement.

So away she went and got some bran and bean-pods and mixed them together. Then she took the mixture and away into the bush till she came to where bush-cow were grazing. There she stopped and put down the food.

When she had waited a while, up came a ferocious bush-cow. The beast ran at her to kill her, but she put down the food and ran off. When the bush-cow saw the food, it ate it up and then went back into the bush. Then she came and picked up her calabash and went off home.

Next day, once again she got some bran and bean-pods, just like the day before. She took it and went and put it down, and again the bush-cow came over from where it was grazing. And when it saw the bran, it didn't attack the woman but ate the bran and then went back to the bush. And the woman went home.

She went on doing this day after day, until she and the bush-

* Cf. III/58, II/12; also an Ethiopian tale quoted by Murad Kamal of a witch-doctor who told a woman to get three hairs from the mane of a living lion.

cow were used to each other. There came a day when she took the bran as usual, and when the bush-cow came along and started eating the bran, the woman started milking it. And before it had finished eating the bran, the woman had milked it.

Then she brought the milk to the malam and said 'Malam, here's the bush-cow's milk I've brought you' and the malam said 'Well! Whatever did you do to get hold of bush-cow's milk?' She answered 'By peaceful persuasion and with no hard feelings.' 'Right' says the malam, 'now, whatever you did to get the bush-cow's milk, you do that to your husband. You'll rule him!' 'Very well' says she.

So she set off for home and when she got there, she set about obtaining all the nicest food. This she would give him, keeping her reasons to herself, and he would eat it. So day by day she continued winning him over, till she had won him and ruled him.

So now you know why people say 'Peaceful persuasion that enables an ox to be led by a thread'.

———————

The Malam and the Chief of Gobir, Bawa-Jan-Gwarzo [I/57]

In the days of the Chief of Gobir, Bawa-Jan-Gwarzo, he heard tell of a malam who had many cures. He was sent for and came, and when he came, a lodging was given him.

Next morning the chief sent to his lodging and summoned him. He sat down in front of the chief, and the chief said to him 'Malam, I've sent for you because I hear that you have a medicine, that has no peer – I want you to give it me.' And the malam answered 'It's – I fear it's a difficult medicine.' Says the chief 'What's difficult about it?' and the malam answered 'It really is – we need three white crows for it.' And the chief said 'Very well! If that's all, that's easy!'

Then he told his *jekadiya* to bring him the little basket that he used for medicinal powders. She went into the compound and fetched the basket. Then the chief undid a little bag, and they brought him live embers in a potsherd. He took a little powder from the bag and sprinkled it on to the hot embers. And as the smoke rose up, there rose up also about a hundred white crows. Said the chief 'There, malam – help yourself!'

And the malam answered 'One who has *that* sort of medicine has no need of anything else in this world. The chief should give thanks to God.' 'I do thank God' says the chief of Gobir, and he gave him a camel fully accoutred.

The Upright Man and the Man who gave up Sin [¹/₆₂]

Once a man came to an upright man who lived in a cave, where he spent his time in worship. The man came and knelt before the man of God and said 'Malam, I have come with a question for you.' And he answered 'May God cause us to know!' The man went on 'I have three occupations – none of them good.' The upright man replied 'Very well – let me hear them' and the other said 'I tell lies, I steal, I commit adultery – which of them shall I give up, that I may obtain leniency from God?' Then the upright man answered 'If you give up lying, I assure you that you will obtain leniency from God.' 'Very well' says the man.

When night came, he arose and went to the door of a house and knocked. And the people of the house called out 'Who's there?' He replied 'I am a thief, I have come to steal.' Whereupon they exclaimed 'Oh, it's a madman. Here, you – be off with you!' And the man said to himself 'I'm giving up stealing.'

Next day, when he got up he made his way to the edge of the market, and stopped a woman in the middle of the road. Says he 'Look – I want to commit adultery with you here.' Says she 'Well! What sort of a fellow is this! Get away with you, be off – you're mad!'

Then he went back to the upright man and said to him 'I'm

giving up adultery, and lying, and stealing. For I now find that if you don't tell lies, then you don't do any of the others either.' And the upright man said to him 'That's what I told you.' Then the man said 'I repent and follow after God' 'Good.' said the other 'May God receive your repentance!' and the man said 'Amen.'

The Thieving Corn-seller of Danja* [$^I/_{112}$]

There once lived a seller of corn in Danja. Whenever someone brought corn to sell to her, she would put one basket on top of the other, first making a hole in the upper one. Then, when the guinea-corn or millet was poured in, it would trickle through to the underneath one, so that there was apparently very little corn for her to buy, and she would say to the villager 'Well, you didn't bring much corn. When you go home, bring a big bag full – look I haven't even got my usual surplus.'† And the villager would swallow it, and next day when he came back the same thing would happen to him. She went on doing this, until people got to know that she was like that.

There came a day when a travelling grain dealer heard about her and said to himself 'I'll find a cure for that corn-seller.' So he threshed some corn and put it in a hide bag, and up on to his donkey, and away he went to Danja market. There he unloaded his bag in front of her booth. Then the corn-seller said to him 'Come and pour it into the basket, and I won't waste any time measuring it for you.' 'Right' said he and pouring the corn into the basket, he went to one side and sat down, watching what she did, until she had finished measuring it. When she had finished, she said to him 'Hey, what sort of a grain dealer are you! Bringing a miserable amount of corn like this – look, there isn't even my usual surplus!' He answered 'Measure what's in the underneath basket! Then I'll give you your extra bit.'

Then in her great embarrassment and shame she began talking nonsense; picked up the baskets, overturned them, talked more

* Twenty miles N. of Zaria.   † Middleman's fee.

nonsense – all indicating that she had been caught stealing. And the people exclaimed 'Hey, come and look at her! She stole the grain dealer's corn.' And she was very ashamed of herself. And now people say 'The mat of shame gets rolled up in madness.'*

The Man who Left his Oil in Safe keeping† [III/155]

There was once a man who was going on a journey. So he took his money and put it in a cooking-pot and heated some oil till it boiled, pouring it in on top, so that the pot was filled to the brim. Then he took it and gave it to his friend, saying 'I'm off on a journey. Take care of this oil for me till I return.' But he never told him that there was money in it.

And so he went on a journey, and it lasted a long time, some ten years. Some while after he had departed, his friend was looking through his things, and came across the oil deposited with him. 'Phew' said he, 'here's my friend's oil gone bad. Just let me see if there is any chance of eating it.' So he shook some of the oil into a calabash, and found that there was money there. He washed the money, collected some gravel, poured it back into the pot and put it aside again.

Time passed and his friend returned. 'Welcome' says the other, greeting him by name. 'We – we thought you were dead, as we had no news of you.' 'It was a long journey' answered the other, 'but God has brought me back.' And when they had finished exchanging greetings, he went to his home.

Two days later he asked for what he left with him, and his friend brought it and gave it to him. He looked, saw that the oil was there as he had left it, thanked him and went his way. He went and did some trading at the market and told those he had bought from 'Come tomorrow for your money.' And, returning, he opened the

* Cf. III/158 and I/102. 'You can put shame away by crazy talk'.
† See J. p. 208.

pot of oil, and found – gravel. Then he put his hands to his head, and said 'I have done a foolish thing. And anyone that I tell about it, will consider me mad.' So he did nothing about it, but grew thin and wasted away.

Another of his friends came and, seeing him, asked 'What's happened to you, that you're so wasted?' And he answered 'Well, you're my friend, I've got something I must tell to someone; come into the bush and I'll tell you.' So off they went, and he said to him 'I've lost my wealth through my folly. I poured a lot of money into a pot, boiled some oil over it, and left it for safe-keeping with a frend, not telling him there was money there. Then, when I got back, he gave it back to me, but when I opened it, I found gravel there. What can I do?' Then his friend said to him 'Is this true that you gave him the money for safe-keeping?' 'It's true.' 'And is the fellow here?' 'He's here.' 'Has he got a son?' 'Yes.' Then his friend said 'If I devise something so that you recover your money, what will you give me?' and the other answered 'We'll divide it into three, and you can take one part.' 'Then point the man out to me.' The other did so, and he took a good look at him.

Then he went and made the image of a man in gum, gave it to the other, telling him to take it and set it up in his hut. He did so and then was told 'Now go and seek a young monkey.' He got a young monkey and next was told to take it and tie it to the image [leaving it there] till it was used to the dummy. He did so, and when it was used to it, he told his friend. 'Is he used to it?' asked the latter. 'Yes' he said, 'he won't leave the dummy.' 'Then go to your friend and ask him to let you have his son to go and hold something for you in the market.' He did this, and the friend said to his son 'Muhammadu, come here. Go with your father* here, my friend, to the market and hold something for him.' And off they went, but not to the market, they went home.

Says he to the friend who was advising him 'Here, I've brought his son.' 'Then take him and hide him somewhere.' And he did so. 'Now take the young monkey', and when he had done so, he went on 'Now go and take it to the boy's father and tell him that Muhammadu has turned into a monkey; that you have seen a miracle happen, Muhammadu has become a monkey.'

And when Muhammadu's father came out of his compound, as

* Hausa classificatory father, not, obviously, the real one.

soon as the young monkey saw him, he jumped down and went and clasped him, and the man who had brought him exclaimed 'There now! Even though he has become a monkey, Muhammadu hasn't forgotten his father.'

Everyone gathered and looked. But if any suggestion of pulling him off was made, the young monkey clung to him the tighter. And his friend said 'Let him be, for it's his son', and presently went home.

The story spread far and wide, and people who heard would come to gaze. And Muhammadu's father began to waste away, being much distressed by this event. So one night he went to his friend's compound. There he made formal greeting, and when the other came out, they exchanged greetings. Then the father said 'For God's sake tell me – did Muhammadu really become a monkey?' 'For shame' said his friend, 'Do you doubt that there is anything wonderful that you may not see in this world? If money can become gravel, why can't Muhammadu become a monkey?' 'Oh' said the other, 'Just so. Send along the pot of oil to me.'

So it was sent along, and he put back the money into it, right up to the brim; and, pouring the oil back on top, took it along and gave it to him. He checked that his property was there, and then said 'Right. Father of Muhammadu, you can send me along the little monkey.' He did so, and our friend tied his little monkey back to the dummy, picked up Muhammadu and took him back to his father.

Then he said to his other friend 'Come along and I'll divide the money up, for I am very grateful to you.' But the other answered 'I don't want your money, for I don't want to be infected by your stupidity. If you're going to give something into safe-keeping, give it publicly, indicating your witnesses.' That's all.

The Judge, the Man and the Frogs [$^{I}/_{141}$]

I have heard tell that once a judge set out on a journey and came to the bank of a river. There he found a man at the edge of the river. Said the judge to the man 'Hey, you there! Let me come in your boat!'

When the judge had got into the boat, he said 'Take me on the river of the water, for I am the river of knowledge.' Then a frog came out of the water and said 'Peace be upon you, oh judge'. And the frog sat down, saying 'Oh judge, I pray you in the name of God, inform me! Inform me what it is that has been and what it is that shall be.' And the judge answered 'Neither of these do I know.' And the frog said 'Oh judge, tell me about these things: things which are forbidden both to do and to omit.' Again the judge answered 'I don't know, but I beseech you in God's name —' and the frog interrupted and said 'Oh judge, I will tell you, spare me your words!'

Then a second frog came out of the water and said 'Hey – you're an ignorant judge – call yourself a judge! Don't you know the answers? Here's a boy asks you for answers, and you don't know, you're baffled by him. Well, the first one we asked you – what has been – that is the World; as for what shall be, that is the Next World; while as for things that are forbidden both to do and to omit, they are the prayers of a drunk man and the ablutions of an adulterer.'

Then the frog said again to the judge 'Three things I have for you. First, I'll kill you. Then, secondly, I'll put my tongue up your nose and drink your blood.' The judge replied 'Have you not heard God's word, that Muslims are brothers one to another, "Do good to your brethren and fear God, that perchance you may obtain mercy".' The frog replied 'There is no greater poverty than ignorance of God's word. You are dead in your ignorance though you seem alive, and I'll drink your blood, oh deluded judge!'

Says the judge 'Frog 'tis you that have not understood the word of God, for the curse of God is upon those who ill-treat others.' And the frog replied 'You ill-treat yourself. How could you come

264

out into the water, when you know nothing about the water?' 'No man' replied the judge, 'can set aside what God wills, and no man can deprive you of what God bestows.'

Then the frog said again 'Oh judge,* prosperity will seek out a slave for his own, or, in just the same way, death may seek him out – for be sure that God will bring prosperity to his slave from where he least expects it. I shall not spare you, but kill you, oh ignorant judge!' But the judge said 'Fear God, oh frog, and do not kill me as you threaten – for know that god is merciful and loves them that are merciful – spare me in the name of God!' And the frog said 'Seek wisdom, oh judge! Cease from pride, for a man is not called learned, that he may be proud' and it added 'I spare you in the name of God Almighty.' Finis.

Falsehood and Truth† [II/11]

Falsehood and Truth were children of the same father. He died leaving them alone.

They tilled their land and had a plentiful crop of corn. And they stowed it safely away in their corn-bin. When they had done this, Falsehood said 'Righto, Truth, let's go and spend the dry-season travelling.' So away they went for the dry-season. Falsehood was the older, Truth the younger.

When they got to a town, Falsehood would go to one side and wait, and Truth would go in and say 'Peace be upon you' and the people would answer her 'And upon you peace.' Then she would say 'We want some food. Let us have some scraps. We tilled our land, and stowed our corn safely away, and have come out to get

* The following passage is obscure in the Hausa, it seems because of a poor translation from the original Arabic.

† Cf. TR. No. 11 and M. No. 16; also Diop, B. *Les Contes d'Amadon Koumba*, p. 127.

corn from others to eat.' And the people would say 'Well! Here's a girl who likes a foolish joke! So! You've tilled your land, have you? You've stowed away your corn, have you? And now you come and tell us to give you food! Well, we won't!' It was the same at each place, for three days' journeys.

Then Falsehood said 'Well, Truth, you must now see why, even before, I told you that if we followed your line, we should die of hunger. Now, today, you let me open the proceedings.'

So she went up to a compound and said 'Peace be upon you!' And they answered 'And upon you peace.' 'We are orphans' she said 'Our father died, and now we have nothing and no one. We are looking for somewhere to live, so that we may not die of hunger.' And the men of the compound said 'We're very sorry to hear that. Come in.' So in they went and were given *fura* to drink and *tuwo* to eat. And they stayed there three nights. And they were both given clothes.

The next day away they went to another town, and Falsehood did as she had done before. And again a third time, so that they were laden with clothes.

And that is why people say 'Falsehood gets food quicker than truth does.' *kungurus kan kusu.*

Patience and Mischief* [II/80]

Two young men met as they were travelling one day, and journeyed together till they came to a town. There they lodged in the same hut. One was called Patience, and the other was called Mischief. Mischief would stay lying in the hut, while Patience went off begging and got corn and money. Then, coming home he would make *tuwo* and say 'Come, Mischief, let us eat *tuwo*.' And Mischief would come and eat the *tuwo*. But when they had done eating the *tuwo*, Mischief would go away, and up on to the bed and just lie

* The style of the Hausa of this tale is somewhat pleonastic.

there, while Patience went off again to beg, and, again returning, would prepare the food. Again he would say 'Come, Mischief, let us eat *tuwo*.' Then Mischief would get off the bed and the two would go and eat. Whereupon Mischief would return to the bed and just lie there.

This continued daily, till Patience bought a rooster, brought it home, and there kept feeding it, until it grew big. Then someone offered him fifteen hundred cowries for it, but he refused, and presently went off begging. Then Mischief saw a dead ram, and called out 'Hey, you people dragging that ram along – bring it here, and help yourselves to this rooster!' 'With pleasure' they said, and bringing over the dead ram, took the rooster and went off. Patience returned from his begging. Says Mischief 'Patience, look at the deal I've done for you!' 'Just so' said Patience, but said nothing else, when he looked at the dead ram lying there.

But before the sun rose next day, that ram came to life, for the sake of Patience. But as for Mischief, he continued to do nothing but mischief. He would just lie there, while Patience went off begging. Then when he had got some money and corn, back he would come, make *tuwo* – and then he and Mischief would eat together. Well one day he went begging as usual, leaving his ram at home, and the ram by now was a fine, big one. Now, while he was out begging, someone offered Patience thirty thousand cowries for his ram, but he refused the offer. Meanwhile Mischief was lying at home in the hut, when he heard a hubbub. For it chanced that some people were dragging along a horse that had died, and they passed close to Mischief's hut. 'Hey there!' called out Mischief, 'You dragging that horse there. Bring it here, and take this ram! 'So they left the horse there and took the ram. And presently Patience returned from his begging. Says Mischief 'Patience – look at the deal I've made for you.' And Patience said 'I see' but nothing more. And so they slept, but in the morning he went and found that the horse had come to life, but was still lying down. So Patience went off and fetched water, and got grass and bran, and took some of the corn that he had got by begging; and bringing all this back, gave it to his horse. Then he went off begging again. And so he would return from begging and go and make *tuwo*, and then rouse Mischief and they would eat. And afterwards he would go to his horse and water him and give him grass and bran and corn; and so off begging again. Again when he got back, he would prepare food for himself and Mischief to eat. And so Patience's horse grew fat and fine and big. Presently someone came along and offered ten slaves for it, but Patience refused. Again, the chief of the town came and offered Patience fifteen slaves for it, but Patience said 'May the chief's days be prolonged, but I'm not selling for fifteen slaves.'

*Well, Patience went off begging one day and Mischief was lying in his hut, when he heard people coming by with numbers of slaves. He went and stood at the entrance of his hut and watched the slaves going by. Now among them was an old woman who, as she walked, was afflicted by diarrhoea. 'Hey, you with the slaves there!' called Mischief, 'Give me that old woman with diarrhoea, and I'll give you this horse in return. Come and take it. And they came and took it, and bringing over the old woman, gave her to him.

Then people began to say 'Mischief, Mischief! How can you live with Patience and yet go on doing him so much harm? And as for him, he bears it all patiently!' 'Mind your own business' he would answer, 'for you see we go on living together, and he still prepares the *tuwo* for our meals. Just leave us alone!'

Well, Patience returned from his begging, and Mischief said 'Patience – look at the deal I've made for you!' 'I see' said Patience, and though what had been done grieved him, yet Patience still said nothing, but just went and made the *tuwo*. And he gave the old woman her share, which she ate; and took the rest for himself and Mischief to eat. Then off went Patience again to beg; and presently came back again, made the *tuwo*, gave the old woman hers and took the rest for himself and Mischief to eat. Then says he 'Mischief, I'm off begging', and so went off. The old woman lay there watching what Mischief was up to, and when Patience returned from begging this time she says to him 'Master, please give me a hundred cowries to buy groundnuts with. Then I can be frying them and selling them; and I shall be able to help you with preparing the food, and you'll be able to rest sometimes.' 'Very well' said he, and fetched a hundred cowries and gave them to her.

And so she started frying groundnuts, while Patience went on with his begging. Now, as it happened, the old woman had a son,

* For this part, cf. TR. No. 29.

and he was the chief of the town she came from. And one day the old woman called Patience aside and said to him 'Master, since you have done me no harm, neither will I you. Let us go to my town' and she named it, 'where my son is the chief. And when we get there, he'll buy my freedom.' 'Very well' said Patience, 'But, listen, this is how we'll do it: you go off as if to sell your groundnuts; and then I, in my turn, will set off as if to beg. Then we can meet and make our journey together, and Mischief won't know.' So the old woman went out, and then Patience did too, and they met on the road.

And as they journeyed, they were in the bush, when the old woman said 'Master, let us stop here by this flat rock.' 'O.K.' he said, and she went on 'Now, look, we're going to this town where my son is the chief. When we get there, if he offers you a thousand slaves for me, don't accept. But say to him that he must give you the stone that he has in his mouth.' 'Right' he answered, and they went on to the town. There everyone exclaimed 'Oh, the chief's mother is back! The chief's mother is back! She who was caught in a raid when she was away in the country.' And the chief sent to meet them and they were taken to their lodgings. Food was prepared, *tuwo* and *fura* and meat, and taken to them.

Then the chief sent for his mother and her master to come to him. And when they arrived, he asked 'Master of my mother, how much must I pay you to buy her freedom?' Says Patience 'Just make me an offer.' 'Then I'll buy my mother's freedom with twenty of every sort of worldly possession.' 'Sorry, no.' 'Fifty of every sort of worldly possession.' 'Sorry, no.' 'I see' said the chief, 'Well, both of you go back to your lodging.' And so they did. Then again he sent, offering to increase his bid to seventy, but Patience continued to refuse and added 'May the chief's days be prolonged, I'll–look, there's your mother, if you want her back, you must give me the stone in your mouth, or rather one of them.' 'Hm. I see' said the chief, 'Both of you can go back to your lodging.' And they did so. But presently the chief again sent, saying that his mother and his mother's master should come back. Back they went, and the chief said 'Master of my mother, I'll buy my mother for a hundred of every sort of worldly possession.' 'Sorry, no' said Patience. Whereupon the old woman said to Patience impatiently 'Come, master, let us go, for he has no wish to buy me. And as for me, ever since you bought me, you have never harmed me. Get up and let us go back where we came from.' At which the chief took out two stones, and giving Patience one, put the other back.

Whereupon Patience rose to go home. Says the old woman 'Come, master, I'll see you on your way.' 'Good' said he. So she went with him and said 'Now master, that stone comes from God, and it is a lucky one. You go back to that flat rock where we stopped and when you get there, you pray to God and his Prophet.' 'I will' said Patience.

So Patience returned to the flat rock and sitting down, set his face to the east. Then, putting the stone into his mouth, he prayed to God. He swallowed the stone, and – behold! – he was in the midst of an enormous town, and he was its chief – right there in the heart of the bush too! Well, soon people began to visit Patience's town and to speak about it.

And presently some people came to Mischief and said 'Hey, Mischief – why are you just sitting there, when Patience is chief of a town? For if you climb to the top of this tree here, you'll be able to see Patience's town in the distance. There you were, continually doing him harm, and he took no notice. And now, look, he's got the chieftainship of a town, and you, for being so wicked, you're here with nothing.' Says Mischief 'Do you mean that Patience himself has been made chief of a town?' 'Climb up and have a look. You'll see' they said. So Mischief climbed up and he saw the town. Says he 'There's a huge town over there right in the middle of the bush, that I can see' and the people said 'Yes, that's Patience's town.' '*Whose* town?' he asked. 'Patience's town.' At which Mischief gave a deep sigh – and died. And that's all for that one.

The Man and his Four Wives [^{III}/$_{83}$]

There was once a man married the daughter of a chief; and also the daughter of a malam; and also the daughter of a merchant and lastly the daughter of a village head.

Well, he went and slept in the compound of the chief's daughter. Very early before it was light, she roused him to say his prayers. And he asked her, saying 'How did you know it was time for prayer?' 'Well' she answered, 'This is how I know; when I am in my father's compound, and it is time, Dad's horses all turn and face the east.' 'Yes' said he, 'you are indeed a chief's daughter.'

He rose and went from there to the compound of the malam's daughter, to spend the night. Very early next morning, before it was light, she roused him to say his prayers. He did so, and then asked her 'And how did *you* know that it was time for prayer!' 'Well she answered, 'when I was in my father's compound, and it was time, all my father's pupils would come along when it was time for the pre-dawn prayer, and get the fire going. That's how I knew it was time.' 'Yes' said he, 'you are indeed a malam's daughter.'

In the evening he went to the hut of the merchant's daughter to spend the night. And again, very early, when it was time for prayer, the merchant's daughter said 'Time to get up and say your prayers, husband.' He did so, and then asked her 'How did you know it was time for prayer?' 'Well' she answered, 'The reason is, that when I was in my father's compound, when the time for the pre-dawn prayer came, the gold and silver would brighten the room as they stirred.' 'Yes' said he, 'you are indeed a merchant's daughter.'

From there he went to the hut of the village head's daughter and spent the night. Next morning very early when it was time for prayer, she said to him 'Time to get up, husband, and say your prayers, for it will soon be dawn.' He did so, and then he asked her 'How did you know it was time for prayers?' 'Well' she answered, 'This is how I knew it. When I was home, just before dawn came, our whole town would make its way outside the town, for excretion. That's how I knew that dawn was near.' 'Get out', says he, 'Get out of my compound, daughter of excrement!' And he laid about her with a stick, and she departed, back to her own town. That's all. End of story.

The Chief and his Courtiers [^{III}/ 168]

There was once a ruler who had many wives, and who found his penis troubling him – sometimes it would stand, sometimes it would not. Seeing this he was apprehensive that his women might leave him, and he thought he would disturb the peace of mind of his courtiers. One day when they were gathered before him as usual he said 'Last night, I made a wonderful discovery; there's a medicine, which I had just a little of – like this – and I didn't give any of my wives the chance to sleep!' His courtiers all bowed their heads. He changed the subject, and presently the gathering dispersed.

Night came and he went inside and went to sleep. Came the Galadima† and touched the gatekeeper. 'Who's that?' said the latter. 'I'm the Galadima. I want a word with the chief.' The gatekeeper went into the compound and coughed. 'Who's there?' said the chief. 'It's me, the gatekeeper. The Galadima's outside, he wants a word with the chief.' The chief came out and said 'Is all well, Galadima, that you come at night like this?' 'Well?' said the Galadima, 'no, indeed it is not.' 'What ails you?' said the chief. 'Something the chief said today' he answered, 'When all those people were there. My penis doesn't stand very well. And as one doesn't get secrets for nothing, I'll give two horses.' 'Go and bring them' said the chief, and the Galadima did so. 'Thank-you' said the chief, 'Now, go back and wait until I've pounded up the medicine. I'll let you know.' Off went the Galadima.

Not more than a day after that, the Vizier came at night to the chief, and what the Vizier had to say was what the Galadima had said. From him too the chief took wealth; and the same for the judge. Then at length the chief felt happier. 'Thank God' said he, 'I'm the same as the rest of my people. They're not better than I, nor I than they.'

So presently he ordered the gatekeeper to summon to him those who had visited him by night, and he did so. They came right into a private part of the compound, and the chief said 'Is that you people?' 'Yes, it's us' they answered. 'We shall get on fine hence-

† A title.

forth, you and I' he said, 'For we're in the same boat. I'm just the same as you, my condition is yours.' And rising, he retired into his inner compound, saying 'Goodnight to you.' All of them rose, much ashamed, and went off home, without the courtesy of taking leave of each other.

And that's the origin of [the saying that] if you refrain from concealing your ailment, you'll find a cure for it.

The Husband, the Wife, the Paramour and the Boy [$^{\text{III}}/_{172}$]

There was once a man who was after the wife of another with adulterous intent. Her husband was away on a journey.

This man got a young lad to accompany him, and they went to the entrance of the compound. Says he to the boy 'Go in and see if she's there, and tell her that I'm here.' The boy went in, the woman saw him. Says she 'Boy, where are you from?' 'I've come with him – he's outside.' 'Go and tell him to come in' she said. He went and returned with the other. Mats were spread for him in the hut and he entered and sat down on the mats. The youngster squatted down outside while the other chatted with the wife.

Suddenly the husband returned. The boy turned, saw him and went into the hut. And the husband came and squatted down with a knife at the hut entrance. The boy, in fear, passed wind loudly. Says the husband 'Whoever broke wind then, let him come out, and he can depart in safety.'

*'It was me' says the paramour, 'I broke wind' And the boy said 'Are you going to snatch my fart from me then?' 'It was me did it' the other insisted. 'So that was why you brought me was it – to snatch my fart from me?' Then the husband said 'The both of you come on out. I don't know which one broke wind – which you're quarrelling about.' Says the boy 'From today I'm not

* cf. I/143

273

coming on any more visiting trips with you. For you've snatched my fart from me.' So he parted from the boy and went off, ashamed.

And that's why people say 'If you're going to do something secret, don't do it with a boy.'

———————

The Blind Man and the Seeing Man* [^{III}/$_{173}$]

There was once a man who had finished weaving a piece of cloth in another town. As he was coming back, he met a blind man in the bush. He was going fast, and didn't notice that it was a blind man in front of him, thinking it was one with sight. So as he went along he bumped into him. Says the blind man 'Have you no eyes?' 'If I had, would I have bumped into you?' asked the other. 'But have you really no eyes?' 'No' lied the other. 'Where have you come from?' asked the blind man next. 'I've just finished a piece of weaving in another town.' 'May I see it?' said the blind man, and the other handed over a length of cloth to him which he took.

Then the blind man hung back and hid in the grass. And there began to crawl away. The weaver stood and waited for a while, then said to him 'Give me my property.' But the blind man remained quietly squatting in the grass. Three times the other spoke and then said 'Look what I've done to myself. Having no eyes, why ever did I give someone else my property?'

Then he went and broke off a piece of wood and began lashing about with it. 'Where can he be?' said he. Eventually he reached a point near where the blind man was and really lashed him. The blind man edged away and again lay down in the grass. 'Ha' said the other, 'That was a lucky one! Seeing that I have no eyes.' He moved on, then swung round and again lashed the blind man. This he did three times in all, and said 'Wherever can I find someone to come and look for this blind man for me?'

But the blind man had had enough of lashing and said 'You're lying. You can see, and all my suffering is quite unnecessary.'

* See J. p. 174. The blind man occurs so often in TATS usually as a Pew-style villain, as to be almost worthy of a separate section.

'If I could see' said the other, 'Would I have bumped into you?'
But the blind man threw down the other's length of cloth and said
to him 'Here – take your stuff. I've suffered enough. And you've
had what you wanted.' And the other picked up his cloth and
departed.

And that is why people say 'All living things oppress others,
except where the power is lacking.'

A Youth [III/186]

There was once a youth who had no other occupation than to tart
himself up and dress like a woman. Then he would go round from
the compound of one chief* to the next, to sleep with their wives.

He went on doing this for some time, and there came a day,
when he went into the compound of a chief and found his wives
about their usual daily occupations. He drew near and mingled
with them.

But while they were there, talking, one of the chief wife's
rings was lost, and word reached the chief. The chief made the
guards close the ways out. Then he ordered that every woman in
the house should have her clothes removed, be left naked as her
mother had borne her, and that they should all be searched, until
the ring was discovered.

The eunuchs went into the chief's compound, and began stripping them. Now the youth was there sitting in the middle of them,
and when this happened he was beside himself with fear, and he
besought God, saying 'God, I know that you created me, and that
before that I did not exist. It was you gave me strength and the
power to reason. If you – by your power – get me out of today's
shame, I on my part swear that I'll never do this sort of thing again.'
And he began saying (reading) a prayer, saying 'Oh thou who
bestowest enduring gifts – let thy gift be enduring!'

* This probably connotes all those of chiefly birth, not only chiefs.

275

Then the Lord heard his prayer, and the ring was found before they reached him. The eunuchs began saying 'Stop stripping them. The ring that was lost has been found.'

Then he set off and went outside. And to this day he has not again behaved in that way. 'Thanks' said he, 'are due to God for saving me from that shame.' End.

The Jackal, the Monkey and the Lion* [^{I}/ $_{140}$]

The jackal came across the monkey and had a word with him, saying 'May God preserve us from words from an unexpected quarter!' and repeated it three times. But the monkey, whom he was addressing, said 'Nothing worries me, for I live at the top of a tree.' (Now by what he said three times he meant a 'frame-up.)

The jackal went off and bought delicious food, three *nakiya*, and kept them till he met the lion. Then he gave the three honey-cakes to the lion, who ate them. The lion asked him 'Where did you get such delicious food from?' and the jackal said 'This food is monkey's excrement.' 'Is monkey's excrement really delicious?' asked the lion. Said the jackal 'Yes, if God so please.' 'Come on' said the lion, 'Are you coming to?' 'Surely I'm coming to' said the jackal. 'Let's go!'

When they got to where the monkey was, the lion looked him up and down and put him down on the ground, saying 'Produce some of your delicious excrement for me!' So he passed some and the lion ate it and didn't find it pleasant. Having eaten it, he said 'Let's tie him up!' And the jackal said 'If you press him, he'll produce his excrement for you.' So the lion pressed him and he produced more excrement, bitter to taste. The lion rubbed it, ate some and found it bitter. Then the lion knew that it had all been a false, malicious tale, and he and the jackal went off home leaving

* Cf. next tale which is clearer than this. It may be that some obscurity has crept in in translating from the Arabic.

The phrase 'frame-up' is a translation of an Arabic one which comes in the saying 'A frame-up from some unexpected quarter brings great grief'.

the monkey sitting there. But because of what had been said at the start of the tale, the jackal went back to the monkey.

And next day the jackal said to the monkey 'May God lighten for us the unexpected things!' and the monkey said 'Amen, amen, amen!'

And from this tale we can see that if any man contrives a plot against another without his knowledge, that other will suffer grief and trouble. That's all.

The Jackal, the Hyena and the Lion* [^{I}/ 87]

The jackal and the hyena were living together. Whenever the jackal stretched himself, he would say 'A frame-up hurts more than spear thrust';† and the hyena would say 'A spear thrust is more painful than a frame-up.'

This went on every day, till one day the jackal went to the market and bought some *nakiya*. He took it away and brought it to the lion, saying 'Mightiest of the beasts, here's a delicacy for you'. The lion took it and ate it, and tasting the sweetness said 'Malam of the bush, where did this delicious thing come from?' and the jackal answered 'Lord of the bush, it is hyena's excrement. But I fear she won't produce it for everyone, just for us boys, and even then only when she agrees to do it.'

Then off went the lion, seeking the hyena. He sought her high and low, till he saw her and seized her. Says he 'Make excrement for me' and she produced some. He took some and ate it but it wasn't sweet, so he said 'Here! Make excrement' and she did. Again he took some and ate it. Again it didn't taste sweet to him, so he pressed her very hard, saying 'Go on, make excrement!' and again she did so, even to the whole contents of her bowels. And still when he took and ate it, it didn't taste sweet to him. So he pressed her and said yet again 'Make some more excrement!' and when she did so this time, she passed her stomach-lining – and still,

* Cf. last tale and TR. No. 6. O. p. 261.   † A regular saying.

when he took and ate it, it didn't taste sweet to him. So he let her go and went off, and she barely managed to reach home.

A little later the jackal arrived, saying 'When I got here yesterday I didn't see you.' 'I was out' said she. They sat for a while, then the jackal stretched himself and said 'A frame-up hurts more than a spear-thrust.' Then the hyena said 'A frame-up hurts more than a hundred spear-thrusts!' and from that day she never again said 'A frame-up hurts *less* than a spear-thrust'.*

The Snake and the Frog [I/23]

It is said that once a snake was riding along on his horse, all coiled around the saddle. And as he went along he met a frog, and the frog said 'Hey, snake, where are you going?' And the snake said 'I'm going for a ride.' Then said the frog 'But you don't know how to ride. Get down, and you'll see how one should sit in a saddle.' The snake agreed and got down, saying to the frog 'Since, then, you know how to ride, come and get on!'

The frog took hold of the snake's horse and, getting on, sat properly, not in the snake's way at all. Then he galloped it for a couple of stretches, without falling off, and came back and said to the snake 'There! Now you see how to ride a horse! Not a bit like your sort of riding, coiling yourself around the saddle.' Says the snake to the frog 'Righto, give me my horse. Anyway, having a thing is better than being able to do one. Maybe you can ride, but as you haven't a horse, it's useless. While I – since I've got a horse – what do I want with knowing how to ride?'

This is the reason people say 'Having a thing is better than being able to do one, like a snake riding. Being able to ride without having a horse is useless to anyone.'

---

* This is obscure, as this wasn't what she had said before, according to this version of the story.

A Variant [^{I}/$_{24}$]

'Having a thing is better than being able to do one, like a snake riding.' The meaning of this is: once a frog met a snake on a horse. Said the frog to the snake 'Hey snake! You can't ride. Get off and you'll see how to sit on a horse!' So the snake got down from the horse, and gave it to the frog, who got up. Away he went at a gallop, for three stretches. Back he came and pulled up with a jerk, saying to the snake 'Now you see how to ride a horse, not like you were!' And the snake said 'O.K. Having a thing is better than being able to do one. Though you can ride, as you haven't a horse, it's useless.' Says the frog 'Yes indeed, that's true – having a thing is better than be able to do one.'

The Duck and the Swift [^{I}/$_{37}$]

The duck and the swift were feeding in the same place, when some hunters came on the scene, to catch them. The swift flew away, leaving the duck there, and they took her. Then said the duck 'Alas and alack! Now I know that a large body is an ill thing. Had I been as the swift, I would't have been taken.' And now you know why a man shouldn't be too fat.

The Cocks and the Hawk [^{I}/$_{38}$]

One day, it is said, two cocks were fighting. One of them suddenly lost his nerve and ran away. Then the other, in his joy, flapped his wings where he was on the top of a high hill.

279

But presently comes a hawk and takes him. And that's why people say 'A man shouldn't boast of his own strength and power' and for a proverb, people say 'Whatever you boast of in the world, there's someone who excels you at it.'

A Variant [$^I/_{39}$]

It is said that two cocks were fighting on a dung-hill, and one of them lost his nerve and ran away and hid. The other, who had caused the first cock to run away, mounted a high hill and flapped his wings in his delight that the other was frightened of him. But presently a hawk spied him from afar and came and took him, and in an instant he was gone.

And that is why, whatever you may have in this world – learning, wealth, strength, fighting power – don't boast about it, because in the things of this world, there's always someone better.

A Hawk and the Chicken [$^I/_{107}$]

The chicken and the hawk had a feud. Whenever the chicken saw the hawk she said 'Look at the tyrant who steals the children of man's chickens for no reason at all!' and the hawk would answer 'When you've hatched out your eggs and the chicks have grown, I'm the one that'll eat them all up.' And, with a scornful noise, the hawk would pass on.

Time passed and the chicken hatched out her eggs and the chicks grew. Then one day along came the hawk, and when he espied the young chicks from high up in the air, in blind rage he swooped down and impaled himself on a sharp-pointed tree stump. So he died before he even reached the chickens.

And that is the reason that people say that if you're going to have a feud with someone who is poorer or weaker than you are, don't press your feud too severely, but with moderation, for you never know, you may be the one to suffer.

The Greedy Dog who Came to the Feast [^{I}/ 109]

It is said that there was once a dog whose master gave a feast, and the dog went and invited a friend of his, saying 'Come to our house, for today we have a feast there, and we shall enjoy ourselves.' And he went along with his friend.

But when they reached the hut where the food was being cooked the cooks saw the strange dog and taking hold of his tail angrily threw him out of the compound. He fell outside, stunned. And he didn't come round, till they had finished eating the feast.

Very early next morning the cooks were going round outside the house when they saw the dog lying there. 'Hullo!' they said 'Where's this dog come from?' They hit it and it got up. Then they saw it and said 'Oh dear! It's that dog we threw out yesterday – his greed brought it on him.'

And that is why people say, whatever else a man does in this world, let him avoid greed. For greed, even if it doesn't bring destruction upon you, will bring you into trouble; and any one who doesn't restrain himself from being greedy, will meet the same fate as that dog – blows or abuse.

The Vulture and the Hawk [^{III}/ 20]

The vulture came and alighted at the gate of a town, waiting for someone to come out and excrete, so that he might go and eat it.

Along comes the hawk. 'Hallo! Vulture' says he, 'what are we up to here?' Says the vulture 'I'm waiting for what God will being me.' Says the hawk 'You, you look for what God gives you; but I – I look for what my strength will bring me.' And the vulture just answered 'We wait for what God brings us.'

The hawk flew up into the air, and seeing a lizard on a tree-stump, swooped down on it. But the tree-stump broke off both the hawk's wings.

Then the vulture lifted his head and saw the hawk lying there. He went over to him. Says the hawk 'Vulture, where are you going to?' And he answered 'Hawk, I've come to eat you.' Says the hawk 'Oh no, vulture, won't you wait till I am dead?' But the vulture answered 'Hawk, I won't wait till you are dead – for you, you came here to kill another creature, to take his life away. Well, now God has given you to me and, this very day, you are my meat.'

And the vulture went and started to eat the hawk, while he was still living, until he was dead; and he ate up every bit of him. That's all.

The Frog, the Fly and the Adobe [III/92]

The fly came to the edge of some water and there found an adobe. Just then a frog put his head out of the water and saw the adobe and the fly. Says he 'Adobe, you and the fly come on in and let's have a bathe.' 'O.K.' they both said.

So the adobe went into the water, reached the frog – and melted away. Then said the frog 'Fly, come and take a piece of grass from my eye.' Up comes the fly and lands by the frog's nose. Whereupon the frog puts out his tongue and licks the fly into his mouth, and eats him up.

Then the frog began to laugh, and he laughed until he lay on his back on the water, and his stomach burst. So all three of them came to a sticky end.

The Lizard and the Chameleon* [III/71]

The chameleon was on her way, going very very slowly, when she saw the lizard scamper by. Says she 'Hey lizard – shouldn't you move slowly and be more cautious of the world around? Look at the way I move. I fear the world.' Says the lizard 'Well, chameleon you – well, one man likes his head shaved *sariya* style, another prefers *kwambe* style†.' And the chameleon departed.

Two days later again the chameleon came by, and again the lizard scampered up. There were people sitting around, and the lizard ran up the legs of one of them. He took a stick and hit the lizard and the lizard died. Then he picked it up and tossed it away.

The chameleon went up to the lizard and said 'Well, lizard, I told you, you know – and not just in the last day or so, either – I was always telling you, that you shouldn't be in a hurry with the world around. But you just answered "Oh no! One man likes his head shaved *sariya* style, while another prefers *kwambe* style." Well, now look – what I told you about has come upon you, and now you're dead. For see – today it is as if you had never existed.' That's all. End of story.

The Song the Hen Sang to the Hawk [III/78]

In the name of God, I shall praise the Prophet. The hen took her ten children outside, when the hawk intercepted her. Says he 'Hen, today you'll have not one left of all those children of yours.' Says the hen 'Even if I don't have one left, I'll thank God for giving me the reward of my sitting.'

---

* A rare character in TATS.   † A proverb.

Dog Meets Dog [^{III}/ 178]

A dog once met another dog as he went along. One saw that the other had in his mouth a fried *waina*, and said 'God's curse on that *waina* and whoever gave it.' And the dog who had it in his mouth said 'Yes, God's curse on it; and God's curse on the man who left it to be found and become a benefit for someone else.'

They say that the point of this story, you know, is that no wise man will reject some small item of wealth, in the hope of getting a big one later.

The Man and the Snakes* [^{III}/ 179]

A man was once taking a walk, when he came across two snakes, fighting, biting each other. He stood for a while watching them. Then he saw a female snake come up, and make peace between them.

Then the man said to the female snake 'It was only because you were even more deadly than they, that you were able to come between them.'

What he meant was that evil men consort with each other.

The Tortoise and the Hare† [^{III}/ 180]

The tortoise and the hare set a target between them to race for. They set a stone. But the hare, knowing in himself that he was a

* Cf. No. I/40.

† This story is written in a very awkward style—possibly translationese (? from Arabic).

swift runner, lay down on the road and went to sleep. But the tortoise, knowing in himself that he was a slow runner, didn't lie down but kept trying to run, so that he even got to the stone before the hare had got up from his sleep. Then the hare woke – and found the tortoise already there. 'Had I known' he said 'I wouldn't have gone to sleep.'

That is to say, the point of this is that one who is strong should not relax his efforts at his work, because he knows that he is strong. For then when he *does* set about finishing it, he'll find himself among the also-rans.

The Hyena and the Lion [III/181]

The hyena went hunting, found some game and took it, rejoicing. Then she set off with the meat. She met the lion and lion took the meat from her mouth. Then the hyena said to herself. 'It's no wonderful thing when a robber is himself robbed. Even if it isn't taken forcibly from him, it won't be of any use to him.'

And the meaning is that whatever you get as the result of oppressing others won't stay long with you; if it does, you won't get any pleasure from it.

PART IV

MEN AND WOMEN
YOUNG MEN
AND MAIDENS

These are tales of marriage and courtship – of jealous fellow-wives – of adultery – of young men and maidens – and simple Rabelasian tales.

How to Tell a Fine Woman [$^{I}/$ xxxvii]

The Hausas say that if you want to choose the finest woman among them, you should look for one who is not too bulky, but not too thin – of middling build. She should have bright eyes, well spaced teeth, dark gums, plentiful hair, and a womanly voice – not a masculine one. She should have long fingers and toes, and her buttocks should be neither too prominent nor yet insignificant. She should not be a great talker, nor a fast walker. This is what the Hausa consider a fine woman – languid, soft-bodied, without elbows.

The Malam and his Two Wives [$^{I}/$ 10]

There was once a malam and his two wives. Now there came a time of hunger, when they could get no food, save a very little. Then he called the wife he liked and said to her 'Together let's get hold of the other wife and give her a certain leaf to eat, so that she turns into a goat. Then we can sell her and buy food.' 'O.K.' says she. So they called her and gave her some medicine, which she drank and turned into a goat.

The malam took her to market and sold her. Then he bought some food and took it home and he and his other wife ate it. After three days, the wife who had been given the medicine and turned into a goat turned back into a woman and came home to the malam's compound.

But after three more days, the malam and his other wife again seized her and gave her medicine. And when she had taken it she turned into a goat. They took her to market and the butchers bought her. And taking hold of her they tied her up to slaughter, when another man came up, who says 'Hey butchers! Give me the goat, I'll buy her and look after her, rather than that you should slaughter her.' So they gave her to him, and he bought her, took hold of her and took her to his home.

Then the goat said to him 'Hi! I'm not a goat, me. I'm a woman. They gave me medicine and when I took it, I turned into a goat. For they didn't like me and sold me to buy food.' Then said he 'If you want to go back to your husband's home, I'll give you medicine to turn you back into a woman and you can go home to him.' And she answered 'Very well, take me there!'

So he gave her some medicine which she took and went home and there she found the malam. Now the wife that he liked had died. And she said to the malam 'I'm back – you, who don't like me and gave me medicine which I took and turned into a goat! So! But you see, another man has given me medicine too and I've turned into a woman again. But since you don't like me, me too I don't like you' and she collected her things together and left the Malam's compound.

And so if a man doesn't like you, have no truck with him!

———————

The Petty Trader and his Wife, and the Old Woman, and Ari*, and the Chief's Son [I/16]

There was once a petty trader who lived in a town with his wife, and in all the town there was no woman so fair as she. And the trader left his wife at home and went off to another town trading.

Before he returned, an old woman saw his wife and was amazed. For she said 'I never knew there was a woman in this town so fair as that!'

And the old woman went home and bought cola-nuts, a calabash full, and scent wrapped them up. Then she went to the trader's wife and said to her 'I'm sent, my girl, to you by the son of the chief of the town.' And she answered 'But how does the son of the chief of the town know me?' And the old woman said

* A common Kanuri name. It is rare to give characters names and so probably significant here that it is a Kanuri name.

'Would he give me cola-nuts and scent to bring you if he didn't know you?' But she said 'Old woman, you're not to bring trouble upon me! I'm just the wife of a humble man.' And the old woman answered 'As for that, it's nothing, here, take them!' And the trader's wife took the cola-nuts and the scent, and the old woman went off home.

A few days later, she pounded up some *nakiya* and bought some strips of dried meat, and, when she had done, took them and went to the home of the chief's son. And she said to him 'Son of the chief, I am sent to you' and, when he asked 'By whom?' she answered 'It's a woman who has sent me with *nakiya* and strips of dried meat, telling me to bring them to you.' Says he 'How does she know me?' And the old woman said 'Whenever you're riding you pass the door of her home and she sees you.' And he was agreeable, and accepted the *nakiya* and strips of dried meat.

Then the old woman returned to the home of the trader's wife, and said to her 'The chief's son says he'll come the day after tomorrow' and she answered 'So be it, if God will.' And again the old woman said to her 'You must prepare *tuwo* and *nakiya* and get together something special to eat the day that he comes' and the trader's wife agreed to do so. She got the food together and put it on one side, before the chief's son arrived. And the old woman put poison into the food and left it there.

Then came the chief's son to the trader's wife, and he sat down. And she gave him *nakiya*. But when he had broken off a piece and eaten, he died. And the old woman said 'Look what has happened – the chief's son has died in your home!' And the trader's wife wept sore.

Then there came up a man, by name Ari, and he asked the trader's wife 'How much will you give me if I rid you of this chief's son?' And she offered him two cows. Then he said 'Done! Bring me a grass mat and some rope!' and she brought them. And he rolled up the chief's son in the mat and carried him away.

From there he went to the home of the head butcher, and said to him 'Here I am!' and the head butcher called out 'Who is it?' and Ari replied 'It's the chief's son, I've come to you because I want some strips of dried meat.' And the other said 'Sorry, I haven't any.' And Ari said 'If you don't give me some, I'll die.'

Then Ari propped the chief's son against the wall and put shoes in front of him, and found himself a hiding-place and lay low. Out comes the head butcher, saying 'Where's the man who wants the dried meat?' and he looked and saw the chief's son propped up there. Then says he 'Oh, hullo, it's you!' and he touched him, whereupon he fell over. Then said the head butcher 'A terrible thing has come upon me today – the chief's son has died at the gate of my home! Whatever shall I do?'

Then Ari came out of his hiding-place, and said to the head butcher 'How much will you give me to rid you of him?' and he answered 'I'll give you twenty thousand cowries and a leg of beef.' Says Ari 'Righto! Bring me a grass mat and some rope!' And he went into the compound and brought him a grass mat and some rope. And Ari rolled up the chief's son, picked him up and went his way.

From there he made his way to the home of a caravan-leader, late at night. Says he 'Caravan-leader, peace be upon you!' and the other came out and said 'Who's there?' Ari replied 'I'm the chief's son. I've come to buy some cola-nuts from you.' The caravan-leader answered 'Oh, but I'm sorry, I haven't any cola-nuts just now.' And Ari answered 'If you don't give me cola-nuts, I'll die,' and he replied 'Very well – die then!' Then Ari propped the chief's son up against the wall, and went to a hiding-place and hid. Then the caravan-leader came out and saw a man leaning against the wall. And he said 'Oh-oh! It *was* the chief's son, come to see me, and I thought it was someone else!' And he touched him slightly and he fell over. Then said the caravan-leader 'God in Heaven! What, oh what shall I do? Here's the chief's son died right at the gate of my home.' Then Ari stepped out of his hiding-place and said 'Caravan-leader, what's the matter?' and the other answered 'It's the chief's son. He came to ask me for cola-nuts, and when he didn't get them, he died! That's how it is and I'm at a loss what to do!' And Ari asked him 'What will you give me, if I carry him away from the gate of your compound?' And the caravan-leader replied 'I'll give you cola-nuts, a whole pannier full.' 'Right' says Ari, bring me a grass mat and some rope!' And he gave him a grass mat and some rope. The Ari rolled up the chief's son and carried him away.

As he went along, he came by the back of his* father's compound.

* I.e., apparently, the corpse's.

He pitched the chief's son over the wall, and the body fell in the compound close to a chicken-pen. The chief heard the noise and drew his sword. Coming out, he saw a man lying close to the chicken-pen, and he slashed him, saying 'Whoever's come into the house, I'll see him in the morning.'

Early next morning, the people gathered and saw that the chief had killed his son. And the chief said 'Since no one but friends and relatives knows about it, go and bury him! It was an honest mistake.'

The Woman who was Jealous and her Husband [I/₃₀]

There was once a man and his wife, who was of an exceedingly jealous nature. She refused to abide a fellow-wife. Whenever her husband married another wife and brought her home, the first wife would give her a poison draught, putting it in her food. And when the other ate it, before the morning she would be dead.

So it was for some time, but there came a day when the husband met another woman he wished to marry. And he said to her 'Well, my girl, I'd like to marry you, but whenever I take another wife, my first wife gives her poison and she drinks it and dies. What can we do?' And she answered 'I suppose you really mean to marry me?' And when he said 'Yes' she answered 'Right, I have a scheme which will stop her killing me.' 'What will you do?' says he. 'I'll sham dumb (deaf-mute)' says she 'while we get married, but don't you say anything, till I come to your home.' 'O.K.' says he.

Then he went off home and said to his first wife 'Well! I'm marrying another wife, but she's dumb. So please, I beg you, just leave her be. Don't talk to her – do you understand?' 'Right' says she, but she added as he went away 'Not a hope! Just wait till we meet!'

After the marriage, the new wife came to his home and for seven days was treated as a bride, and the other said nothing to her. Twenty days passed, but when the first wife thought that the dumb girl felt herself to be at home, she took poison and put it in the food. But the other saw her doing it. So when she gave it to her to eat, knowing there was poison in it, she didn't eat it, but put it aside. Then when it came her turn to cook, she took the one with the poison in it and mixed it with the one she had cooked, and gave the whole to the first wife, all unsuspecting. Then the first wife ate the food, ate all of it, and began to feel dizzy. So she made signs to the other, meaning 'I suppose you haven't given me any of that food I gave you?' Then the other denied it, shaking her hand. The first wife collapsed, vomiting and died. Then the pretended dumb wife said 'Now we can live at peace!'

A Neighbour and a Neighbour [^{I}/$_{48}$]

There were once two neighbours who had their huts next door to each other. One had a wife, the other was a wifeless man.

Someone told the one with a wife that his neighbour was after his wife and when he questioned it he was told 'If you don't believe me, one day you tell your wife you're going on a journey. Then go off in the morning, and in the evening, come back and hide. You'll see!' He agreed to this, and next morning said to his wife that he was going on a journey in the morning. 'See you when you return' says she and off he goes.

When it was dark, he came home, entered his hut, got on to the bed and lay down. Presently her lover comes out and makes to enter the hut. 'May I come in? says he, 'and the husband said 'Who are you?' It's me' says the other. 'What do you want now, at night?' 'Oh, I've come to get some firing.' 'What's wrong with the fire in your own hut?' 'Oh, it's not hot – this one has more heat.' 'Very well' said the husband,' take it in your hand and go.' And the lover picked up the firing with his hand and made off at a run, back into his hut.

Next morning, he couldn't face the other, he was so ashamed. And he fled the town and never came back.

The Farmer and his Three Wives* [$^{I}/_{65}$]

A farmer had three wives who used to help him with his farming.

But the time came when they refused to work on the farm, doing their work very slackly. So he said to himself 'Let me see if I can trick them into doing a little work.' So he made three loincloths and called his chief wife secretly and gave her one, saying 'Put on this loincloth! It has a special magic power – but don't tell the others.' 'Right' says she.

He called another one and gave her one too, saying the same to her as to his chief wife. And to the youngest he did the same.

Then when they were on the farm, he would say 'Speed up, the one with the little loincloth! Speed up, the one with the little loincloth!' and they would work faster at their hoeing, vying with each other till they were tired. So that it got beyond them.

Then said the chief wife to her fellows 'I'm sick of this little loincloth, I'm giving our man back his property.' Whereupon the others said 'But we were given them too!'

So they went home and said to him 'So you gave us these loincloths, did you, so that we would work fast for you, eh?' And he answered 'If I hadn't done so, you wouldn't have worked fast.' To which they replied 'Here, take your loincloths, we don't want them.'

Wake, Chief of the Gwari his Wives and the Young Man [$^{I}/_{67}$]

In the days when Wake was chief of the Gwari and living in his court, he had very many wives; some of them he wouldn't see for two years, and they were all kept in the compound, not allowed to go out.

* Cf. TR. No. 49.

There came the day when they gathered and put their heads together to discuss the matter. They said 'Let us send the *jekadiya* out, secretly to find us a man, to come in and visit us in turn, to make life more bearable.' The *jekadiya* agreed and went off to the market. There she saw a handsome young man. She called to him 'Hey young man, come here and carry some wood for me, and take it home for me!' When he agreed, she went ahead and he followed her. She bought some wood and helped him put it on his head. And he took it for her, right into the compound, without anyone seeing them. They came to the chief wife, and he put down the wood. Then the *jekadiya* said 'Here you are – here's a young man, I've brought for you. Don't let anyone hear about it!' And they promised.

The chief wife found a hiding-place and put him there. Then, in the evenings he would come out, and each night spend the night with a different wife. They gave him fine food and they washed him and anointed his body. And he had no work to do.

So he lived in the compound of the chief of the Gwari for about eight months and no one knew of it.

Then one day the chief came into the compound, sticking his nose into the women's huts. In one of them he looked up, and he saw some spit on the purlin of the roof. Then he said to himself 'There's a man in this house! A woman couldn't spit right up on to the purlin and make it stay there. Only a man could do that'. Then he went and stood in the middle of the compound and commanded all the women of the house to collect.

And they all collected in the middle of the compound. Then he said 'Where is the man who is in this compound? Let him come out – I won't kill him, I want to ask him some questions.' They brought him out, and he asked him how many months he had been in the compound. 'Nine' says he. 'Who brought you in?' says the chief, and he answered 'The *jekadiya* told me to carry her wood for her and bring it here. I brought it right into the compound, and then the women kept me and wouldn't let me go out, and I'm still here.'

Then the chief sent for the *jekadiya* and said to her 'Was it you who brought a man into the house?' Says she 'It was your wives who complained that they hadn't a man and asked me to get one for them to keep in the house. That's why I brought him. But I thought he'd gone by now. Just fancy! He's still here.' Then the chief killed the *jekadíya*, and from that day till he died, he never appointed another one. But he dismissed the young man, who went his way.

The Husband and Wife [^{I}/$_{73}$]

A man and his wife were lying down asleep at the dead of night once, when the wife got up and said to her husband 'I'm going out to relieve myself.' 'O.K.' says he, 'bring me some news, when you come back.' She made no objection to this. 'Righto' says she.

She went outside and round behind the hut. As she was squatting down, relieving herself, she heard someone outside the compound talking. 'Tomorrow at this time' he was saying, 'this town will be nothing but ruins.' He was a scout, it seemed, who had come to spy out the town, leaving his army hidden close at hand.

As for the woman, when she heard that, she went into the hut and said to her husband 'Well, here's the news I've brought you.' 'What did you hear?' says he. And she replied 'I heard a man outside the compound saying "Tomorrow at this time, this town will be nothing but ruins".' 'What!' says he, 'is that so?' 'Yes indeed' replied his wife. 'Right' says he. 'Then we'll pack our things and get out without any delay.' And away they went. And before dawn the army had sacked the town.

The Father of the Daughter and the Three Men* [^{I}/$_{76}$]

There was a man who had a daughter, and in all the town there was none so fair as she. There came a man who said he wished to marry

* Cf. TR. No. 47.

her. He promised her to him. There came a second and he too
sought her in marriage – and he promised her to him. And there
came yet a third, seeking her – and to him too he promised her.
Three men that was – and they all brought him money which he
took. Thus he obtained the money of all three of them.

Time passed and the girl was old enough to be married, and
people said to themselves 'Let's see what this fellow will do with
only one daughter and three accepted suitors!'

Then he went off and visited an old malam and said to him
'Malam, I've come to see you..' 'Well?' says the malam. 'I've
got only one daughter, but I've taken money from three people;
and I promised her to each of them! And now the girl is old
enough to be married.' 'Just so' said the malam. 'Now, when you
rise to say your prayers, draw your sword, and leave it handy by.
When you have made a bow and lifted your head again, if you see a
bitch passing across in front of you, then quickly take your sword
and slash her, cutting her in two. You'll see what you want there.'
'Good' says the other.

When the time of prayer came, he rose and began his prayers, and
he had made a bow and lifted his head again, when he saw a bitch
come and run quickly in front of him. Then swiftly he picked up
his sword and cut her in two. And then, behold, two maidens rose
up in front of him, fair as his own daughter. So he took them home,
and prepared them for marriage,* the two of them and his own
daughter too. Then, having solved the problem, he gave each
man his bride.

Time passed, and after about three months, he went and said to
the malam 'What shall I do in order to know my own daughter
among them?' Says the malam 'You must set out and visit all their
homes, and greet them all, until you discover which among them is
your daughter.' 'Very well' said the man.

So he set out and he came to the home of the first husband, he
who had married the bitch's front end. He found them quarrelling,
from morning to early afternoon, ceaselessly. When the people
there saw the father, they said to her 'Here! Have patience, be less
quarrelsome; see! Your father has come.' Says she 'I won't –
good-for-nothing father indeed!' And the father said 'This one
isn't my daughter' and he went on.

* Lit. 'put them in henna'.

Then he went to the home of the next husband, the one who married the bitch's back end. When he got there, he made formal greeting, and then found that his daughter wasn't there; that she hadn't been there for three days. Then he asked the people of the house 'Where's the girl who was brought into this house two months ago?' And they said 'Oh, her! She's a good-for-nothing girl. Ever since she was brought here, she has never slept for seven days in one place. She's away there, after men.' And he went on.

Then he came to the home of the man who had married his very own daughter. When he got there, he made formal greeting, and received reply. He was given a fine place to stay. He was treated with great respect, given *tuwo* and meat to eat, and *fura* and milk to drink, and all other tokens of great respect were paid to him. Then he knew that he was now at the home of his very own daughter.

The Man and his Three Daughters [I/93]

Are you listening? Well, there was a man who had three daughters, each from a different wife: one from his favourite wife, one from his least favoured wife and one from the wife in between.

They grew up and none of them had yet a husband. Then said their father to them 'Be off with you and seek husbands, and get yourselves married!' 'Certainly' they said, and going forth from their home, they set off.

And as they went, they came to some weavers, who spied them coming and called out 'Hullo! There are some girls!' And the daughter of the favourite said 'Do you mean me?' 'No, not you' said they. And the daughter of the least favoured wife said 'Do you mean me?' 'No, not you.' Then the third girl said 'Do you mean me?' and they answered 'Yes, you, come here!' So she went up to them and they gave her a narrow strip of cloth, saying 'Take this and go and make it up into a cloth.' 'Very well' said she and took it and brought it over to the others. Then said she to the daughter of the favourite 'Here, you take it and keep it, and let's go!' 'I won't' said the other to her, 'for you very well know that at home my mother is superior to yours.' Then she gave it to the daughter of the least favoured wife, saying 'Here, you take it and keep it, and let's go!' And she said 'Give it here! One good turn deserves another' and she took hold of it, and away they went.

Next they came to some tailors, and these said to them 'Hey, look! Some girls!' and the daughter of the favourite said 'Do you mean me?' 'No, not you.' And the daughter of the least favoured wife said 'Do you mean me?' 'No, not you.' And then the third girl said 'Do you mean me' and they answered 'Yes, you. Come here!' So she went up to them and they said 'Give us your strip of cloth, we'll sew it up for you.' She took it and handed it to them. And they sewed up a cloth for her and gave it to her. She took it and off they went again.

And as they went they came across some dyers, who said 'Hullo! There are some girls.' Then the daughter of the favourite said 'Do you mean me?' 'No, not you' they said. And the daughter of the least favoured wife said 'Do you mean me?' 'No, not you.' Then the third said 'Do you mean me?' 'Yes, you' said they. 'Give us your cloth, we'll dye it for you.' So she gave it to them and they dyed it and returned it to her. And away they went again.

Next they came upon some blacksmiths, who said 'Hey look! Girls! And just look at that lass!' And the daughter of the favourite said 'Do you mean me?' 'No, not you.' And the daughter of the least favoured wife said 'Do you mean me?' and they said 'No, not you.' Then the third said 'Do you mean me?' and they said 'Yes, you. Come here!' And she went over to them and they made silver armlets for her and gave them to her. So on they went again.

They travelled for a while, till they came to a town. They entered it, and, as soon as they had entered, the son of the Galadima* and the chief both saw the third girl and fell in love with her. Well, it was the daughter of the least favoured wife that the son of the Galadima married. As for the favourite wife's daughter, she married a blind man. But the third girl, whom both the chief and the son of the Galadima had fallen for, the chief married her.

Time passed and their father arrived at the town, wearing a gown

* A title. It may be that 'son of' is a mistranslation, as *Dan Galadima* is also a title.

made from palm-leaves* performing dances in the market. Where-upon the daughter in the chief's compound sent a slave-girl to the market to see him and report on him. When she got home, she told her, saying 'I saw a man with a gown made from palm-leaves in the market and he was dancing – just like a chicken he was!' Then her mistress knew that it was her father, and taking a gown, she gave it to the slave-girl, saying 'Here, take this and take it to the old man you saw in the market; and tell him to come here.' Then she took it and brought it to him.

And the two of them came back. He stopped at the entrance of the compound, while the slave-girl went in and told her. Then she, in her turn, told the chief, saying 'My father and yours is here.' 'Where is he?' said the chief. 'In front of the compound' says she. 'Let him come in' said the chief, and he came in and they greeted him. The chief brought a horse, fully accoutred, and gave it to him – and a slave-woman, and a slave-boy to gather grass for it – all he gave him. And his daughter went and brought other presents too and gave them to him, and she brought cloths and gave them to him, telling him to take them to her mother.

Then her elder sister, the wife of the son of the Galadima, brought a gown and a turban and a pair of trousers and gave them to him; and three cloths which she told him to take to her mother. But as for the daughter of his favourite wife, he neither saw her nor her husband. He asked after her and was told 'Oh, she married a blind man.' Now he had thought that she would have married the best husband, seeing that her mother was his favourite wife. When this daughter† heard that her father had come, she made *tuwo* from bran (*i.e.* inferior stuff) and brought it to him and he cursed her for a good-for-nothing girl.

So he returned home and he told all their mothers about it: he told them what their respective daughters had done for him and what their husbands had given him. Then his favourite asked him where the presents her daughter had given him were, and he answered 'There are none, for she gave me nothing.' Then he said to them 'In a year's time, all of you must go and each visit your daughter to see how she is.'

Time went by and a year passed. Then they made their prepara-

* A very unusual garb which he wore in order to be noticed.
† I have emended the punctuation here and read *sai ta for suka*.

tions and off they went. When they reached the entrance to the town, there they saw horses standing waiting. For, it seemed, that news of their arrival had been received and the chief and the son of the Galadima had sent to receive them. So they entered the town, and the least favoured wife went to the home of the son of the Galadima. When she reached it, presents were brought and given to her. The next wife went to the chief's house, and there she was lodged and given a huge collection of assorted presents.

As for the favourite wife, she went to her daughter's home and put up there. She found that her hut was roofless, without even a few thorn branches for thatch, and she herself had no cloth, but was clad in rags which she had patched together to cover herself. And she cursed her, at which she burst out crying. But the least favoured wife and her fellow wife each year from then on they would make a visit to their daughters. That's all. *Kungurus kan kusu.*

The Man and his Wife* [I/96]

There was once a man who had lived together with his wife for nine years.

There came a day when his wife said 'Husband, what sort of a man are you indeed?' 'Well, what do you think?' said he. Then she answered 'What I think is this – am I going to be all alone in this household apart from you for ever? Aren't I going to get a fellow-wife?' 'Oh-oh' says he doubtfully, 'better not bring in a fellow-wife, it'll only cause trouble.' 'No, indeed' said she, 'I'll find another wife for you.' 'O.K.' he says, 'I think that's a good idea too. Off you go and find one for me!'

So off she went and found him a widow (*or* divorcee) and brought her to him. He took her into his hut and they discussed the matter and came to an agreement. Next day when it was light, the marriage was sealed and she moved into her husband's home. And there the two of them lived together. And anything he got – money or cola-nuts or clothes – he would bring to the hut of his bride, bringing nothing to the hut of his senior wife.

* Cf. TR. No. 52.

Time passed, till the day came when he bought two calabashes of cola-nuts and five phials of perfume of roses, which he mixed with musk. These he put by till it was night. Then, the whole of that night he spent in his bride's hut, chatting, chewing cola-nuts, putting scent on themselves – till midnight came and still they didn't go to sleep. All the while his senior wife was listening and kept from sleeping.

At last she got up and said 'Husband, since it was I who arranged this marriage for you, let's cancel it – I don't like her, let her go away and leave us.' 'Is that so?' said he. 'Yes' says she. And he answered her 'Now, listen – before, when there were just the two of us, you and me, *I* never said to you I wanted to marry again. It was you who insisted on my getting a fellow-wife for you. Now, since you found her and brought her here and I've married her, I'm not going to drive her out. On the other hand, you, be off with you! I divorce you!' and he drove her out. Then said she to herself 'Alas, I have done something that has brought trouble on me. Had I but known, I would never have said that!' and she added 'Whoever mounts the horse of "Had-I-But-Known" suffers trouble.'

The Paramour who was Given Away by a Boy [I/ 111]

There was once a man living with his wife. Now the husband travelled away from home a lot, trading in village markets.

There came a day when he said to his wife 'Look, tomorrow I'm going to a market that is a long way off, and perhaps I shan't come back, but spend the night there.' Now he knew that whenever he travelled, his wife would fetch her paramour and he would spend the night in her hut. So the husband waited till the sun had set before he left the other town, and before he reached home everyone was asleep.

The wife summoned her paramour, and he was lying in the hut, when the husband arrived home. 'Peace be upon you' said he, and the woman hearing her husband's voice realised that he had returned and said to her paramour 'Get up and get under the bed, here's my husband come.' So the paramour got into the space for lighting a fire under the bed, stretched out and lay there. Then her husband came into the hut, not knowing that the other was there too. Says his wife 'Welcome back'. 'Thank you' says he.

Then she brought him food, and he started eating it. And she and their son were both eating theirs too, when the boy said 'Oh! Here we are eating our nice, steaming *tuwo*, mother and father and me, and the one under the bed hasn't got his'. So spoke the boy as they ate their *tuwo*, and the husband said 'What! What do you mean –the one under the bed?' and the boy replied 'What! Can't you see him there with his eyes blinking?' Then said the husband 'How long has he been here? How did he get under the bed?' And the boy answered 'He came in as soon as you left. He went to bed with mother. Then when they heard you coming, she told him to get under the bed.' Then the husband said 'Well, well, well! Boys don't lie' and her paramour said 'Kill me and be rid of me.'

The Woman who was exceedingly Jealous [^{I}/ 120]

There was once a man who had three sons, two from one wife, the third from a different one.

The day came when they were men, and their father said to them 'Each of you go and seek a wife and I will arrange for you to be married.' So the eldest went and found himself a wife and came and told his father. 'I've found a wife, Dad' said he. 'Good' said his father, 'what's her nature?' And the son replied 'Her nature is to chase men.' 'If that's all, no matter' said his father and produced the money and they were married and she came to his compound. Now when they made a hut for her, they made a little hole in the compound wall just beside her hut. When she went round behind her hut she saw this, and said to herself 'Well, I suppose somebody's told them that I chase men, that's why they made this hole close to my hut so that I can go in and out. Very well! I'll give up being promiscuous, I won't do it any more.' And so she lived happily at home.

A little later the second son said to his father 'I've found a wife, Dad.' 'What's her nature' said his father. 'Her nature is stealing' said he. 'No matter' said his father, 'if that's all' And he produced the presents needed for the marriage, and the marriage was arranged and she was brought to the compound. Whereupon the father said 'Collect all the things in the compound and take them to her hut – money and all other possessions.' So all these were collected and taken to her hut. And she said 'Well! It must be because they've heard that I steal, that's why they've brought all their wealth and left it in my hut. Very well! I'll give up stealing, I won't do it any more.' And so she lived happily at home.

Soon after the youngest son also found a wife and came and told his father. 'What's her nature?' said his father. 'Nothing worth mentioning' said the boy 'But she's very jealous.' 'Don't you marry her' said his father. So the boy went into the compound and told his mother, saying 'Mother, when I told Dad the wife that I have chosen, he told me not marry her.' 'Well!' said she, 'it's because your mother is different from theirs, when you tell him of the wife you've found, just because she's jealous he says don't marry her. And this one married a thief, and that one married a promiscuous woman, and no one stopped them – no, it's only you he prevents. All right – you *shall* marry her. And let what comes, come!' Then the boy went back to the entrance of the compound and told his father. Says he 'Dad, I'm *going* to marry the one I said.' 'Very well' said his father 'You've refused my advice, you've listened to your mother. Go ahead!' and he produced the presents needed for the marriage. She was brought to the compound, and they began to live together, man and wife.

There came a day when her younger sister came to visit them. And the younger sister and the husband* began to flirt with each other, until one day he began stroking her breast. His wife was to one side, at work pounding, and she saw this. Whereupon she

* They were in 'joking relationship' by Hausa custom.

305

lifted up her pestle and struck her husband on the head. He fell, with his head cracked.

When the father heard the women in the compound crying he quickly came in. And when he saw what had happened, he said 'There! I told you. I said that the boy shouldn't marry this woman. But you, his mother, you said he should marry her. And there you are – there's the cause of his murder – excessive jealousy.' Then the wife was sentenced to be taken and put to death. But when they were on the point of killing her, she said 'Even though the monkey is being killed, the damage is already done!'* God preserve us from a woman who is excessively jealous!

A Man called Arli and a petty Trader, his Wife's Paramour [$^{I}/_{127}$]

There was once a man at Sokoto called Arli, who had married a wife. But he was a very jealous man. Every morning he would catch his father's donkey, put a pack-basket on and two water pots in that and drive it down to the stream to fetch water and bring it to her. This he would repeat twice, before he relaxed and sat down. Then she pounded *fura* and mixed it for him to drink, and not until the early afternoon would he go off to the market. But before sunset, he would be back home again, anxious lest anyone might enter his compound and see his wife.

Well, all this while, as it happened, his wife was very friendly with a petty trader, and he was fond of her. In fact, when she was a girl, it was with him that she used to sleep. Now he had gone off to Lagos, and when he got back found that she was married. When he asked who her husband was, he was told 'Oh, her husband is a very jealous man, he doesn't let anyone see his wife' and the trader said 'Oh yeah? Look, *wherever* she is, no one will stop us getting together.'

So he waited till the early afternoon, when her husband had gone

* Proverb.

to market to get ingredients for the soup. Then, coming to the compound, he stuck his head in. And the wife said 'Here's my elder brother returned from Lagos, and my husband gone to market. But come on in, let's hear your news.' And the trader went into her hut, and she took a round mat and spread it close to the door. Then getting on the bed, they took their pleasure, and he departed. All without any one the wiser.

When the husband came back from the market, one of the women said to him 'Oh, your wife's elder brother came when you were at the market. But he went to her hut and visited her. And he said when you returned he would come and call on you.'

Then his father sent to enquire from the wife's parents, saying 'We hear that your daughter's elder brother has returned from Lagos, and we send him our greetings.' To which someone there said 'What nonsense is this! She has no other elder brother in the whole of this town, except me, and I haven't even been to Bod'inga, let alone Lagos.' So he knew it was her paramour who had come back from Lagos, and had said he was her elder brother so that they could commit adultery. And her husband took a cudgel and beat her.

But when night came again, the trader went round behind their compound, and taking a stone tossed it on to her hut, thud. The woman heard it and taking up her clothes went out, while her husband still slept. Then she followed the trader to his house and spent the night there. When she got up, she went to her parents' home, and they brought her back to her husband.

Then her husband took a complaint against the trader before the judge. The judge addressed the trader, saying 'As for you, why did you enter the hut of a woman and her husband and break the law? Very well! You will be locked up for two months and then given thirty lashes.' 'That's bad!' said the trader. 'But even though you kill the monkey, he's already done the damage.'

The Man who had Two Wives, one who Smoked and one who Didn't [I/ 135]

There was once a man had two wives: one was a smoker, the other wasn't.

Whenever their husband went to market, he would buy tobacco for the one who smoked.

But after a while, the other wife – that didn't smoke – said to her husband 'Seeing that I don't smoke, just give me the money for myself. If you buy her ten cowries' worth of tobacco, give me five for my tobacco, but as I don't smoke, I'll buy myself perhaps groundnuts to eat.' He agreed to this.

So from that day on, if he set out for the market, he would give her five cowries saying 'Here you are! Since you don't smoke, buy something else with them' and she would take them. Well, when she received the money, she didn't spend it, but had a tall corn-bin made inside her hut, and there she would put the tobacco money whenever it was given her, continually adding to what was in the bin.

This went on and continued for years, until she had collected enough cowries to fill the bin. She looked in and when she saw it she said 'Praise God, my purpose is fulfilled.' Then she said to her husband 'I want you to buy a slave-girl for me.' 'Where have you got the money to buy a slave-girl?' said he. 'You just bargain for one and bring her along to me. You'll see where I'll get the money.' 'Righto' said he.

Setting out, he went to the market, and going to where the slaves were sold, he bought a slave-girl for two hundred and fifty thousand and he took her back to his wife. 'Where are her owners?' said she. 'There they are' he answered. And she said they were to come and get their money.

When they entered the compound, she smashed the bin, and began collecting the cowries and, as she took them out, poured them on to the floor, and the others began counting. They counted till they had reached two hundred and fifty thousand, which they gathered up and departed.

After they had gone, the other wife and the husband asked her 'Where did you get that amount of money so that you were able to buy a slave-girl?' She answered 'Oh, ever since that time some years ago, the tobacco money that you have been giving me, I've been collecting, until it has accumulated like this. For I said to myself, each person has his own special heart's desire – my fellow-wife's is smoking. But as for me, I collected money to buy someone who would help me in my chores.'

Then said the other wife 'Good God! I'm giving up smoking from today,' and taking her tobacco-box, she took it to the dung-heap and threw it away. And so great was her irritation that she left the household. But the other stayed on, she and her slave-girl. Finis.

The Man and his Mistress [^{I}/ 136]

We heard a tale of a man in Bida, who lived with his mistress. He was a tailor, and he finished his trading capital. So he said to his mistress 'If you've got, say, ten shillings,* I'd like you to give me a loan, so I've got some capital. When I've invested it and got back the proceeds, I'll pay you back.' 'O.K.' said she, and putting her hand to her head she pulled out ten shillings and gave it to him.

When it was night, she came to him to sleep. They lay down, but as soon as he knew that she was asleep, he took his sword and sharpened it. Then he struck off her head at a blow, and taking up the head, quickly undid the hair, meaning to see if there was any more money he could take. But he found nothing there barring a threepence. For she had given him all she had, the ten shillings. Then he went out in the night, leaving her there dead.

Next morning, when they looked in his hut, they found a woman there dead. But though they tried, they could think of no reason why he should have cut off the woman's head. Then one of them said 'Perhaps it was her lover, seeing his money on her head,

* One of the very rare references to the new money in TATS.

wanted to get it back. For it must have been he that beheaded her, for, look, her hair is undone.' They all agreed with this and buried her. As for the man, they sought him in all the villages, but he hasn't been seen to this day.

The Husband who Counted the Spoonfuls [I/138]

We've heard tell of a man who couldn't stay married because he counted spoonfuls. Whenever he married a wife, after she had been a week in his home, he would wait till she had prepared the *tuwo* and was preparing to dish it out. Then he would come up close, squat down, and as she dished it out, count the spoonfuls.* Then when she had finished, he would say 'Such-and-such a number of spoonfuls you've dished out today.' She would ignore this, but next day he would repeat it, and the next day, till he had driven her out. Then she would leave the compound and not return.

He continued doing this, when one day he heard tell of a woman who was the fairest in the whole town, and he went off to her home to seek her in marriage. He told what had brought him, and she answered 'We-ell – I'm not refusing you, but, even if I marry you, there's one thing that will cause us to separate.' 'What's that?' said he. 'Your only failing' said she, 'is counting spoonfuls.' To which he replied 'If *that's* all it is, I won't do it again, since you say that that is what you don't like.' 'Very well' said she.

So they were married and she moved into his compound, and they dwelt together. And for about three months he ceased counting the spoonfuls. Then one day he came and sat on the edge of the bed, when his wife was dishing out the *tuwo*. She had dished out eight spoonfuls and had taken out the ninth, but hadn't yet put it into the calabash, when some called him from the entrance to the compound – 'Hey, Tagwayi!' and he answered 'Nine!' But his wife paid no attention. She went on serving out the *tuwo*, while he went

* Actually pieces of broken calabash used for the purpose.

and dealt with the caller, and then came back. Meanwhile she had reached eleven spoonfuls and had taken out the twelfth, when he said to her 'If I hadn't told you that I had given up counting spoonfuls, I should say that that was the twelfth that you were putting into the calabash.' 'You did it just now' she said 'And I took no notice, pretending not to hear, for I thought that you had just forgotten. But it seems that you are back to your old tricks.' She added 'That's the finish of our marriage. I'm not living with a husband who counts spoonfuls.' And going out she went away and never returned to his compound.

And he – he never got another wife till the day he died.

The Man and his Wife [¹/₁₅₂]

There was once a man and wife. And every night before she would let him lie down beside her, she would make him carry her round on his back for a while. So he would pick her up and put her on his back and walk around with her inside the hut until he was dripping with sweat. Then, when he put her down, and not till then would she agree to let him lie down with her. Night after night this went on, till he became quite wasted away and thin.

So he told a friend about it, and his friend said 'Leave it to me. I've got a cure for that.'

A few days later, his friend said to him 'Today I'm coming to your hut, or rather not your hut, your compound. When I come to your compound, then I'll come into your hut, but don't you worry, just keep calm.' 'Very well' said the other 'Roll on, evening!'

In the evening the friend set out and cut himself a tough stick and holding it in his hand made for the home of his friend. He went in, right into the compound, and coming to the door of the hut, he listened. He heard her saying 'Carry me round a little more before we lie down.'

Then he burst into the hut and began beating the woman, saying What sort of useless, bloody husband are you, that you let your wife make you carry her on your back, so that word of it has reached even the chief? Tomorrow, woman, I'll take you before the judge, so that he can deal with you.' Then the husband said 'I beseech you to have patience. For I know she won't do it any more now.' And she was afraid and said 'God knows I'm very sorry, I won't do it again.' And the friend said 'Very well – I'll let you off this time. But if you start again I shall hear of it.'

Well, from that day she never again made him carry her on his back. And next day he had a fine appetite,* and said to his friend 'Thank you very much. My! I feel better now.' And that was the trick that those men played on a wife who made life troublesome for her husband.

The Husband, his Wife
and her Paramour [$^I/_{155}$]

This is the tale of a man and his wife who lived once upon a time in the city of Kano, and they were very short of food. Then the wife said to her husband 'You know, I think we'd better go and pay a visit to my parents.' 'Righto' said her husband. 'When shall we start?' 'The day after tomorrow.' 'Good. That's fine' said he, 'I'll go and buy something to take them.' Says she 'Buy some cotton. We'll put it in a gourd and take that to them.' 'Right' said he and set off to market. There he bought some cotton and put it in a gourd on that very day.

Meanwhile, she sent for her paramour. 'Well' said she, 'My husband and I are going a journey in a few days.' 'What do you advise?' said he. 'Well' said she 'The best thing is for me to empty the cotton out of the gourd, and for you to get inside it. Then, when you're in, I'll put cotton back on top of you. Then, when my husband somes, I'll have him carry it. Thus you can come along

---

* This is preferable to the literal 'felt hungry' which seems pointless here. *A da* in the next sentence is also obscure. I have also transposed the inverted comma after *mijinta* to after *lafiya*.

with us, and I'll fix it so that he doesn't see you.' 'Good. That's fine' said he.

Then her husband returned and she said to him 'Let's pack and be going.' 'Very well' said her husband. 'You can carry the gourd' said she. 'Very well' said he.

So he picked it up and off they went, he and his wife. And whenever they reached a town, she would tell her husband to sleep in the entrance-hut. But she would go into the compound with the gourd and have it with her all night. In the morning she would tell her paramour to get back into the gourd, and putting back the cotton on top of him, would call her husband to come and carry it.

She continued to do this whenever they stopped at a town, until they reached her parents' home. Then she said to her parents 'My husband's bashful, he won't want to come and sleep in the compound. Just let him sleep in the entrance-hut. But I'll bring this gourd with me into the compound and have it where I sleep, so that it doesn't get stolen.' 'Fine' said her parents, and pointing out a hut to her they said 'You sleep there.'

So, picking up the gourd, she took it into the hut, with her paramour inside it. And every night he emerged, and they would spend the night together; then in the morning he would get back into the gourd.

This went on for seven days. Her parents brought corn for them. 'You must be packing up to return home now' said they, and bringing along a donkey, they loaded it up with corn and gave it to them.

Then the wife went back into the compound and taking the cotton, put it back on top of her paramour in the gourd. Then she carried it out and put it down in front of her husband. 'Husband' says she, 'this cotton that we've brought them – they refuse to accept it. For they say that we being city people it is for *them* to bring *us* cotton, and when we bring it to them they won't accept it. We'll have to take it back home.' 'All right' said her husband, 'Let's take it home. We can use it.' So they took their cotton home. *Kungurus kan kusu.*

The Husband, the Profligate Wife
and her Lover [$^{II}/_8$]

There was once a man whose wife was a harlot. As for him, his only means of livelihood was a charm: if anyone touched this, he turned into a donkey, and the man would take him off to market and sell him and bring home the money. This was his regular practice.

Now his neighbour was after the wife. And once, when she was in the neighbour's compound, he said to her 'I say, hasn't your husband any regular trade? He never seems to lack money.' She answered 'Oh, he's got a charm. If he touches a man with it, he'll turn into a donkey. Then he takes him to market and sells him.' 'I say, won't you steal it for me? Then I can have a day at the market.' 'Very well' she answered, 'Wait till you hear him say "Bring me water to wash with". Then go out and stand close to the grass matting fence, and I'll throw it over to you.' 'Righto' said he.

The husband came out and took off his clothes and went to wash himself. His wife took the charm and threw it over to her lover, but it fell on to his ear and he turned into a donkey. And as the husband was washing, what should he hear but a donkey braying and farting nearby.

When he had finished washing himself, he got up and taking his clothes, put them on. Then, sticking his head out, what should he see but a donkey with a charm on its ear. So he undid the grass matting and took hold of the donkey, and bringing him in, tied him up. Then he took a pestle and going up to the donkey, beat him till he was tired. Then he put back the pestle, and went into the entrance-hut.*

Then the wife, coming out, began saying 'Donkey, donkey, I *am* sorry! You poor, poor donkey!' Whereupon the husband came from the entrance-hut into the compound, and she busied herself with her pounding again. Again he took up a pestle and began beating the donkey. Then, having giving it a thorough drubbing,

* I.e. the living room for the men of the compound.

314

he put back the pestle, and returning to the entrance-hut, stood there peeping out at his wife. She came up to the donkey and said 'Donkey, donkey, I *am* sorry! I never knew this would happen, that when I threw the charm it would land on your ear. I *am* sorry!' Says her husband 'Here, what are you crying for?' 'I'm not crying' says she. 'If you're not crying, then what are the tears I see in your eyes?' But she persisted that she wasn't crying.

Then the husband took hold of the donkey, led him to market and sold him. Then he found himself another wife, married her and brought her home. And he said to his first wife 'Pack your things and get out – and don't come back to my house!' And that's the end of that tale.

The Cripple, the Profligate Wife and her Husband [II/ 26]

There was once a cripple, who was rich, and there was a beautiful but profligate wife. Her husband went a journey, and leaving the compound during the day for a walk, she made her way to the cripple. 'You there, walking along,' he called. 'Who, me?' she answered. 'Yes' he said and she went over to him. 'Here are five thousand cowries' said he, 'I want you, but I can't walk. I get carried out evenings. But at sunset you come and carry me.' 'O.K.' she said, and taking the money went off home.

So when it was sunset, she went and lifted the cripple on to her back and took him back to her hut. Later, during the night while they were there, she heard sounds of her husband coming. So she picked up the cripple, put him in a pumpkin* and put him on one side, saying 'I'll come presently and pick you up and take you home.' 'All right' said he. Then she and her husband went into the hut and started chatting.

Soon the cripple got tired of just sitting and being bitten by

* Sic.

mosquitoes, so he said 'You people in the hut there!' 'Listen' said the husband, 'There's someone speaking.' 'No' said his wife, 'there's no one.'

Then the cripple crawled up to the doorway of the hut and said 'Hey, you, woman! If your husband is back, won't you come and pick me up and carry me home? Just because you see your husband, you have to desert me, leaving me for the mosquitoes to eat. Don't forget I gave you five thousand cowries. Come and carry me away; for the whole town knows that I can't get to anyone else's house, unless I'm carried.' 'You're lying' she answered, 'When did you give me five thousand cowries?' 'For shame!' said he, 'just because you see your husband, you think you can deny that I gave you the five thousand. Come on out and take me home!'

Well, they left the cripple there, they wouldn't take him home, for the whole night. The husband didn't know what to say, for he said to himself that he couldn't let the wife carry the cripple to his home; for he feared that when they got there, the cripple would lie with her. On the other hand why should he, the husband, carry the cripple home, when it wasn't he who had brought him?

The Jealous Man, his Wives and the Man with the Meat [II/47]

This is the tale of a man who had two wives, and he was a very jealous man indeed. For he wished no one even to look upon his wives. So going into the bush he made his home there. And from there he would come into the town to make his purchases at the market and take them back to his wives.

Well one day, the chief said 'Is there no one able to cuckold him?' Whereupon a man there rose and said 'May Allah prolong the chief's days! I'll go – and I'll spend several days and nights in his compound.' 'Do you think you can?' said the chief and 'Certainly' he answered.

Well, he went off to the market. There they had slaughtered a bull, and he bought a leg. Then he got a bun made on his head, and put on a head cloth and body-cloths*; and, picking up the leg of beef, he set off.

He travelled till he reached the compound of the jealous man. When he got there, he made formal greeting to those in the compound, and they called out 'Welcome'. Now the women of the compound knew him, and he said 'Here's meat I've brought for you to buy; for being in the bush here, you don't get meat. Bring me a knife.' And the husband got up and fetched him a knife.

Then the seeming woman with the meat cut some off and gave it to the women. 'Here' she said, 'Make some soup for the master.' And the master of the house expressed his thanks, saying 'God bless you.' And his wives took the meat, while the visitor said 'Won't you buy what is left, sir? I'll call for the money some other day, when I'm back here.' And his wives encouraged him to buy it, saying they would contribute to the cost. So he bought it.

Then all the flesh was stripped off, leaving the bone. And the meat-seller said that, as the daughter of a butcher she could never part with a bone. Now the husband was due to sleep that night in the hut of his senior wife, so he said 'Go to the hut of my younger wife and sleep there' to the visitor. 'Very well' said she, 'I think I'll take my bone though.' And picking it up 'she' took it into the hut with her.

Night came, and presently from the hut where the visitor was came the voice of the younger wife, calling out the visitor's name with excited squeals. Her husband heard and came running out, saying 'What's this? Are you dreaming? Or is it that bone?' And he took it away from her.

On the morrow he moved into the hut of his younger wife, and the visitor into the senior wife's hut. And that night the excited squeals and calling on the visitor's name came from the senior wife. Her husband came running out of the other hut and said 'You too – are you dreaming with that bone?' And so for four nights the visitor remained with them.

The senior wife went down to the stream, leaving the visitor behind. And he was overcome by sleep – for he had not slept for four nights. But when the husband entered the hut, he was sleeping on his back, and his cloth had opened, revealing to the husband his

* I.e. woman's clothing.

penis. Whereupon the husband picked up an axe and made for the stream.

But when his wife saw him coming, she let go of her pitcher, which fell and smashed. And she began to lament loudly. When her husband came up, he said 'Here, what's the matter with you?' Says she 'Someone has just gone by and told me that all my relatives, on both my mother's and my father's side, have turned into men.' And he answered 'Stop crying! For, look, that woman who is visiting us has also turned into a man. So, cheer up and be quiet!' And she returned to the compound and, hitting the visitor said to 'her' 'Here! Get up! You've turned into a man.' And up 'she' got.

The visitor said it was time for him to go home. When he got there, he said to the chief 'Well, I did what I said I would – cuckolded him, and spent four nights in his compound. Last night was the fourth.' And that is the end of that story.

The Chief, the Wife of his Servant and Lami* [II/50]

There was once a chief had a servant, and the servant had a beautiful wife. Said the chief to his servant 'Hey, I've an errand for you into the country.' For the chief wanted his servant's wife as did all his senior officials.

So when the chief had sent her husband away on an errand, when the sun had set, she was visited by Lami.† But while they were conversing a message was brought to her from the Chiroma.

'Oh-oh' says Lami, 'are the likes of the Chiroma after you too? Wherever shall I hide, with the Chiroma just coming?' 'Get under the bed there' says she. And he did so.

Next the Sarkin Rafi‡ came and sent his servant to tell her that he was just coming. And when he told her, the Uban Dawaki

* Cf. R. No. 1 (p. 38).

† Or Dan Lami, is a name given to a boy born on a Thursday. He seems to be the only non-official visitor that she had. The reason for his inclusion comes at the end of the tale.

‡ Lit. 'Chief of the Stream.' There is an obvious lacuna here, which the reader can easily fill.

said 'Oh-oh! Are the likes of Magajin [sic] Rafi after you too? Wherever shall I go?' And she said to him 'Get under the bed there.'

Next comes the Galadima and word was brought to her that he was approaching. Then says the Magajin Rafi 'Oh-oh! Are the likes of Galadima after you too? Wherever shall I go?' 'Go and get under the bed' said she.

But while she and the Galadima were sitting chatting, the Vizier approached and sent word to tell her that he was coming. Says the Galadima 'Oh-oh! Are the likes of the Vizier after you too? Where-ever shall I go?' 'Go and get under the bed' said she.

But while she and the Vizier were sitting there, who should come along but the chief, and he sent word to tell her that he was on his way. Then says the Vizier 'Oh-oh! Are the likes of the chief after you too? Wherever shall I go?' 'Go and get under the bed' says she, and the Vizier did so, just before the chief arrived.

But presently as she and the chief sat chatting, who should return but the chief's servant, her husband; and while all those senior officials were there in her hut, he came back from the errand on which the chief had sent him. They heard a horse coming up, and he entered the compound. Says she to the chief 'I'm afraid that's my husband returned.' Says the chief 'Oh – what a shameful predicament! – wherever can I go?' 'Go and get under the bed' says the wife.

So the chief got under the bed and there found all his senior officials, but he held his peace.

Then said the woman to her husband 'You're late back, I'll get you some *fura*'. And fetching *fura*, she gave it to him. And she fetched water too and gave that to him. And she said 'Here's some more, rather poor quality stuff.'*

Whereupon Lami spoke out 'There's a damned woman for you! Here's the Chief, the Galadima, the Vizier, the Magajin Rafi and the Uban Dawaki. And am I the only one you're going to give away to your husband?' and, pushing over the bed, he came out; and the whole band of them came tumbling out. That's all.

---

* = *dan lami*. A pun in Hausa. Lami thought she said 'There's a certain Lami here.'

The Maiden and the Two Youths [II/ 53]

Another story. There was once a youth courting a maiden, but another youth came along and ousted him from her favour, so that she now went regularly to *his* compound to sleep, and no longer visited her former young man.

Well, one day it rained very heavily and the ground became very slippery. Says the girl to her young man 'Look, today I shan't be able to walk; it's raining and very slippery. You'll have to carry me.' 'O.K.' says he and picking her up, set off through the water. And so he went all the way to his town. Now their way took them by the entrance of the compound of her rejected suitor.

When they got there, she said 'Let's go in here' and they entered the entrance-hut. 'Go ahead. We'll go right in' says she, and so he went on, right to the door of the other young man's hut. He was awake. 'Put me down here' says she to the other, 'And get off home. I'm going to stay here tonight.' And he ducked and went out without a word. But she spent the night with the other, and next morning went home.

Well, the next day was the Festival. The procession to the place of prayer was finished and everyone was home again; evening came and the fun and games began. Our maiden set out for where they were being held, but took with her a baobab fruit.

Everyone had gathered for the fun, including her companion of the previous night, who had had his head newly shaved.* She went up to him and said 'Well, well! You've just had you head shaved!' and again 'Take your turban off, and your cap too. I want to crack this baobab fruit, for I can't wait to get at its contents.' Then he submitted his head to her, and she smashed the fruit on it; and then took it and gave it to the other young man – the one who had carried her when it was raining. 'Here' says she, 'Here's something tasty for your to suck.' And he put out his hand and took it. Now, which of those two young men had the worst of that exchange?

---

* The normal style for Hausa men.

The Man with the Spoon, his Wife and his Wife's Paramour [$^{II}/_{71}$]

Here's another tale. There was once a man cleared some five farms, all for himself. But he didn't wield the hoe himself. For you see, he had a special sort of spoon. And it was this he would take to the farms.

When he reached one of them, he would throw this instrument on to the land, and say 'Farifas.' Whereupon the spoon would set to work hoeing the ground, and in no time at all the farm would be hoed. Then he would say to it 'Dangarama',* and it would topple over and lie still. Then he would go over, pick it up, and take it to the next farm. There he would repeat the word, and in no time that farm too would be hoed.

Day after day this happened, and people saw how his farms seemed to keep hoed, without his ever bending his back to work. And they marvelled.

Now this fellow with the spoon had a wife, and she had a lover. Well, one day this paramour of hers said to her, puzzled, 'How come that your husband – even though we never see him at work hoeing – never takes more than an hour to get his farms hoed. Just one hour!' 'Oh that!' she answered. 'Well, you see, my husband has a sort of spoon; and when he goes off to farm, he picks it up and throws it on to the farm, saying "Farifas", and then in no time at all it hoes up all the farms.' 'Well!' said he, and then 'I say, couldn't you get hold of it for me. If I could even have the use of it for three days! Please, I beg of you.' Says she 'You must have more farms first.' 'All right' says he, and off he goes, rallies his neighbours to help, and clears the bush to give himself more farmland.

The time for sowing arrived, and he did his sowing. Then one day as he went out to his farm, he met the faithless wife. Says she 'Have you got more farmland?' 'Yes,' 'Good. Then as soon as my husband has finished his hoeing, I'll get the spoon and bring it over to you. Then, when you have done hoeing, you must return it to

* I am presuming that this, like *farifas*, is a mere open-sesame, but in fact it is given in the dictionary with several meanings, none very relevant here.

me.' 'Very well' he replied. And she duly brought him the spoon and left it with him. Away he went – but forgot what the word was that he had to say to it.

So he returned and went along to their compound, lurking close by till he saw her. Then he said 'Hey, what is it that you have to say to it, to this spoon?' And the woman said to him 'When you get back, just say to it "Farifas" and sit back. Then when it has nearly finished the work, say to it "Dangarama".' 'Thank-you' said he.

Back he went, and said to the spoon 'Farifas', and the spoon set to work hoeing. Then when it had nearly finished, he went up to it, and it moved over and started on the farm of someone else. Then he said to it 'Dangarama' and it toppled over. He bent down, picked it up and took it home, where he said to the woman 'Here's the spoon' and gave it back to her. Says she 'But when the time for the second hoeing comes, when he has finished, I'll bring it and give it to you again.' 'Fine' said he.

The second hoeing came, the heads of corn formed and the grain appeared on them. Her husband finished his second hoeing, and took the spoon home and left it there.

And that same day along comes the other fellow and asks her for it. She went and fetched it and gave it to him. And off he went to his farm, where he said to the spoon 'Farifas' and it set to work hoeing. It hoed up the whole place. But then he forgot that he had to say to it 'Dangarama' and instead began saying to it 'Farifas'. So it continued hoeing – the whole farm, so that there wasn't a weed left; and then started hoeing up the corn. Whereupon he began to yell out 'Oh dear! Good people, come and help me to stop Farifas, Farifas.'

It cleared his farm completely and then began on the neighbours' farms; he was yelling the while, and his yells were heard through all the cultivated land, and right into the town.

Well the husband was at home, when he heard someone saying 'Hey, fellows, there's a thing there in the fields cutting down all the corn, and they call it "Farifas"'. Then he got up and went and looked in the place where he had left the spoon. When he didn't see it, he made his way to the fields and there saw his spoon hard at cutting down the corn. 'Dangarama' he ordered it, and picked it up.

Getting home, he asked his wife 'Where's the spoon?' 'Where you left it, I suppose' said she. 'Then go and get it' says he. She went and found that it wasn't there. 'Husband' says she, 'I didn't see it there.' 'Pack your things' he replied, 'and be off to the compound of your paramour.' And she did just that. But when she got to the other compound, her paramour picked up a stick and drove her out again. That's all. *Kungurus kan kusu.*

The Chief's Daughter and the Malam's Daughter [II/85]

A chief and a malam each had a daughter. Said the chief 'Malam, bring your daughter and I'll put her with mine and keep them in a fine hut, secluded, and keep them well fed.' 'O.K.' said the malam, and bringing along his daughter gave her to the chief. And the chief had them put in a hut, and thereafter none but he brought them food; none but he brought them cola-nuts; none but he brought them honey; and he it was, too, took them tobacco-flowers.

Well, one day the chief's daughter peeped out of the window and saw a man on his way to market 'Hey, there! You going to market – buy some cooked foods for me.' 'Very well' said he, and went on to the market and bought some cooked foods and brought them back. And when he got there, he threw them in by the window. And they took them in and ate them.

This happened regularly for some time. Then the man said to her 'How can I get to see you?' and she answered 'Oh' and went on 'Here we are and, as you can see, we are shut in here, and not allowed out; and as for how you can get to see me – that's up to you, you'll have to devise some way.' 'Very well' said he, and went off. Then he wrapped up some money, ten thousand cowries, and set out for the compound of an old woman. 'Old woman' said he, 'I want you to help me.' 'Is all well, my son?' she asked. 'How can it be?' he asked, and he told her what he wanted, adding 'But I don't know who can help me to get it.' She asked for details and he said 'Listen, there's a girl in the chief's compound' and he named her, 'and I must get in to talk with her. Look, I've brought ten thousand cowries.' 'Is that all the trouble?' asked the old woman. 'Yes' said he. 'Oh, that's easy' she said and fetched a mat, and spreading it out, said to the man 'Come and lie down here.' So he lay down and she rolled him up in the mat. And picking it up she went and said to the chief 'Chief, I've brought you this for safe-keeping. I want you to keep it for me somewhere where no one goes.' 'Oh' exclaimed the chief, 'Old woman, there's nowhere in this compound where no one goes, except in that hut over there where I keep my daughter and the malam's daughter secluded.' 'As you will, chief' answered the old woman, 'In any case, there you are. I'm leaving it with you.' 'Bring it here, old woman' said the chief. And so the old woman brought over the mat and handed over the man in it. And the two girls received him – all without the chief's knowledge.

Then said the chief's daughter to the malam's daughter 'You must move from here now into that small hut; and leave this one to me – me and my man here. For after all it is my father's.' So the malam's daughter moved into the small hut and took her bed there, leaving the other hut to the chief's daughter with her man.

Well, the man spent seven days there and, as it turned out, made the chief's daughter pregnant. And the old woman, seeing that seven days had passed, set off again and returned to the chief and said 'I want back what I deposited with you.' Then he was rolled up again in the mat, as he had been before, and handed back to her. She received it and took it back home and there set it down. Then she unrolled the mat, and the man rose and went off back to his compound.

Well, before long the girl's pregnancy was far advanced, but no one else knew of it, save herself and the malam's daughter. And presently the chief's daughter bore a child, a son. Now they had no hoe, not even a little one, nor did they have an axe, and it was a hard, beaten floor. Well, the chief's daughter took a knife and, killing the child, cut off his head and his feet. Then said she to the malam's daughter 'Please – in the name of Allah and of the Prophet – keep my secret; and take the head and the feet and eat them, while I eat the rest.' To this the other girl agreed, and so between the two of them they consumed the boy.

Then, after a while, there came one to the town in search of
learning, and he came to the compound of the father of the other
girl, who was with the chief's daughter. Says he to the malam
'Malam, please let me have your daughter in marriage.' But the
malam answered 'My son, 'tis not me that you must ask, but the
chief; you go along and see him.' 'Very well' said the other, and
rose and went along to the chief. 'May your life be prolonged' says
he. 'Amen, my son' said the chief, and the other continued 'The
girl you adopted from malam' and he mentioned his name – 'I
want you to give her to me in marriage.' 'What!' exclaimed the
chief, 'Oh, yes – surely I'll give her to you, be assured of that' and
he dismissed him. So the student went and collected the presents
requisite for a marriage and took them all along. And the chief
had the girl duly bathed; and chose out a slave-girl to accompany
her. As for the other girl, his own daughter, he took her and gave
her in marriage to the son of a former chief.

So they settled down in their new homes. But there came a day
when the malam's daughter found herself with nothing to make
tuwo with. So she sent off her slave-girl, saying 'Go to the chief's
daughter and say that if she has rice or guinea-corn or bulrush-
millet, please will she lend you some. Then when my husband gets
some we'll pay her back.' 'O.K.' said the girl and went along to the
compound of the chief's daughter and said to her 'Please, the
malam's daughter has sent me along to say that if you've some rice
or bulrush-millet or guinea-corn, would you give it to me to take to
her.' But the chief's daughter answered 'No, I'm not giving her
any. I've got flour, and rice and guinea-corn and millet, but I
shan't give her any. Go and tell her that.' Now, all the while she
was speaking, her husband was lying there on the bed. Then the
girl went off and told the malam's daughter, who couldn't believe
it and told her to go back again. And so three times in all the girl
went with her request. But the chief's daughter would not grant
it. And all the while there was her husband, lying on the bed
listening to the message that the malam's daughter kept sending.
At last the malam's daughter said to the girl 'Go back this time and
say to the chief's daughter that she should remember, please, the
day when the head and the feet were eaten.' Back went the girl and
repeated these words to the chief's daughter, who promptly rose
and took some flour, and some rice, and some millet, and some

acca, some salt, and some *daddawa*, some peppers and some oil, and said to her 'Here, take these to her.' But at this point, the chief's son, listening on the bed, rose and stopped her. Says he to the girl from the malam's daughter 'Go back and tell your mistress to come along with you.' 'Very well' said she, and went and did so. And the malam's daughter came along.

Meanwhile the husband of the chief's daughter had been asking her 'Hey, what's this about remembering the day when the head and the feet were eaten?' 'Oh, nothing!' she answered, 'Something we did when we were children.' But when the malam's daughter came, he said to her 'Malam's daughter, I sent for you.' 'Well, here I am' says she. Then said he 'I've got a question for you. You sent your girl to ask for rice or bulrush-millet or guinea-corn as a loan until your husband had bought some, when you would return it. She wouldn't give it to you; and then you sent again and told her to remember the day when the head and the feet were eaten – at which she fetched some rice. and all the other things and gave them to you. Now, if you don't tell me what is the meaning of this, I'll take my sword right now and cut off your head – yours, and hers too, both of you.' At this the malam's daughter in some fear exclaimed 'Oh, no! Don't do that, for it's not worth the losing of heads. Here's what happened when we were young. When the chief confined us in that hut, she peeped out of the window and saw a man on his way to market; and she commissioned him to buy cooked foods for us from the market. He went and got them for us. This happened regularly, until one day an old woman brought something to the chief for safekeeping. It must be kept, she said, where no one would come. And the chief said that the only place like that was where we two girls were, for only he visited us. And so they brought the man wrapped up in a mat. He spent seven days, and made her pregnant. Time passed, the pregnancy advanced, at last she was delivered. Then she cut off the child's head and feet and giving them to me told me to eat them. And she ate the rest of his body.'

'That's enough, you can go' said the husband of the chief's daughter. Then he took them before the chief. 'Chief' said he, 'Here's your daughter. I don't want her, for this is what she did' and he told him. Says the chief 'Let the old woman be called.' She was called, and he questioned her. Says the old woman 'That's how it was, chief. Your daughter spoke with him, and he told me to bring him to her, and I did so.' Then said the chief to his daughter 'There, where you are standing, take off all your cloths and leave them there. Then put on just your head cloth.' She did as he told her, and he went on 'Now be off, into the bush' and she departed, into the bush. Then he said to the malam's daughter 'All the things that were given her, and the slaves – they're all yours' and he dismissed the malam's daughter with his blessing. That's all for that story.

The Husband, his Wife's Paramour and the Charm [II/91]

There was once a man had a wife; and another man became her lover. So that whenever she made *fura*, she would divide it in two and take half to her paramour. And whenever she made *tuwo*, she would divide that in two and take half to her paramour. The husband perceived this for some time, but at last it became too much for him.

So he went to see a malam, and said 'Malam, listen to the way my wife is behaving with' and he mentioned the name of the other man. He went on 'I hear what is going on, and I even see it. For she makes *tuwo* and carries it out, saying she is going to take it to her family; but she takes it to her paramour, and the same when she makes *fura*.' 'All right' said the malam, 'Go and get some paper and bring it to me. Then I'll do something for you: I'll make a charm and give it to you. Then, when she pours the *tuwo* to take to her family, you must devise some way to deceive her and get her out of the way – perhaps send her into a hut – and then take this charm and slip it into the *tuwo*. Do you understand?' 'Certainly' said the husband, and went off and soon got some paper and brought it to the malam. The malam wrote on it for him and folded it up. Then he took it and gave it to him, and the husband hid it away.

That evening his wife made *tuwo*, and taking out his portion

327

gave it to him. Now previously he had taken the little gourd water-bottle he used for his ablutions and left it round behind the hut. And he said to her 'Please fetch my water bottle from outside the hut and get some water in it, so that I can say my prayers when I've had my *tuwo*.' 'O.K.' she said and went and fetched it. Whereupon he got up and slipped the charm into the middle of the *tuwo*, and added some soup to hide the traces. Then she came back with the water in the water-bottle and gave it to him.

Then she picked up the *tuwo* and went out, meaning to go to the compound of her lover. But on the way she met him and he asked her 'Where are you going?' to which she replied 'No, where are *you* going?' He repeated 'Where are you going?' and she repeated her words. [So there they stood repeating themselves] and someone went and told her mother and father, and they sent along her younger brother, saying 'Go and ask her what she is doing there and tell her to be on her way.' But when the boy got there, all he could say was 'Mother says, says, says; mother says', and he went on saying that. So presently her mother came along, very angry, meaning to scold them. She got there and began saying 'Daughter, this is shameful, this is shameful; daughter, shameful, shameful; daughter, shameful, shameful; daughter, shameful.'

Then word was brought to the father, and he got up and picked up his axe meaning to come along and kill them all. But when he got there and lifted up his axe to strike, he began to say 'I'll kill you with my a—, I'll kill you with my a—. I'll kill you with my a—.' and just stood there saying that. Until word reached the chief of the town, and he came along.

When he reached the scene, he intended to say to them 'Hey, all of you! Disperse now!' but all he managed to say was 'The matter's before the chief, the chief; the matter's before the chief, the chief; the matter's before the chief, the chief.' At last the malam sent to the husband, telling him to remove the charm now.

So he went along and, pushing his way through the large crowd, went and lifted the mat lid that covered the *tuwo* and took out the charm. At which everyone went off to their own homes. That's all for that tale.

The Woman, her Daughters and the Man and his Daughter [$^{II}/_{92}$]

There was once a woman had two daughters, and she was beautiful and they likewise. And there was a man sought her, and she became his mistress. And after that he sought her elder daughter, and she too became his mistress. And so too with the other daughter.

Now this man had a ring, and one day the younger daughter had spent the night with him, and in the morning went off with his ring. She went off to wash herself, taking the ring off her hand and into the hut, where she left it. When she returned from washing, she picked up the ring and started cleaning it, and when she had finished she put it down again. At which point her mother came into the hut, and her elder sister also came in – and saw the ring. Says the last 'Hullo! Who brought that ring into this hut?' 'Oh!' said her mother, 'Do you know that ring then?' 'Oh, yes' the replied, 'It belongs to' and she mentioned his name. 'I see' said her mother, but to herself she said 'So. He got me to be his mistress, and then went after both my own daughters, and got them too. He thought he could make me and my daughters his mistresses at the same time. Very well. But I'll be revenged!'

Now he had two wives of his own. The senior wife had a daughter. And the woman who had sworn revenge went to him one day and said 'In future let us be just good friends, who consult each other in everything. All right?' 'O.K.' said he. 'I mean' she went on 'let us not sleep together any more; but just help each other with friendly advice. For both of us are getting on now you know.' 'O.K. my dear – that's fine' said he. So she left him alone for a while.

But two months later she returned to him, and said 'Look, I've a request to make of you. Let my take your daughter and look after her, for she is my daughter too.'* 'For goodness' sake' he answered, 'Do you have to ask me? Just go and take her!' And he became

* This – to us – impossible statement has meaning for a Hausa, where the same term of address is used to an aunt, a mother and any female relative of the same generation.

quite abusive to her. So she rose and went and took away the girl. And she went with her to another town, where she stayed for about a year. Then she returned and again went to the man and appeared before him crying bitterly. 'Hullo! What's the matter?' he asked. 'Well' she said, 'It's the girl that I took away with me – she is no more!' 'For goodness' sake' he said again, 'Just because a daughter has died, do you have to come and cry to me? Look, there she was living there – well? If the appointed time for her death comes, *I've* no cure for it. Be quiet and stop crying!' 'Very well' she answered, and went home. And there she stayed for a while.

But a month later she returned to him. Says she 'My elder brother has a daughter, whom I have bespoken for you as a bride. But I didn't mention it when I was here before, because of the death of that girl. I didn't think it would be timely.' 'What? Nonsense' says he. 'Was that worth a thought? But, look – you and I – our thoughts are very close; for I had been looking round for a maiden to marry.' 'Oh, but this one isn't of age yet' she answered, 'You'll have to be patient for a while – about a year and a half.' 'Ah well' says he, 'if we are spared, what's a year and a half? Just a few days!' 'That's right' she said.

And from then on he lavished presents on her, which she put away till the girl was old enough to be married. Then she sent for him and said 'Now you must build a new hut, for I shall be going to fetch your bride and bring her to you. All right?' 'Yes' says he, and then, 'But let me fetch the money for the bride-price.' But she answered 'For shame! Here are you and I such good friends, and when I get a maiden for you to marry, you go and say that you'll pay bride-price! No, I'll pay it.' 'Fine' said he, and off went the woman again. Then he had a fine hut put up. And they added a grass extension as a verandah to it; and pounded the floor of the hut, and of the verandah too.

And the woman, when she reached the other town, found that the girl was old enough for marriage. So she had them wash the girl, and she brought her back with her, and took her to him in his compound. Straight away he kept her in seclusion, and she soon became pregnant by him. Then one day, when her pregnancy was well advanced she came out to the edge of the verandah and was sitting there. Her mother's fellow-wife saw her and said 'Well!! If the dead ever returned, I should say that that girl was' and she mentioned the daughter's name. Along comes the girl's mother, and she too examined the girl in silence. 'My!' she said at last 'She's her double!' Then the other woman went up to the girl and said 'What town do you come from, girl?' And the girl gave them the name of their own town, saying also that her father had two wives, and giving their names and her father's too. Whereupon her mother's fellow-wife exlaimed 'So! What all this means is that we are fellow-wives to our own daughter! At which the girl's mother collapsed, and the other packed her things and went out. She reached the compound entrance and the husband saw her. 'Everything all right?' says he. 'Ugh! You beastly, shameful fellow!' she exclaimed, and went on 'You have gone and made us fellow-wives of the daughter of our own wombs – whom you fathered! So that was why you sent her to be cared for elsewhere – so that you could bring her back and marry her, back into our compound as our fellow-wife! For it is' and she mentioned the girl's name 'that you've married here.' He jumped up and ran as fast as he could, till he came to the chief's compound, and there he told the chief. 'Hey there, guards!' said the chief, 'Quickly, get up and take chains and go off and arrest' and he gave them the other woman's name.

Along came the guards at the double, but as they were about to put the chain round her neck, she said 'Just a minute! This isn't a case where I should be chained. Come along, we'll go together' and she led the way. So they went and came to the chief's compound, and the husband repeated what he had said. 'Take her before the judge' said the chief, so they were both taken to the judge's place. And when the man got there, he again told his story in front of the judge. Then the judge said to her 'Well, what's the reason for this?' 'Well, judge, may your life be prolonged' she answered, 'I was his mistress ever since he came to manhood and I was yet a virgin; and even after I married I didn't desert him; nor even when I had two daughters. And when he saw me with a baby on my back and joked saying "How about giving me something in return for the baby on your back?" I would answer "Oh no! You must be patient, for we have known each other a long time." "All right, all right" he would say, "Get along with you. I'll be patient." Well, judge, when he got home, he seduced both the daughters that I bore, both of them. Ask him if that isn't true. And send for them too, my children. He wronged me, he did. And that is why I did to him what I did, judge.' 'You have right on your side, woman' said the judge. 'And as for this man, you've made him lose his case.' That's the end of that story.

The Husband and his Wives* [^{II}/$_{97}$]

There was once a man had three wives. Now, though he did not know it, two of them were witches. But the third one was not. Now the two witches plotted together, but the other – the one who wasn't a witch – was not privy to their plotting. And they devised a plan to devour their husband.

But the third wife heard what they were saying, and she called her husband and told him. Now he had a friend who used to drum on a *dundufa* (long, narrow drum), and this friend said to him 'When you get home, tell them that you're going on a journey. Then when you have packed, come back to my compound here and stay here, while I go out playing. Then I'll roll you up in a mat, and while I'm drumming, you can hear everything they are saying. Then we shall be sure whether they are witches or not.' 'All right' said the other, and went home and told his wives 'I'll be for setting out on a journey tomorrow, and it'll be seven or eight days before I get back.' 'Very well' they said.

Next day when it was light, he packed up† his things for the journey, and set off. But when he had gone a little way, he went round back by another way, and so to the home of his friend. And the friend rolled him up in a mat, and picking up his drum, took it out into the open space, and there sat down, having laid down the mat. Then putting one foot on the mat, be began drumming. And all the women asked their husbands if they might go and join the dance. And their husbands gave them leave. But, as for the three whose husband was away, they sent to ask their husband's friend who was drumming if they might come and join in the dance.

* Cf. TR. No. 92.   † *Shirya* seems a more likely reading than *shirga*.

'Surely, come along' said he. 'Good' they said, and along they came. The one who wasn't a witch led the way, and the two witches followed her, and so they reached the open space.

The wife who wasn't a witch joined the dance and began to sing 'Allah, give me money to pay the *dundufa* drummer.' Then the drummer changed the beat, and with his drum said 'Mat of mine, listen, and hear what the women say.' The first wife left the dance, and one of the witches came in. She began to sing, and these were her words – 'What shall I give my drummer? May Allah give me a man's liver to give my drummer, or perhaps a heart.' Again the drummer changed the beat, and said 'Mat of mine, listen, and hear what the women say.' Then the other witch too entered the dance, and sang 'May Allah give me a man, so that I may give my drummer the liver or the heart.' And again the drummer changed the beat, and said 'Mat of mine, listen, and hear what the women say.' So they went on drumming and eventually the dance ended. The drummer had them take his drum home for him, but took the mat himself, and picking it up, went off home.

Next day, again, he again went out drumming for the dance. And again the wives came and repeated their words of the day before; and again for seven days. Then the drummer said to his friend 'Well, you'd better be getting home now.' But the other said to his friend 'Not till you've come with me into the bush, and I have cut myself some clubs.' So they went into the bush, and he cut them and brought them back to his friend's home. Then he did them up in a grass mat, and picking it up, went off to his own compound.

When he got there, they welcomed him, and fetching *tuwo* and *fura*, gave them to him. He ate the *tuwo* and drank the *fura*, and then took water and rinsed out his mouth. Then he went and sat on the floor of the hut and said, singing 'Allah, give me money to give to my drummer.' And again he sang 'What shall I give my drummer? Allah, give me a man, so that I may give my drummer the liver or the heart.' And he repeated it, 'Allah, give me a man, so that I may give my drummer the liver or the heart.'

This brought those two wives of his to their feet and over to where he was. 'Husband' said they, 'Where did you get that song?' 'Oh' said he, 'at the place I went to, I saw some women in front of a drummer, they were dancing and singing those words.' At which

333

they went at him to attack him, but he quickly drew out his clubs and set about them, driving them from the compound, and so all the way to their parent's compounds. After that he settled down with the other wife, who wasn't a witch. That's the end of that story.

The Woman, her Husband and her Paramour [$^{II}/_{99}$]

There was once a very jealous man, and whenever his wife went anywhere, he would say to her 'Don't you go astray now, and let anyone treat it badly.' 'Of course not' she would answer, 'However would I do that?' And he would insist 'I'm just telling you – if you take it to anyone and let them treat it badly, it always tells me.'

Well, one day he said he was going on a journey, Now, it so happened that another man was after her. She was going out, and her husband said 'I shall have gone before you get back.' Then he went out, and round behind the compound, broke through the fence, and went and entered the hut. There he got under the bed and hid. And there he was when she returned from going out. Now it chanced that she had met with her paramour, and she said to him 'My husband has gone off on a journey.' Then she came back home, as he said 'I'll be along in the evening.' 'Good' said she.

Off he goes to market, and buys ten cola nuts, and tobacco flowers; musk, perfume and a cloth. To these he added five thousand cowries and gave them to someone to take to her. And they were duly brought, and the bearer said to her that they were sent by her paramour 'Who told us to bring these things; ten cola-nuts, tobacco-flowers, musk, perfume, a cloth and five thousand cowries.' 'Thank you' said she and, accepting them, gave the customary present in return. Then, when his servants had left, she uncovered some calabashes and, fetching the cloth, put it in one, and so too the musk, the perfume, the cloth [sic] and the five thousand cowries – the whole lot she put into calabashes. Then she took the cola-nuts and put them in the sand beneath the water-pot*; and the tobacco-flowers she took and put in a little earthenware bowl and fetched water and sprinkled it over them.

Then again her paramour bought fifteen hundred cowries' worth of meat, with salt and *daddawa*. And these too were brought to her with a 'Here's meat and salt and *daddawa*, that he told us to bring you.' 'Thank you very much' said she. And all the while there was her husband, under the bed, seeing what was going on – and every one of the presents that were brought her.

Evening came, and the other man came to her compound, and right into her hut. He sat himself down on the bed, but she said 'Oh no! Get up and go away! Wait until nightfall, and then, when the night is well advanced, then you can come back.' 'O.K.' said he and off he went. And she picked up a pitcher to go off to the well. And while she was at the well, before she got back, out came her husband from under the bed. Then he went out and leant his bow up by the entrance to the hut, and hung up his quiver. And presently she returned from getting water. 'Oh, husband!' said she, 'So you've come back!' 'Yes' said he, for I met the man I was going to visit on his way to another town.' At which she got *fura*, and stirring it, gave it to him and he begun to drink.

But, as she sat there, her husband began to speak 'Eh? What's that you say? Let me come closer. She was given ten cola-nuts? And tobacco-flowers? And musk? And perfume? And a cloth? And five thousand cowries? And she's put the money and the cloth and the musk and the perfume into calabashes; but the cola-nuts are beneath the water-pot in the sand, and the tobacco-flowers in the little bowl? And the meat? Oh, there it is in the cooking-pot, cooking.'

Then the husband said 'Did she take you where you got treated badly? What? No, she didn't?' and then again 'Good' said he.

At which his wife gasped, flabbergasted and overcome with shame; for here was her husband detailing every present that her paramour had sent her. Says she to herself 'It's my vagina telling him all the presents that I've been given.' She went out of the hut, and the other man saw her and began to speak to her, but she made signs to him with her hand, pointing with her finger at the front

* Where it was cool and damp.

of her body, to tell him that if anyone spoke with her, her vagina would tell her husband. After that she never went after other men again. That's the end of that story.

The Husband, his Wife and his In-laws [III/11]

There was a man and a wife living together. One day she said to him 'Husband, won't you take me on a visit to my home?' 'Surely' he replied, 'but wait till the end of the month, when I've finished my work. Then we'll go.' 'Good' said she. And he went off and worked away at his corn crop, till he had finished.

Then he said to her 'O.K. I've finished with the corn. Up you get, and let's be off. I'll take you home.' 'Right' said she, and packed up her things, and lifted them on her head. And so they went to her parents' home, and found them busy making bean-cakes.

When they reached the compound, the wife went on to the inner compound, and her husband was taken to the hut in which was the mixture for making the bean-cakes. There he was brought *fura* and *tuwo*.

His mother-in-law offered to give him a little of the mixture there, but he answered, that he never touched the stuff, finding it too sour.

Night came and the mixture began to smell very good. He got up, meaning to put his lips to it, in its container, which was hanging from the roof, and take a drink, but spilt it all over his head and body.

Up he jumped and began to yell 'Where's the bean-cake mixture kept? Take me to the bean-cake mixture.' For he realised that he had done a shameful thing in the home of his in-laws: there was the mixture, spilt all over the hut, and he himself – he was bathed in the mixture. So he went on yelling and shouting 'Take me to the hut where the bean-cake mixture is!'

At which his wife said 'Oh dear! Mother – I forget. They have taken the man to the hut where the bean-cake mixture is! And he has some jinns, which don't like bean-cake mixture! If they see any, they bathe him in it!'

Whereupon the mother and father turned on the girl and up-braided her violently, saying 'Since you knew this, why ever did you not tell us right at the start? However, it is you that has done this, quite deliberately. Now, if you can, calm him down, and both of you set off and go home, before it gets light. For you know, if it gets light and he comes back to his senses, he will feel shame – and when it wasn't any of his doing too!' So the two of them departed home.

Now, when they got home, the wife chanced to break wind in the presence of her husband's mother. Thereafter, if they began to quarrel and the husband threatened to abuse her with the title of 'Breaker of wind in the presence of your husband's mother,' she would reply with 'Then I'll call you the man to whom they offered bean-cake mixture, went so far as to say that he never touched it, and *then*, when he came to steal it, gave himself a bath with it!' 'Well!' he answered, 'surely you would not make public a little thing that happened a long way away. However, so far as I'm concerned, I don't propose to quarrel with you any further.' That's all. That's the end of that story.

The Woman who Refused to Marry Anyone who Couldn't Play with Words* [III/15]

There was once a woman who got married, but left the compound of her husband, saying that he couldn't play with words.

So she went and married someone else. They lived together for a while, but presently she left his compound too, saying that she wouldn't marry anyone, except a man who could play with words. Whereupon she went and married a dyer.

They lived together for a while. Now when he was away at the dyepits once, her mother fell ill. She lost consciousness, and his

* See note p. 339.

wife set off to where he was, and coming near the dyepits, said to him 'You there on the dyepits!'* But all he said to her was 'Ashes or dregs of indigo?' She said again 'Didn't you hear?†' But again he answered 'I have chickens, but they're not for sale.' So she went home, but before she got there, her mother died.

So she went back and said to him 'You there on the dyepits'* and he answered 'Ashes or dregs of indigo?' Again she said 'Didn't you hear?†' and again he said to her 'I have chickens, but they're not for sale.'

Next she said to him 'Hey – the old lady has gone before us to the house of truth.'‡ He answered 'The house of the Judge.' Again she said 'The old lady has finished hoeing her farm'‡ and again he answered 'Well, she never got very much from it!'

Again she said to him 'Look – the old lady had a big feed, and when she went to excrete, died.' Still he answered 'Couldn't she have moderated her eating?' and again 'When she went to excrete, she strained – that's why she died; but at least now she won't have to spend any more money on headshaving.'§ At which his wife got angry and went off.

Then other people asked him why he had acted in this way, and he answered 'Well, she used to say that she wouldn't marry anyone who couldn't play with words; and she had left two other husbands. I'm the third, and even I have not shown her how I can play with words – until today.' That's all.

The Husband and his Father-in-Law in Zaria [III/III]

Here's a tale from Zaria. A man went to seek a wife for himself; found someone to supply one; the marriage was made, and having been given the bride, he went off home with her.

* Or 'Take the contents of the dyepits.'
† Or 'Aren't there any chickens?'
‡ Normal euphemisms for 'died'.
§ An indication of the antiquity of the tale. Hausa woman – unlike some women on the Bauchi Plateau – no longer shave their heads.

They lived together for some time, but one day his wife went off in a huff, back to her parents' home. When she got there, she told them that the husband that she had married couldn't play with words (*or* didn't know proverbs).* 'Really?' they said. 'Yes' she answered, and they said 'Well, stay then.'

News of this reached the husband. 'Is that so?' said he, and set off to go the parents' home. Now they had sowed okra by the entrance of their compound. And he went in amongst them, creeping stealthily about.

Presently the girl's father saw him. 'Hey!' he said, 'Who's that rustling about in my soup?' And the other answered 'Oh – it's the salt and the *daddawa* – they're what's rustling about in your soup.'†
And coming out, the father saw that it was his daughter's husband. He went back into the compound and, taking a stick, he took his daughter and gave her a beating. Then he took her and gave her to her husband. 'Here's the little bitch' said he. 'It seems you were lying' he said to her. 'your husband has a supply of words inside him,' and to the husband 'Take your wife.' Turning to the girl he said 'Don't you come back here again – for look, just this minute, right away he played with words when he spoke to me.' That's all.

The Jealous Husband
and the Paramour‡ [III/28]

There was once a man had two wives. He used to live in the town, but he was very jealous, and so moved out into the bush, and there built himself a compound, where no one would come.

* *Karin Magana* (Proverbs, playing with words). One of the Gaskiya Corporation's booklets which contains a selection of these has always had a ready sale, especially it seems among young men, who are expected to be able to quote them – as part of the ritual of courtship.

† Like okra, essential ingredients of the 'soup' that goes with *tuwo*. They have, in fact, a right to be there.

‡ Cf. the next story.

One day those who were gathered outside the chief's compound began discussing men and women who were jealous, and someone mentioned this man's name, saying 'He's the one to be jealous for his wives. Look, he's even moved his compound out into the bush!'

At which one of the chief's foot-soldiers said that he would go to that compound and sleep with the man's wives. 'Do you really think you can?' asked the chief. 'Yes' said he.

So our soldier counted out two thousand cowries, and went and got some ash and washed with it. Then he made his way to the compound, and when he got there made formal greeting.

Says the husband 'Hey, where do you come from?' 'Never mind, I'm here now' said the other, 'and I want somewhere to sleep.' 'There's a shelter there behind the compound' said the husband, 'You can go and lodge there,' and again he said 'But, guest, what is your name?' 'My name is Bututu' said the other.

Now that day it was the turn of the chief wife to prepare the meals. So she prepared food and carried his over to the guest.

And he counted out a thousand cowries, and said to her 'Here's my money, a thousand cowries. While I am on top of you, just keep saying "Hey, Bututu, hey there, Bututu, hey, Bututu, are you there?" ' And she did so, until he had finished what he was about.

Then the wife said 'Well, I've never seen such a man for sleeping before. Here have I been calling to you ever since I came, and it has taken you all this time to get up. Here – here's *tuwo* for you, which my husband said to bring you.' And she went out and back into her compound.

Next day, he was there inside again, and the other wife made *tuwo* and carried it to him. And once again Bututu put down a thousand cowries.

When she arrived he said to her 'See these cowries? There are a thousand of them and they are yours. I gave your fellow-wife some yesterday, and these are yours. When I get up on top of you, just keep saying "Hey, Bututu, hey there, Bututu" – like she did yesterday.' 'Is that all? That's easily done' said the woman and took the cowries and heaped them on to a mat-lid.

Then Bututu got up on to her, and she began saying 'Hey, Bututu, hey there Bututu' but presently her words changed to squeals of delight.

Whereupon her husband heard and came running out. Up

jumped Bututu, and coming out of the shelter, set off at a run too.

But the husband said to him 'Hey – come here, stop running. Come and help me carry my stuff, for we are moving back into town.'

So that was that – he moved back into the town and lived there. That's the end of that one.

The Jealous Husband
and his Wife's Lover, Bididi* [$^{III}/_{29}$]

There was once a man married a wife, a real beauty, without a peer in the town. But he, the husband, was a jealous man.

Well, one day the young fellows of the town had gathered to exchange the news, and they said that this man's wife was the most beautiful in the town.

And it happened that one of them decided to become her lover. He went home, and there counted out two thousand cowries. These he took to an old woman, and said to her 'Old woman, here are two thousand cowries that I've brought you. Now I've given them to you, because I want you to go and tell the wife of' and he mentioned his name 'that I send her greetings and that I am in love with her.' 'Is that so?' said the old woman. 'Yes' he replied. 'Very well then' said she.

So the old woman set off and went to the girl's compound, and when she got there said to her 'Look, girl, a young fellow called' and she gave his name† 'Has sent me to you to bring you his hearty greetings; moreover he has given me two thousand cowries, and added that if you go to him, you have no idea what he will give you.' 'Very well, old woman' she said, 'But when you get home ask him what his name is.'

---

* Cf. last story. Also see J p. 201.

† But see below. Perhaps the Hausa should read *wani* not *wane*, which could be rendered 'a certain man.'

Off went the old woman and made her way home. 'Well, I went, my boy' she said, 'and delivered your message, but the girl asked me what your name is.' 'My name?' said the boy. 'Yes' said the old woman.

And he was just going to speak, when the old woman said 'Hey, stop, you fool – I'll give you a name. Your name's Bididi, don't say your own name.' 'Oh, very well' said the boy.

But the girl's husband, when he saw the old woman enter his compound, got up, collected all his things together, and moved out, away into the bush. And when he got there he made himself a shelter there in the bush.

But there came a day when their salt and *daddawa* ran out. Now the husband had a sore tooth and was in bed, so he said to his wife 'Get up and be off into the town and buy us some salt and *daddawa*.' 'O.K.' she said.

So she went off into the town, nor did she stop till she reached the old woman's compound. As soon as the old woman saw her, she made her very welcome. Says the girl 'Old woman, where's Bididi?' 'Bididi's in his home' said the old woman and went on 'Let me go and call him.'

Then she went to him and said 'Bididi, I've good news, what'll you pay for it?' 'Cola-nuts'* said Bididi. 'Well, the girl you're after has come.' 'Old woman' said the boy, 'let me fetch you a little present.'

And he went and counted out seven thousand cowries. Says he 'Old woman, this is yours – two thousand; and this is the girl's – five thousand. Let's be going.'

So they went along and the boy and girl greeted each other. Says the old woman 'Take her along to your compound, why not?' 'No' said the boy, 'for I've heard that her husband is a jealous man; so I'm sending her off to hurry home.'

He went on 'But I'll be coming out to your compound. So when you get back, get your husband to put up a grass shelter some way from the one that you and he use.' 'O.K.' said the girl.

Then the girl went on to the market, made her purchases, and then went home.

Time passed, and she continued quietly living with her husband; then she said to him 'It's too bad, husband! You should really

* The standard reply to the question.

put up a little grass shelter, so that if a leper or a wandering scholar comes this way, he can have somewhere to sleep.' 'Very well, I will' said her husband.

Then her husband set about erecting a grass booth, and when it was done showed to her. 'Fine' said the girl, '*Now* if a travelling student, or some leper comes, now they've got somewhere to lodge.' 'Quite so' said her husband, 'that's true.'

Shortly afterwards, the young fellow said to the old woman 'Old woman, go off to the compound of those people and see whether the booth I asked her to get made, has been made.' 'Very well' said she. And she went off, taking *daddawa* and salt, and reaching the compound, made formal greeting.

The girl saw the old woman and said 'Welcome, old woman.' 'Greetings, girl' said the old woman. The husband was absent.

Then the old woman said 'The young man has sent me, to see whether the booth he asked for has been set up.' She went on 'And I see that it has.'

So she set off home again, and went and told the young fellow. Then he took a little gourd waterbottle and filled it with guinea-corn, and some heads of bulrush-millet, which he held, and a skin mat which he put over his shoulder. Lastly he took a stick and off he went along the road.

But when he got near their compound, he left the road and cut through the bush. And when he reached the entrance of the compound, he said 'God reward you, good people of this compound. If you have fed, perchance you have left a fragment of *tuwo*, or some dregs of gruel.'

Her husband said to her 'You heard the student begging. Get up and take him some alms.' And the girl took some dregs of gruel and gave them to him.

But as he finished drinking them, he fell to the ground, groaning. Says the husband 'Hey – the scholar – don't you hear? He fell down and he's groaning.'

And he went over to the boy and took his hand, but the boy was unable to rise. 'My boy' said the husband, 'What's your name?' 'Bididi' said the boy. 'Well!' said the husband to his wife, 'Did you hear that? He said his name was Bididi.' 'Just fancy!' she answered, 'Bididi. We must filter water through ash and let him have that.' So they did that.

Then the husband took it and said 'Bididi, get up and drink some ash-water.' But Bididi just went on lying there, taking no notice of the husband.

Evening came and the girl made *tuwo*. Says she 'Let me take some to that young scholar, Bididi. Perhaps he'll eat now.' 'What!' said her husband, 'A boy that I took ash-water to and tried to get him to drink it and he wouldn't – but go and take him *tuwo*.'

Along she went and 'Bididi, hey there Bididi' says she. 'Yes' said he, and then 'So it's you is it?' 'Yes' said she.

And Bididi got up and mounted the girl, saying 'Keep saying "Bididi, get up and have some *tuwo*." '

Bididi kept at it, and the girl kept saying 'Bididi, get up and have some *tuwo*; Bididi, get up and have some *tuwo*' again and again.

But just as Bididi was about to ejaculate, the girl changed her tune and began 'Oh! oh! Bididi! Bididi! You're killing me! Oh, Bididi! Oh!'

At which her husband, hearing it, came out at the double, and seized Bididi's hand, saying 'For shame! Won't you stop there! But don't tell anyone. For the sake of God and His Messenger, don't let my shame be known! Come now and help me carry my things and we'll move back into the town.' And they packed up their things and moved back into the town.

And from that day on, he gave up being jealous. That's all.

The Caravan Leader, his Wife and his Friend* [III/ 39]

There was once a caravan-leader had a friend. They were always together, except when the caravan-leader went on a trading journey, then only were they separated, for the friend stayed behind at home. Now the caravan-leader had a wife who would have nothing to do

* See J. p. 216.

with men. Even when they made approaches to her, she would refuse them, keeping herself for her husband.

But one day the caravan-leader and his friend had an argument about women. Says the caravan-leader 'My wife will have nothing to do with another man.' 'No' said his friend, 'she'll pursue the men.' 'She won't' said the caravan-leader. And his friend said 'Very well, since you argue the point, I'll sleep with your wife. If I don't, here's my slave-girl and my horse. They are yours.' And the caravan-leader answered 'And I, if you do sleep with her, when I next go on a trading journey, when I get back, I'll give you my donkeys and what they are carrying, my mules and what they are carrying, my ponies and what they are carrying, and all the goods I bring back from my journey – the whole lot.' 'Really?' said the other 'Yes' said the caravan-leader.

Well the day came when the caravan-leader loaded up his merchandise for the journey, and set off along the road, but without saying anything to his wife about the argument he had had with his friend. So he started off on his journey.

But his friend went and counted out ten thousand cowries and gave them [to a servant] with instructions that they were to be taken to the caravan-leader's wife. Three days passed, and he again counted out ten thousand cowries, and sent them to her. Yet another three days passed and once more the caravan-leader's friend counted out ten thousand cowries and ordered that they be taken to the caravan-leader's wife.

Thus he sent her money five times, ten thousand cowries each time.

At length the wife sent someone to ask him what he wanted, adding 'But tell him that I shall be pleased if he will come himself,' and so the friend came.

Then said the caravan-leader's wife 'Good sir, I sent for you, for you keep sending money to me and I am grateful. But let me ask you, now we are alone together, what is that you want?' And he answered 'I love you – this is the reason.' Then she asked him and asked him three times 'What do you mean – love?' And he answered 'Lady, you have asked me three times. Well, what I want is to sleep with you.' And the caravan-leader's wife answered 'What! Is that all? And when I asked you, you would not answer? Wait till this evening, and when the sun has set I'll be along. Where shall I find you?' And he answered 'The hut is just inside my compound, close to the entrance-hut. In my boy's* hut, that's where you will find me.' 'Right' said she.

So, shortly after sunset, the caravan-leader's wife called her slave-girl and gave her body-cloths and shoes, saying 'But whatever happens to you, don't say anything, until you get back home.' Then she fetched perfume and rubbed it all over the girl's body, and even on the cloths. Then off went the slave-girl of the caravan-leader's wife.

Meanwhile the friend had got hold of a razor and had it in his hand. Presently the wife's slave-girl entered the hut, and the two of them got on to the bed, he thinking it was the wife, when really it was her slave-girl who had come in her place. And so the caravan-leader's friend had his will of the slave-girl of his friend's wife. But, as he got up, he took the razor and slashed the girl's thigh. Then he went out and the girl followed, her blood pouring forth. And her mistress tended her wound until she recovered.

Well, the day came when the caravan-leader returned and found his friend in great spirits. Three days passed and his merchandise remained unpacked.

Then along came his friend and says to the caravan-leader 'I've been waiting for you to send along all my goods, but I find that you haven't done so.' The other answered 'My word! Do you mean that argument that we had? Do you mean you managed to do what you said you would?' 'Yes' said his friend. 'But where is the proof?' asked the caravan-leader. 'Call your wife' replied his friend, and so the caravan-leader sent for his wife.

Says he 'Wife, I am told that you have slept with' and he named his friend. 'No, husband' she answered, 'and don't you reject this sort of tale when anyone brings it to you?'

At which the friend said to her 'Let's see your thigh.' For shame, sir' said she, 'My thigh?' and she continued 'But let me call my slave-girl.'

Now the caravan-leader, up to this point, was in some fear that the wealth he had spent months winning was all going to someone else.

But his wife returned with her slave-girl. 'Show us your thigh'

* Or 'servant'.

346

says she to the girl, and the girl bared her thigh, and there was the place where the man had slashed it with a razor.

Then said the wife to her husband's friend 'Well, now you see where you left your goods – and not with me.' She turned to her husband. 'Did you have an argument?' she asked. 'Yes' he answered.

'Well' she said, 'then let him give you what he promised.' 'Certainly' said the caravan-leader. 'He was to give me his slave-girl and his horse. As for me, I said that when I got back from my trading journey, if it was true that he slept with you, he might come and take all these beasts of mine home with him.'

The friend became very ashamed, and the caravan-leader's wife said 'Very well, let him bring you the slave-girl and the horse.'

And her husband said to his friend 'Well, bring me the slave-girl*, but I'll let you off the horse.' And his friend went and fetched the slave-girl and gave her to the caravan-leader.

But the latter took the slave-girl and gave her to his wife. 'This is your slave-girl' he said. But his wife said to him 'You should be ashamed, husband! For though you hear of men who chase women, the woman always have a say in the matter. If a woman doesn't approve of him, a man won't sleep with her.' That's all. This with peace.

The Youth and the Girl† [$^{III}/_{54}$]

There was once a man had a daughter of stunning beauty, who would have nothing to do with the boys.‡ She would reject all who courted her.

But one day a youth heard of it, and left his home and came to the compound of her father and settled there, and for three years worked on his farm.

Then one day he said 'Master, I would like you to give me your

---

* The less valuable of the two things.   † Cf M. No. 4, and TR. No. 10.
‡ Lit. 'never indulged in *tsarance*', for which see BABA.

daughter in marriage – permit us to be married.' 'Very well' said her father, 'Take her. She's yours.'

But the town had a river that ran beside it, which must be crossed if one would reach the youth's own town.

And the girl had two bangles on each arm. Says the youth to her 'Give me your cloths' and she did so. 'Sit down' said he – and she did so. Then he pulled off her bangles, and the anklets from her legs too, and tied them up in the cloths.

Then he went down the path, into the river and began to swim. But when he reached the middle, something seized him and they began to struggle. Down they went to the bottom, but he got himself out of that and escaped, emerging on the bank nearest his home.

He heard a voice from in the water, saying 'Why did you let him go?' and another saying 'Oh' he'll be coming back.' But the young fellow stayed right there.

The some hyenas set upon the girl, and the townspeople stood by and watched. For they said 'No one is to go to her; for the girl would have nothing to do with us. Ignore her.'

But the youth called out to her 'Keep still – don't move from there. I'm coming.' Then the girl replied 'Don't go into the water. Look what difficulty you had getting out before – and you heard them say you would be coming back!' But he answered her 'Nothing happens to a man without God's knowledge. God will get me out of it.'

And so he went into the water and reached the girl, and the two of them went home. That's all. *Kungurus kan kusu.*

The Youth and the Maiden [^{III}/60]

There was once a lad who was courting* a girl, whom he used to visit, going to her town every day.

But one day he arrived at night, and came to her compound.

* For *tsarance* see footnote on previous page.

348

And as he got there, the girl's mother was saying to her 'Get up and close the hut, so that we may go to sleep.'

The boy made formal greeting, and the girl answered 'Welcome' 'Come along, let's be going' he said, but the mother said 'Going? Where?' The boy answered 'To my compound.' 'Oh no' said she, 'Since you didn't come early, before night fell, and have left it till now to come – I won't have a hyena eating up my daughter!' 'Oh no' said the boy, 'for, you see, I have some spears.' At this she agreed, and the girl went out and they set off.

They walked for some way and had come into the bush, when a hyena intercepted them. The boy hurled a spear at the hyena, which leapt up – and the spear landed on the ground. The hyena rushed at them, and the boy took another spear and threw it at the hyena. Again the hyena leapt aside and the spear landed on the ground. Again the hyena came at them.

Says the boy to the girl 'Be brave and stand still. I'm going to wrestle with this hyena.' 'Very well' said the girl.

So she stayed there, while the boy went and grabbed the hyena, wrestled with her, and threw her to the ground. The girl began to cry, but he said to her 'Here, stop crying, for I have got the hyena down – look, I'm on top of her', and he took hold of the hyena's ears and began to twist them.

Next he told the girl to come over, and she did so. Says he 'Put your hands there and hold on,' and the girl took hold of the hyena's ears.

Well, actually, the hyena was dead and had been from the time the young fellow threw her, but they didn't know it. And he said to the girl 'Hold on tight. For if you relax, the hyena will escape from your hold and eat you up. So, provided that you don't relax – you'll see your mother again. As for me, I am – as you see – on my way.'

And off went the boy, leaving the girl holding on to the hyena. The night had barely begun when he went, and there she spent the whole night, until daylight came and some people came along that way. And they sighted the girl there in the bush, squatting.

'Is that a madwoman over there?' they speculated, and decided not. So they went over and saw the girl sitting there with her hands on the hyena. They asked 'How did you come to be here, girl, and holding a hyena?' And the girl answered 'It was my young man –

my mother tried to stop him taking me out, but he said it would be all right. It was he left me here and went off on his own.'

Then said they 'If you follow men, one day they'll destroy you. That's all there is to it.' Again they said 'Let the hyena go – for, you see, she's dead. Then get up and come home with us.' That's all. This with peace.

Two Young Men and their Girls [III/ 101]

There were once two young fellows, who used to go regularly to another town and fetch their girls and bring them home at night.

One day the mother of one of the boys said to him 'Look – you stop travelling at night like this! Have a care for the hyenas, for fear one of them eats up someone else's daughter.' 'Nonsense, mother!' he answered. 'What hyenas?'

But one day, they set off as usual, and this boy brought home his girl, as did his friend. But a hyena met them, and sprang at our hero's girl to sieze her. Then he told her to take him on her back. She did so and ran off, carrying him on her back, with the hyena after them.

After a while the hyena turned back towards the other young fellow – who had made no boast. When the animal reached him, she was about to seize his girl, when he drew his sword, and took the girl's hand and held it. And when the hyena came on, the boy slashed at her with his sword – and kept breaking wind!

At which the other young fellow, riding along on his girl's back, said 'Ha! For heaven's sake, my dear! Listen to old' and he mentioned his friend. 'May he rot! Listen to him – he's so frightened that he's breaking wind.' The other boy fought with the hyena until daybreak; but his friend was carried home by his girl. That's all. That's the end of that tale.

The Two Young Men and the Girl* [$^{III}/_{118}$]

There were once two young men, who had shared a hut ever since they were boys. Now they were grown to young men and each had his own hut in the compound, but still one would leave his own hut and go and spend the night with his friend, such was their friendship.

Later they would go and bring home their girls as *tsarance* partners, and when they fetched them, they would all go to the compound of one of the two boys and there spend the night. But one day they didn't bring the girls back. Now one of the boys had a girl who was fond of him, and would sleep in his hut regularly, by herself.†

Well, on this day, he set off home and reached his hut at night, and going into it, heard movement. He drew his sword and slashed the top of the bed, thinking it was a snake. But in fact – though he didn't know it – it was the girl. Then he went and fetched some embers, and kindling them in the hut, saw that he had divided the girl in two with the sword. There they were – and he didn't know what to do, for he had committed murder.

He went outside and so to his friend's compound, and addressing him by name, said 'Listen to what I've done today: I heard movement on the bed and drew my sword and struck.' He went on to say that it was the girl he had killed unwittingly. Then his friend said 'Come along, let's go and dig a hole and bury her, just the two of us.'

And they went into the hut and dug a hole, there in the night, and buried her in the hut, and went about their business. The girl's parents kept looking for her, but not finding her, resigned themselves.

Four years passed, and one day the young men went to the farm of the mother of the boy who had killed the girl. As they hoed, they were laughing, laughingly loudly, when the boy's mother brought them out food to where they were working. Says she 'What are you laughing at so loudly?', and they answered 'Mother, it was

* Cf. III/19.   † Presumably when the young man was in his friends' hut.

something that we did once, that we remembered.' 'What was that?' she asked, and they told her 'You see, that girl that they looked for and never found, it was' and they named her son 'who killed her in his hut, without realising it.' 'Alas and alack!' said the old woman, 'Did you really kill the girl they were looking for?' And crying bitterly, she went off to the town.

She was asked 'What are you crying for?' 'Oh dear!' she said, 'You know the daughter of' and she mentioned his name, 'Well, she was killed by' and she named her son.

So they went and told the chief. 'Where are they?' said he. 'Away at the farm' he was told, and horsemen were sent to arrest them. But they, when they saw the horses, made use of charms of invisibility, vanished and went off to travel through the world. That's all. End of story.

The Man and his Two Wives [III/79]

There was once a man had two wives, to whom he gave out corn each day to thresh and share out. Now it happened that one of the wives used to turn into a goat. When their husband gave them the corn and they had threshed it, they would divide it into two and each would take her share. The other wife would take her water-pot and go off to get water; whereupon this wife would change herself into a goat, enter the hut of the other wife, and eat up all her corn. So that it even came about that the husband scolded her, for he kept saying 'Well! What sort of wife are you, that whenever I give out corn to you both, yours is used up straight away. Now look – I'll give you both corn; but if you,' addressing the other wife, 'Waste yours, then we shall have words, you and I.' 'Very well' said she.

So their husband fetched corn and gave it to them, and they threshed it and divided it out. Each of them took her share and put it in her hut.

Then the innocent wife said 'With God's help I'll catch that goat hat is being such a trouble to me, eating up my corn; and I'll take her to her mistress; for whenever we are given corn, that goat comes and eats it up.'

Another night passed, and the innocent wife said to the other 'Hey, keep an eye on my hut for me, I'm going to the stream to get water; see that that goat doesn't come and eat up my corn.' 'Right' said the other.

Off she went, but she hid herself, and waited. Then her fellow-wife turned herself into a goat, went straight into her hut, and when she got there began eating the corn. Back comes the other wife, straight into the hut, and blocks the way for the goat. The goat began to tremble and the wife said 'Well, goat, God has caught you at last. As for me, I'm taking you to the market now. Whoever owns you can come and find me and I'll pay his price. For all the damage that this goat has done me, I'm taking her to the butchers this very day for them to slaughter her.'

Next she began to call to her fellow-wife, pretending that she didn't know that it was she who had turned into a goat. So she called and got no reply.

Then she began pulling the goat along, the goat bleating, saying 'Me-e', until she reached the market and the place where the butchers were. 'Hey' said she, 'Come here. I've got a goat for you to buy and slaughter – but I want half the meat.' 'Really?' said they. 'Yes' she replied.

So the butchers came up and took hold of the goat to slaughter her. Whereupon she turned back into a woman. At which they began abusing her, on hearing her fellow-wife's account of the damage she had done. They went home and she told her husband. Then he drove away the wife who turned into a goat. And after that lived with just the other wife – just the two of them. That's all. That's the end of that tale.

The Husband, his Wife
and her Elder Brother [$^{III}/_{85}$]

A man once went and married a girl, and took her off into the country, saying that he was going to till a farm. He put up a hut in the middle of his farm. Now, whenever he made his wife prepare food, he would go off to market and buy meat, and it would be fine food; but then he would tell his wife to dish it all out, leaving none in the pot. 'All right' she would reply, and dish the whole lot of *tuwo* into the wooden bowl. Then he would come and pick it up and say that he was going to take it off to the dead. Then he would go off, sit down and eat up the lot, leaving his wife to eat the scrapings.

This happened regularly. And if she made *fura*, he would tell her to mix it all up and not to leave any, and she would do so. Then he would take it and go and sit down and drink it all up.

This continued daily, until one day her elder brother arrived, and saw how his sister had grown thin. 'Hey' says he, addressing her 'What's the matter with you?' I'd heard you were here on the farm, working – is it the work that has made you get thin like this, no fat left, just bones?' 'Well, she said, 'You see, ever since I have come to his compound, whenever I make *tuwo*, my husband tells me to dish it all out, and not to leave any; for he says he's going to take it to the dead.' 'Which way does he go?' asked her brother, and the girl pointed out to him the way her husband would go, showing him exactly the way.

Her brother went off to the bush and cut two sticks from a tamarind tree, and brought them back and hid them. Next the husband returned, and finding her brother there, gave him a warm welcome, to which he replied.

Evening came and she prepared the *tuwo*. Her husband said to her 'Serve some *tuwo* out for your brother, a little, not too much.' 'Very well' she answered, and gave the first serving to her brother. Then she dished out all that was left and poured the gravy on to it. Her husband took it and set off along the road; reached his usual place, and put it down.

Meanwhile the girl's brother rose and taking some ash, rubbed it on his body; then set off along the road. Presently he reached the spot where her husband was sitting, eating his *tuwo*. He struck him with the stick, at which he got up and ran away. 'The dead!' exclaimed the brother, 'Dead your mother – you!', beating him severely and repeating these words, until his whole body was covered with blood.

The girl's brother returned home and quickly washed himself, telling the girl of the drubbing that he had given her husband. Presently the latter returned with his body streaming blood, and told his wife to prepare hot water for him to wash with, telling her 'Phew! Those dead people! Usually when I go I take it to the chief of them, but today when I went I took it to the lesser ones; at which their chief leapt up, attacked me and gave me a beating. So, from today, I shan't go again, lest by any chance they should see me and beat me.'

And from that day on he never went to take *tuwo* and *fura* to the dead. That was that. So her brother cured her husband for her, and from then on she was able to get some food to eat. That's it. This with peace.

The Husband, the Wife and the Husband's Friend [III/86]

A young fellow once got married. But when he brought his bride home, she said that they never had *tuwo* in her home, and she had never made it, all she could do was cook beans. And so every morning and evening that's what she cooked – beans.

Then one day a friend of his came and asked him after his wife. He answered 'There she is. But, ever since she came, she's never prepared *tuwo* for me. All she cooks for me is *gakaiwa* [cooked beans].' 'What's *gakaiwa*?' asks the friend. 'Guinea-corn [sic]* that

---

* This and the next reference to guinea-corn seem obscure, as contrary to the whole point of the story.

she cooks' answered the other. Then said his friend 'Very well. Just let me cure her.' 'O.K.' said her husband, and his friend said 'Go and tell her that a law has been made forbidding people to draw water during the day, and that only after sunset may anyone do so.' 'O.K.' said the other, and he went and said to his wife 'Look, they've made a law today, that no one is to go and fetch water during daylight – only after sunset.' 'Very well' said she.

His friend went into the bush and cut a stick from a tamarind tree, and brought it home and put it aside. Evening came and she took some guinea-corn, poured it into a cooking-pot, and began to cook it. The sun set and taking a water-pot she set off to get water.

Meanwhile, the husband's friend mixed red earth and indigo and whitewash, and flicked it all over his body. Then he rose and took his stick and went off to a spot close to the well. The wife was drawing water. He suddenly appeared through the grass, saying 'Is this the one who cooks *gakaiwa*? She's the one I'm after.' He went towards her, and she ran off making for the town. He went round and intercepted her, and began beating her with the stick as he came, saying 'I'm going to give this cooker of *gakaiwa* a drubbing – will you cook any more *gakaiwa*?' And she began wailing and saying that she wouldn't cook *gakaiwa* again. So he beat her and she cried, and all her body was covered with blood. Then he returned to his home, back to normal. And she reached her home, crying.

Her husband asked her 'Hey, what's the matter with you? Where's the pot you took to get water?' But as soon as she got in, she took corn and began to grind it; put a pot on the fire, and made *tuwo*; she gave it to her husband and he ate it.

And from that day forward she never again cooked *gakaiwa*, but made her husband *tuwo* every day. And that was that. His friend had used his cunning to help him and cured his wife. That's all.

The Two Fellow-Wives and their Children [III/ 88]

There were once two fellow-wives, both with children. And the husband loved one of them, her and her daughter, but not the other. And anything that he acquired from time to time he would keep from the one, giving it all to the other one and he daughter. In fact he never went into their hut. And so mother and daugher came to lack even a cloth between them. All they had was one single ragged piece.

Then one day a female friend of this wife came to see her. Says the friend 'My dear, what on earth's the matter with you. You look terrible.' 'Ah, just so' said the other, 'for my husband dislikes me and dislikes my daughter too; he only loves that other wife – why, he doesn't even give us food.' Then her friend said 'Let me go and get some money, a hundred cowries, to lend you.' 'Thank-you' said the other.

So the friend went off and bought her cotton worth eighty – and ten cowries, – and ten cowries' worth of spindles. Then she returned with the cotton and gave it to them. Then the mother and daughter fell to spinning the cotton, and very quickly turned it into thread.

When the friend next came, they took the thread and gave it to her, and she went off to market and sold it for a hundred and eighty cowries. Then she bought them sixty cowries' worth of corn, spindles for thirty and more cotton, a hundred cowries' worth.* This corn they ground and made themselves gruel, which they drank.

In no time they turned the hundred cowries' worth of cotton into thread, and when the friend next came, they gave it to her. She took it off to market and sold the thread for two hundred cowries, all of which she spent on more lint, which she brought back to them. And very quickly they turned all that too into thread.

So when the friend next came they gave that to her and she took it to market and sold it for four hundred cowries. Then she

* Sic.

bought them cotton lint for three hundred, and spent a hundred on corn for them. Then they spun that three hundred worth of cotton into thread, and sold it for six hundred.

Again they bought six hundred cowries' worth of cotton, went and spun that, and taking it to market sold it for twelve hundred cowries. With a thousand of these she bought some more cotton, with a hundred she bought corn for themselves; and she took the remaining hundred and went and paid back the loan that the old woman had made her. She took the corn and the cotton home, and once more they quickly turned the thousand cowries' worth of cotton into thread.

Again came her friend and again took the thread to the market, and there sold it for two thousand cowries. With this amount she bought cotton and took it back to them, and once again they spun it all. They took this thread and sold it for four thousand, and the friend brought them back cotton to the value of that amount. Back they went to work and turned it all into thread.

Next time the friend came she took the thread and sold it for eight thousand cowries at the market. Five thousand she spent on more cotton, fifteen hundred on corn for them; and also five hundred on salt, seven hundred on *daddawa*, and meat too to the value of three hundred. And putting all that lot up on to her head she took it to them.

They took the cotton and went back to work, and continued until very soon they had spun that lot too. And when that was taken to market it was sold for ten thousand cowries. And once more she brought back cotton for them.

And so it went on. She even bought cloths for them and they were able to make trips outside. She got finery for the girl; they bought two slave-girls, and the mother got plenty of basins and calabashes for her daughter.

Then one day two young men came looking for wives. One was the son of a rich merchant, the other the son of a poor man. The merchant's son married the favourite daughter; while the poor man's son married the other daughter. Now the favourite daughter received the usual fine show of calabashes – but not a basin of metal among them. But the other daughter didn't have her fine things brought for another seven days; and then they were taken to her new home at night, when her husband was out.

When he returned, he saw basins a-plenty, and calabashes and carpets of eastern manufacture. He said nothing but went out and along to the house of the merchant's son. There he saw calabashes, but not a basin among them, nor any fine carpets. He chatted into the night with the other, and at last said 'Well, I must be getting home. Now that I've visited your home, won't you come and see mine?' And the other answered 'I'll be along to your compound tomorrow.'

Next day, in the evening the merchant's son set off and made his way to the poor man's compound. As soon as he put his head inside, he saw basins everywhere – more than there were calabashes even – and there too were her two slave-girls sitting.

Then he ran as fast as he could back to his own compound. There he gave his wife a good beating, until she ran off to her own home. Then he went and got a hammer and smashed the calabashes and the cooking-pots and the water-pots. Says he 'Good-for-nothing slut – you and your mother too, your father's favourites and you haven't even any decent utensils! While the daughter he doesn't like – and her mother too – why, she's got a hut full of things!'

Then the girl's father rose and went to find the wife whom he didn't like; and set to beating her, accusing her of being the cause of his daughter's getting a drubbing. That's all. *Kungurus kan kusu.* I ate the rat, not the rat me.

The Blind Man and the Man and his Wife [III 95]

Here's another. A blind man once went off begging at night. He came to the compound of a man and said something, but the man ignored him and didn't speak.

But the wife answered him. Says the blind man 'Is your husband away?' 'Yes, he's away' she answered. 'I see' said he.

He moved a little farther into the compound and said again

'Lady, is it really true that your husband's out?' 'Yes' she repeated, 'He's out.' Meanwhile her husband was lying quite silent on the bed.

'Lady' said the blind man again, 'Look, I've four hundred cowries here, which I'll give you, if you'll lie with me.' 'Oh no!' she answered, 'We mustn't do that, for fear my husband comes and catches us lying together.' 'Never fear' says the blind man, 'Come on, let us lie together.' But she continued to refuse. Whereupon he offered her five hundred cowries.

The blind man came to the edge of the bed and groped. He felt what long hair the woman had, and said 'Curse this blindness! Here's a beautiful woman, and me with no eyes to see her!' He addressed her again 'Look! I'll give you more – I'll give you six hundred; only please be a little kind to me.' 'Shame on you blind man!' she answered, 'If I am kind to you, and my husband comes back and catches us both together – what am I going to say to him?' 'No, but –' said the blind man, 'Look – we'll be very quick – before your husband comes back.' 'No' she said, but the blind man made as if to sit on the edge of the bed.

At this point the husband said 'Hey! Who's this here? What brings you here?' 'Oh!' said the blind man, 'I was begging, and I came to shelter from the rain.' 'You're lying, blind man' said the husband, 'Now you can just give me that white gown of yours, and those white trousers of yours – with their embroidery and narrow ankle-bands* – and that white turban of yours; oh yes – and those six hundred cowries that you said you would give my wife. I'll have the lot, thank you. And if you refuse to hand them over, I'll lock you up here and now.'

Up got the husband and took all the blind man's things, leaving him standing there with just his staff and wearing only his loincloth. And so the blind man went off home just like that. So that was that, that was the end of that tale. Well, which of the two – husband or wife – occurred guilt in his treatment of the blind man?† That's all for that story. This with peace.

---

* *Gidan tara* is a particular embroidery pattern.
† For *dauki alhaki*, see II/CI

The Man with the Large Penis* [III 98]

There was once a man whose organ was seven cubits long. Before he got up on to his horse he had to lash it to his backside.

One day he visited another town, and lodged at the home of a certain woman, who had no husband of her own. There he saw a woman come by, a very beautiful one. So he gave his hostess twenty thousand cowries, saying 'Here's forty [sic]† thousand cowries to take to that woman that I saw and asked you about; for I have fallen for her.' 'Very well' said she and took the money. But she took it and put it away in her hut.

So the man saw no more of the other woman. Then he fetched out another eighty thousand cowries and gave them to his hostess, telling her to take all that money to the woman he had seen. Then his hostess thus addressed her guest 'Hey, my friend, don't tread in the water that you're drawing.' Says the man 'I don't understand that sort of talk. Won't you tell me plainly? Speak in clear words and don't hide your meaning.' 'Well' said she, 'this is why I said to you "Don't tread in the water that you're drawing". For I'm a woman, and yet you send me off to another woman. Well – aren't I one?' 'Yes, hostess' he answered, 'Surely you're a woman. All right but – do you think that you'll be able to –' 'Yes, I'll be able to' she answered, 'I'll come along to your hut this evening.' 'Good' said he.

Evening came and the sun set and the guest took a ring and put it on his penis, so that only that part of it up to the ring could enter the woman's vagina.

The woman came into the hut, and heard something lashing the bed. It was his penis, which, scenting a woman, had begun to rise and was lashing the bed. Says the woman 'What's that hitting the bed?' 'Oh' said he 'That's – well it's rising.'

At this point he said that he was going out to relieve himself, and collected it and took it all out, went and relieved himself and came back. Then before he sat down, he let down the whole lot on to the

* Cf. M. No. 50.   † This is made clear below.

bed, and then sat down himself. 'Hey!!' said the woman, 'What's that?'

'Oh' he answered, 'That's all my organ – all of it.' 'I see' said she, 'And how much of it goes into a woman's vagina?' 'Well' he said, 'You see I took it to the blacksmith's, and they put a ring on it to mark that point.' 'Where's the ring?' she asked, and he answered 'Do you see as far as this ring here? From the end down to there, no further, that's what I put in.' 'Huh!' she said, 'When you start, you can take that ring off; for I can accommodate the whole thing. It'll all go into my vagina – and its appurtenances* here too!' 'Really' said he. 'Yes – but just let me go and relieve myself first. Then it'll be able to go in.'

But as soon as the woman got outside, she ran off fast. She didn't return to her compound all night, but spent the night in someone else's home. She slept late and it wasn't till after midday that she set off home. There she found her guest had made his preparations to set out; but he was delaying setting off until she came.

She arrived and was about to speak, when he interrupted her. 'Well I'll be —! Now what are you going to say? Look, what I've got to say to you now is this: if there's been no smithing done, what's used up the charcoal?' 'I don't take your meaning there' she answered. 'Better be plain and tell me.' 'Well' said he, 'here's why I said that to you. You began by saying to me "Don't tread in the water that you're drawing". Well, now it's my turn to say to you "If there's no smithing done, what's used up the charcoal?" Here's for why. There I was, your guest. I saw a woman I wanted. I go and give you twenty thousand cowries, as reward for fetching her. Then, for her, I give you another forty thousand to take to her; and on top of all that another eighty thousand. That's a hundred and forty thousand good cowries – and you really thought that you could absorb the lot! Well, why did you run away? So now you can give me my money and I'll be on my way, for not a glimmer of sleeping with you have I had. Had I put even the head of my penis in, the money would lawfully be yours. As it is, you don't get even two cowries, and you can give me my money and I'll be going.' So the woman brought the fellow his money and paid it all back. He rose to his feet, saddled his horse, and putting foot to stirrup, mounted.

* Lit. 'children'.

There was a man just by and our friend said to him 'Pass my organ up to me. I must be getting along.' And it was duly dragged over and handed up to him; and clutching it in his arms, he went his way. That's all. This with peace.

Two Friends and their Wives [^{III}/₁₀₂]

There were once two friends who both had wives. One said that his wife was addicted to adultery, while the other denied that his was. Whereupon the former said 'My friend, better not hold any brief for a woman; they are all bad. Just you leave them as you find them!' But the other persisted in defending his wife. 'Very well' was the rejoinder, 'try a trick on her and see.' 'What sort of a trick can I play?' And his friend said 'Go close to the road and make a hole. [Get in and] when you're right under the middle of the road, come up.' So he went and did so, and lay down on his back, and pushed his penis up [through the hole].

Along came the women to fetch water, his wife among them. Each of them noticed it, but all passed by. But she, when she got there, she said 'Hey! What's this?' The others spoke sharply to her 'Here, come on, let's be going. Were you the only one of us to see it?* Of course we all saw it, but we didn't say anything – except for you.' Then she moved on too.

They went and got water and took it home, but she waited behind them. 'Keep going, I'm coming' she called to them. Then, picking up her pot, she came along, but when she reached the spot, she said 'Let me put the pot down and relieve myself.' Then she went up and began to touch it, saying 'Naughty thing, I wonder how it came here.' She was just preparing to put it into herself, when her husband said 'You good-for-nothing bitch!' At which she snatched up her pot and ran off as fast as she could.

When he got out, he went back to his friend and said to him

* I have replaced the semi-colon by a question mark.

'You were right.' 'Of course' said the other, 'I told you to hold no brief for women. Anyone who stands up for them will be destroyed by them.'

And that is why wise men don't trust women – however much a man may like a woman. That's all.

The Husband and Wife [III/ 123]

There was once a man who set off on his travels, and when he came to a town, he would say 'Where is the virtuous woman?'* When no one answered him, he would pass on and go to the next town, and say 'Where is the virtuous woman?' – and there too no one would answer him. And so he travelled for four years.

Then he came to a town and asked his usual question, and a girl came up and said 'You there – what do you want?' 'Well' he said, 'I've been travelling for four years, asking for the virtuous woman.' Says the girl 'What a man! Or are you a simpleton? The virtuous woman is in her husband's hut.' He came a little closer to the girl, and said 'What was that you said, girl?' 'Well!!' said the girl, 'I said that the virtuous woman was in her husband's hut.' 'Did you really say that, girl?' asked the man. 'Yes' said she.

Then the man sat down and waited till the girl's father came back from the town. Then he said to him 'Good sir, will you not give me this daughter of yours in marriage?' 'Very well' said the other, 'I'll give her to you – but I don't know what town you hail from.' Says the man 'No matter. If you bestow her upon me, I'll go to the chief of this town and ask him to give me a compound and a farm, and settle down here.' 'Then go and do so, for I give her to you' said the father.

The man rose and went to the chief of the town. The latter found a compound and gave it to him, and also a farm. The man put the compound in order, and went and did the same to the farm. And when the hot season came, and the sowing rains, he went and sowed his farm. The seedlings appeared, and he did his

* *mata* means both 'woman' and 'wife'.

hoeing. Harvest came and people began cutting down the corn. And he too cut down his, removed the heads, and took them home, a fine crop.

Presently the girl was of age to marry, and she was duly married to the man. Her father supplied her with household goods, and also a cushion that he filled with dried excrement. And he said to her 'See here – all your life, if ever you hear your husband say that this cushion stinks, you get your things together and come home – for that husband of yours will have grown tired of you.' 'Very well' said she, and went to her husband's compound with the cushion. And her husband used it for his head. They lived together for ten years. Then her husband was after another woman.

And one day her husband said to her 'Ugh, this cushion! It stinks!' 'Really?' she asked. 'Yes' he said, and she fell silent, saying nothing more. Her husband rose and went off into the town about his business. Then the girl got up, packed her things, and going to her father's compound, moved back in there.

The husband returned home later, and when he got there looked into the compound; saw the hut with no one there, no calabashes – not even a cooking-pot. So he went out again, and to the home of his in-laws, to find the girl.

Her father came forward and the husband said 'My wife has left me and come home. And yet we haven't quarrelled!' 'Is that so?' said the other, and when the husband affirmed that it was, the girl's father had her fetched. She came and sat down. Her father asked her about it and she answered 'Yes, he has tired of me. He said the cushion stank. But I know it wasn't the cushion that was smelling bad to him, but me. So I left, removing myself from his compound. He can go and get someone who smells nice. As for me, someone else will come along and I'll smell nice to him.' And the husband got up and went home.

And this is the way with husbands and wives – if a man tires of his wife, he will do much evil to her. And a woman too, if she tires of her husband, she will do much evil to him. Well, you've heard all there is of that tale. That's it. This with peace.

The Jealous Husband and his Wife* [$^{III}/_{140}$]

There was once a jealous man who went and married a wife and he was exceedingly suspicious of all that she did. So, whenever he took a bundle of corn out of the bin and gave it out, when it had been threshed, before going off to the farm, he would first measure to see how many measures there were.

But his wife would give the corn its first pounding and then tip it into a cooking-pot. Eventually she filled all the pots, and had a bin built for her in the hut, and she would take the pounded corn, and tip it into the bin – until eventually that too was full.

Now her husband had a horse. And when his corn was all finished, he said 'Could I but find someone to buy my horse, I'd sell it and buy corn for us to eat.' His wife said 'Take him to market, and if you get an offer for him, come and tell me.' 'Right' said he.

So he led the horse along to the market, but nobody made him an offer. Next day he again led the horse to market. Someone made him an offer of a hundred [thousand], which he wouldn't accept, and returned home, telling his wife 'I was offered a hundred [thousand] for the horse, but I refused it.'

Next day he went back again, taking the horse, but no one made him an offer. The horse spent the day there, and when evening came he led it back home again. Next day, in the morning, again he took the horse and went to market with it; again someone offered him a hundred [thousand], and again he led the horse home.

When he got there, he said to his wife 'It looks as though the horse will fetch a hundred thousand.' 'Really!' said his wife. 'Yes' he answered, and she said 'Then give him to me; I'll pay you that.' 'O.K. – there he is' he answered.

Then the woman called her husband over and showed him the bin full of pounded corn. They made a hole in the bin and the corn came pouring out, and her husband saw the corn, shining

---

* Perhaps 'suspicious' would be nearer. On the other hand, checking the corn might indicate he was making sure it wasn't being used to feed any but he. In these stories, a normal concomitant of adultery seems to be feeding the paramour. Cf. "I, the Lord . . . am a jealous God."

white. And his wife took the horse to her parents' compound and asked them to keep it for her. And they tied it up there for her.

And so they ate of that corn, until harvest came and he could use the corn he had grown. Then his wife went to her parents compound, and fetched the horse back and gave it to him, saying 'I'm giving him to you to ride whenever you want.' And he said 'Well, I'll – I'll never deal jealously with a woman again; whatever she pleases she may do, and whenever she pleases. I'll not again be jealous.' And nor was he. That's all. This with peace.

Shekara and Shekarau* [III/10]

There was once a youth, who had a girl that he was dating.† She used to come regularly and sleep at his place, and eventually he married her. And so they continued until they were both old. His name was Shekarau, and hers Shekara.

But one day Shekarau said 'Look, Shekara, we are both old, you and I. So I want to marry a strong girl, who will be able to prepare our food for us, both of us, to eat.' 'Oh, no, Shekarau!' she answered, 'for I am quite strong, you know.' 'O.K.' said he and let the matter drop.

But again one day he said to her 'Shekara, I'm going to marry again, so that we can have someone to prepare our food for us to eat, you and me and her.' 'Oh, no, Shekarau!' she said. 'for I'm quite strong.' 'Very well' he replied, 'if you're strong, let met get up on to the roof‡ of the corn-bin, and you can carry me, together with it.' 'O.K.' she said, 'up you get.' So he climbed up on to the bin, and grasping the top, held on. And she went over, and putting her head under it, lifted the cover and set off with it. But she grew tired and said 'I'm tired out, I'm tired, Shekarau.' And he answered 'If you really are tired, Shekara, take me home and I'll marry again.' But she said 'I'm not tired, Shekarau, he-man among men; I'm not tired. Let us go on.'

* Cf. next tale   † For the exact significance of *tsarance*, see BABA, p. 256.
‡ Of thatch.

And on she went, but presently again began to grow tired. Says she 'I'm tired out, I'm tired, Shekarau.' And he answered 'If you're tired, Shekara, take me home and I'll marry again.' But she said 'I'm not tired, Shekarau, he-man among men. I'm not tired. Just let us go on.'

They went a long way and turned back, and she said 'I'm tired out, I'm tired, Shekarau.' And he said 'If you are tired, Shekara, take me home and I'll marry again.' But she said 'I'm not tired, he-man among men. I'm not tired. Just let us go on.'

But as they went along, she fell. Shekarau jumped off, but she – she was dead. So he went off home, and married again. That's all. *Kungurus kan kusu.*

The Jealous Wife* [III/148]

A jealous wife heard that her husband was going to marry again. So she put a charm on him to prevent it. Then he went to consult a malam, who told him that he wouldn't be able to make the marriage here – only in some other country.

He had a camel, and he rolled up all the furnishings of his hut, and loaded them on to the camel.† But his wife told him to take them off and put them on to her. This was done, and so they travelled – he on the camel, she on foot, carrying the load on her head.

They went some way, and presently she had sunk into the sand up to her knees. Said she 'I'm tired, he-man among men.' Said he 'If you're tired, wife of men, let me take you home and make a new marriage.' But she said 'I'm not tired, he-man among men.'

On she went, until the sand had reached her navel. Says she 'I'm tired, he-man among men.' Says he 'If you're tired, wife of men, let me take you home and make a new marriage.' And she said 'I'm not tired, he-man among men.'

* Cf. last tale.
† This sounds like a nomad tale. See also below for the sand.

On she went, until the sand reached to her neck. Says she 'I'm tired, he-man among men.' Said he 'If you're tired, let me take you home, and make a new marriage.' Then she said 'I'm not tired, he-man among men.'

On she went, and now the sand was up to her neatly plaited hair. Says she 'I'm tired, he-man among men.' 'If you're tired' he said, 'Let me take you home and make a new marriage.' And she said 'I'm not tired, he-man among men.' Then her husband saw that the sand had swallowed her up.

He picked up his load, put it on his camel and went on with his journey. Presently some blacksmiths came along, looking for charcoal*, and saw the neatly plaited hair; and one of them started to dig a hole to get her out. He called a friend over and the two of them dug till they had got her out. 'What happened to you?' they asked. 'Jealousy' she answered. 'And will you go on being jealous now?' 'Yes' she replied. And that is how blacksmith's wives came to be jealous.

A Case of Fornication† [III/156]

A certain chief once ordered that a law should be made that anyone who committed fornication should be arrested; and that the two offenders should be killed and all their relatives fined.

Time passed and then a certain blind woman became pregnant. And word was brought to the chief, telling him of it. 'Let her be taken to the judge' said he.

But she got news of this, and went to a malam. Says she 'You must devise something for me in this matter; for even if they kill me, they mustn't take my relatives' wealth and leave them paupers all for something that is my fault.' And the malam replied 'If I devise something for you, and you get off, what will you give me?' 'A hundred thousand [cowries]' she answered, and the malam said 'If the judge summons you and addresses you, you must say to him

* ?='wood for charcoal'.

† *Farka* connotes any illicit intercourse outside matrimony. For the story see J. p. 221.

"I'm afraid I can't see, but the voice of the man who slept with me and made me pregnant, was just like your voice. I think it was you" '
'Right' said the woman. 'And thank you.'

Presently they came and summoned her and took her to the court. There she was sitting outside, when the judge sent a servant to question her. He did so and she answered 'I'm afraid I can't see, but the speech of the man who made me pregnant was like your voice. I think it was you.' At which the fellow went back to the judge and said 'I can't make out what she is saying.'

Says the judge 'Let her come closer to me,' and she did so. Then he asked her 'Girl, who made you pregnant?' and she answered 'I can't see, but the voice of the man who made me pregnant was just like your voice. I think it was you.' At which the judge said 'I can't make out what she is saying either, properly, I'll have to go to the chief.'

So he went and told the chief, saying 'I can't understand exactly what this woman says.' The chief answered 'Tut, judge. I hear that this woman's relatives have much wealth, and now here you are trying to throw away the case! Go and bring her. I'll ask her.'

So the judge went and fetched her. 'Where is she?' asked the chief. 'Here she is' said the judge. 'You girl' said the chief, 'who made you pregnant?' She answered 'I'm afraid I can't see, but the speech of the man who made me pregnant was just like your voice. I think it was you.' 'Now then' he said, 'I'm the chief of the town that am talking to you.' 'Have I got eyes to see with?' she asked, 'I've only got ears to hear with.'

Then the chief said 'Call the judge over' and he was summoned and came over. Says the chief 'This woman says she has no eyes, but claims to have ears. Well, I don't agree – she hasn't any ears, and she's quite mad. Let her go!' So the judge dismissed her and she went off home.

The malam heard about it and rose and went to her. 'Peace be upon you' says he. 'Welcome' she answered. 'I hear' he said, 'That God brought you out of that business. Where's my hundred thousand?' And she answered 'Not only do you make me pregnant, but now want a hundred thousand from me?' 'What!!' said the malam, 'me too?' 'Have I got any eyes?' she asked, and the malam said 'God's curse upon you, and may he prevent the return of your sight a thousand times.'

And he rose and went about his business. He went and told a friend, who said to him 'God showed you favour.* For whoever makes deep the hole of wickedness that he digs, will fall into it himself.† Don't you do it again!' And he answered 'I'll not again teach tricks to people so long as I live.' That's the end of that tale.

The Simple Minded Wife [^{III}/₁₆₂]

A man once had several wives, one of whom was a simple one. The husband fell ill, and his illness didn't leave him till he died in the simple wife's hut. When he was dead, she got up and took a knife and cut off his penis, complete with testicles, and hid them. Then she went and said to the other wives 'Come here, for your husband is dead.' They came and, finding it was true, burst out crying.

Everyone came along and found the wives crying; but the simple one was smiling. Then the people took up the corpse and buried it. They offered their condolences, saying 'May God give you patience.' And as they dispersed, they said 'That one wife has a brave nature, she bore it all without crying.'

At first, while the business of the death was with them and the compound was full of people, she had no opportunity to turn to what she had hidden safely away. Eventually, after three days had passed, she had the chance and went to her treasure, and found – that it had rotted. Then she dissolved into tears.

And everyone said 'That wife who was so brave before, that's her crying now – that's her voice.' And they came running, and when they reached her, found her with her hoard in front of her, crying and saying 'Alas! My husband is dead.' 'God's curse on you' they said, 'You're a stupid woman; so your bravery was baseless.' And she said 'I thought I hadn't suffered any loss; but now I see that I have.' That's the end.

---

* Because he didn't suffer anything worse?   † Proverb.

Another Simpleton* [$^{III}/_{163}$]

There was another simple woman lived with her husband. A famine came, and her husband just sat there without making any effort. Says she to him 'Hey you! The other husbands are all going and getting something to eat on credit, and you just sit there, while we die of hunger!' For her husband had nothing.

This angered him and he went off to where people were getting food on credit, and found some trading going on. He had no cash, but he took off his trousers and sold them and bought some corn. The corn wasn't more than a cap full.

He put it on his head and set off home, but on the way he got soaked by rain, so that even his penis shrunk into his body, leaving only a little of it outside. He reached home, put his foot on the smoothed floor of the hut, slipped and fell.

His wife came out and supported him and expressed her sorrow and concern for the exhausting day he had had. Then she led him into the hut and made him lie down, unable to take her mind off the condition of his penis. So her husband had a good rest.

She brought in the little cap with the corn in and asked 'Is this all you got?' 'Yes' he answered. 'And where has your penis disappeared to?' 'What do you think I bought the corn with?' he answered. Then she burst out crying, loudly for all to hear.

People gathered and found her saying 'This deal mustn't be, I won't agree.' They tried to calm her, but she kept saying 'It's too much!! To lose the penis for a cap full of corn!' 'You're right' they said, and turning to her husband 'Why did you make this deal?' 'She told me' he answered, 'to go and use what I could to buy corn; I had nothing else, so I sold my penis.' 'Well, go and cancel the deal' they said. 'But I can't walk' he said, 'Hunger has taken all my strength.' So they told her to make some gruel for him, so that he might recover sufficiently to go back.

In great haste she made the gruel and gave it to him. He drank it all down, his strength came back and his penis emerged again. He called her over and said 'Well, you've told me to go and cancel

* Cf. M. No. 49.

the deal – but isn't this the penis that you're used to?' Then she looked, saw that it was and gave a shrill cry of joy.

People came running up again and said to her 'One moment you make a scene, the next you're shrilling for joy.' Says she 'My husband didn't lose anything on the deal after all; that's why I've stopped making a scene, and why I'm making sounds of joy.' And the people dispersed, laughing.

———————

The Hunter, his Wife and her Lover* [III/166]

There was once a trapper of guinea-fowl, who would take out his trap regularly, catch three guinea-fowl and then return home. His wife would cook them, give him one and eat two herself. Filling herself up in this way, she grew huge.

Now there was a young fellow lived near them, a greedy fellow. He saw what was going on, and set about becoming the woman's lover. And whenever the trapper went off to trap, she would go over to the young man, and found great pleasure in him.

So when her husband brought back the three guinea-fowl, she would cook them, give her husband one, eat one herself, then taking the other, go and thump the *zana* fence. Her lover would jump up and come over, and she would hand it over to him, and he would go and eat it. Eventually her husband spotted what was going on and was very sore at it. So he got himself a cudgel and hid it away.

Previously he had gone trapping in the afternoon, but now he deliberately changed to the morning. He caught his three guinea-fowls, but didn't return with them till midday, and said to her 'Hurry up, so that you're finished before night falls.' So she made haste and cooked the guinea-fowls. It was nearly evening when the food was ready.

* Cf. J. p. 185.

Reaching the compound he played a trick on her. Says he 'Leave everything that you're doing, get some water boiling. I want to prepare some medicine to take to the chief's place.' She imagined that if he went off to the chief's place, she would have her opportunity. So she quickly put water on, and when it had boiled, he said to her 'Pour it out and give to me.' And she did so.

He took the water round behind the hut and struck the *zana* mats, in the spot where she would do so to hand the fellow his guinea-fowl. Hearing the sound, the young man rose and approached the spot. Then he held out a calabash over the top of the *zana*, and, as he did so, the hunter let him have all the water at once on his head. The other's skin peeled off and he fell to the ground in a dead faint. All without anyone else knowing.

He came back round to the front of the hut, and returned the calabash to her. 'Now you can finish getting your food ready in your own time' he said. She was overjoyed, thinking that she now had her chance.

He went out of the compound and round into the other's compound. When he got there, he saw the spot where he had thrown the water over him, and saw that he had crawled over into his hut. Then he squatted down just there with the cudgel in his hand.

His wife finished getting the food ready and picking up her lover's, came over and touched the fence. He rose and she passed the calabash over to him. He held out his hand and took it. 'Here's something for you' he said, and she straightened up as if to take it. Whereupon he struck her on the forehead with the cudgel, and she fell there, behind the hut.

Off he went and ate up his guinea-fowl; had a drink of water, and came home as usual. When he got there he found everyone wailing. 'What's happened?' said he, and his people said 'A very strange thing, you wife finished preparing the food, and went round outside her hut, and then suddenly fell down, crying. And we went and found her – with her forehead smashed in' 'Who did that?' he asked. 'We don't know' they answered. He asked her, but she couldn't speak.

Then he sat down and began to cry, and people came and offered him comfort. 'For shame' they said, 'To behave like a woman.' But he said 'My only wife – and someone goes and cracks her head –

374

and I don't know who it is!' And they went on offering comfort.

He spent the night in this state, refusing to eat.* Then he began giving his wife medicine and gradually the wound healed.

As for the other, the young fellow, no one saw him for some time. Midnight came and they said that they hadn't seen him all day. His mother told them to look in his hut, in case he was sleeping. They went into his hut and found him with his skin all peeled off. Then the whole compound began to wail [asking him] 'What happened to you?' But all the skin of his mouth was burnt and he couldn't speak. And so they treated him, until he recovered.

Now, where they farmed too was in one place, no distance apart. Came the hot season and they set out to sow. The trapper of guinea-fowls caught his three for his wife to cook, and then went off to sow, saying to her 'When you've finished, bring them to me on the farm.' She prepared the food and took it to him on the farm, and rose [to go].

He looked over at his neighbour, the young fellow, and said to him 'Young man, come over and help me eat this.' 'Who's that?' asked the woman. 'That young chap' her husband answered. 'Never' said she. 'He's never going to eat my food.' And the young man said 'If yours was the last food left in the world, I wouldn't eat it.' 'You bastard!' said she. 'Bastard yourself!' he answered.

The older man interposed, saying 'Whatever has brought you foul of each other?' The boy said 'She's not fit for me to eat her food.' 'And you're not fit to eat it' she answered, and the boy went off.

The older fellow ate up his guinea-fowl, without again asking her what was between them. Nor did he question the boy again.

And that's how it is – if you're going to play tricks, don't play them on an old man, who sees through them. End of story.

---

* Having just had a whole guinea-fowl.

375

The Mother and her Son [III/ 187]

A woman once had a son and she said 'Oh, what a handsome boy this son of mine is! I don't wish him to look on any girl, any woman but me.' And whenever God brought night, she would go into the hut, and lie incestuously with the boy. This happened regularly and the boy remained under the impression that it was his mistress. Presently the mother became pregnant, and when people asked her how she had become pregnant when she had no husband, she would put them off with a non-committal answer.

Presently the son, realising, said 'So it is my mother that I have been sleeping with! But we have done a very shameful thing.' Then he called his friend and told him that he was going to leave the town, for he felt that no one had ever done such a thing before. Then he took his trousers,* and went out of the town gate. His friend went with him some way, and then said 'May God bring us together again one day!'

He travelled till he came to another town, far away in the east. He kept asking people [what he should do], for he said 'I have made my mother pregnant.' 'Study the Book' was their answer. And he settled down and became a student, and God granted that he came to know the whole Book.

Meanwhile the mother had given birth to a girl, who grew rapidly and before long there she was, a maiden.

Some people were going off on a trading journey, and her mother gave her some money and put her in the care of the people. So they set off, but presently the woman to whom she had been entrusted died, it being God's will, on the road. And the man who was travelling with her said 'Well, girl, you may come and stay with me until God brings us to the end of our journey.' And the girl was with him until God brought them to a town. And when they got there, she had her first period (became adult).

Then the man, whom she was with, said 'See now, you are of age. Let us contrive to have you married. Then, even if you go

---

* This apparently unconnected remark, and his previous words, which seem rather in a vacuum (no *ya ce*) may indicate that something is missing.

home, your mother will rejoice at your coming.'* And the girl answered. 'Let it be as you will. I have no mother and no father – only you. Let it be as your heart bids.'

Word was brought to the son of a malam, saying that there was a girl to be married, and he thanked them for offering her to him, but said 'There is a young student in my compound – let her be given to him.' 'Very well' said the man.

The girl was told and said 'As you will', and the man said 'Well, today you will be put in henna.'† 'Very well' said the girl.

Then the girls of the town were collected and came to her. The midwife‡ was fetched; she put the girl in henna and they washed her. Says her 'father' 'You know, the marriage of travellers should be expedited.' 'When shall we take her to his compound?' they asked. 'Tonight' answered her 'father' 'If God spares us.' So they took the girl along and brought her to his compound and the young malam expressed his gratitude.§

They lived together for some two months, and the girl said 'You ought to come back with me and visit my parents. 'O.K.' said he, and they prepared some food for the journey.

The malam, in whose compound the young fellow lived, said 'You must hasten back, for it is nearly time for the rains to start.' 'Right' said the boy.

They set off from home, and after some days of travelling, without trouble, God brought them to the town where the girl's parents lived. The girl saw her mother and the mother looked and said 'But that's my son!' and she¶ expressed great surprise. That night she couldn't sleep for thinking of this matter, for it filled her mind.

Next day when it was light, she took her cloth and a gourd water-bottle, and went to the compound of her bondfriend. Then she told her what had happened saying that it was between them alone.

---

* ? I.e. 'will rejoice the more.'

† I.e. prepared for the marriage ceremony.

‡ I do not think it is usual for a midwife to be involved in this ceremony. The spelling *unguwanzoma* (for *ungozoma*) may be folk etymology or may indicate an earlier stage of the word. There are a number of linguistic and stylistic peculiarities in this story (e.g. *waushe* (for *yaushe*) three lines on.)

§ This was a 'marriage of alms' (see BABA).

¶ This apparently refers to the mother, not the daughter.

And the mother went on to say 'Only when I'm dead – no, even when I'm dead, you mustn't let anyone hear of it.' And she went out saying 'Come and see me on my way.' And her friend came with her and travelled a long way accompanying her. Again the mother said 'For God's sake, for the sake of the Prophet, for the sake of the Lord that made us, don't tell anyone!' 'Very well' said the other. They said goodbye to each other with a 'May God bring us together again.'

But the friend remembered all that she had been told, intending to go and tell it. She thought over what she had been told, recalling every word of it and said 'Pouf! Bondfriendship doesn't mean a thing, does it?' Then the Lord God – even as she was saying this – she vanished, and turned into a shrew-mouse!

Well, that was that, but people say 'For this reason, if you have friend, and if you are not very close to him – don't tell him too much.' That's all, that one's finished.

PART V

DILEMMA TALES

These end with a question to the audience, usually 'What would you do here?' They are related in many ways, and easily converted to the Cases at Law, which follow in the in the next section.

The Digger-Out of Ground Squirrels and his Son and the Arab* [$^I/_{29}$]

There was once a man who did no other job but dig out ground-squirrels. And one day he and his son went out to dig some up. Says he to his son 'You stop up the back entrances, and I'll dig 'em out' and the father set about digging out the ground-squirrel's hole; whereupon the ground-squirrel came out where the son was and made off. Then the father hit his son with the handle of his hoe and knocked him out.

A little later up comes an Arab, who was taking a stroll in the evening, and he saw the boy who was just coming to his senses. Now this Arab had never had any children. And he picked up the boy and tok him home. His nostrils were full of ants, and the Arab blew them away and had him bathed in hot water. And the boy recovered completely. And he put on him a black and white gown, and a heavily indigoed gown as well and embroidered trousers and a turban twenty cubits long and twenty strips wide.

Now the rich merchants' sons used to ride out and gallop in the race-course, and this Arab had a saddle ornamented in gold and silver brought out, with brass, Tripolitanian stirrups, and all the other trappings for a horse. Then he told the boy to get on, and said to him 'When you get to the racecourse, whatever you see the other riders do – you do it too!' So the boy joined the rich merchants' sons and went along with them.

Then there arose some arguments among the people, when it was asked whose son he was. Some said 'He's the Arab So-and-So's son' and others said 'No, he's not.'

After this, when the merchants' sons got home, each one said to his father 'There's an Arab who has a son who has more finery than we have.' And their fathers answered 'No, it's not his son. That's false.' But they added 'All the same, if he is his son, to-morrow when you go riding with him – let each one give away his horse and equipment before he comes home. Then we'll see!'

So they went for their ride, and afterwards they gave away their horses. And he, before he went home, he too gave away his horse.

* Cf. TR. No. 67 and No. 68; also R. No. 19; F. p. 90 D.; No. 109

After this the merchants gave their sons other horses, each worth a million cowries, to ride, and told them 'When you go riding, before you come home, cut down your horses!' And the other boy was given a horse worth ten thousand* to ride. Away they went. And when they had had their gallop, each one took his sword and cut down his horse. Then the boy, without even troubling to take the saddle off, cut down his horse and went off home. And they said 'Did you see? He cut down his horse' and again 'Well! the boy didn't even take off the horse's equipment; he left it there'. Then people said 'So it seems he is his son after all!'

Time passed and the Muslim festival was at hand. In the morning, the usual mounted procession took place, and in all the town there wasn't a youth whose horse was fitted out to touch his. And as they were coming back from the place of prayer they [passed among] the common people who had come into the town for the prayers, from the country.

Well, it happened that the father of the boy, the digger-out of ground-squirrels, came to the house of the Arab, where his son was. When he saw him, he exclaimed 'Hey! Get down from that horse – it's bloody well not your father's, you rascal! Look at your brothers there – one of them has killed nine ground-squirrels, one of them ten, and you – here are you in dissipation and idleness!' And the Arab said to him 'Please, please keep it to yourself! Here – take your son!'

And in the evening, he chose two horses and saddled them up picked out two gowns, a black one and a white one, and gave them to the boy's father. And he gave him twenty thousand cowrie shells and provisions for the journey. Then Arab too mounted, and the boy also.

They passed out of the town and came into the bush. Then the Arab produced a sword and gave it to the boy, saying 'Now! Either me or your father – cut down one of us!'

Well that's the question† – the Arab, who had given him so many things? Or his own father, who had struck him unconscious because of the ground-squirrel? Which should he kill?

* Or 'ten million' if *zambar* is understood (which is probable).
† Cf. the end of III/72.

Iblis*, the Girl and Her Young Man† [III/74]

A youth once saw a maiden and told her that he loved her; and she saw him and told him the same. And the young fellow went and picked up his mat, and took the girl by the hand and they went off into the bush. There the boy spread out the mat and invited the girl to sit; and so they sat and chatted.

Along comes Iblis, siezes the boy and kills him, and cuts off his head. And there was the girl sitting on the mat lamenting.

Meanwhile her mother and father were searching for their daughter; and the boy's mother and father were searching for him. An old woman told them where they should go to find their children. 'Thank-you' said they, and went off along the road. There they found their son killed, with his head taken off. At this the boy's parents too began to lament.

Up comes Iblis again. When he gets there he makes a river of fire, and a river of water and a river of black-hooded cobras; and bringing a land-monitor, he put it in the river of cobras.

Then he went up to where the girl's mother and her father, and the boy's mother and his father, and the girl herself were. Says Iblis to them 'Would you like me to help you over your son and bring him back to life?' 'Yes' they answered. 'Very well' he said, 'You, the boy's mother, must go into the river of fire, and then into the river of water, and then into the river of cobras, and go and seize the land-monitor and bring it out – there it is over there in the river of cobras.' But the boy's mother answered 'No! I'm not going into a river of fire to be burnt up; I'm not going into the river of water to be swallowed up; I'm not going into the river of cobras, to be thoroughly bitten.' Says Iblis 'Had you gone and captured the land-monitor and brought it out, I'd have helped you over your son.' Whereupon the girl said 'Is that so? If that land-monitor is captured and brought here, will the boy come to life?' 'Yes' said Iblis.

Up jumped the girl, and into the river of fire. She swam until she was through it. Into the river of water, and swam and swam till she was through that. Then into the river of cobras; and pushing

* A devil.   † Cf. TR. No. 65.

aside the cobras, she seized the land-monitor. Back she came through the rivers, and gave the land-monitor to Iblis.

Then said Iblis 'So! So you've got the land-monitor for me?' And the boy came to life and stood up. Then Iblis said again 'Now – this land-monitor – if it is slaughtered, the boy's mother will die; but if it isn't slaughtered, the girl's mother will die.'

Well then now – is the boy going to slaughter the land-monitor, so that his own mother dies? Or on the other hand, will he spare it, so that the girl's mother dies? Which of the two will he choose do you think?

The Chief's Son, the Poor Man's Son and the Chief's Daughter [$^{II}/_{43}$]

There was once the son of a chief who heard tell of the daughter of another chief and set off to visit her.

And as he travelled, he met a young fellow. Says he 'Young fellow, I'd like you to come with me, for I'm off to seek a wife.' 'Oh no' said the other, 'for I have a father who has neither gown nor trousers nor loincloth; and this leather loincloth that you see me wearing is all that we have between us, my father and I. If my father is going out from our hole in the baobab tree, then he takes it and puts it on; and I do, when I'm going out' 'Where is your father?' asked the chief's son. 'Over there, in the hole in the baobab tree.' 'Take me over. Let's go.'

And off they went, the young fellow leading, till they came to the hole in the baobab tree. When the boy got there, he said to his father 'Dad – look, as I was taking a walk, I met the son of a chief, who said he wanted me to go with him to seek a wife. But I answered that I must come and tell you first; and hear whatever you had to say about it.' 'By all means go along with him' answered his father. And the chief's son said 'Take the leather loincloth off and give it to your father.'

And the chief's son had a kitbag opened and a gown taken out, and trousers, and a turban, and a cap, and a sword, and a sword-sling, and all these together were given to the other. And he had him shaved and bathed too.

And so they took the road and travelled till they reached the other town. And word was brought to the chief's daughter that she had visitors. So they were taken to lodgings, where they put up. And she had *tuwo* prepared, and *fura,* and three rams were slaughtered, and chickens too. In short, food of the best was prepared and taken to them. And then the chief's daughter too rose and came to them.

But when she got there, her heart went out to the servant of the chief's son – he whose father lived in the hole in the tree. And she spoke and said that he was the one she loved. 'No, no!' says he, 'I wouldn't dare. See, here's my master.' 'No' she answered, '*You're* the one I love.' But again he protested that he and his father had nothing, but lived in a hole in a baobab tree, and added 'Even the clothes that I'm wearing were given me by the chief's son here.' 'Oh' says she, 'is that all?'

And she sent home to her father's compound, asking for two kitbags, one with a gown, and one with trousers; and she sent too for a turban. And her wishes were conveyed to her father, who fetched all that she had asked for and handed it over, and it was brought to her. Then said she 'Take those things off, and return them to him; and take these and put them on. 'Very well' he answered and did as she had said, and collecting the chief's son's clothes, returned them to him.

And the chief's son set off home, leaving the son of the man with the leather loincloth. For the chief's daughter had decided that it was he that she loved. Then she went and told her father, saying 'Dad, I want to be married today.' 'Very well' said he, and so they were married.

Time passed and her father died. His estate was duly divided and she inherited, for he had no sons, she being his only child. And she inherited much wealth. Her mother left the chief's compound, and had a separate compound built for herself. Then the girl said to her husband 'Where is your father? Let someone go and fetch him, and let him and my mother be married.' And he answered 'He's back there in the hole in the baobab tree.'

They they went and fetched him, and when they returned, the marriage duly took place. And so they lived for some time.

But after a while there came a day, when the elder couple had a quarrel and he knocked her down, striking out one of her eyes. Then said the girl to her husband 'Look – your father has quarrelled with my mother and knocked her eye out. If you value our marriage, you'll go and put out one of your father's eyes. If you don't here's your leather loincloth, and you and your father can go back to your hole in the baobab tree – that's if you don't put his eye out. But if you do, then let our marriage continue.' Well, here was a nice problem! He had been quite destitute. If he put out his own father's eye, he might continue to live with his wife; but if he didn't then he must go with his father back to the hole in the baobab tree, whence they had come!

Two Youths, Two Girls and the One who Thought he could Frighten Them [II/44]

Here's another. Two young men set off for a walk, and going to another town, collected two girls and came home with them.

Now having become acquainted with the girls, they soon made a regular practice of going for them and fetching them home. And their elders said to each other 'Those boys go off every night and fetch home the girls – what shall we do to scare them?' And one of them said '*I'll* scare them.'

Now there was a big tamarind tree, underneath which the path passed, and it had many branches. And the man, who had said that he would scare them, went at night and climbing the tree got on to a branch that hung over the path, and sat there. Presently along came the two boys and the girls, one boy leading and one behind, with the girls in between.

They passed under the tamarind tree, and the leading youth and the two girls went on. Now both the boys had a plait on their heads,* and the fellow up the tree put his hand out and grabbed the plait of the boy at the back, and held it fast. The boy stopped still, but didn't say anything.

The other went on with the two girls, not knowing that his friend had had his plait caught and held. And they reached home. But when he called out to his friend, there was no answer. And one of the girls said 'Oh, he stopped, and afterwards never caught up with us.' 'Was it far back that he stopped?' asked the boy. 'Yes, a fair distance' she answered. 'Go into my hut and sit down, both of you' said the boy, 'and I'll go after him, to see if there is anything the matter.'

Back he went, following the path till he came to the foot of the tamarind tree, and there was his friend. Says he 'How come? We went all the way home and missed you. Is all well?' 'Put your hand on my head and you'll see.' Then the other felt and found that his friend was held by his plait and said 'What the —! You never told me that something had hold of your head.' And again 'Whatever it is – devil or man – we'll have it out with him now!'

Then he took off his gown, hitched up his trousers, went to the trunk of the tree, and taking hold of it began to climb. He caught hold of the man up the tree, and they were about to fall to the ground, when the man said 'Here! What the —! I'm —' and he mentioned his name. But the young man said 'Oh no! Whatever would bring him here at this time? You're lying.' Whereupon the fellow let go of the boy's plait, and they both came down. Well, now – which of them d'ye think showed the most determination? That's all.

———————

* The tuft on the male head is referred to a number of times in TATS. In recent years among Muslim Hausa this style has been very unusual. At F. p. 88 we are told that a sharif is privileged to have one on the crown, and a budding malam one in the front; but that after the British occupation these distinctions were much disregarded and many kept the tuft as a receptacle for coin.

The Beautiful Maiden, the Five Young Men and the Chief* [II/₅8]

Here's another. There was once a maiden who had no peer for beauty. Whenever she came to where the others were dancing, the boys couldn't take their eyes off her. She lived alone with her mother, and the fame of her beauty spread far and wide.

And there were five young men who swore that they would go regularly to where the dancing was, just to watch her; when she went there, they would follow, and when she left, they would leave.

This went on for some time, until the chief of another town heard about her. Then he sent horsemen with instructions to go and seize her and bring her to him. So his horsemen set out and reached her town, where the girl had just reached the space where the children danced and played. The five youths were there watching her, as she played.

Whereupon up rode the chief's horsemen, and seizing her, set their horses to the gallop and rode off.

Then the five said to each other 'Alas! She whom we came to watch has been seized and taken away' and again 'Well, what can we do?' and they went back to their homes.

But the girl's mother came and asked them about it, and they told her 'Oh, some horsemen came and took her away.' 'Is it even so?' says she. 'Yes' they replied, and she went off home.

But the young men decided to put their heads together and go and seek the girl who had been taken away.

And one of them spoke up and said 'I'll undertake, when we set forth, that I'll get food for us to eat at any town we stop at'. And another said 'And I'll get mats for us to sleep on.' And the third said 'As for me, when we enter a town, I'll show you a trick that will get us lodging.' And the next promised that when they had got into the town and found somewhere to stay, he would steal back the girl. And the last said that when they had taken back the

* Strictly, not a Dilemma Tale, because of the last few lines. It is perhaps a Solved Dilemma.

girl and left the town, even if a thousand horsemen came after them, he would fight them. And so they decided to set off.

So they took the road and travelled till they came to a town. And the first youth told lies to the people of the town and quickly got them some food. And the second went into the town and borrowed mats and brought them back to them, enough for all to lie on. And these two – one getting *tuwo* for them and one getting mats – continued their work until they came close to the town where the girl was.

Now they had gourds, staves and little calabashes, and when they came to the outskirts of the town, the youth who had promised that when they got to the town he would get them lodgings, told them to close their eyes. They did so and made their way to the entrance of the chief's compound; and going into the mosque, they all sat down. 'Hullo!' said someone, 'here are some visitors, blind men. I wonder where they are from?' And another said 'Go and tell the chief that five visitors have arrived, blind men.' So someone went and told the chief that there were five men, all blind, in the mosque, and the chief commanded that they be summoned to him.

Then the cunning one told his friends to open their eyes, and they did so. And the messenger from the chief came to fetch them, saying 'Hey there! You blind men, come along!' So they rose and went, their eyes open, in front of the chief. And the chief asked them 'You there – what's brought you here?' 'May the chief's days be prolonged' they answered, 'We – well, we heard of your name; and we heard the name of your town. So we felt we must come and see you. We were blind, but when we reached your town and were sitting in your mosque, our eyes were opened. So, you see, we have to thank God for your town; and we thank his Messenger, and indeed we thank your town; for in truth we travelled for forty-four days before we reached your town.' Then the chief ordered that they should be taken to lodgings. So they were given lodgings and set down all that they were carrying.

Then the thieving one made a cloud of smoke and got up and went into the chief's compound – in daylight, without anyone seeing him. But the girl saw him, and he asked her 'Where's your hut?' 'There it is.' 'Where's the chief's hut?' 'Over there.' 'Well' he said, 'When night comes, I'm coming to steal you away, so that we can go back to our town.' 'Good' says she. 'And' he said, 'Get out the things you want and pack them up.' 'O.K.' said she.

Night came and the thief went and entered the compound. He found the girl lying beside the chief. So he roused her, and they went out, and so to his lodgings, where they found his friends. Then they all rose and set off, got out of the town and travelled until dawn broke, all without the chief knowing anything.

But as they travelled, the chief woke – and saw no girl! Then he sent to the compound where the visitors were – and they had gone. Then says the chief 'Saddle up at once! Sound the drum for mounting!' The drum was beaten, everyone mounted his horse and set off at a gallop, and presently they overtook the fugitivies.

Then the youth that had promised to fight them, fought them and fought them and fought them, and defeated them and routed them completely. And so the five got home and took the girl back to her mother. 'Mother' said they, 'here's your daughter.' And her mother said 'Now – out of these five young men, which shall I choose for you and which reject?' And turning to the girl, 'Choose a husband for yourself from among these five youths.' 'Hm' said the girl. 'Well – this one, wherever we went and stayed, cheated to get *tuwo*. I'll not marry him. And this one's a liar, I won't marry him – in case one day, if I married him, he goes and tells a lie about you* and gets you arrested. As for this one—well, I'm not marrying a thief, in case he goes and steals something, and people say that it's for my benefit. And this fighter – I won't marry him. For if I do, one day he'll be practising his profession and get killed – and I'll be left in mourning. But this fellow – the one who borrowed mats, wherever we stopped for the night, and next morning took them back – he's the one who'll suit me best.' And so it was. End of story.

---

* Lit., but I suspect she means 'me'.

The Chief's Daughter and her Husband and the Chief's Son [$^{II}/_{63}$]

Here's another tale. The son of a certain chief was married to the daughter of a former chief, and he had a horse, a light grey one.

They had been married for some time, and the husband, before entering the hut was in the habit of saying 'Grey horse, grey horse, you're worth more than the women of today, these modern women.' Then, when he got into the hut, his wife would say to him 'You can kill that grey horse, before you approach me.' 'Don't stir yourself' said he, 'But I'm not killing the grey.'

This went on for some time, until one day another chief's son heard of it. Now he also had a grey horse. And he put some gowns together, into a kitbag, and mounting his grey horse, set off. When he got to the town he put up at the compound of an old woman. And he asked her 'Old woman, what's the news?' 'Such as about what?' says she. About the chief's son and the old chief's daughter' said he. 'Oh that' said she' 'Yes, they were married. But he hasn't yet slept with her. For she says he must kill his grey horse; but, on the other hand, he sings his grey horse's praises without fail every night.' 'Is that so?' said he, 'Tell me, what sort of gown does he wear, this chief's son?' 'A black and blue check gown, embroidered trousers,* a dark blue turban are what he wears.'

Well, that day the young husband was away to visit the compound of a friend of his, and sat there with him, chatting, late.

But this other chief's son went into his compound, having put on a black and blue gown, embroidered trousers and a dark blue turban. And as he went to her hut, he said 'Grey horse, you're worth more than the women of today, these modern women.' And she, as usual, said 'You can kill that grey horse, if you want to come to me.' 'Is that all?' said he. 'Yes' she said. And he went and drew his sword and slew the grey. So the grey died.

Later that night the chief's son returned home, and entered the compound; and there he found his horse, killed. Says he 'It's someone who had a grudge against the grey has killed him.' And

* She mentions the particular embroidery pattern – *gidan tara*.

his wife said to him 'You've lost both ways – you've lost your horse and you've lost what was yours by rights.' 'Hm. I see' said he. 'But don't say a word' said she, 'just keep quiet. I'll take revenge for you – don't you disturb yourself.' Then she got herself a razor, and put it into a basket, and collected some cloths and put them in the basket; and in went a little hide box of antimony, and a mirror, and her cola-nuts and her tobacco-flowers. Then she took the basket and gave it to one of her girls to carry for her.

And she set off along the road, enquiring the way till she reached the town where he was. And there she found him together with his courtiers. Said they 'Well!! *There's* a girl! Is she married?' 'No' said one, and they agreed that she couldn't be married. And then another of them said 'But she has been married before.' Says the chief's son 'I want her. Take her to my compound.' And away they went with her and took her to the compound of the chief's son.

The sun set, and the chief's son returned to his compound. And when night fell, he threw himself on the girl. And when they had finished, he was overcome by sleep. Whereupon the girl got up quietly and taking her razor, seized his penis and cut it off. The young fellow started awake and leaping up, tried to stand, but fell back; and again a second time, but again fell back, and so died. But she put the penis into her basket, and gave it to her girl to carry for her. And so they once again took the road, and made their way home.

Meanwhile the young men who were friends of the chief's son entered his compound and came up and found him dead. So they went and told the chief. And the chief summoned his horsemen, saying 'Seeing that there is no horse in the whole town so fast as that of the boy that has been killed, go quickly and tell his younger brother to saddle up the grey, and let him get quickly after the fugitives, before the others come up with them. And when he catches up with her, let him take his sword and slay her.' 'Very well' said his younger son.

And mounting the horse, he galloped and galloped until he had overtaken them. Now they had reached close to where there was a deleb-palm. He drew his sword to kill her, but said to himself 'Surely a girl like this ought not to be killed?' and again 'Look, girl, let us lie together, you and I, and then I'll release you by some other road, before my friends catch us up.' But the girl answered with spirit 'No! What, right here, out in the open! No, I certainly won't lie with you. I'm afraid you'll just have to kill me. But' she went on, 'if you climb that palm-tree and cut down some of its large leaves – look, there are three of them up there – and then come down, why we can spread them out, and then you can lie with me.' 'My – is that all?' said he, and proceeded to take off his gowns, his trousers, his turban, until he was wearing only a loin-cloth, and carrying his sword with which to cut off the leaves. Then he climbed the palm tree and reached where the leaves were. But when she saw him make his first slash, she picked up her slave-girl and put her on the horse; and herself putting foot to stirrup mounted too. And so she spurred the horse and escaped. And there was the young man, and all he could do was say 'Come back, please, please come back, for God's sake and the Prophet's. I won't kill you. Only give me back my horse!'

So there he was, squatting up the tree, when the other horsemen came up, right to where his horse had stood. And one of them said 'Hey, look! Here are hoof marks where a horse stood, and a girl's close by. Perhaps he killed her.' But another said 'Not likely! For if he had killed her, we should have seen blood here–and there isn't any.' Whereupon one of them lifted his head and saw him – squatting there up in the tree – and said to the others 'Well, for— look, there he is, up in the palm tree!' 'Well!' said the others in surprise, 'However did you come to be in that position?' 'Well – you see – she took my horse' he answered. Then the others all said 'That girl's not to be trifled with! We'd better not go any farther.' So there they stopped, and suggested to him that he got down. That done, they made one of his brother's servants dismount, and gave him the horse. He got up, and so they returned home.

But the girl went on, and so returned to her husband. 'There you are' she said, 'I said I would take revenge for you, didn't I? Look – I've done so, I've cut off his penis, and I've brought you his horse, which no one could distinguish from yours. They're like twins.'

Well now, which of the three of them would you say got done – the girl, her husband the chief's son, or the other chief's son? And that's the end of that one.

393

Abdu, his Father and his Rich Father-in-law [$^{III}/_{72}$]

There was once a man had three sons. His eldest son was called Abdu. Now Abdu went and got together money so that he could marry. Whereupon his father took the money away and used it for the marriage of Abdu's younger brother. But Abdu didn't feel sore at this – at least he did, but only just a little.

Once again Abdu went off and got together money so that he could marry. Once again Abdu's father took the money away and used it for the marriage of his other, youngest brother. At this Abdu was very upset and he decided to go off and seek his fortune. So he set off along the road and began to walk.

He reached another town and settling there, set to acquire some more money. Then he sought the hand of the daughter of a rich man. The latter favoured his suit and arranged the marriage. And in due course the couple had a child, a boy.

Well, the rich man, Abdu, the girl and the child set off, walking, and presently coming to a tamarind tree stopped and were resting there – when up comes Abdu's father.

Abdu's father goes up to them, takes hold of the hand of the little boy, and dashes the infant against the tree, killing him.

Thereupon the rich man seized Abdu's father and the two began to struggle, struggling till they both fell to the ground. Abdu drew a knife. Then said the rich man to Abdu 'Give me the knife, so that I can stab him.' And Abdu's father said 'Hey, Abdu, don't you give him that knife, to kill your father with!'

Well? Which of the two was Abdu to choose? Should he give the knife to the rich man, or to his father? You've heard the situation. Which of the two people should he give the knife to, to kill the other? That's all.

The Husband, his Wife and her Lover [III/69]

There was a man and his wife, and the man had a load of salt. Now the wife's lover was by the edge of the water, which lay in front of them.

They came up, the husband leading, the wife behind. Her lover was at the edge of the water washing himself.

The husband girt up his loincloth.* Whereupon his wife's lover, from where he was washing, says to the woman 'Well, just fancy my dear! I never knew what rough buttocks your husband had! Just let me rub a little mud on them.' And taking some mud, he rubbed it on the buttocks of his mistress' husband.

And so, what people ask is this: should the man with the salt throw his load of salt into the water and fight his wife's lover – or should he ignore him? Well, there you are – that's the sort of thing.

The Hunter, his Wife
and the Chief's Son [III/112]

There was once a hunter, who had no other occupation but to go out into the bush hunting. A chief's son had cast his eyes on the hunter's wife and would come and commit adultery with her. This would happen regularly whenever the hunter was away in the bush.

Moreover whenever he came to her, the chief's son would say to the woman 'How's that damned rascal of a husband of yours?', and the woman would answer 'Now then! My husband's worth more than your father.' Then he would say 'What!! Do you mention your husband and my father in the same breath?' To which she would reply 'Well, I don't know your father, but I know my husband.'

* To wade through.

395

They were talking thus, when her husband arrived back from the bush, and the chief's son said to her 'Now here's your husband come back from the bush. So what's to do?' Disgusted she said 'You useless coward, get up! You'll see.' And again 'You squat down over there.' And the chief's son squatted down, whereupon she took a mat and covered him over.

Then she said to her husband 'Man of my house, listen – I was with the wife of your elder brother, and someone came and told us that the meat you kill and bring home – that in fact you don't do so, but someone gives it to you.' 'Who says so?' he asked, and she said 'That's what was said to us. But I think that – do you see that mat there? – well, if you shoot at it, and your arrow doesn't go right through it (?), I shall know that the meat you bring home is given to you.' But he answered 'For shame! Woman of my house, I'm not shooting at that mat, sending an arrow right through it (?).' But she said 'Well anyway, take your bow and your arrow, and shoot at it for me to see. Then we can all relax.' He still wouldn't, and she again pressed him to shoot at the mat.

Then he picked up his bow and arrow. At which there came a diarrhoeic sound from the chief's son. The hunter strung (?) his bow, set (one end) on the ground, and braced his foot against it.* Then he said 'Woman of my house, have a look and see what's there.' Then he drew the bow till the bowstring reached his chest – and let it go. She said 'I swear that if you don't shoot that mat, I'll no longer be your wife.' 'Do you mean that?' he asked. 'Yes' said she.

Then he took an arrow and put it in the bow, and drew, to shoot at the mat – whereupon there came an even longer and more lavatorial noise from the chief's son – he had, in fact, excreted in his trousers! 'Well done, man of my house!' said the hunter's wife, 'Now please just shoot that mat.' But he answered 'No. Woman of my house, don't make me become the cause of burning down the town! For look – if I shoot through that mat, it will pierce through the walls of ten huts, and the whole town will catch fire.' But she said 'Look, you know my father has a hundred slaves, and my mother has fifty slaves. Please – just shoot the mat.' And once more came a plop from the chief's son.

* The Hausa is rather cryptic here, and would seem to imply a longer bow than is general now.

Then the hunter's wife went and lifted off the mat, and there was the chief's son squatting, his whole body stinking of his excrement.

Then the hunter's wife said 'Man of my house, I thank you. For you have managed to cause the chief's son to foul his own trousers.' And turning to the latter, she said 'Chief's son, get up and go home.' And he rose and set off home. And that was that. Well – which of them all played the worst trick on one of the others? That's all.

The Maiden, the Two Young Men and the Lion* [III/114]

There were once two young men who went to visit a girl, just one girl; and they came home with her. On their way they passed through the bush, each of them with two spears.

A lion waylaid them. Whereupon the girl fell down to the ground, saying that her stomach was paining her. The lion leapt at them, and the first youth threw his spear at the lion, but the lion dodged and the spear fell to the ground. So he threw his second spear at the lion, and that too fell to the ground.

So the second young fellow, in his turn, stepped forward and threw a spear at the lion; but it fell to the ground without hitting the lion. Then, taking his other spear he threw that too, but again missed the lion, and it fell to the ground. So all their spears were used up; they'd thrown them at the lion, and hadn't hit him.

Then one of the two youths said to the other 'Hurry up! Run home, and in my mother's hut, at the head of the bed, you'll find some spears. Bring them, and get some water in a calabash; and bring some potash too.' Off went the boy, fetched the spears, the potash and the water, and brought them back.

Meanwhile the other young fellow leapt at the lion, and after a struggle, threw him, and taking his knife cut his throat. Then he

* Cf. R. No. 15.

397

lifted the lion into a squatting position, and the girl got up and came over, and lay down beside the lion. The youth getting behind the mane and hiding.

Presently the other youth returned with the spears, the water and the potash, and reaching the spot where he had left them, failed to see them. He went on a little, and came upon the lion crouching there, with the girl in front of him. Says he 'So that was his trick on me was it? To go off and run away, and leave the lion to kill someone else's daughter! Very well then, I can but die here.' And throwing away his spears and his little calabash of water and the potash, he threw himself full tilt at the lion. He grappled it – and the lion fell over. And up got the girl, laughing; and the other boy too rose from behind the mane.

Well then – which of the two, the boy who killed the lion, or the other boy who went and fetched the spears and the little calabash of water and the potash – which of the two of them showed the greater pluck?

The Four Champions* [^{III}/127]

The Horny Head champion,† the Penis champion, the Wind-Breaking champion and the Testicles champion set off on a journey together and came to a town, where they lodged in the compound of the chief of the town. Then bundles of corn [to feed them] were duly issued from the chief's compound – but the town had nowhere to thresh it!

Then the Horny Head said 'May the chief's life be prolonged! Here are we, and yet they're looking for somewhere to thresh! Let them come and do it on my head!' So they came and undid the bundles on Horny Head's head.

But then arose the problem of a piece of wood with which to

* Cf. II/96. Were it not for the last paragraph this would classify as a Tall Story.

† In his dictionary, Bargery, a doctor, suggests a scalp disease (impetigo?) for *kora*. It is also the horny excrescence on a guinea-fowl's head.

thresh the corn, and Penis said 'May the chief's life be prolonged! Here we are now, and yet they're looking for something to thresh with! Just give me a bit of room and you'll see!' And pulling out his penis, he began threshing, and presently the corn was threshed.

But there was no wind, and word was brought to the chief that, though the corn was threshed, there was no wind and so winnowing was out of the question. Then said the Wind-Breaker 'May the chief's life be prolonged! Here are we, and yet they're looking for wind!' And he unveiled his anus, and let rip. And all the chaff was blown away, leaving just the grain.

But they had no skin bag in which to put the grain, so Testicles said 'May the chief's life be prolonged! Here are we, and yet they're looking for a container for the grain!' and opening his scrotum he said 'Bring the grain and pour it in here.' And they did so, and so he carried the corn home.

All right, among the four of them that exercised his special gift, which was the champion? Horny Head? Or Penis? Or Wind-Breaker? Or Testicles? Let's hear who was the greatest, for each of them exercised his speciality.

A Source of Dispute for Hausa Youths [^{III}/ xII]

Here's something the Hausa tell. A man, they say, once bought a mare for two hundred [thousand] cowries, but at the same time he had sent others to arrange his marriage to a maiden. But she, the girl, had another man who had also come to marry her.

Now the first man – if he marries her – this mare of his, the one he paid two hundred thousand for, is going to die; but if he doesn't marry her, the mare won't die.

Well that's the point at issue. One says 'Better let the mare die, but complete his marriage arrangements.' But another will say 'Better for his mare to live, not die.' Well, you've heard that argument.

The Man, his Womenfolk, the Well and the Soldier [III/169]

A man was once on a (trading) journey with his mother, his younger sister, his wife and his wife's mother. They had travelled some way and the heat of the sun made them very thirsty. Reaching the foot of a tree, they sat down.

The husband looked out and saw what seemed to be a well, and said to his sister 'Go and see if there is water in that well. If so, draw some and bring it.' She went and peered over the edge of the well, and one of her eyes fell out, down into the well. She held on to the other one and squatted down there.

A little time went by, and she hadn't returned, so the wife said 'Let me go and see what's happening to that girl.' She went over and found her squatting there. Says she 'What's made you squat there without drinking water? Isn't there any?' And going up, she peered into the well – and one of her eyes fell into the well. Then she too squatted down there.

Next, the man's mother* said 'What's making them take so long?' and she went after them. When she got there she asked them what had caused them to squat down there like that. 'Isn't there any water?' she added. And she peered down into the well – and one of her eyes dropped down into the well. Then she took hold of the other one and squatted down.

Finally the man's mother went after them, saying 'What can have delayed them like this?' She asked them 'What's made you all squat down here? Isn't there any water?' She peered down the well – and one of her eyes fell out into the well.

More time passed, and the man said 'Well! This is very strange! Can all be well? Just let me go after them and see.' He did so, and when he got near the well, he said 'What's the matter with you, that you are all sitting there like that?' His wife tried to turn him back with her hand, but he took no notice and peered into the well, and one of his eyes fell down into it. Holding on to the other

* From the context, it must be 'mother-in-law'. Perhaps *mijin* is an interpolation.

one, he too squatted down. And there they all were, moaning, with one eye each.

Presently a foot-soldier came upon them out of the bush, and the man saw him. The soldier too saw them and came towards them. 'Stop there, my friend, till I get you' said the man. He obeyed, and the man came up to him, still holding his eye. Says he 'I've stopped you to prevent you coming to this well. I, my mother, my mother-in-law, my wife and my younger sister, all of us now have only one eye each, from peering into the well.' 'Really?' said the soldier, 'Then you couldn't have heard about this well. There's a jinn in it.' 'I didn't know' said the other. Says the soldier 'If I go into the well and fetch out your eyes, may I take one of them?' 'Yes' said the man.

Down went the soldier into the well, which was more than a hundred cubits deep. But presently he emerged with all five eyes. He handed the man four, and put one in his pocket and went off. The husband took one and replaced his own.

That left three. Well, who would you give those three to? Who would you *not* give them to? People argue about this.

And that is the origin [of the saying that] if you want something don't be in too much of a hurry to make an offer for it.

The Man, his Wife, his Mother and his Mother-in-law† [III/170]

A man was once going along with his wife, his mother and his wife's mother – four of them. And as they walked, thirst seized them, so that they were nearly dead with it. They came to a well, but had no bucket.

So they wanted to devise some way in which they drink the water. The wife's mother said 'Let me go in. You, mother of my son-in-law, hold on to my foot. If I reach the water, I will draw some. If I don't reach it, your son can hold on to your foot. If we

† Cf. last story.

401

still don't reach it, my daughter can hold on to her husband's foot, and then we can draw water and drink.' And so they did.

And there the girl was, all alone, holding on to her husband's foot. Then she heard a splash, and asked her husband, 'What did I hear that sounded like something falling?' Says he 'I think it was your mother, slipped from my mother's grasp and fallen into the well.' 'No matter' said she, 'Loose hold of your mother and let them both go. Then I'll pull you out and we can be on our way. If you refuse, I'll let you all go and go off on my own.' Well, what would *you* do?

The Man in the Latrine
and the One with the Stone [^{III}/188]

There was once in a compound a latrine that was full up with ordure and a man went along to it to excrete, not knowing that the top was rotten. He sat down forcibly and it caved in, and he fell in, up to his chin.

Along comes an enemy of his, and when he gets there, sees him in it and says 'I'll have my revenge.' Then he picks up a big stone and throws it. Well, there was the fellow, in the faeces, and the stone was coming straight for his forehead.

Well, should he duck down into it – or stay upright? Which would be better? Some say he would be better to duck, others that he would be better to keep still. They are still arguing, and we still haven't found who's right.

A Variant [^{III}/XIII]

A man once went to the latrine. When he got there, he squatted down – and fell into the pit. He fell, not prone but upright. Now it chanced that the pit was deep, so that the ordure came right up to his chin. And, before he realised it, another man had picked up a stone to throw it at his head. And then – there was the stone on its way.

Well, what to do? Should the man duck into the excrement? Then his nose, his eyes and his ears would be full of faeces. But if he doesn't duck, then the stone will crack his head for him. So, there is much argument which of these two the man will choose. Will he choose to duck? Or to get his head cracked?

Dividing the Inheritance* [^{III}/XIX]

A man once had three children (sons), and when he died, he left twenty thousand and one cowries. Well how were the cowries to be divided, so that no one was treated unfairly over the single one?

Along comes a Kano fellow. Getting there, he asks 'How much is the inheritance money, to be divided?' and is told 'Twenty thousand and one cowries.' 'Right' says he, 'Bring them here, and tell the sons to come.' The money was brought and given to the young Kano chap. 'O.K.' says he, 'Come here, boys.'

Then he went and sat down, the Kano fellow, and counted out three lots of 5000 cowries each. 'Each of you come and take one of these' said he. That left 5001.

He counted out 3000 in three lots of 1000, and said to the boys 'Come and take 1000 each.' That left 2001. Next he said 'Let me count out 500 each for you.' He did so, and told them to help themselves. That left 501.

* Another resolved dilemma but it might have come under the Character of Kano Men, or Legal Cases.

'Now!' said he, 'let me count out 350* each for you.' He counted out 300* and divided them into three lots of 150 each. That left 51 cowries.

Next he said 'Now take 15 each' – and they did so. 'And that' said he 'Leaves six cowries. Each of you take two.'

Twenty thousand and one cowries – and the Kano man divided the inheritance correctly, without anyone being unfairly treated. But only a Kano man could make that calculation.

---

* Something is wrong here!

PART VI

CASES AT LAW

———————

Potentially any story of social deviation in a Muslim context comes into this category, but I have limited these to stories in which the main part occurs in a judge's (*alkali*) court, or before a chief, sitting as a judge. Often there is in these stories an embryonic whodunnit interest, otherwise hardly occurring in Hausa tales. Unlike in the West, there is never any doubt who did the murder or how he did it. In fact, most accused in murder trials in modern Nigeria tend to plead guilty, if they are permitted to.

The Honey-seller
and the Keeper of the Gate [I/8]

One day a man selling honey came by night from market, and when he came to the gate of his town, he found the gate shut. Then he called out for the gatekeeper. Up comes the gatekeeper and says 'Who's there?' And he answered 'It's me, I was selling honey and I've travelled late.' Then said the gatekeeper. 'How much will you give me to open the gate for you?' And the other answered 'Here's honey – help yourself!' So he opened the gate for him and he came in. Then he gave him some honey which he ate – and fell down dead.

Then the gatekeeper's wife, when she heard no sound, came after him to the door, and coming there found him dead, and there beside him the rest of the honey. She screamed for help and people gathered saying 'What's the reason for all this?' And she said to them 'It was just now he left the compound; he came to open the gate for a man, who was selling honey. Then I heard no sound and came after him, and when I got here I found that he had died suddenly. And there's the rest of the honey sitting there!'

And the people said 'In this town there's no one who sells honey except So-and-So.' And they went to his home and found him, and he was summoned to court. The judge asked him 'Seller of honey, why did you put poison in the honey and give it to the gatekeeper to eat, so that he died?' And the seller of honey said to the judge 'Well, you see, I didn't know that there was poison in it.' And the judge said 'Kill him!' But some people said 'Let him not be killed but rather ask where he got the honey.' So they asked him, and he said to the judge 'Me, I bought the honey from a pagan, to sell for profit. Why should I give it to someone to eat so that he died?' And the judge sent out to ask people, and to say 'Where is the pagan who gets the honey?'

Then the pagan was brought in front of the judge, and the judge asked him 'Tell me, pagan, where did you get the honey from?' And he answered 'I got it out of a hole in a tree.' Then people were sent with him, and he led them to where the hole in the tree was, and they found the honey up in the hole. But they also discovered, above the hole, a snake lying there. And whenever it belched, poison ran into the honey. So it was clear that no one was to blame for giving the gatekeeper the honey that caused his death, and the judge said 'Do not kill the seller of honey, nor the pagan, but kill the snake, for he killed the gatekeeper, and they but brought him the honey, not knowing.'

———————

The Old Woman in Egypt
who Washed Corpses [$^I/_{79}$]

There was once an old woman who lived in Egypt whose business was washing corpses. Whenever a woman died, she would go and wash the body.

One day a woman died who was still a girl, and the old woman was sent for to come and wash her. She went along and started to wash the body. As she did this she patted the private parts with the back of her hand and said 'This one has taken its pleasure in the world'. Whereupon the old woman's hand stuck to the private parts. The old woman let out a yell and people gathered and asked her how it had happened. They tried to prise her hand away, but failed. It was firmly stuck there. Then they were quite at a loss what to do next.

Then said one of the wiser among them 'You must go to the house of Malam Abdullahi, son of Mas'uda and tell him what has happened.' Now this malam was an old malam who never went out, nor did he speak with anyone, unless some grave matter arose.

So they went to his house and made formal salutation. He told them to come in, and when they went in, he asked them 'What troubles you today, that you have come to my house?' Then they said to him 'Something happened today in our home which has given us great wonder. One of the women died, and an old woman came to wash her body, but when she put her hand on her private parts, the hand stuck there. We have tried in every way to prise the hand away, but it remains firmly stuck to the corpse's private parts. This is why we've come to you'. Then said Malam Abdullahi, son of Mas'uda 'Go and get a whip and start whipping the old woman. Go on until you have given her eighty lashes, and then see.' 'Very well' they said and off they went.

They got a whip and started whipping her, counting as they did so. When they reached eighty, the old woman's hand came away from the dead woman's private parts. They went back to tell Malam Abdullahi, son of Mas'uda and said 'We did what you told us to and the old woman's hand came away.' 'Ah' says he, 'you see? The old woman had slandered the dead woman falsely. And the penalty for one who slanders another falsely is eighty lashes. That's the law.' And they said to him 'How should we have known that, if we hadn't come to you?'

The Lion and the Hyena [$^I/_{82}$]

The hyena had a slave-girl and the lion had a slave. And the lion's slave married the hyena's slave-girl. Then they had a son, and the lion said it was his, and he gathered together the beasts of the bush to give judgement for them. Each one of the beasts came and when he saw the lion, he said 'The son is the lion's.'

After that they sent to the jackal to come and give judgement, but he said he was menstruating, and they returned and told the lion who accepted the reply.

But afterwards the jackal came out and stood there, keeping his distance. The lion saw him and called to him 'Malam of the bush! Where are you off to?' And he said to the lion 'I'm off to get some leaves, for my father has had a baby.' The lion answered 'Whoever heard of a man having a baby!!' and the jackal answered 'So men don't have babies! You told the hyena the boy was yours. Now, just you give the hyena her son!' Then the lion went running off and gave the hyena her son. Then the meeting dispersed. That's all of that one.

A Variant [$^{I}/_{84}$]

The hyena had a slave-girl and the lion had a slave. The lion's slave married the hyena's slave-girl and they had a son. Then the lion claimed that the child was his, and he gathered together the beasts of the bush to give judgement for them. Each one of the beasts came, saw the lion and said 'The child is the lion's.' The jackal was sent for and told to come, but he answered that he was menstruating. This was told to the lion who accepted it.

A little later the jackal came out and stood afar off. The lion seeing him said 'Malam of the bush, whither away?' and he answered 'I'm off to get leaves for my father has had a baby.' Says the lion 'When has a male ever had a baby?' and the jackal replied 'Oh, so males don't have babies, eh? But you said the hyena's son was yours. Very well, be off and give the hyena her son!' and he ran off. Then the lion gave the hyena the child, and the meeting broke up. That's all.

The Slippery Trader and the Boy* [$^{I}/_{98}$]

There was once a travelling trader in Kano. He set out for Gwanja,† and seeing a young fellow just then, he said to him 'Here, you, my lad! Come here' And the young chap came over. 'Will you be my companion as far as Gwanja?' asked the trader. 'Sure – I'll be your companion' said the youth. 'Good' said the other 'When we've been to Gwanja and returned, I'll give you something to get meat with.' 'All right' said the boy, and followed the trader, driving his donkey till they got to Gwanja, and back again to Kano.

When they got back, after three days, the trader brought a little knife and gave it to him, saying 'Here's something to get meat with.'

* Cf. I/162.   † In the region of Ashanti, to buy cola-nuts.

'Right' said the boy, and taking the knife, he went to the home of the judge. Said he to the judge 'I bring you my complaint against a trader. I went with him to Gwanja, driving his donkey for him, and after getting there, we came back here. Now before we set out, he told me that if we got back from Gwanja he would give me something to get meat with. Well! Now we're back, and this is what he has given me – a little knife – saying this is to get meat with.'

The judge sent for the trader. And when the trader came before him, the judge asked him, saying 'Now you employed this boy, and he went with you to Gwanja, driving your donkeys, and then you came back here. When you came home, what did you give him as recompense for his trouble?' And the trader answered 'I gave him something to get meat with.' 'Spare me your jokes' said the judge sternly. 'This little knife here that you gave him – is that his wages?' And he went on 'You will not leave this place, till you have produced six hundred thousand cowries to be paid to this boy as fair wages for his trouble.' And the trader at once produced six hundred thousand cowries which he paid over. But from that day the trader didn't take another boy on a trading journey with him, unless they had first made an agreement over wages, right there in Kano before they set out.

The Corrupt Judge who Accepted Presents at Night to Change the Course of Justice [$^{1}/_{99}$]

There was once a man and his wife living together, till there came a day when they failed to agree. Then there arose a violent quarrel between them which grew so bad that she took the matter to the judge.

The judge sent for the husband and, when he came, asked him saying 'What is the trouble between you and your wife, that she should bring the case here?' And the man answered 'Well, if you have a quarrel with someone who lives in your house, what do you do? You have your differences, but you go on living together.

Now, since it happens that she has complained about me to you, I want you to win her round and make it up between us.'

However – though he didn't know it – the night before his wife had given the judge three strips of cloth, which the judge had accepted. So he answered the man 'No – the wrong you have done your wife will not admit of making it up between you. My opinion is that you and your wife should be divorced.' Then the man answered the judge 'Very well, but I must go and consider the matter a little.'

He went home and gathered his friends, and said to them 'Listen to what the judge did to me today the minute my wife complained to him against me: he made no enquiries, but straight away divorced us.' One of his friends was a bold, shameless fellow and he said 'Let's go to the home of the judge, so that I can see just how he means to divorce you and your wife.'

They went back to the judge's home and the judge said 'Oh, you've come back.' 'Yes' they said. 'Well, have you considered the matter?' said he. 'Yes' said the bold friend. 'We have considered it, and we hear that you are divorcing our friend and his wife.' 'Yes' said the judge. 'That's right.' 'Then' said the other, 'We are divorcing *you* from you wife.' 'What have I done' asked the judge 'That I should be divorced from my wife?' 'What has this man done that he should be divorced from his wife?' 'He broke the law' answered the judge. 'And you have done the same' said the other. 'In annulling the marriage.' Then the bold friend said to the judge, 'If you don't give this man back his wife, you won't hear any more cases today' and he took a firm grip of the judge's gown with both hands. Then the judge said 'Let go of my gown and I'll give you back your wife.' Which he did and they departed.

As they went along, he said to the husband 'There – you see. Nothing like a bit of roughness to get what you want.'* If we hadn't done that, we should never have achieved our desire of getting your wife back.' But from that day the judge would only hear cases if he was surrounded by guards. Then, if anyone tried to cause trouble for him, they could help him.

----

* Lit. 'the soup is only tasty if the ox is out of temper.'

The Blind Men and the Householder* [¹/₁₄₂]

Here's a tale of a blind man who used to beg. One day he went out begging to get himself something to eat, and came to a house with a staircase† and began begging there.

Then the master of the house looked out of the door and said 'Come on up!' and the blind man said 'But I can't see.' 'I'll come and take your hand' said the other, and going down he took his hand and led him up the stairs. Then he asked him 'Well, what do you want?' 'Alms, that I may buy something to eat today, in God's name.' But the householder replied 'Well, of all – why didn't you ask me before we came up here? Anyway, I have nothing for you that you could eat today.' 'Very well' said the blind man, 'show me the way out.' But the other replied 'There's the way just in front of you.'

The master of the house went back into his house, and the blind man felt his way down with his feet, but when he was about ten steps from the bottom and nearly down, he missed the step and fell, cracking his head. Whereupon the master of the house came out and stood at the door, laughing. And the blind man grew very angry, biting his fingers in vexation.

Then he set off home, but the householder followed him all the way to the blind man's compound. Arrived there he gathered his mates, two other blind men, and began telling them what had happened to him. And the other was hiding close by, listening.

When they had finished talking, they went into their hut, and he followed them right in there. They they brought out their food and began eating – and moving very quietly he too put his hand in and began eating with them! But they heard him move and said 'Here! What's that moving in this hut?' And getting up they groped round the hut, all over it, but found nothing, for the other had climbed up and hidden under the thatch.

Then the blind men, hearing nothing once more, shut the door

* Cf. J. p. 178. This is the Barber's Story of His Third Brother from *A Thousand and One Nights*.

† Indicating non-Hausa origin of story. Such are rare in Hausa compounds.

and taking out their money – about twelve hundred pounds,* began counting it. Whereupon the other put out his hand to take some, and they heard him move. And springing up they seized him and began beating him and shouting at the tops of their voices 'Help! Help! Thief!' And hearing them, the people came running to help them.

Now when the householder heard them all come, he shut his eyes, just like the others, and began to bellow like them. The door was still shut. 'Open the door' said the people, 'so that we may see the thief.' So they opened the door for them, and there they saw – four blind men. 'What's this?' they exclaimed, 'Here you are, all of you blind, living in the same hut – how can there be thieving among yourselves?' Then the householder said that he had a complaint against his brothers, the other blind men, but he wished to make it before the chief of the town. 'Very well – certainly' said the people.

So they took them before the chief of the town, and told him 'These four are all blind. We heard them quarrelling and shouting "Thief." When we got there, there they were, all blind, three of them holding the one and calling him a thief. Coming up, we spoke with them, and he said he had a complaint, but that he would only make it before the chief.'

Then the chief asked him to tell his story, and tucking his legs under him and leaning respectfully forward, the householder began 'May God lengthen your days, oh chief. 'Twill be best for you to order us to be given a hundred strokes of the whip each – but let them begin with me.' 'Very well' said the chief 'Let them begin with him.'

They began to whip him – one, two – whereupon he opened his eyes, and said 'We four, we're all blind, but each morning one of us goes out begging. And we keep all the money we get together in one place. We've got about twelve hundred pounds now. So we discussed it, and decided to divide it up, each to take his share. But the other three plotted together to deprive me of mine, and we got fighting and they beat me. And this money isn't just what we've got by begging, for we're not really blind. We've shut our eyes, pretending to be blind, and we go into people's compounds, begging. And if we get a chance to do so, we steal too. That's

* An addition by the teller to keep his story up to date.

how we spend our days, doing wrong to people. Look at them now – if you have them each given a hundred strokes with the whip, you'll see they'll open their eyes just as I have.'

Then the chief ordered that they should each be given a hundred strokes with the whip. And while this was being done and they were yelling, the householder stood on one side and said 'Open your eyes and make it easy for yourselves, as I have' and again 'Don't be afraid of what the world will think, but consider what will be your fate in the next world, which is more important.' But they just went on yelling, while he was laughing. And they were beaten within an inch of their lives.

Then the householder came and lay down before the chief and said 'May God lengthen your days!' 'Amen' said the chief. 'Let them be now' said the other, 'seeing that they have chosen the censure of the next world for that of this world and, whatever you do to them they won't open their eyes. But let the chief give judgement now.'

Then said the chief 'Where is the money?' And it was given to him. Then he divided it into four parts, and giving the householder one part, kept the other three, and drove away the three blind men. And they went off very indignant and amazed at the way the householder had tricked them. But he went off home, laughing and delighted at the money he had got. That's all of that one.

The Head Butcher and the Lepers [II/15]

Some lepers came and spotted the compound of the head butcher. Now the head butcher was busy pounding groundnuts. Then he added some salt, small red peppers, Melegueta pepper, black pepper and other sorts of peppers, and then went and applied the mixture to the strips of meat we call *kilishi*. And afterwards the lepers came and took some, and going off home, consumed it.

Well! Next morning when the head butcher came back, he saw footprints. Says he 'Hm – I wonder if this is the work of men or jinns. However, I must catch whoever is drinking my broth.'

So he went and bought a basket of small red peppers. Then he got some soot. Next he went and collected* some ash. Then collected the ingredients in the usual place, brought some water and poured it on. Lastly he mixed the soot and the red peppers and the ash.

When night fell, the head butcher came to the entrance of his hut and squatted down. Presently along came the lepers, two of them. As soon as they arrived, one of the lepers put his hand in and took some. Soon the fieriness of the mixed peppers and soot and ash went right through the leper.†

His friend asked him 'Is it nice?' 'Very nice' he answered, 'more so even than usual.' So the other leper put his hand in and the fieriness of the mixed peppers and soot and ash went right through him too. Then said he 'Phew! You never told me it was as hot as this' and again 'Phe-ew! I shall have to scream.' The other said 'If you scream, we'll be caught, And if we are caught, we'll be taken to the chief's compound.' But the second answered 'Oh! Oh! It's not the chief's place but the other world I feel I'm bound for! Oh dear! I'm going to scream – AOW!' and he screamed.

Whereupon the Head Butcher came running out and caught them. 'There' said he, 'I said I would catch you' and he put them in the hut and guarded them till it was light. Then he took them to the chief. The chief sent them before the judge. So they were brought to the judge's compound, and there they were tried and fined. That's all.

The Chief and the Wife of his Slave‡ [^{I}/$_{146}$]

There was once a chief, who would sit on his roof looking about and around. And his eyes fastened upon a girl in the compound of a neighbour, a girl of surpassing fairness. Then he asked whose wife she was and was told 'She's the wife of your slave.'

So he called his slave and gave him a piece of paper, saying 'Go and take this to such-and-such a town, and wait for an answer and bring it back to me.' The fellow went off, and when he went to bed,

---

* Conjecturally emending *tarara* to *tara*, or possibly *tattara*.
† Lit. 'into his stumps.'   ‡ Cf. J. p. 193.

laid the paper by his bed. Next morning he forgot to take the paper with him. Meanwhile the chief eagerly waited for the departure of his slave.

When he saw that he had gone, he got up and went to the hut of the wife of his slave and found her there. She got up and paid her respects to him and spread a mat for him, saying 'Is all well, that my husband's lord should come here? Indeed I am fearful that this visit betides some ill.' And he replied 'My visit is to you, for I love you.' 'Gracious God!' says she. 'Would you think to drink in the place where your dog drinks? That were not fitting for you.' And the chief was ashamed and hung his head, and getting up, went off quite forgetting his shoes. And that was the last of the chief for the moment.

As for his slave, morning came as he was travelling, and when he looked for the paper he couldn't find it. So he returned and found the chief's shoes in his hut. Then with angry surprise he realised that the chief had given him his errand, because of his wife. But he kept quiet and went and returned. When he got back the chief gave him a hundred dinars. Then, going to the market he bought a collection of the things that women like and returned to his wife. 'Make yourself ready' said he, 'to pay a visit to your home.' 'What's all this?' says she. 'Why, the chief has given me a present, and I should like your father to know of it.' 'Well! That's fine!' said she.

So she set off and went to her father's home. And he was delighted to have her visit him. She stayed there for a month, and her husband never sent for her. His friends said to him 'We don't understand what has made you angry.' 'No matter' said he but refused to have her back.

So they haled him before the judge. The judge happened to be in the presence of the chief, and they came to him and said 'Judge, we gave this fellow a farm, a fine fertile one, bearing fruit, and now he has returned us the farm with no fruit.' And the man said 'Judge, I gave them back their farm, until it shall exceed what it now is.'* 'Return to your farm, young man' said the judge. 'Judge' said he, 'I am afraid, for I saw the tracks of a lion in it. I fear the lion may kill me.' The chief was leaning on his elbow, then got up,

* The Hausa seems obscure. Perhaps (so Johnston) 'and in better condition than it was'.

saying 'That lion hasn't touched anything in your farm. He didn't stay, but made the tracks as he was leaving – and, by God, I've never seen a farm to match yours!' 'I see' said the slave, 'Then I'll return.' But neither the judge, nor the wife's relations knew what was behind their words.

The Blind Man and the Seeing Man* [^{II}/$_{93}$]

There was once a man went to market riding on his ox. He bought a number of things and, wrapping them all up, mounted his ox and came away. But as he made his way home, he met a blind man who was suffering greatly from the heat of the sun. He was lamenting the heat that afflicted him, saying 'Oh God, oh God! Here I am and I can't see. If only I could see, I would go under a tree and sit down and rest.' Then the man on the ox came up with him and dismounting, he said 'My poor fellow (lit. 'slave of Allah'), come, let me help you on to my ox.' The blind man answered 'God bless you, man with eyes.' And so he helped the blind man on to his ox, and going in front, led the way with the blind man bringing up the rear on the ox.

As they walked along, they chatted, and the blind man began fingering the other's purchases, all wrapped up as they were. 'What's this one?' says he. 'That's salt.' 'How about this one?' 'That's *daddawa*.' 'What about this?' the blind man asked again. 'Oh, those are peppers.' 'And this one?' 'pounded baobab leaves.' 'What about this?' 'Oh, that's potash.' 'And this?' 'Ginger.' 'How about this one?' asked the blind man. 'Oh, that's peppers with seeds in.' But there was one package hanging there that the blind man didn't find (*lit.* 'see'!). And so they reached the town.

Then the seeing man said 'Well, blind man, we've reached the town; come, let me help you down, for I have to go on from here.' But the blind man began to yell, and people gathered. Says he 'This man who can see is trying to take my ox from me.' 'Well!' said the other, 'for God's sake, speak the truth, blind man.' 'It's the truth I'm telling' said the blind man. 'Seeing man, you're

* Cf. next tale and S. p. 193.

trying to snatch what belongs to me.' 'Is that really so?' said the other. People said 'Let them be taken to the chief.' So they took them to the chief's compound, and the chief said to the seeing man 'Let me ask you how it all began.' 'No' he answered, 'don't ask me. Ask the blind man.' So the chief turned to the blind man and said 'What brought you and the seeing man together?' 'Well' he answered, 'you see, I was begging and picked up this ox. I went to market and bought a few things – salt and *daddawa*, peppers and shea-butter, potash and ginger, peppers with the seeds in and *kimba** peppers (*sic*). Just you look and see whether there aren't eight packages.' They looked and saw nine packages. Then the chief said to the blind man and the seeing man 'You'll be taken to lodge now, but tomorrow come back, and you will hear what we have to say.'

Then the chief had two wooden bowls of *tuwo* prepared; oil was poured over them. Then boiled meat was brought and added, added to both the bowls. *Fura* was brought, and then buttermilk and honey added to that. Next they brought two bowls of fried meat, and the chief said 'Here, take all this to the seeing man, and to the blind man too. Give each of them his portion. And when you've done that, you're to hide and listen to what they say.' So those who had taken the blind man his food, hid; and those who had taken the seeing man his food hid too. The former ones heard the blind man say 'Bloody fine! Here I get my *tuwo*, with oil and meat, and fried meat too; and I drink *fura*, with buttermilk and honey – and then on top of it all, before the sun is up I shall acquire an ox!' At which those who were listening, rose and went and told the chief what the blind man had said. 'Very well' said the chief. 'Let us await those from the seeing man's hut, and hear what they have to say.' Well, the seeing man said 'Ugh – food! How can I eat any sort of food now, seeing that they are going to take away my ox wrongfully, perforce? I won't eat their food, for I can't stomach it.' Then those other listeners too rose and made their way to the chief and told him all that the seeing man had said. 'Good' said the chief, 'You may go home now, but come back in the morning.'

Next morning, when it was light, they came again, and the chief said to them 'Go, and each one of you bring back the wooden

* *Xylopia aethiopica.*

419

bowl that he took.' Well, the ones that had been taken to the blind man had been cleaned up completely – all that he had left was the wooden bowls and the calabash. They took these to the chief. 'Right' said he, 'we've seen the blind man's. Remain those of the seeing man.' So they went and brought them back too. And there they were just exactly as they had been when they were taken to him: the seeing man hadn't even lifted the lids off to inspect them. And they picked them up and took them back to the chief to see. Says he 'Good people, the ox belongs to the seeing man; for it was grief that he was going to lose his ox wrongfully that prevented him eating his *tuwo*. As for the other, you can see that he has eaten up every bit of the food. Go and fetch them, and let us hear. Remember the blind man said this his purchases consisted of eight packages; but we saw nine of them.'

So they called the seeing man and asked him, saying 'How did you and the blind man come to be together?' 'Well' he answered, 'I went to market and bought some things there. He said that there were eight packages, but I know that there were nine. The ninth was some herbs – that one wrapped up there. But it was hanging down, and that is why the blind man didn't notice it; he asked me about all the others, and I told him what was in them.' At this the blind man exclaimed 'You're lying! There are only eight packages.' And the seeing man said 'May the chief's life be prolonged – let that package be opened, and you'll see.' It was opened, and there were the herbs. Says the chief 'Blind man, you are lying. Those who brought *tuwo* to you, and *fura* and meat, returned and told me what you said. You said "Bloody fine! A fellow gets *tuwo* to eat, with oil and meat, and *fura* with honey; and then before the sun is up next day, he gets an ox into the bargain!" But the seeing man said "How can I eat any sort of food, when they are going to take my ox away?" and, as for the food that was taken to him, he never even lifted the lid to inspect it. Yes, blind man, you're lying. Guards, sieze him and take him away and kill him, for he is a thief.' Says the blind man, 'Chief, in the name of Allah and his Prophet, spare me. For I confess that it was deliberate. But I'll never do it again.' 'Very well' said the chief, 'let him be,' and then to the other 'Here, take your ox.' And that's the end of that story.

The Owner of the Ox
and the Blind Man* [III/174]

A man with an ox was travelling from one town to another when he fell in with a blind man. Says he 'My poor fellow,† where are you going to?' 'I'm travelling to another town.' 'Is it far?' 'I don't know' said the blind man. 'Then why not let me mount you for a fee?' 'Surely – let's settle on one.' And they agreed on a fee of a thousand cowries. He helped him up on to the ox. And when he had done so, presently they came to the entrance to the town.

When they got there, he said 'Get down here.' But the blind man said 'Why? Just because you see that I am blind, do you think that you can cheat me?'

Some of the chief men of the town came along and said 'What has happened?' Their answer was‡ 'Something has indeed happened. We both came through the bush. I saw him on the road, and then I agreed to let him ride for a thousand cowries. I put him on my ox. But then, when he saw that I was blind, he tried to trick me.' And the chief ordered that they should be taken to two separate compounds.

This was done, and *tuwo* was got ready. When it was ready, some was taken to the blind man and some to the other. Says the blind man 'Let me eat my *tuwo*, for tomorrow I shall be given my ox that I got by trickery.' And the other, the one who could see, said 'I'm afraid I have no appetite for this *tuwo*. It was my ox, and I gave him a ride, and we agreed on a price for the ride.'

Then the chief of the town said 'Let them be brought before me. The blind man began swearing that what he said was true, but the chief said 'The ox is not the blind man's, but the other's.'

And he had the blind man given fifty lashes and driven from the town. And so he departed.

As for the other, he was given his ox and told 'From now on,

* Cf. last tale
† Lit. 'slave of God', elsewhere translated as 'pious man' etc. The blind, like the learned, are presumably God's special care.
‡ It seems that this is the blind man speaking.

even if you see a blind man in the middle of the bush, don't give him a lift; leave him, let him die. Another time one may play a trick on you, and though on this occasion you received the verdict, on another occasion you might not.' That's all.

And that's the origin of the saying 'There are times that call for caution quite in excess of one's normal amount'*

The Man who had a Female Camel, and the Three Young Fellows† [III/2]

There was once a man, whose female camel strayed. And she set off along the road and travelled for some way; and as she went she pulled off the leaves from trees and ate them.

But her owner met three young fellows, and said to them 'Hey there! You've not met with a female camel here, have you?' And one of them answered 'Oh – do you mean one that's in foal?' 'Yes, that's her' said the owner. Another of them said 'Oh – do you mean the one that's only got one eye?' 'Yes, that's her.' And the third said 'Oh, you mean the one with a sore on her back?' 'Yes, that's her' said the owner again. And they said 'Brother, by God, we've not seen her.' And the man went on, whenever he met anyone, asking them; until at last he had travelled for a day and a night, without coming across any who said that they had seen her.

So he turned and started back, and came and began asking for those three young men, until he found them.

Then he took them to the chief's compound, and the chief asked him 'Did they give you a description of her?' 'Yes, indeed they did' he answered. 'Boys' said the chief, 'Is this true?' 'Yes' they answered, 'May the chief's life be prolonged. He asked us and we told him – but we never saw her.' Says the chief 'That is false – there is something crooked here. Take them to the judge's compound.' And they were taken to the judge's compound.

* Or, perhaps, and more literally, 'The wisdom that is given you once in a while is worth more than all your day-to-day judgement.'
† Cf. M. No. 2.

The judge asked the owner of the camel about it, and he told the judge what had passed between him and the boys. Then the judge asked them, saying 'Well. How was it that you could describe the camel's appearance, without seeing her? How is that possible?'

One of them answered 'Judge, may your life be prolonged. The reason that, when he asked me, I said "Do you mean one that's in foal?" – to which he replied "Yes" – the reason was that a camel that is in foal, if it stales, scatters its urine widely. If I'm lying, judge, you go and take a look at a camel in foal – you'll see. That was how I deduced that she was in foal – I saw where she had staled.' 'Very well' said the judge. 'So much for your account.'

And he turned to the next one and asked him for his. Says he 'May the judge's life be prolonged. This is how I realised that she has only got one eye. The whole length of the road we followed, we noticed that she was eating grass on the one side – and that's why I said that she only had one eye.' 'Very well' said the judge, 'So much for your account. How about you?' turning to the third, 'How did you know?'

And he answered 'Well – may the judge's life be prolonged – my reason for saying that she had a sore on the back was that whenever she pulled up some grass, she would put her mouth round to scratch the place. For I kept seeing grass that had fallen on the other side. And that, judge, is why I said what I did.'

Thereupon the judge said 'My boys, go your way, you have told the truth. As for you' turning to the owner of the camel, 'Get along and seek your camel.' And he went off and found her. That's all. This with peace.

The Man who had a Bull, his Neighbour and the Chief [III/5]

Here's a tale of two neighbours. One of them had his bull stolen. So he went over to his neighbour and addressing him by name, said 'Look – I've had my bull stolen.' 'Really?' says the other.

'Yes.' 'Well, the man who stole it is in' and he named the town.
To which the owner added 'If that's where he is, he's a butcher.'
'Right' said his neighbour, 'Let's be going,' and off they set along
the road.

They travelled till they came to the town, and, going to the
chief's compound, told their story. 'Very well' said the chief,
'I've heard what you have to say. Now you will be taken to lodgings,
until tomorrow when you must come back.' 'Very well' they said
and were taken to their lodgings.

Evening came, and they were brought *tuwo* and meat, which
they ate. Says the neighbour to the owner of the bull 'It's dog that
we have just eaten!' Says the other 'And the *tuwo* that we've eaten
was made by a woman who was menstruating.' And his neighbour said again 'Well, I – I say, the chief of this town is a bastard.
His mother had him as the result of adultery.'

Well, it chanced that a slave-girl of the chief's compound was
on the other side of the *zana* fence while they were talking. And,
returning to her compound, she went and told the chief. Says she
'May the chief's life be prolonged, but this is what those strangers
said. They said that the flesh of that ram, that it was dog. And they
said too that she who had prepared the *tuwo* was menstruating.
And then also they said that you were a bastard, and that your
mother committed adultery, and so conceived and bore you.'
'Is that so?' said he. 'Yes' said the slave-girl, 'That's what I heard
them saying.'

So the chief had his mother summoned. And he asked her
privately 'Mother, in those days, how did you come to conceive
me?' And she answered 'Aye, 'tis true. My husband had gone off
to war. And I took the milking calabash, and went off to the
corral to milk. But when I got there, I found the herd all alone
with the cattle; and he called me over. So I went, and he slept with
me. And Allah caused me to conceive you. And now you know how
I came to bear you.' Says the chief 'Yes. So much for that one.'

And then he had the woman that had stirred the *tuwo* sent for,
and asked her. And she too replied 'Yes. while I was stirring the
tuwo, my period began.' 'So' said the chief, 'So much for that one.'

Then said the chief 'Well! Where are the owners of that ram?
Send for them!' They were summoned, and the chief asked them,
and they replied 'Yes. When that ram was quite young, its mother

died, and he attached himself to a bitch and was suckled by her.'
'Yes' said the chief, 'those men spoke truly.'

But as he was going out of the entrance of his compound, he
had someone squeeze a lime for him, and tossed it into his pocket.
Then he went out to the clear space in front of his compound,
and said 'Let those men be summoned, the ones who accused my
head butcher of stealing their bull – send for them, to come.'
So they were sent for, and came.

Then the chief said to them 'Which of you is the owner of the
bull?' 'I' said the owner. 'Then' said the chief, 'I have a question
for you.' 'May the chief's life be prolonged' said the owner of the
bull, 'God grant that I know the answer!' 'What' said the chief, 'is
in my pocket?' And the owner of the bull answered 'Something
green, something juicy.' And his neighbour added 'Of course,
it's a lime.' Then said the chief 'Hey – chief butcher! Get up and
give them their bull.'

So the head butcher went and gave them their bull. And they
went their way. That's all. That's the end of that story.

The Chief, the Judge, the Chief's Daughter and the Pauper* [$^{III}/_{35}$]

There was once a chief had a daughter, whom he kept in purdah.
And he offered her to the judge to be his wife. Says the judge 'I
suppose, chief, that the girl isn't a nymphomaniac by any chance?'
'For shame, judge' said the chief, 'A girl – my own daughter – who
from the time she was small until she was grown, has never been
out of the compound – and you suggest that about her!' 'Oh, very
well, chief' said the judge, 'I accept her.' So they went and prepared†
the girl, and she was taken to the judge's compound.

But a pauper, a ragged fellow without a cowrie to his name,
went into the judge's compound at night; and into the chief's
daughter's hut.

* Cf. next tale.   † Lit 'washed'.

425

Presently the judge heard them talking. He rose and went and found the pauper together with the girl. And he took a shackle and hammered it on to their legs, one end on a leg of each of them, fastening them together.

Then the judge went to the compound of the chief, though it was night, and when he got there, said 'Chief, did you say that your daughter wasn't a nymphomaniac? Well now, I have caught her with a man, in my compound.' 'Can this really be true?' exclaimed the chief, 'Is this so, judge?' 'This is the truth, chief' said the judge.

Then said the chief 'Very well, judge. Go home now, but in the morning you bring her to me, with this fellow.'* Says the judge 'But they're there now, in my compound, and I've fastened them together.' 'No, you just go home now, and bring them in the morning, judge.' 'Very well' said the judge, and went off home.

Meanwhile the pauper said to the girl 'Well, I must be on my way. Wake whichever of your slave-girls you trust and tell her to come.' She woke one of them and the girl came over.

Then the pauper opened the end of the shackle on his own leg, and put it on the slave-girl's leg.

'Now' said the pauper, 'As you go, I'll be sitting at the compound entrance. When you get there, contrive to push against me. Understand?' 'Yes' said the girl.

Morning came and the judge went into his compound and to the girl's hut. And when he got there, he found the girl fastened to her own slave-girl. And so he took them to the chief's compound.

But the girl, as she was about to enter the room, saw the pauper, who had borrowed a gown which he was wearing. Whereupon the girl pretended to stumble and saved herself from falling by pushing against the pauper.

'Judge' said the chief, 'But you said that you caught this girl with a man, so that you even shackled them. But look – it's her slave-girl that she is with.'

Now the judge had a Koran, on which if anyone forswore, they died inevitably.

Says the chief 'Fetch it and let her swear.' And the judge went and got the Koran.

* *kato* (lit. 'huge') seems strange; but it may be used simply for 'rough fellow'. ? Read *kwarto* (=paramour).

The girl made her ablutions and came back. Then she said 'I swear by Allah and His Messenger that ever since I have been in the judge's compound I have not been touched by any man, save only that one that I pushed against just now – the one I pushed against when I was falling. And if I have known any other man as a man, then let the Koran strike me.' And the girl pressed the Koran, pressed it three times.

Then she said 'And if it is desired that I swear four times, I will add another.' But they said 'No. For the rule for a Muslim is to swear three times.'

'Judge' said the chief 'You called me a liar.' And he took him and cut his throat.

And that is why, now, if a man is being given the oath, and he inserts other words – then he is guilty of what he is charged with. But if he follows the words exactly, adding nothing – then he is not guilty, for he has sworn by Allah and His Messenger. That's all. This with peace.

The Arab, his Wife and the Boy* [III/40]

Here's another. An Arab had a daughter, and another Arab came along and sought her in marriage. In due course she was named; more time passed, and she was of age to be weaned. Then the Arab who had sought her, asked that she might be given to him, to take away and keep in his own compound. 'For' he said, 'if she grows up at home with her mother, her mother will teach her scurvy tricks.' So the girl was given to him.

He had been living in the town, but now he moved out of the town and built himself a new compound. Presently the girl grew up. Now her husband used to make regular visits to the town, to the chief's compound, to pay his respects and spend some time in the chief's presence, before going home.

Well, one day he set off, and presently another young Arab,

* Cf. M. No. 47 and the last story.

who had saddled up his horse and put on his gowns, came by the compound and the girl saw him as he was passing. She called to him, inviting him in.

The boy came over, and the girl told him to dismount. He dismounted and she took his horse and set up a tethering post for it, and tied it up.

Next she and the boy went into a hut – but at this point her husband returned. At which the girl went to the entrance of the compound and said to her husband 'While you were out, on your way, the chief sent you a horse – look.' And he answered 'Then let me go back and take my thanks to the chief.'

And she went back into the hut, she and the boy, and the two of them finished what they were about. After that she went and pulled out the tethering-post and led over the horse. But she said 'Now, listen. They'll take us to court. When you get there, sit close to the entrance to the compound, so that I may touch you.' 'Right' said the boy, and he mounted his horse and departed.

Then she took a broom and wherever the horse had trodden, she swept, right to the entrance of the compound.

The husband returned and asked the girl 'Where's the horse?' 'What horse, sir?' said she. 'The horse that you said the chief had sent me.' But the girl denied any knowledge of such a thing. At which the Arab got up and was on the point of giving the girl a beating, when she protested, asking what the beating was for. So he took her to the judge's compound.

Meanwhile the boy, the young Arab, had returned home and dismounted. Thence he went to the judge's compound and sat down at the entrance of the building. Up comes the husband with the girl. The latter, as she was entering the building made as if to stumble and pushed against the boy. Then she went in.

Her husband accused her of having another man in his compound, but the girl denied it, saying that she had never known any male other than he, who had weaned her. Then her husband demanded that she be given the oath.

But the girl, when she came to take the oath, said 'Ever since I was born, since my husband weaned me – and after that I grew up in his compound – if I have known any other man apart from him, saving only the young man whom I pushed against when I fell just now, may the Koran strike me dead.' And the girl repeated the oath three times. And so she was adjudged to be speaking the truth. But the Arab, her husband, said 'So it seems that women are born with their scurvy tricks [and don't have to learn them].'

And that's the reason that, even when a woman has taken the oath, it never strikes her dead. That's all. This with peace.

The Hare and the Guinea-fowl [III/62]

Another fable. The hare and the guinea-fowl shared a farm which they were hoeing together. If the hare went off to the farm, he would travel afoot along the road; as for the guinea-fowl, he would flutter his wings and fly off to the farm, up in the air – no travelling afoot for him.

The day came when all the hoeing was done and it was the harvest. They went and made a corn-bin, and fetching in their corn put it in the bin.

Then the hare went and took a complaint against the guinea-fowl before the judge, Judge Jackal. The guinea-fowl was summoned before him, and the judge asked him 'What has been your association with the hare?' 'We shared a farm' said the guinea-fowl; 'we hoed it together, and harvested the corn, and put it in a corn-bin.' He went on 'But he won't let me have any corn, and now he has brought me to court.'

Then the judge asked the hare what road he had followed to the farm. 'My path is there to see, along the ground' answered the hare. And the judge ordered that this be inspected.

It was inspected and duly reported on to the judge, who turned to the guinea-fowl and asked 'And where is the road that you followed, when you went to the farm?' But he answered 'Me, I used to flap my wings and then fly to the farm.' 'Guinea-fowl' said the judge, 'you lie, and the hare speaks truer than you. Be off with you; for you have tried to cheat the hare.'

Well, one day the hare went and brought back a load of salt.

And as he came back from buying the salt he grew tired. Up comes the guinea-fowl. 'Hare' says he, 'let me relieve you of that burden, for they are tiring things as you know.' 'Thank you' said the hare. So the guinea-fowl took over the hare's load of salt and went off with it.

So the hare took a complaint against him before the judge. The guinea-fowl was summoned, and the judge told the hare to state his case. The hare did so, and the judge asked the guinea-fowl, in turn, for his version. Now it chanced that the load of salt that he had taken over had made a horny place on his head.*

Says the judge 'Hare, come here and let me see your head.' So the hare proffered his head, and there it was, smooth as smooth could be.

The guinea-fowl in its turn was called to show its head. He did so – and there was the horny place. Says the judge 'Hare, the load belongs to the guinea-fowl, for – look – he has carried a load, so that he has got a horny place on his head. Be off with you, for he speaks truer than you.'

And that is why the guinea-fowl has a horny place on his head even now – because he carried the hare's salt.

The Man who Tricked the Judge [III/160]

An accused man was once brought before a judge. He pleaded his case, and the hearing continued. The judge saw that the case would go against the man,† and said to him 'What have you to say?' He indicated three portions with his hand, saying that he had no ability with words. But seeing it, the judge gave a false decision [for leniency]. Then the court rose.

When the judge got home, he was sent three pumpkins. Now the judge had thought that the man had indicated three goats, so he

* See footnote to III/127.

† Or, possibly – depending on vowel length – 'involve the death sentence for the man'.

sent for him. 'You're a deceiver' said the judge, 'You've tricked me. God's curse upon you! Get up and be off!'

And when he got outside he said 'The trickster doesn't like being tricked.'*

The Ka-fi-gamba,† the Ostrich and the Judge [^{III}/₁₆₄]

A *ka-fi-gamba* came across an ostrich egg and squatting down on it, said that it was hers. The ostrich returned and found her, and said '*Ka-fi-gamba*, get up! I don't want to have a quarrel with you.' 'It's my egg' the other answered, 'I'm not getting up.'

Contemptuous of the little bird, the ostrich took the matter to the judge. The *ka-fi-gamba* was summoned. She came along, and when the judge questioned her, said that it was her egg. The judge looked at the ostrich, then at the *ka-fi-gamba*, and saw that there was something funny somewhere. So he ordered the egg to be brought.

His men took a large calabash and fetched the egg. ‡ '*Ka-fi-gamba*,' said the judge, when they had brought it, 'Is this your egg?' 'Yes, it's mine' she said. 'Very well' he said, 'Take what is yours.' At which she said 'I give up the case', and getting up, she departed, her lies at an end.

---

* In another version the proverb *wanzami ba ya son jarfa*, 'the barber doesn't like being tattooed' is used.

† The racquet-tailed, purple-rumped sunbird.

‡ *Kwai* could mean 'egg' or 'eggs' throughout this tale.

The Man with the Load
and the Dumb Man* [III/175]

There was once a man walking along, who met another on the
road, with a lot of stuff to carry. Says he 'Is your load too heavy for
you?' and the other replied 'Very much so.' 'Then give me half
and let me take it for you.' So he put down his load and, dividing
it in half, gave half to the other, who took it.

On they went till they came into the city. 'This is the quarter
where I am staying' said the one, 'Give me my things.' But the
other made the inarticulate sounds of a dumb man. Whereupon the
owner took hold of the load, and the other did the same. They
began to struggle, the one saying to the 'dumb' man 'Let go of my
things', and the 'dumb' man continuing to make inarticulate
noises, as a dumb man would, such as no one could understand.

People came up and tried to separate them, but failed. So they
were taken before the judge. The one who could speak was
questioned and he said 'I was coming back from a journey and I
overtook this fellow on the road. He said to me "It looks as though
your load is too heavy for you." I said it was, very much so, and
then he told me to give him half which he would carry for me. I
put my load down and gave him half to take for me – which he did.
We reached this town, chatting as we came. Then when we got
into the town, I said to him "Here's the quarter where I am lodging.
Give me my things." Whereupon he began to make noises like a
dumb man. We started to struggle, and people came and tried to
separate us, but failed. Then they brought us before you, judge.
That's all I have to say.'

The judge asked the people what they thought and they said
'Because he saw that he was a dumb man, he intended to play a
trick on him. For when has anyone ever heard of what he says as
happening?' Then the judge asked him if he had any witnesses.
'No' he answered, 'we were the two of us.' 'Go away. You're
lying' said the judge. And away he went, and settling in the town,
sold the rest of his things.

* Cf. J. p. 191 and I/17.

A friend of his, a sharp fellow, came and found him. Addressing him by name he said 'When you passed me, you had a lot of stuff. But now I see you have hardly anything left in your possession. How did it happen?' 'Owing to my folly.' 'How? Folly?' So he told him, 'I was coming back and overtook another man. Says he "You've got a tough task." "Very much so" I answered. "Give me half and I'll take it for you." So I did. But when we got here, he behaved badly, pretending to be dumb. We went before the judge, and the judge rejected my complaint.' 'You're quite sure he spoke with you?' asked his friend. 'Quite sure.' 'Is he here in the town?' 'He's here.' 'Well, I understand deaf-and-dumb talk. Go back to the judge and tell him that you have found someone with this ability.' He did as he was told.

The judge laughed, and had the 'dumb' man summoned. He came, and the judge said to the other 'Say on,' but he answered 'I have told my side of it. Let the dumb man give his.' Then the 'dumb' man was touched by someone and he began to make the same noises again. 'Stop' said the friend, and they stopped the 'dumb' man. Then the friend rendered it for the judge, saying 'The dumb man is abusing you, judge.' 'When?' said the 'dumb' man [indignantly]. And so that one came unstuck!

The judge arrested the 'dumb' man, and had him whipped – heavily. And he returned the other man's property to him.

And that is why they say 'Don't enter upon something unknown, just in order to shirk difficulty.'

Appendix

TABLE OF CROSS REFERENCES TO THE ORIGINAL EDITION

As the three volumes are to be published over a period of eighteen months, it is not possible to complete all index references until the final volume; thus 'B' refers to items in Volume II, and 'C' to Volume III.

TATS	Page	TATS	Page	TATS	Page
I/1	B	I/37	279	I/73	297
I/2	B	I/38	279	I/74	B
I/3	3	I/39	280	I/75	97
I/4	B	I/40	B	I/76	297
I/5	58	I/41	252	I/77	252
I/6	5	I/42	B	I/78	99
I/7	8	I/43	159	I/79	408
I/8	407	I/44	B	I/80	161
I/9	10	I/45	176	I/81	225
I/10	289	I/46	97	I/82	409
I/11	227	I/47	B	I/83	14
I/12	157	I/48	294	I/84	410
I/13	69	I/49	160	I/85	71
I/14	240	I/50	243	I/86	72
I/15	B	I/51	B	I/87	277
I/16	290	I/52	B	I/88	100
I/17	182	I/53	B	I/89	B
I/18	89	I/54	183	I/90	B
I/19	158	I/55	209	I/91	B
I/20	59	I/56	C	I/92	73
I/21	184	I/57	258	I/93	299
I/22	11	I/58	B	I/94	6
I/23	278	I/59	B	I/95	91
I/24	279	I/60	B	I/96	302
I/25	B	I/61	179	I/97	B
I/26	222	I/62	259	I/98	410
I/27	178	I/63	179	I/99	411
I/28	251	I/64	180	I/100	162
I/29	381	I/65	295	I/101	B
I/30	293	I/66	189	I/102	207
I/31	13	I/67	295	I/103	243
I/32	241	I/68	C	I/104	246
I/33	242	I/69	194	I/105	B
I/34	257	I/70	B	I/106	C
I/35	B	I/71	224	I/107	280
I/36	B	I/72	204	I/108	247

TATS	Page	TATS	Page	TATS	Page
I/109	281	I/154	130	I/XXXVII	289
I/110	B	I/155	312	I/XXXVIII	C
I/111	303	I/156	61	I/XXXIX	C
I/112	260	I/157	17	I/XL	C
I/113	B	I/158	B	I/XLI	C
I/114	B	I/159	78	I/XLII	210
I/115	B	I/160	19	I/XLIII	206
I/116	B	I/161	169	I/XLIV	C
I/117	B	I/162	164	I/XLV	C
I/118	110	I/I	C	I/XLVI	C
I/119	74	I/II	C	I/XLVII	C
I/120	304	I/III	C	I/XLVIII	C
I/121	253	I/IV	C	I/XLIX	C
I/122	B	I/V	C	I/L	C
I/123	B	I/VI	C	I/LI	C
I/124	B	I/VII	C	I/LII	C
I/125	B	I/VIII	190	I/LIII	C
I/126	228	I/IX	C	I/LIV	C
I/127	306	I/X	C	I/LV	C
I/128	B	I/XI	C	I/LVI	C
I/129	75	I/XII	C	I/LVII	C
I/130	B	I/XIII	C	I/LVIII	C
I/131	C	I/XIV	C	I/LIX	C
I/132	98	I/XV	C	I/LX	C
I/133	242	I/XVI	C	I/LXI	C
I/134	B	I/XVII	C	I/LXII	C
I/135	308	I/XVIII	C	I/LXIII	C
I/136	309	I/XIX	C	I/LXIV	C
I/137	B	I/XX	C	I/LXV	C
I/138	310	I/XXI	C	I/LXVI	B
I/139	B	I/XXII	C	I/LXVII	C
I/140	276	I/XXIII	C	I/LXVIII	C
I/141	264	I/XXIV	C	I/LXIX	C
I/142	413	I/XXV	C	I/LXX	C
I/143	B	I/XXVI	C	I/LXXI	C
I/144	15	I/XXVII	C	I/LXXII	C
I/145	247	I/XXVIII	C	I/LXXIII	C
I/146	416	I/XXIX	C	I/LXXIV	C
I/147	77	I/XXX	C	I/LXXV	C
I/148	B	I/XXXI	181	I/LXXVI	C
I/149	229	I/XXXII	C	I/LXXVII	C
I/150	163	I/XXXIII	C	I/LXXVIII	C
I/151	129	I/XXXIV	C	I/LXXIX	C
I/152	311	I/XXXV	C	I/LXXX	C
I/153	16	I/XXXVI	C	I/LXXXI	C

TATS	Page	TATS	Page	TATS	Page
I/LXXXII	C	II/40	113	II/85	323
I/LXXXIII	C	II/41	B	II/86	B
I/LXXXIV	C	II/42	B	II/87	B
I/LXXXV	C	II/43	384	II/88	B
I/LXXXVI	C	II/44	386	II/89	80
I/LXXXVII	C	II/45	B	II/90	B
II/1	110	II/46	194	II/91	327
II/2	112	II/47	316	II/92	329
II/3	B	II/48	B	II/93	418
II/4	132	II/49	B	II/94	B
II/5	138	II/50	318	II/95	C
II/6	92	II/51	B	II/96	C
II/7	B	II/52	95	II/97	332
II/8	314	II/53	320	II/98	201
II/9	134	II/54	76	II/99	334
II/10	141	II/55	B	II/100	B
II/11	265	II/56	B	II/101	B
II/12	22	II/57	142	II/I	C
II/13	102	II/58	388	II/II	C
II/14	B	II/59	B	II/III	C
II/15	415	II/60	B	II/IV	C
II/16	B	II/61	B	II/V	C
II/17	B	II/62	B	II/VI	C
II/18	B	II/63	391	II/VII	C
II/19	B	II/64	B	II/VIII	C
II/20	141	II/65	26	II/IX	C
II/21	B	II/66	B	II/X	C
II/22	B	II/67	B	II/XI	C
II/23	24	II/68	B	II/XII	C
II/24	B	II/69	B	II/XIII	C
II/25	B	II/70	B	II/XIV	C
II/26	315	II/71	321	II/XV	C
II/27	B	II/72	41	II/XVI	C
II/28	B	II/73	B	II/XVII	C
II/29	B	II/74	B	II/XVIII	C
II/30	24	II/75	B	II/XIX	C
II/31	B	II/76	B	II/XX	C
II/32	B	II/77	B	II/XXI	C
II/33	103	II/78	B	II/XXII	C
II/34	B	II/79	B	II/XXIII	C
II/35	185	II/80	266	II/XXIV	C
II/36	196	II/81	115	II/XXV	C
II/37	B	II/82	B	II/XXVI	C
II/38	B	II/83	B	II/XXVII	C
II/39	B	II/84	144	II/XXVIII	C

TATS	Page	TATS	Page	TATS	Page
II/XXIX	C	II/LXXIV	C	III/7	145
II/XXX	C	II/LXXV	C	III/8	28
II/XXXI	C	II/LXXVI	C	III/9	244
II/XXXII	C	II/LXXVII	C	III/10	367
II/XXXIII	C	II/LXXVIII	C	III/11	336
II/XXXIV	C	II/LXXIX	C	III/12	B
II/XXXV	C	II/LXXX	C	III/13	B
II/XXXVI	C	II/LXXXI	C	III/14	B
II/XXXVII	C	II/LXXXII	C	III/15	337
II/XXXVIII	C	II/LXXXIII	C	III/16	117
II/XXXIX	C	II/LXXXIV	C	III/17	B
II/XL	191	II/LXXXV	C	III/18	B
II/XLI	C	II/LXXXVI	C	III/19	B
II/XLII	C	II/LXXXVII	C	III/20	281
II/XLIII	C	II/LXXXVIII	C	III/21	B
II/XLIV	C	II/LXXXIX	C	III/22	B
II/XLV	C	II/XC	C	III/23	B
II/XLVI	C	II/XCI	C	III/24	31
II/XLVII	C	II/XCII	C	III/25	B
II/XLVIII	C	II/XCIII	C	III/26	33
II/XLIX	C	II/XCIV	C	III/27	198
II/L	C	II/XCV	C	III/28	339
II/LI	C	II/XCVI	C	III/29	341
II/LII	C	II/XCVII	C	III/30	104
II/LIII	C	II/XCVIII	C	III/31	119
II/LIV	C	II/CXIX	C	III/32	B
II/LV	C	II/C	C	III/33	B
II/LVI	C	II/CI	C	III/34	165
II/LVII	C	II/CII	C	III/35	425
II/LVIII	C	II/CIII	C	III/36	B
II/LIX	C	II/CIV	C	III/37	B
II/LX	C	II/CV	C	III/38	36
II/LXI	C	II/CVI	C	III/39	344
II/LXII	C	II/CVII	C	III/40	427
II/LXIII	C	II/CVIII	C	III/41	230
II/LXIV	C	II/CIX	C	III/42	82
II/LXV	C	II/CX	C	III/43	B
II/LXVI	C	II/CXI	C	III/44	65
II/LXVII	C	II/CXII	C	III/45	B
II/LXVIII	C	III/1	B	III/46	B
II/LXIX	C	III/2	422	III/47	120
II/LXX	C	III/3	160	III/48	62
II/LXXI	C	III/4	116	III/49	B
II/LXXII	C	III/5	423	III/50	B
II/LXXIII	C	III/6	B	III/51	B

TATS	Page	TATS	Page	TATS	Page
III/52	B	III/97	B	III/142	108
III/53	166	III/98	361	III/143	127
III/54	347	III/99	52	III/144	B
III/55	B	III/100	B	III/145	151
III/56	B	III/101	350	III/146	55
III/57	B	III/102	363	III/147	B
III/58	83	III/103	B	III/148	368
III/59	202	III/104	106	III/149	153
III/60	348	III/105	B	III/150	67
III/61	36	III/106	B	III/151	87
III/62	429	III/107	B	III/152	B
III/63	B	III/108	46	III/153	B
III/64	B	III/109	249	III/154	B
III/65	B	III/110	B	III/155	261
III/66	B	III/111	B	III/156	369
III/67	B	III/112	395	III/157	B
III/68	C	III/113	121	III/158	B
III/69	395	III/114	397	III/159	B
III/70	B	III/115	B	III/160	430
III/71	283	III/116	B	III/161	C
III/72	394	III/117	50	III/162	371
III/73	170	III/118	351	III/163	372
III/74	383	III/119	B	III/164	431
III/75	177	III/120	147	III/165	231
III/76	173	III/121	123	III/166	373
III/77	B	III/122	B	III/167	234
III/78	283	III/123	364	III/168	272
III/79	352	III/124	B	III/169	400
III/80	B	III/125	147	III/170	401
III/81	B	III/126	B	III/171	B
III/82	B	III/127	398	III/172	273
III/83	271	III/128	B	III/173	274
III/84	B	III/129	255	III/174	421
III/85	354	III/130	215	III/175	432
III/86	355	III/131	B	III/176	128
III/87	B	III/132	84	III/177	128
III/88	357	III/133	124	III/178	284
III/89	B	III/134	126	III/179	284
III/90	B	III/135	232	III/180	284
III/91	B	III/136	86	III/181	285
III/92	282	III/137	B	III/182	248
III/93	B	III/138	B	III/183	B
III/94	B	III/139	C	III/184	B
III/95	359	III/140	366	III/185	B
III/96	40	III/141	B	III/186	275

APPENDIX

TATS	Page	TATS	Page	TATS	Page
III/187	376	III/XII	399	III/XXVII	C
III/188	403	III/XIII	403	III/XXVIII	C
III/189	B	III/XIV	C	III/XXIX	C
III/190	B	III/XV	C	III/XXX	C
III/I	B	III/XVI	C	III/XXXI	C
III/II	B	III/XVII	C	III/XXXII	C
III/III	338	III/XVIII	C	III/XXXIII	C
III/IV	C	III/XIX	403	III/XXXIV	C
III/V	C	III/XX	C	III/XXXV	C
III/VI	C	III/XXI	C	III/XXVI	C
III/VII	C	III/XXII	C	III/XXXVII	C
III/VIII	C	III/XXIII	C	III/XXXVIII	C
III/IX	C	III/XXIV	C	III/XXXIX	C
III/X	C	III/XXV	C	III/XL	203
III/XI	C	III/XXVI	C	III/XLI·	C

For Product Safety Concerns and Information please contact our EU
representative GPSR@taylorandfrancis.com
Taylor & Francis Verlag GmbH, Kaufingerstraße 24, 80331 München, Germany

www.ingramcontent.com/pod-product-compliance
Lightning Source LLC
Chambersburg PA
CBHW050552270326
41926CB00012B/2025